Sport and the Transformation of Modern Europe

In the modern era, sport has been an important agent, and symptom, of the political, cultural and commercial pressures for convergence and globalization. In this fascinating interdisciplinary study, leading international scholars explore the making of modern sport in Europe, illuminating sport and its cultural and economic impacts in the context of the supra-state formations and global markets that have reshaped national and transnational cultures in the later twentieth century.

The book focuses on the emergence and expansion of media markets; high-performance sport's transformation by, and effects upon, Cold War dynamics and relations; and the implications of the Treaty of Rome for an emerging European identity in sport as in other areas (for example, the influence of soccer's governing body in Europe, UEFA, and its club and international competitions). It traces the connections between the forces of ideological division, economic growth, leisure consumption, European integration and the development of European sport, and examines the role of sport in the changing relationship between Europe and the USA.

Illuminating a key moment in global cultural history, this book is important reading for any student or scholar working in international studies, modern history or sport.

Alan Tomlinson is Professor of Leisure Studies and Director of Research in the Centre for Sport Research, Chelsea School, University of Brighton, UK. He has authored and edited numerous works on mainly sociological, but also historical, aspects of sport, leisure and consumption.

Christopher Young is Reader in Modern and Medieval German Studies in the Department of German and Dutch, Faculty of Modern and Medieval Languages, University of Cambridge, UK, and a Fellow of Pembroke College. He has authored and co-edited eight books on German language, literature and culture, and a further five volumes and journal special issues on international sport.

Richard Holt is Professor of History in, and Director of, the International Centre for Sports History and Culture, De Montfort University, Leicester, UK. He has previously worked as a Senior Research Fellow at the University of Leuven (Belgium) and as a Lecturer in History at Stirling University. He has written general histories of both British and French sports.

Culture, Economy and the Social
A new series from CRESC – the ESRC Centre for Research on Socio-cultural Change

The *Culture, Economy and the Social* series is committed to innovative contemporary, comparative and historical work on the relations between social, cultural and economic change. It publishes empirically based research that is theoretically informed, that critically examines the ways in which social, cultural and economic change is framed and made visible, and that is attentive to perspectives that tend to be ignored or sidelined by grand theorising or epochal accounts of social change. The series addresses the diverse manifestations of contemporary capitalism, and considers the various ways in which the 'social', 'the cultural' and 'the economic' are apprehended as tangible sites of value and practice. It is explicitly comparative, publishing books that work across disciplinary perspectives, cross-culturally, or across different historical periods.

The series is actively engaged in the analysis of the different theoretical traditions that have contributed to the development of the 'cultural turn' with a view to clarifying where these approaches converge and where they diverge on a particular issue. It is equally concerned to explore the new critical agendas emerging from current critiques of the cultural turn: those associated with the descriptive turn, for example. Our commitment to interdisciplinarity thus aims at enriching theoretical and methodological discussion, building awareness of the common ground that has emerged in the past decade, and thinking through what is at stake in those approaches that resist integration to a common analytical model.

Series titles include:

The Media and Social Theory (2008)
Edited by David Hesmondhalgh and Jason Toynbee

Culture Class Distinction (2009)
Tony Bennett, Mike Savage, Elizabeth Bortolaia Silva, Alan Warde, Modesto Gayo-Cal and David Wright

Material Powers (2010)
Edited by Tony Bennett and Patrick Joyce

The Social after Gabriel Tarde: Debates and Assessments (2010)
Edited by Matei Candea

Cultural Analysis and Bourdieu's Legacy (2010)
Edited by Elizabeth Silva and Alan Ward

Milk, Modernity and the Making of the Human (2010)
Richie Nimmo

Creative Labour: Media Work in Three Cultural Industries (2010)
Edited by David Hesmondhalgh and Sarah Baker

Inventive Methods: The Happening of the Social (forthcoming)
Edited by Celia Lury and Nina Wakeford

Rio de Janeiro: Urban Life through the Eyes of the City (forthcoming)
Edited by Beatriz Jaguaribe

Sport and the Transformation of Modern Europe: States, Media and Markets 1950–2010 (forthcoming)
Edited by Alan Tomlinson, Christopher Young and Richard Holt

E·S·R·C
ECONOMIC
& SOCIAL
RESEARCH
COUNCIL

Centre for Research on
Socio-Cultural Change

Sport and the Transformation of Modern Europe

States, media and markets
1950–2010

**Edited by Alan Tomlinson,
Christopher Young and
Richard Holt**

LONDON AND NEW YORK

First published 2011
by Routledge
2 Park Square, Milton Park, Abingdon, Oxon OX14 4RN

Simultaneously published in the USA and Canada
by Routledge
711 Third Avenue, New York, NY 10017

Routledge is an imprint of the Taylor & Francis Group, an informa business

© 2011 selection and editorial material, Alan Tomlinson, Christopher Young
and Richard Holt; individual chapters, the contributors

British Library Cataloguing in Publication Data
A catalogue record for this book is available from the British Library

Library of Congress Cataloging in Publication Data
Sport and the transformation of modern Europe : states, media and markets,
1950–2010 / edited by Alan Tomlinson, Christopher Young and Richard Holt.
  p. cm.
1. Sports—Europe—History. 2. Sports—Social aspects—Europe. 3. Sports and
state—Europe. 4. Mass media and sports—Europe. 5. Sports—Economic aspects—Europe.
I. Tomlinson, Alan. II. Young, Christopher, 1967– III. Holt, Richard, 1948–
GV603.S525 2011
796.094—dc22
2011001923

ISBN: 978-0-415-59222-2 (hbk)
ISBN: 978-0-203-80716-3 (ebk)

Typeset in Times New Roman
by Keystroke, Station Road, Codsall, Wolverhampton

Contents

Notes on contributors

Maarten van Bottenburg is Professor of Sport Development in the School of Governance at Utrecht University, the Netherlands.

Alexander Brand is Lecturer in the Department of Political Science at the University of Mainz, Germany.

Robert Edelman is Professor of Russian History and the History of Sport at the University of California, San Diego, USA.

Xavier Ginesta is a Lecturer in the Department of Communication at the University of Vic, Barcelona, Spain.

Richard Holt is Professor of History in, and Director of, the International Centre for Sports History and Culture at De Montfort University, Leicester, UK.

Nikolaus Katzer is Professor of Nineteenth/Twentieth Century History (Central/Eastern Europe) at Helmut-Schmidt University, Hamburg, Germany, and Director of the German Historical Institute, Moscow.

Chris Kennett is MBA Manager and Lecturer at BES La Salle Universitat Ramon Llull, Barcelona, Spain.

Anthony King is Professor of Sociology at the University of Exeter, UK.

Lindsay Sarah Krasnoff is a Historian in the Office of the Historian, US Department of State, in Washington, DC, USA.

Simon Martin is a Visiting Researcher at the University of Hertfordshire, UK, and the British School at Rome.

Toby Miller is Professor of Media and Cultural Studies at the University of California, Riverside, USA.

Miquel de Moragas is Adviser to the Director of the Centre d'Estudis Olímpics i de l'Esport, Universitat Autònoma de Barcelona (CEO-UAB), Barcelona, Spain.

Arne Niemann is Professor of International Politics in the Department of Political Science at the University of Mainz, Germany.

Roy Panagiotopoulou is Professor in Sociology in the Faculty of Communication and Media Studies at the University of Athens, Greece.

Kay Schiller is a Senior Lecturer in the Department of History, Durham University, UK.

John Soares is Adjunct Assistant Professor of History at the University of Notre Dame, Indiana, USA.

Georg Spitaler is in the Department of Political Science at the University of Vienna, Austria.

Stefan Szymanski is the Stephen J. Galetti Professor of Sport Management at the University of Michigan, USA.

Alan Tomlinson is Professor of Leisure Studies and Director of Research at the Centre for Sport Research, Chelsea School, University of Brighton, UK.

Christopher Young is Reader in Modern and Medieval German Studies in the Department of German and Dutch, Faculty of Modern and Medieval Languages, University of Cambridge, UK, and a Fellow of Pembroke College.

Acknowledgements

We are grateful to the Arts and Humanities Research Council (AHRC), UK for support that enabled us to hold a symposium from 6–9 January 2010 on the contribution that sport has made to the making, shaping and transformation of Europe and its culture; and on the economic, social and political currents that have influenced sport cultures in Europe. This was the third symposium in the funded Network 'Sport in Modern Europe – Perspectives on a Comparative Cultural History' (see www.sport-in-europe.group.cam.ac.uk). Special thanks go to those contributors who braved the snowy weather conditions to get to Pembroke College, Cambridge, and to those who were foiled by the wintry conditions but nevertheless delivered material electronically that symposium participants were able to discuss as planned.

There can be no better location for a focused, participatory symposium than the wonderful Thomas Gray Room at Pembroke College, or the more modern Nihon Room, and all symposium participants as well as the book's editors are indebted to Pembroke College staff for the efficiency, service and care that allowed the event to progress as planned.

Tony Bennett, Penny Harvey and Kevin Hetherington are the series editors of the Culture, Economy and the Social series in which this book appears. The series is an initiative of the Economic and Social Research Council (ESRC)-supported Centre for Research on Socio-cultural Change (CRESC), and we are pleased that the book is appearing in such an innovative list, with its interdisciplinary concern for the place of culture in both society and the economy. In many respects, sport's significance in political economy and cultural politics is yet to be adequately acknowledged, and we are grateful to the series editors for bucking this trend, and placing the book in the series. Thanks to the editors, too, for their sharp, incisive and perceptive comments on the initial manuscript.

Our final thanks go to Marcus Hunt, who has worked with successive versions of the developed chapters, and has shown tireless patience and diligence in spotting anomalies, identifying and chasing up missing material, and shaping and reshaping the contributions into consistent format and style.

Alan Tomlinson (University of Brighton)
Christopher Young (Pembroke College, Cambridge)
Richard Holt (De Montfort University)
5 January 2011

Introduction: sport in Europe 1950–2010

Transformation and trends

*Richard Holt, Alan Tomlinson
and Christopher Young*

Sport in Europe: socio-cultural change and transformation

Whether in the home, the café or the stadium, watching sport has become an increasingly central and ubiquitous element of European culture since the 1950s. 'Transformation' is a daunting word but an appropriate one in this case. Changes in the delivery, scale and structure of European sport since the Second World War resonate with the fundamental etymological meaning of the word: the roots 'trans' and 'formation' convey the sense of movement – across, beyond, above – a particular set of socio-cultural characteristics. Whilst the word is not conspicuous in dictionaries or encyclopedias of ideas or of thought, there is no doubt we can talk the language of transformation when looking at the tempestuous history of both political and socio-cultural change in Europe in the second half of the twentieth century. In everyday technical life we are also familiar with the function of the transformer, which is to connect and potentially redirect currents and forces. The process of societal transformation can usefully be thought of in comparable ways, as rival sets of ideological values clash, connect and coalesce to generate change across cultural, social, economic and political spheres.

In historical terms, the analysis of socio-cultural change requires that we track key moments and events in that change process; in social scientific terms, this requires what Randall Collins (1999) calls a 'sociology of the long run', in which a synthesis of understanding emerges from historical and social scientific work conceived as part and parcel of the same intellectual challenge and academic project. In this volume, we collect and interrelate the scholarship of the historian, sociologist, anthropologist, economist, political scientist and media analyst to examine selected aspects of sport's contribution to the transformation of Europe in the long run of the Cold War and the post-Cold War period.

Why this focus upon Europe, and why now? Peter Berlin was sports editor of Europe's English-language newspaper the *International Herald Tribune* from 1995–2010, a period in which the European Union (EU)'s membership expanded dramatically with the inclusion of Eastern Europe's former communist states. When asked 'Is there such a thing as European sport?', he instantly amended the question and elaborated upon the characteristics of 'sport in Europe', as manifest in European organizations, governing bodies and competitions.[1] But the sports that he pointed to first, other than football, were volleyball, basketball and handball. In these sports, he claimed, there is what he called a 'European familiarity', in that neighbouring countries produce teams that matter in significant competitions, in stark contrast with the USA, where international competitions matter much less than internal, domestic competition. In the USA, for instance, the World Series has a much higher profile and status than does the World Baseball Classic, the most recent two of which have been won by Japan, staged in California. From Berlin's perspective, sport acts as a form of catalyst for expressing social commonalities. On his European sport journalist's beat, he recalls a camaraderie of transculturalism and not just professional likemindedness – 'European sports journalists know each other' – in their contribution to the reporting of the European scene. They share a sense of the importance of sport, of its 'social and cultural functions'. Here, Berlin echoes the discourse of sport generated by its supporters at the European policy level.

In the European Commission's 2007 *White Paper on Sport*, the 'specificity of sport' was identified in the competitive balances of European sporting competition, and the pryamidical sporting structure of European sport, from the broad base of grassroots organization to regional, national and Europe-wide sporting federations (European Commission, 2007: section 4.1). The following year, the European Presidency (Council of the European Union, 2008: 21) published a *Declaration on Sport*, stating it to be 'essential to European society', important for its benefits beyond mere economics, and particularly valuable for its potential effect on young people through 'combined sports training and education'. The emphasis here, after decades of debate by lobbyists within the European political body, was upon values for participants, not just sporting markets and spectators/consumers. Such a high-profile – though no doubt diplomatically diluted – statement on the Europe-wide significance of sport confirmed the apposite timing of our bringing together contributions illuminating the European sporting question in the second half of the twentieth century. The European sporting scene may have spawned a professional network of media professionals and political/policy lobbyists, but what has sport really meant to the peoples of Europe in the period under scrutiny?

In a poll of twenty-five EU states in 2004 (TNS Opinion & Social, 2004), 78% of respondents recognized the health benefits of sport, and 39% the importance of sport as fun. Sport's potential to promote the integration of immigrant populations through creating cultural dialogue was recognized by 73%. Smaller or newer member states (Cyprus, Malta, Greece and Poland) supported the prospect of more EU intervention in sporting matters, and 63% backed more EU cooperation with national governments and national sporting organizations. Those least keen on the inclusion of a sport-related clause in any future European constitution were Danish and German respondents. This provides a mixed picture of European citizens' views of the significance of sport, but confirms the perceived importance of sport's potential contribution to cultural development and social policy.

Previous studies have examined aspects of sporting culture in the European context, but none with this book's interconnected analytical concerns with states, markets and media. Stephen Wagg and David L. Andrews' (2007) edited collection provides valuable case studies of particular sports and events. Neil Blain, Raymond

Boyle and Hugh O'Donnell's (1993) *Sport and National Identity in the European Media* collected studies of the media discourses of sport within European nations, but these valuable studies stood relatively alone and highlighted national distinctiveness. J.A. Mangan, Richard Holt and Pierre Lanfranchi's (1996) journal issue/book *European Heroes: Myth, Identity, Sport* examined selected cases of sporting figures from several European countries. Wladimir Andreff and Stefan Szymanski's (2008) *Handbook on the Economics of Sport* has shown the specific economic characteristics of European sporting institutions and competition. Anthony King (2003), a contributor to this book, has analysed European football as ritual. Philip Dine and Seán Crosson's (2010) edited collection recognizes how sport mobilizes millions of people across Europe as practitioners and/or spectators; their focus is on representation and selected aspects of the mediation of sporting practices and spectacles, and the historical net is widely cast, from the mid-nineteenth century to the present. More generally, studies have reflected on the wide-ranging political dynamics of the European project; these have included Chris Shore's (2000) anthropological approach identifying cultural actions as the top-down strategies of European elites.

The *Journal of Contemporary History* (Volume 38, Number 3) has featured sport in a special issue on sport and politics, with an introduction by Jeffrey Hill and a review/commentary by Mike Cronin: most of the articles in the collection dealt with examples of state-building and the constitution of a national community through sports, though not specifically with the pan-European context. Nevertheless, the collection raised important theoretical and methodological questions: Cronin urged the development of a 'total history' (Cronin, 2003: 503), and Hill reprised Eric Hobsbawm's (1995) call for a 'concern with social totalities' (Hill, 2003: 358). We are in agreement with the need for such emphases in contemporary historical work, and they inform the Europe-wide perspective that we adopt in this book.

While these publications have provided invaluable understanding of the national dimensions of sport, have demonstrated interconnections between respective national models and ideologies of high-profile sport (most often in the case of football), and have confirmed the importance of sport in the constitution of some forms of pan-European identity, no text has explored the interconnectedness of the cultural, the social and the economic in the making and, in part, remaking of European sport. To do this, this book brings together original research generated by the Sport in Modern Europe Network's January 2010 symposium (Arts and Humanities Research Council, AHRC and the universities of Cambridge, Brighton and de Montfort; www.sport-in-europe.group.cam.ac.uk). The symposium explored the forces of ideological division, economic growth and European integration as they have been articulated in the development of sport in post-Second World War Europe, from the emergence of the Soviet Union and its satellite states as key players in world sport, to the fall of the Berlin Wall and beyond. Contributors concentrated on three areas: (i) the emergence and expansion of media markets and the globalization of sport; (ii) high-performance sport's transformation by, and effects upon, Cold War dynamics and relations; and (iii) the implications of the Treaty of Rome (1957) for an emerging European identity in sport as in other areas, particularly in relation to the formulation of statements and declarations on sport and its pan-European characteristics and significance. These interrelated themes were considered in the context of shifting patterns of media consumption and the changing framework of sporting competition and markets in both Western European liberal democracies and the changing Eastern Europe in the post-Soviet era. The relationship of Europe with the USA, and the different influences on the shaping of sport in those respective geopolitical contexts, were also considered. Where appropriate, international scholars who were not at the symposium have contributed chapters on topics central to the core themes of the book.

Sport in Europe: phases and trends

Sport as spectacle has become increasingly visible and prominent in contemporary European popular culture. This took place in two distinct phases. First came the long post-war boom of the third quarter of the twentieth century, which brought television not only to the capitalist democracies but also to the communist bloc. The Cold War and the broadcasting of sport on mainly state-controlled terrestrial television went hand-in-hand until the late 1980s. Then came a sharp break around 1990 and the beginning of the second phase. This began with the collapse of the Soviet Union and its satellite states, creating new democratic regimes throughout Eastern Europe. This dramatic ideological and political change coincided with a remarkable technological breakthrough in satellite broadcasting. A transnational and global market for European sport, especially football, suddenly came into being. This new 'electronic box office' provided unprecedented access to high-performance sport and generated vast income flows across national frontiers. Hence the successive impact on European spectator sport of ideology, technology and regulation forms the subject of this collection, which is concerned primarily with three topics: the impact of the Cold War on European sport; the transformation of televised sport; and intervention of the EU as a market regulator.

The writing of post-war European history has been rooted in the different perspectives and priorities of the nation-state. This applies with particular force to spectator sport, which has been such a powerful vehicle for civic and national identity. Hence there is no general history of European sport in the way that there is of the European economy, the EU or the Cold War. Europe is 'a patchwork of memory landscapes that are partly isolated and partly in touch with each other' so that 'genuinely transnational investigations into European social and cultural history that go beyond the history of international relations and wars are still rare' (Jarausch and Lindenberger, 2007: 5–6). Even periodization and terminology are a problem. For some French scholars, '*histoire contemporaine*' still begins in 1789 whereas for Germany or Italy, 'contemporary history' tends to start with the fall of Hitler and Mussolini. In Eastern Europe, the dividing line is either the imposition of Soviet control after the Second World War or, increasingly, its collapse in 1989. Most accounts of recent European history begin with1945, the period's 'year zero' in a way. Tony Judt's (2005) magisterial account of recent European history is entitled simply *Postwar*.

This works well for some aspects of sport, though not for others. Clearly the establishment of two opposed armed camps in Eastern and Western Europe had a profound influence on the shape of European sport. As Katzer shows in Chapter 1, the Soviet model of mixed physical culture and sport was extremely important in the new Communist states of Eastern Europe. This was embedded in a wider communist and socialist youth culture, as Schiller's account of the World Youth Festival in East Berlin in 1973, in Chapter 3, reveals. But in other ways the political division of time is less helpful. The extraordinary economic growth that swept Western Europe from the mid-1950s for twenty years – and was also felt more modestly in the East – was crucial. As Wakeman remarks, 'of all the upheavals of the twentieth century, this "golden age" may, in retrospect, be the defining event precisely because it involved a whole new material world and with it, a new society and culture that transformed the lives of Europeans almost beyond recognition' (Wakeman, 2003: 6).

This is a persuasive argument, but requires historical qualification. The striking success of participant and spectator sport in the 1950s had its roots in the rapid growth of teams and clubs in the inter-war years. Whether in the democratic states of Western and central Europe or in fascist Italy and Germany, organized sports such as athletics and swimming or ball games, especially association football, spread beyond their elite origins in the late nineteenth century to be taken up by the mass of clerical and manual workers. This was mainly confined to men, but increasingly attracted girls and younger women. Hence the growth of sport in the 1950s might be better understood in terms of continuity and development rather than marking a sharp break with the past. In the long twentieth century, codified modern sports have moved from their bourgeois beginnings through a popular but still restricted process of democratization to a mass phenomenon spanning age, class, gender and ethnicity in the early twenty-first century. This view accords with the wider argument of van Bottenburg's contribution to this collection (Chapter 12), which underlines the pioneering role in European sport of private clubs and voluntary associations, often provided with state subsidies, in contrast to the American model of high school and commercialized college sport.

In both continents, however, it is television that has made sport a truly mass phenomenon, followed by tens of millions of armchair spectators whose playing days are long in the past or who might never have played at all. Association football is the most striking example. Television arrived in the 1950s at the same historical moment as the formation of the Union of European Football Associations (UEFA) in 1954 and the signing of the Treaty of Rome in 1957. The year 1954 saw the birth of the 'International Inter-City Industrial Fairs Cup' under the aegis of UEFA (the 'Fairs Cup'), which became the UEFA Cup (and in the 2009–10 season became the 'Europa League'); the following year, in 1955, UEFA inaugurated the European Champion Clubs' Cup, popularly known as the European Cup. This brought the Real Madrid of Puskas, Di Stefano and Gento from the enclosed world of Franco's Spain to a wider European public, winning five successive titles and beating Eintracht Frankfurt 7–3 in Glasgow in 1960, in what many commentators considered the best game of club football ever played in Europe.

The UEFA Champions League is now the world's most popular and profitable club competition, and its final match of the 2008–09 season attracted 2009's biggest worldwide television audience of 109 million dedicated viewers, with 97 million more looking in at the action – more than the Super Bowl.[2] What was once a treat, an occasional mid-week black-and-white broadcast, is now virtually a weekly fixture for much of the year, in brilliant colour and with frequent replays and analysis, followed not just across Europe but around the world by satellite subscribers. Just as television viewers are increasingly transnational, so more active and committed fans can take advantage of cheap flights to move to and fro across national frontiers to follow their team. Low-cost airlines hardly enter the calculations of players and managers at the highest levels of the game, who can hire private jets to whisk them around Europe or increasingly to Africa or South America to play for their country or fulfil a family engagement. The geographical and social mobility brought about by television revenues is unprecedented, and is an important aspect of our second analytical theme running through this book.[3] First, though, we turn to the Cold War.

Cold War sport

Instead of concentrating on the founding liberal democracies of what is now the EU, we have chosen to give a major place to Eastern Europe, which is often overlooked. Katzer's chapter on Soviet sports culture over the whole twentieth century (Chapter 1) and Edelman's account on sport and Soviet television (Chapter 6) are supplemented by Schiller's evocation in Chapter 3 of the communist youth culture of East Germany. Another distinctive feature is the presence of North America in a book about Europe. Soares (Chapter 2) shows how the Cold War cultivation of ice hockey in the Soviet bloc and in Scandinavia had profound effects on North America. Sport was not a one-way street. American influence through media-driven models of consumption and broadcasting was undoubtedly important. Yet the distinctiveness and resilience – the 'stickiness' – of national cultures is another theme of this collection. Whilst there has been a certain convergence at the business level and in styles of sports presentation, Europe and North America are still very different, as van Bottenburg's overview in Chapter 12 explains.

Sport, perhaps more than any other cultural form, offers an obvious route to explore the interaction of East and West. There have been many accounts of the tensions in Cold War sport, intricately staged by both sides, and the era still holds its fascination. Recent work on East and West German sport, from the 1950s to the era of détente from 1969 onwards (*Ostpolitik*), has shown that there is no easy mapping of the relationship between sport and politics; sport often runs ahead of politics and sometimes floats free of it. Its essential paradox – that it is claimed to be non-political, but is political to its very core – means that sport can be used both to oil the wheels of politics and to throw sand in the machine.

Katzer's account in the opening chapter of the Soviet sports model sets the scene. After the Russian Revolution, the Soviet Union developed a distinctive form of physical culture. This drew on the German and Czech traditions of gymnastic exercise, but was blended into a distinctive revolutionary body culture to express harmony and optimism. Competitive sport at this early stage was marginal, but became increasingly important with the ascendancy of Stalin and of 'socialist modernism'. Sport was to be enlisted in the great patriotic task of building a more efficient and dynamic Soviet Union. This in turn paved the way for the Soviet Union to enter the international sporting arena, which began tentatively with the tour of the Dinamo Moscow football club to Britain in 1945. However, the increasingly hostile rhetoric and the formation of two opposed armed camps profoundly divided over the future of Germany meant that the Cold War established a new ideological and strategic framework as international sport resumed after the Second World War. As a massive airlift was mounted to supply the citizens of West Berlin trapped behind the 'iron curtain', the Olympic Games of 1948 were held in London.

Unsurprisingly, the Soviets did not take part. Rather than risk their international reputation in what they had previously dismissed as bourgeois sporting nationalism, they waited for the following Games in Helsinki with the intention of proving the superiority of Soviet communism through sport. Their intervention was dramatic. Despite finishing second in the medals table to the United States, 'at the end of the Olympic Games in Helsinki, *Pravda* (*Truth*), the official newspaper of the Communist Party, proclaimed victory without reference to point totals, reporting simply that "the athletes of the Soviet Union took first place."' (Parks, 2007: 39). This rhetoric and rivalry continued more or less stridently, depending on the international situation, until the first post-Cold War Games in Barcelona in 1992. In 1960, as Martin shows in Chapter 5, the Rome Olympics took place in the shadow of the spy-plane trial of Gary Powers in Moscow, the furious confrontation of Krushchev with the USA, and the looming missile crisis in Cuba. China had recently left the Olympic movement over Taiwan. Cold War themes underlay the contact of US and Soviet athletes, and Cold War discourses dominated the build-up to the Rome Games in the world's media, which were also used by the Italians to shore up the Christian Democrat majority, assisted by the Vatican. The Olympics continued to be dominated by Cold War rivalries, and later marked by Cold War boycotts, first by the United States of the 1980 Moscow Games and then tit-for-tat by the Soviets in Los Angeles in 1984.

The Soviet Union and its Eastern European allies built up a formidable athletic machine that remorselessly delivered Olympic medals. However, it was Soviet success in ice hockey, as Soares (Chapter 2) shows, which particularly shocked North America. Hockey was Canada's national sport. It was a defining passion, especially in Quebec, but hockey also enjoyed remarkable success in the United Sates. After baseball, basketball and American football, hockey made up the 'Big Four'. Until the 1950s, North Americans took their superiority in this sport as axiomatic. However, the politics of the Cold War brought a formidable Soviet team to the fore, which developed a new style of collective play. The Soviet Union won the Olympic gold at the first attempt in 1956 and subsequently six Olympic gold medals and twenty world championships between 1963 and 1990. But this was not simply a Cold War phenomenon. Hockey was a European as well as an American sport. Its success went beyond the Soviet Union to encompass Sweden,

Finland, Germany and Switzerland, revealing that Europe could compete with the commercialized world of professional North American sports without the backing of a Communist political and military machine. Within the Soviet bloc, success came at a price. The USSR had deliberately sabotaged Czech hockey in the immediate post-war years to improve its own chances, and hockey re-emerged later as a focus for fierce anti-Russian sentiment after the failed anti-Soviet uprising of 1968.

This undercurrent of national rivalry and resentment was a problem for the communist states. Their leaders sought to promote fraternal solidarity amongst socialist nations through initiatives such as the World Festival of Youth (WFY). As Schiller shows in Chapter 3, the WFY was founded to promote peaceful inter-nationalism, but was quickly dominated by the Soviet bloc. With only two excep-tions, the WFY was held in Eastern bloc capitals, first in Berlin in 1951 and again in 1973. The communist German Democratic Republic (GDR) sought to combat the success of the Munich Olympics for the Federal Republic by hosting a 'Wood-stock of the East' – a festival of music, dance and sport amidst massive street decorations, with a five-petal flower as the Festival symbol to rival the five Olympic rings. This was partly an attempt by the new President of the GDR, Eric Honecker, to rebrand the regime. This 'deformalization', however, was more apparent than real. In fact, the full force of the communist state was marshalled to police the event. At the same time, it was important to win over youth by making certain limited concessions to popular culture, especially in the area of pop music. Hence there was a certain licence for large numbers of young people to have fun and to socialize, playing music, talking, sleeping out in parks and enjoying a moment of freedom, including sexual freedom, not normally permitted by the regime.

There is clearly an element of *Eigen-Sinn* here, in the sense of a limited appro-priation of an ideologically driven event by the participants themselves, exploiting the opportunity to flout the strict norms of communist culture without appearing to do so or putting themselves at risk. Schiller's detailed study, however, reveals how tricky it is to 'read' such an event in terms of *Eigen-Sinn*, or resistance. For the WFY seems to have been genuinely popular despite the covert presence of the secret police, and was warmly remembered in East Germany by many of those who took part for a brief euphoric moment.

Schiller's study leads us more generally to Uta Balbier's (2007) linkage between East and West Germany in the 1960s in terms of the emergence of sports policy. Although both states approached the issue from different ideological bases, changes in one led to inevitable catch-up moves in the other. Against the normal flow of influence from West to East, on this occasion it was the East that took the initiative in sponsoring high-performance sport. Always lagging some way behind, the West was nonetheless dragged up, like a second climber attached to a leader by rope.

France was a striking example of this process of response, as Krasnoff's con-tribution in Chapter 4 shows. The successes of the East and the West Germans sharpened the French sense of failure. De Gaulle's assumption of power in 1958 and the creation of a more powerful and presidential Fifth Republic brought with it a new agenda for national competitiveness – '*la France qui gagne*' – and led to a government outcry over the poor performance of France at the 1960 Olympics.

As Martin notes in Chapter 5, Rome was the first Games to be widely screened on television, with simultaneous broadcasting to eighteen European countries and delayed 'live' broadcasts to the USA and Japan. Humiliation was global and instant. This led to a new manifestation of a long-standing discourse of decline, which was taken up by the Gaullists, who formally legislated in 1975 to provide public funds for the identification and training of elite athletes. The message was clear. Success in sport was increasingly an indicator of international prestige. It allowed smaller nations such as the GDR to punch above their weight and to exercise 'soft power' on the world stage within the shadow of superpower dominance.

The Olympic performances of both Germanies – the Federal and the Democratic Republics – was superlative. Evelyn Merten (2009) has looked at the relationship of East and West Germany to the Soviet Union. Here, the pressure of growing East German success on the track – and, one might add, the détente incentives of increased trade links – actually encouraged the Soviets to seek friendship and even institutional cooperation with West German sports bodies. Jutta Braun's (2009) recent article on trends and fun sports (golf, jogging, karate, windsurfing, skateboarding, triathlon) and fan culture in the GDR in the 1970s and 1980s shows that recreational sports lost massive material ground to performance-oriented Olympic sports, which provided crucial symbolic capital for the state. The lack of adequate resources devoted to alternative sports, and the fitness boom that reached the GDR from the West, posed a significant challenge to the regime. To a certain extent, jogging was successfully appropriated within the established structure of sport, but windsurfers managed to reject the regime's embrace and carve out a semi-legal sphere for themselves. Karate (popularized because it was practiced by the stuntmen in GDR films) was banned because of the threat to medal-winning judo squads. This did not stop its practitioners risking imprisonment for their sport. In a certain sense, then, these 'Pacific-rim' sports (or what Bourdieu [1986] dubbed *les sports californienne*) were the punk rock of bodily culture: they opened up spaces of freedom and protest.

Representing European sport: television

If taking part in sport left open the possibility of individual or collective self-expression, sports broadcasting placed control in the hands of the state or, more accurately, the particular broadcasting agency through which it operated. As Edelman reports in Chapter 6, in his consideration of football and Soviet television, little of the violent or drunken fan culture surrounding Russian football got onto the screen. The television set, so often perceived as a quintessential item of Western consumption, was one of the few consumer goods available in plentiful supply in the Soviet Union. As in the West of Europe, most Soviet homes had one by the 1980s and could watch five or six sports broadcasts a week across all time zones. These were usually football or ice hockey matches, with blanket coverage of the Olympic Games every four years. Soviet state control in this area took an unusual form. Whilst transmissions might occasionally be suspended if there was crowd trouble, there was little attempt to manipulate football politically apart from a systematic refusal to acknowledge the wider symbolism of the rival Moscow teams: Dinamo, with its secret police associations, and the more populist Spartak. As Edelman observes, most televised sport in the Soviet Union was remarkable only for 'its utter ordinariness'. Soviet football was embedded in male culture and offered the opportunity to express divergent identities in a politically unthreatening way. Televised Soviet sport was a 'slippery tool', less obviously propagandist than might be imagined – a force for inertia rather than for *Eigen-Sinn*.

Szymanski's overview of television markets (Chapter 7) begins with a comparison of the United States and Europe. The European model differed strikingly from the American, which was based on competing commercial broadcasters – NBS, CBS, ABC – working through networks of local affiliates with access to bandwidths regulated by a federal authority. In Europe, there was closer state regulation and resistance to commercialization. Governing bodies for sport, for example the Football Association and Football League in England, were strongly opposed to the broadcasting of live sport, which they believed would lead to the collapse of attendances at matches. In the United States, the National Football League (NFL), representing a small number of clubs in a large continent, had no such fears. The NFL set out to sell itself through television in the 1950s, with team owners co-operating to create a 'good product', by which they meant one where results remained uncertain and (unlike in Europe) no single team or groups of teams could dominate for too long.

European sports broadcasting was quite different. National broadcasters were far less market-driven, and grouped together in a cartel, the European Broadcasting Union, to avoid bidding for rights against each other. Moreover, until the 1960s, European television was relatively indifferent to the popularity or potential of sport on television. However, as Szymanski points out, 'the accumulation of audiences started to bring changes', notably in the selling of Olympic rights. However, the stand-off between those who governed professional football and the various national television networks persisted into the 1980s. It was the technological breakthrough in satellite broadcasting, which defied national regulation and control, combined with a directive from the European Commission legitimizing the right of new trans-national European media businesses, that broke down the old system of national restrictions and regulations and had an immediate and dramatic effect. In 1995 there were three subscriber sports channels in Europe; by 2000 there were sixty. Sport, as Rupert Murdoch recalled in 1996, had been an effective 'battering ram' to penetrate the terrestrial television audience. England led the way. The English 'Premier League', a group of elite clubs which broke away from the Football League to profit from the new opportunities for media-generated wealth, agreed to televise sixty games in its first season of 1992–93. By 2006, this figure had risen to 138. The value of the product has been similarly exponential. From a £304 million deal between Sky and the Premier League in 1992 for five years, Sky and Setanta between them paid £2.7 billion for national and international rights to the English Premier League from 2007 to 2010. This figure has continued to rise.

However, it is misleading to assume that the brave new world of satellite sport created a uniform product and reaction. In fact, the impact of subscription television, whether by satellite or cable or internet, varied significantly across Europe, as the case study of Spanish football by de Moragas, Kennett and Ginesta (Chapter 8) reveals. Spain has resisted the wider pattern of collective selling of rights, and maintained a legal requirement that at least one major football match from La Liga is broadcast weekly. The Spanish courts banned collective selling in 1993 in favour of individual clubs marketing their own rights. This precipitated a 'football war' between different media companies from 1996–2009, beginning when Telefonica, the main Spanish telecommunications provider, and its rival, the Sogecable/Prisa group, each tried to outbid the other in deals with individual clubs. Neither gained enough subscribers, and large losses led to a merger in July 2002. In 2006 a new company, Mediapro, challenged this arrangement and by 2008 had secured rights to the games of thirty-eight of forty-two clubs in the top two Spanish divisions for around €500 million per season. In addition, Mediapro signed deals with Barcelona for €1 billion and Real Madrid for €1.1 billion over a period of seven years.

At the level of the biggest sporting phenomena of all, the men's Fédération Internationale de Football Association (FIFA) World Cup and the Olympic Games, European cities have hosted these events as they have been transformed from relatively low-key occasions covered by a few specialist journalists into the biggest media events in world history.[4] This initially favoured small as well as large European cities. In the 1950s, a small city such as Helsinki (1952) could host the Summer Olympics, and World Cup Finals with just sixteen national teams took place in small European nations (Switzerland 1954, Sweden 1958). Within two decades, this would be inconceivable, as the value of the mega-sports event rose and media technologies improved immeasurably. Along with the raised media profile, a politics of representation informed the ceremonial side of Olympic events, with the flag of the post-Soviet expanding European entity flying alongside the International Olympic Committee (IOC)'s flag at the Games of 1992. In Chapter 5, Martin notes the 'epic coverage' of the Rome Games on television, which culminated in a feature-length documentary film made by a fascist-trained film-maker, Romolo Marcellini, in which was presented both a vibrant image of a new Italy and a prolonged tourist advertisement. In reviewing the Athens Games of 2004 (Chapter 9), Panagiotopoulou poses the question of whether such a branded and globally marketed event can even be considered distinctively European at all. The accountants of Greece's collapsed economy, however, might like to point out the local, European economic consequences of such aspirational cultural and economic strategies.

Making the new Europe: regulation

The sudden change in the structure of sports broadcasting led the European Commission and the European Court of Justice to intervene to regulate the market. This was both to ensure fair competition under European law, and to protect member states and European citizens from the loss of all their most important events to subscription television. This initiative is set in a wider context in Chapter 10, where King examines the post-war history of regulation in terms of a switch from Keynesian management by the nation-state in the third quarter of the century through to the neoliberalism and deregulation of the late twentieth century. Here Niemann, Brand and Spitaler, in Chapter 11, make a useful distinction between 'Europeanization' and 'EU-ization' in the sense that transnational networks were established in European football well before the Treaty of Rome. This was especially important in Central Europe, where there had been extensive movement of players within the multi-national Habsburg monarchy, notably the triangle of Vienna, Prague and Budapest and the creation of a 'Mitropa Cup' as early as 1927.

This early transnationalism was reinforced in new ways by the interventions of the EU in what became known as the Bosman ruling, which revolved around the constraints imposed by UEFA/FIFA and backed by national federations and clubs on the free movement of labour and freedom of contract under European law. The Bosman ruling of the European Court of Justice in 1995 banned the imposition of quotas for players of EU origin by national football authorities. The implications of such a change were enormous, but reaction to it varied significantly. Whereas this ruling was widely contested in most European states, in Germany it was embraced. The Germans even extended Bosman beyond the EU to cover all the fifty-two member states of UEFA. Germany, Niemann *et al.* argue, were not only good Europeans, but also in the process of reunification and wishing to keep an open door to the East. More pragmatically, they were also keen to be able to sign non-EU players, mostly from Eastern Europe, for relatively modest transfer fees. Austria, with its tradition of central European migrants, took a broadly similar line. However, under pressure from the right-wing nationalist parties, the Austrian FA required teams to have at least nine Austrians out of eighteen on the team sheet and provided additional funding for teams with eleven or more Austrian nationals in the squad. Both countries were concerned about the impact of the influx of foreign players on their national teams. But each reacted rather differently. Proposing nationality quotas and generally banging the national drum was politically sensitive in post-war Germany, whereas a more inward-looking, even xenophobic nationalism remained more acceptable and more influential in Austria.

Of greater concern to Germany was the second element of the Bosman ruling banning the charging of fees for out-of-contract players and effectively giving freedom of movement to professional footballers of EU origin. Germany was alarmed at the implications of this ruling for the stability of the Bundesliga. The Germans joined with other major European powers, notably the UK, to petition the Commission to provide compensation to clubs for the costs of developing younger players. This was a success. The Commission modified its position whilst maintaining the principle of freedom of contract. During these negotiations, the Austrians remained on the sidelines, believing their league was too small to be seriously affected by the proposed changes.

However, it is misleading to see EU regulation only in terms of the imposition of free market legislation on the movement and hiring of players. The exclusive 'collective selling of sports rights' ran into difficulties under EU competition law. The ownership of broadcasting rights for the European Champions League, for example, might suit the seller and the purchaser, but it was not necessarily good for the citizens of Europe or for fair competition between bidders. Exclusivity was critical, and in a 1997 revision of the 'Television Without Frontiers' Directive of 1989, member states were permitted to 'list' events that had to be available on free-to-air television. Here the Commission intervened to 'unbundle' collective rights and to ensure that a range of bidders was able to compete for smaller slices of the cake, and to see that a monopoly commercial provider did not unreasonably deny EU citizens free access to major sporting events across Europe. This in turn brought new problems as governing bodies sought to maximize the value of their sport and resented the loss of income from listing or from undermining collective selling. The EU appeared to be infringing the rights of individual clubs to dispose of their own product.

The English Premier League was a huge beneficiary of collective selling; so, too, were UEFA (through the Champions League) and the German Bundesliga. These bodies lobbied strongly with top-level political support, and the Commission agreed to modify its position in return for a limited redistribution of matches to a broader range of providers. The wider point here is that there was no single 'European position', as Niemann *et al.* show in their comparison of Germany and Austria. The Germans were heavily involved in contesting the Commission decision, whereas the Austrians, who had a much smaller league and no significant economic interest at stake, were passive observers of the struggle. The Commission had to walk a fine line between different kinds of freedom: the freedom to compete without restrictions in an open market; the freedom of national federations to operate profitably for their member clubs; the freedom of some fans to subscribe and the freedom of others to watch a range of sport on free-to-air television in the traditional way.

Transforming trends

Modern sport in Europe began with the creation of codified rules, national structures and international competition in the late nineteenth and early twentieth centuries. This was the first 'revolution'; the second, media-led 'revolution' began modestly in the era of Cold War confrontation and black-and-white television broadcasting by national monopolies. Whether in Edelman's Moscow apartments or in the living rooms of London, live sport was broadcast without frills on small screens for most viewers until the 1980s. Around 1990, the fall of the Soviet system coincided with the technological transformation of broadcasting, and Murdoch's 'battering ram' opened up a new media business with huge subscription and advertising revenues. This assault on state-controlled televised sport was combined with a further weakening in national regulation through the Bosman ruling on freedom of movement and freedom of contract. From closed national markets, football in Europe had been transformed into 'European football', with the best teams from across the continent regularly playing each other. Being 'in Europe' is what really counts. Other sports remain more nationally focused but the broader pattern of European and global competition is undeniable, and there are thriving basketball and handball leagues, and high-profile European championships in, for instance, aquatics and athletics (track-and-field).

Sport is becoming a transnational, media-driven business at an astonishing pace. History seems to be speeding up; sport is getting bigger in economic terms with every year that passes. More does not mean worse, as standards of play and performance seem to go from strength to strength. But how long can it go on? The economics of European sport, especially football, are precariously balanced, indebted and buoyed up by the banks or by vastly rich individuals who can withdraw their investment as quickly as they made it. Such massive changes at the top have left ordinary fans behind, struggling to keep up with the twists and turns of sport as a global business whilst sticking loyally and obstinately to their allegiances to club or country despite the spiralling costs of being a supporter. Will new generations of Europeans develop new loyalties that cross frontiers as easily as their favourite players? Will we develop multiple identities: local, national and European? Football certainly gives Europe something to share and to celebrate collectively. But can other sports follow suit? Will national 'stickiness' prevail or will sport eventually bring us closer to the elusive idea of a common European culture? These are big theoretical questions, deserving of the kind of empirical investigation that we have brought together in this volume.

Together, then, the chapters in this book have explored the core processes and dynamics – economic, social, political – underlying the story of sport and its contribution to the transformation of Europe. Central to this is an understanding of the tension between commercial and media-driven pressures for convergence, and sport's innate national stubbornness, on the threshold of the globalization of cultural markets. The studies in the book locate, problematize and illuminate sport and its cultural and economic impacts in the context of supra-state formations and global markets that have reshaped national and transnational cultures in the later twentieth century, and in varying degrees have contributed to the transformation of European culture and identity. Sport in the European context is shown to be a significant element in the cultural economy, demonstrating, as Ferdinand Braudel has put it, 'the mobility and resourcefulness of a capitalism' which is 'often sick but never dies'.[5] The European focus of the book produces historical and spatial case studies that analyse cultural trends over the second half of the century and into the current century, what some see as the '*longue durée*' of the post-Second World War period.[6]

We conclude with three theoretical or interpretive comments. First, sport's place in the contemporary European and global marketplace – from the styles and fashions of sports goods to the explosion of sport's presence in mainstream and new media – has been of increasing significance in the post-Second World War period and, especially, the post-Soviet period.[7] Sport has embodied the spirit of capitalism as the neoliberal politico-economic agenda has boosted a particular model of the global sport market. This has involved a form of intensified 'financialization' of institutions, as billionaires from Russia or India, as well as the USA, have become owners of and investors in European sport. It has also embraced a model of sport as modernity, in the branding of places, individuals and practices.

Second, the reconstitution of national identity and the dynamics of the transnational have both been informed by the meteoric growth of the sport–media partnership. This has both produced lucrative European formations in pan-European sporting competitions in numerous sports, and fostered a sense of national identity among, in particular, the newly formed or reconstituted states of the former Soviet-dominated societies and countries. International sporting competition, intangible as its values and consequences might sometimes seem, contributes in some part to the articulation and manifestation of a European identity. Sociologist Georg Simmel, reflecting on Europe–USA relations in the early years of the First World War, wrote that 'in addition to our Germanness, we also have to think of ourselves as a European state, sharing a certain unity with all other European states' (Harrington, 2005: 69). Almost a century on, Europe has no shared language, no shared currency, no shared religion; perhaps sporting rivalry with neighbours, as suggested by Peter Berlin, relayed regularly in accessible media forms, has much still to offer to the cultural transformation of European life.

Third, sport has made significant contributions to the social reordering of culture within urban settings, in European cities and locations throughout our period under study. The Cold War was a huge influence for much of the period, but cultural flows were not simply one-way. Mega-sporting events, such as the Olympics, the men's football World Cup and the Commonwealth Games stimulate and symbolize in unparalleled ways new geopolitical configurations and economic orders, presaging a potential new world order of sport culture. For much of our period, the world order was contested between the Cold War superpowers of the USA and the USSR. Perhaps at the end of our period power is swinging away from Europe. Socio-cultural change can be planned and produced by the potential transformation of public spaces. Several contributions to this book, focusing on cities and events, inform such analytical and theoretical concerns. As the Soviet Union gave way to both a revived capitalism and a renaissance of separate nationalisms, sport itself was reframed in a post-Cold War economic and political landscape that was defined by a more assertive free market ideology. But towards the end of the period under review, the spatial dominance of Europe in staging such events was without doubt under challenge: from 1896–1996, Europe staged 54% of Summer Olympic Games, and from 1930–98, 50% of men's football World Cup Finals (European Commission, *c*.1998); of the Summer Olympics 2000–14, Europe won just two (40%), and of the World Cups 2002–22, Europe was awarded just Germany 2006 and Russia 2010 (33%). The decision of FIFA, in December 2010, to award the 2022 World Cup to Qatar ahead of the USA (with no European candidate permitted) was a sign – emitted, ironically, from the heart of Europe at FIFA's Swiss base – that any sense of European hegemony over dominant sporting spaces and events was increasingly misplaced.

The twelve chapters in this book reflect the thematic structure of this introductory chapter, ordered in a sequence according to the primary themes and topics of the volume: the Cold War, media developments and regulation. The final, twelfth chapter by van Bottenburg is a further reminder that not all things European are homogenized by global economic and political change and the cultural and economic influences that flow outwards from the USA. But the central question of socio-cultural change informs all the studies in the book, and the empirically embedded chapters speak to more than just one of the core themes. They could be shaken and stirred, to Cold War warrior James Bond's distaste, and still constitute a tasty mix. An afterword by Miller offers provocative reflections on the globalization process through which states, media markets and cities have transformed the context in which the post-1990 pan-European sporting landscape has emerged. Overall, the chapters illuminate sport's place in the contemporary history of post-Second World War and Cold War Europe; reaffirm the interconnectedness of the cultural, the social and the economic in the sporting trends of the period; and highlight sport's neglected contribution to the remaking and continuing transformation of Europe.

Notes

1   Interview with Alan Tomlinson, Friday 11 December 2010.
2   See Tomlinson (2011).
3   This is a collection about the state, politics and the media. It is not a 'bottom-up' study of sport as mass culture. Other volumes can and should be compiled on the grassroots spread of sports participation across Europe. The provision of sport was an important component of both the long-running Christian Democrat-dominated coalitions of Germany and Italy, and the governments of the social democratic left. There was a tacit understanding, which in some cases became an explicit consensus, that sport was 'a good thing'. This, however, is not a collection about the place of sport in 'welfare capitalism' of left or right. Rather than looking at European sport in the now familiar terms of a culture of participation and consumption, these chapters offer an innovative approach by concentrating on the ideological, technological and regulatory context that underpinned it.
4   See Schiller and Young (2010).
5   See Braudel (1980).
6   For a discussion of the *longue durée* as related to sport's development in Europe 1880–1939, see Tomlinson and Young (forthcoming).
7   See CRESC website, www.cresc.ac.uk. The second phase of the CRESC project has identified five primary themes: spirits of capitalism; reframing the national/transnationalism; material powers – culture and social ordering (including urban spatialization); topographies; and culture, participation and inequalities. The interconnected case studies and overviews in this book contribute to this five-point research agenda, so it is appropriate to conclude this introduction with commentaries on the first three themes of this agenda, compatible as they are with the core considerations of the AHRC symposium (states, media and markets) upon which this book is based.

References

Andreff, W. and Szymanski, S. (eds), (2008), *Handbook on the Economics of Sport*, London: Edward Elgar.

Balbier, U., (2007), *Kalter Krieg auf der Aschenbahn: der deutsch-deutsche Sport 1950–1972*, Paderborn: Schöning.

Blain, N., Boyle, R. and O'Donnell, H., (1993), *Sport and National Identity in the European Media*, London: Leicester University Press.

Bourdieu, P., (1986), *Distinction: A Social Critique of the Judgement of Taste*, London: Routledge & Kegan Paul.

Braudel, F., (1980), 'Will Capitalism Survive?', *The Wilson Quarterly*, 4 (2), 108–16.

Braun, J., (2009), 'The People's Sport? Popular Sport and Fans in the Later Years of the German Democratic Republic', *German History*, 27 (3): 414–28.

Collins, R., (1999), *Macro-History: Essays in the Sociology of the Long Run*, Stanford: Stanford University Press.

Council of the European Union, (2008), *European Council Declaration on Sport, Annex 5, Presidency Conclusions 17271/08*, Brussels, 11 and 12 December.

Cronin, M., (2003), 'Review Article: Playing Games? The Serious Business of Sports History', *Journal of Contemporary History*, 38 (3): 495–503.

Dine, P. and Crosson, S. (eds), (2010), *Sport, Representation and Evolving Identities in Europe*, Oxford: Peter Lang.

European Commission, (*c*.1998), *The European Model of Sport*, Brussels: Directorate General X.

——, (2007), *White Paper on Sport*, COM (2007) 391 Final, 11 July (last update 9 January 2009).

Harrington, A., (2005), 'Introduction to Georg Simmel's Essay "Europe & America in World History"', *European Journal of Social Theory*, 8 (1): 63–72 (includes Simmel's essay, pp. 69–72).

Hill, J., (2003), 'Introduction: Sport and Politics', *Journal of Contemporary History*, 38 (3): 355–361.

Hobsbawm, E., (1995), *The Age of Extremes, 1914–1991*, London: Abacus.

Jarausch, K. H. and Lindenberger, T. (eds), (2007), *Conflicted Memories: Europeanizing Contemporary Histories*, New York/Oxford: Berghahn Books.

Judt, T., (2005), *Postwar: A History of Europe since 1945*, London: Heinemann.

King, A., (2003), *The European Ritual*, Aldershot: Ashgate.

Mangan, J. A., Holt, R. and Lanfranchi, P. (eds), (1996), *European Heroes: Myth, Identity, Sport*, London: Frank Cass.

Merten, E., (2009), *Sowjetisch-deutsche Sportbeziehungen im 'Kalten Krieg'*, Sankt Augustin: Academia.

Parks, J., (2007), 'Verbal Gymnastics: Sports, Bureaucracy, and the Soviet Union's Entrance into the Olympic Games', in Stephen Wagg and David Andrews (eds), *East Plays West: Sport and the Cold War*, London: Routledge: 11–26.

Schiller, K. and Young, C., (2010), *The 1972 Munich Olympics and the Making of Modern Germany*, (Berkeley: University of California Press.

Shore, C., (2000), *Building Europe: The Cultural Politics of European Integration*, London: Routledge.

TNS Opinion & Social, (2004), *The Citizens of the European Union and Sport*, Special Eurobarometer 213, Wave 62.0, Brussels: European Commission.

Tomlinson, A., (2011), *The World Atlas of Sport: Who Plays What, Where, and Why?* Berkeley: University of California Press.

Tomlinson, A., and Young, C., (forthcoming) 'Sport in Modern European History: Trajectories, Constellations, Conjunctures', *Journal of Historical Sociology*, 25 (1) (e-copy December 2011).

Wagg, S. and Andrews, D. L. (eds), (2007), *East Plays West: Sport and the Cold War*, London: Routledge.

Wakeman, R. (ed.), (2003), *Themes in Modern European History since 1945*, London: Routledge.

1 Soviet physical culture and sport

A European legacy?

Nikolaus Katzer

Twenty years after the collapse of the Soviet Union, the achievements and failures of the first communist state in world history have become the subject of intense academic debate. Cultural historians, political scientists, sociologists and economists have begun to assess the Soviet experience, and of the many 'achievements' ascribed to Soviet socialism (e.g. industrial development, elimination of backwardness, its educational system, and victory over Germany in the Second World War), sport is one of the less contentious. Indeed, it is arguably the most established and celebrated. Although its structures did not survive the *perestroika* years, its reputation remains intact for many Russians. The athletes and officials might have broken free from the political and ideological restraints of the system, but they lost the privileges and financial support they had previously enjoyed. With the end of the Cold War, the socialist 'body machine', which produced one record-breaking performance after another, had lost the contest with 'bourgeois', Western sport. But we should pause and ask if Soviet sport was really 'socialist'? Did the essentials of Soviet physical culture (*fizkul'tura*) differ as much, say, as the overall social and political order undoubtedly did from Western Europe and the United States? As prominent, high-profile characteristics of the 'Soviet Modern' (the ambiguous and conflicting culture of state socialism as a certain incarnation of modernity), *fizkul'tura* and sport seemed to have more potential for transnational relations with the outside world than other sectors of post-revolutionary society. Sport's propensity for direct, 'non-political' and emotional communication presented an ideal opportunity to intensify foreign contacts, and it is not surprising that sport under Stalinism was upgraded to an important tool in foreign relations (Prozumenshchikov, 2004). After emulating Western patterns in the inter-war period, sport's universalism offered attractive ways of asserting national power in the international arena (Keys, 2006).

'Soviet sport' remains an object of nostalgia and admiration. Obviously post-Soviet governments, not least the Putin administration, have tried to revive one of the most impressive and successful products of the socialist era, and this has generated a view of the miserable state of sport in contemporary Russia, the post-Soviet sporting system having become a subject of widespread public criticism. On the one hand, Soviet-era sport complexes such as the Podolsk Olympic training centre near Moscow are crumbling. Yet on the other, the International Olympic

Committee entrusted the Russian Federation with the organization of the Olympic Winter Games in 2014 in Sochi at the Black Sea, prompting the government to spend billions of dollars on rebuilding the athletic machine. On the eve of the 2008 Beijing Olympics, the political leadership was told to plan several thousand new sports facilities. Heralding a revival of its former status as a major sports power, the political and economic elites seem to be speculating on the country's hunger for international prestige. But can the revival of a dynamic social and cultural force be managed only by political will? Historians must consider the extent to which the Soviet sports infrastructure was an element of an autonomous area of social change shaped by physical activities, and then set this carefully against the government's power to act as a catalyst to transform society through body and leisure politics. It is not necessarily self-evident that the Soviet sports complex represented a 'system' that was fundamentally different from others (Graham: 1998, XI–XIII).

This chapter seeks to answer this question by focusing primarily on selected aspects of Soviet physical culture and sports, debating them in the context of the new, internationally comparative approach to sports history, which has emerged in recent years. By exploring Russian experiences during the first half of the twentieth century, which are crucial to an understanding of the ambiguous development of Soviet sport after 1945, the chapter outlines the breaks and continuities, the landmarks and contexts. In order to clarify the contribution of Soviet civilization in general and Soviet sport in particular to the Modern Age in Europe, a deeper engagement is needed with the question of how physical culture and sport are affected by specific environments. Consideration must be given too to how, and if, these contextual influences change sport and physical culture's universal meaning. Soviet sport can be seen either as a social construction that genuinely differs from the British, German and other cases, or as one that generally follows the same lines. Since it emerged under Western influence and was developed by a permanent, interrelated transfer of modes and methods, sport could be used for diplomatic purposes, not because it was peculiarly 'socialist' but because of its 'sportive' universalism.

Fizkul'tura: a Soviet *Turnen?*

Alongside German *Turnen* (Krüger, 1996) and Czech *Sokol* (in English, 'Falcon') (Ruffini and Sivulka, 2005; Blecking, 1991), Russian *fizkul'tura* represented a third variation of the modern physical education that was prominent in Central and Eastern Europe before and after the First World War, and connected gymnastics and other non-competitive body activities with social ideologies. In general, all three physical forms have their roots in national movements and the process of industrialization. To date, the Soviet variety has been researched only in part. German *Turnen* associations, most prominently the school of '*Turnvater*' Friedrich Ludwig Jahn, and elitist British sports clubs, are held to have had a formative influence. These were accompanied by a whole series of popular champions of gymnastic and sporting education (Riordan, 1977a; Read, 1996; McReynolds, 2003:

87–95), most notably biologist, anatomist, educationalist and social reformer Petr F. Lesgaft (1837–1909), whom Soviet scholarship hailed as the 'founder of the scientific physical education' (Samoukov, 1964: 230). Each of them fostered and encouraged an explicitly masculine cult of the body.

The Bolsheviks broadened this pre-revolutionary legacy, giving it far-reaching utopian (as well as practical) expectations that were of central importance to their political aims and goals. In the 1920s, the *avant-garde*'s visions of disciplined masses of workers transformed by industrial metronomes into a huge and elegant *corps de ballet* had not yet come to dominate sports discourse and the practice of festivals. Rather, the kinetic visions were multiple, complex and conflicting. Ranging from eurhythmics and expressive dance to paramilitary formation exercises and human pyramids, or even modern and imported or native and traditional physical culture pastimes (Stites, 1989: 145–64), many of them nonetheless shared similar ideas of communality and collectivism, a cult of steel, (electrical) energy and technical standards. At the same time, they expressed themselves in images of strong, healthy and beautiful bodies that represented the self-conscious, harmonious society of the future (Bowlt, 1996). On the eve of Stalin's revolution, the overlaps were such that it would have been impossible to determine the borderlines between the nationalist Russian, internationalist Soviet, and modernist European elements of the physical culture movements.

Early Bolsheviks viewed 'science-based' adult education programmes as an effective vehicle of social change. But the mass literacy campaign 'Away with Illiteracy!' (*Doloi negramotnost'!*), the reading cottages (*izby-chital'ni*) in villages, and the worker faculties (*rabfaki*) and Party schools (*partshkoly*) could only deliver political training in a general sense and at a more abstract level through verbal and visual forms of knowledge dissemination (Holmes, 1991; Fitzpatrick, 2002). As in the world of children's education, therefore, there was a need to occupy time outside the classroom and to inculcate citizens with 'rational leisure' – to subject all manifestations of culture to a spatial and temporal ordering, from the workplace to music, theatre and domestic life. One important way of doing this was to encourage 'physical culture' (*fizkul'tura*), a 'sport for health' movement that drew on the contemporary obsession with prophylactic medicine (Starks, 2008: 73–76, 191–93). This movement had its roots in the Civil War, during which the Central Board of Universal Military Training (*Vseobshchee voennoe obuchenie, Vsevobuch*), founded on 7 May 1918, had been given the task of bringing all conscriptable men up to the requisite standard of physical fitness.[1] These militaristic and masculine origins (only 4% of the organization's 143,563 members in 1921 were women) were diluted during the later development of the *fizkul'tura* movement following criticism from hygienists that *Vsevobuch* was too 'sportist' in its emphasis. Thereafter, *fizkul'tura* had two branches: competitive sport and the mass performance of collective exercises, described contemptuously by one of sport's most influential supporters, Nikolai Semashko, Director of the Supreme Council of Physical Culture, as 'the semolina pudding of hygienic gymnastics'.[2] In his capacity as People's Commissar of Health, however, Semashko often appeared a staunch supporter of discipline in the schoolhouse, the special colonies for abandoned children, the workplace and the home. Differences remained as to how socialist body politics should best proceed and what counted as 'soft' and 'hard' exercises or 'useful' and 'damaging' practices. Whatever one's view of such social experiments in early Soviet Russia, attempts to ignite a genuine 'communist' physical culture were met with little enthusiasm. Apart from numerous campaigns, directives and resolutions that sought to incorporate a centralized 'system' of physical activities, the transformation of Soviet life via modern sport followed a variety of directions. On the ethnically diverse peripheries, modern body culture diffused at different rates. Women exploited the emancipatory potential of sport in various ways, coming into conflict with both the strict patriarchal order and the central party's changing notions of womanhood (Goscilo and Lanoux, 2006). The conflict between non-competitive gymnastics and competitive sport continued, and the protagonists and spectators of popular sports such as boxing and football hardly offered themselves for easy assimilation to the noble goals of 'healthy' and 'hygienic' bodily culture favoured by the state. Although the 1930s saw the establishment of a canon of officially desirable sports disciplines, a range of others – more or less tolerated, or even disapproved of – developed their own dynamic with particular fan cultures and social milieus.[3]

The *fizkul'tura* movement, then, was highly ambiguous, containing a mix of different native and foreign cultural traditions and codes of bodily practice (Borenstein, 2000; Zlydneva, 2005). To retain credibility, the champions of a normative Soviet body culture could not ignore the dilemma of having to combine modern sporting elements with a widespread preference for notions from the nineteenth century, which rendered any exclusive focus on gymnastics impossible. Nonetheless, the countless other functions that were heaped upon *fizkul'tura* (paramilitary training, prevention of disease, the acculturation of peasant migrants to the process of mechanical labour via production gymnastics or the assimilation, *korenizaciia*, of non-Russian ethnic minorities to the 'Soviet family') aroused such diverse associations and expectations that the 'unity' of the concept could be achieved only with the extreme ritualization of public and private, individual and collective bodily practices.

In as far as the original aim of Soviet *fizkul'tura* was to provide an 'all-round' education, equal in physical, mental and spiritual terms, it is possible to conceive of it as a variant of *Turnen*. Equally, the aim of producing an instrument of Soviet nation-building echoed older models. But what emerged in the 1930s as a collective state form of multiple associations turned *fizkul'tura* into an unmistakable characteristic of Soviet culture that survived into the late period of socialism. On the one hand, *fizkul'tura* aimed to bring the Soviet population up to the fitness levels required by a modern industrial state and, more sinisterly, to ensure its preparedness for civil defence (*boevaja gotovnost*); the public parades by trim young *fizkul'turniki* with their human pyramids and mass exercises were also intended as powerful representations of a fit new society and the healthy state of the Soviet body politic (Atwood and Kelly, 1998: 267–68).[4] On the other hand, the identification of socialism with Soviet state-building in the 1920s was challenged by cultural and national autonomy promoted by the authorities themselves. Clubs and circles generated more or less independent activist milieus, enthusiasts and fans crowding the sports scene with agendas other than those of the official festivities. These non-conformist grassroots cultures invented their own traditions, partially competing with the radical political and social changes that followed. After the death of Stalin and the cultural 'thaw' under Khrushchev, the emergence of both a deviant youth culture and informal intellectual groups led to an ironic turn in the perception of the Soviet craze for massive sports spectaculars (Makoveeva, 2002).

The winning spirit of the 1930s

One phrase that often recurs in post-Soviet nostalgia is the notion of the 'winning spirit of the 1930s'.[5] In some discourses, the 'victory of socialism' is told as a series of achievements and portrayed as a precondition of the Red Army's triumph in the Second World War. In this version of the past, there is no alternative to high-performance sport. In point of fact, *fizkul'tura* and competitive sport never actually functioned as a workable unit. Corresponding with the power struggle in the Communist Party and the sharp ideological debate on how the backward country should be transformed into a modern industrial power (Halfin, 2007), the rivalry between the two concepts of body politics intensified sharply. A parting of the ways began at the end of the 1920s. The Moscow *Spartakiad* of 1928 was the last time that the Olympics (in Amsterdam) were openly challenged by the rival claim to supremacy of 'true' sport and international solidarity (Gounot, 1998; Heeke, 2003: 88–89). Concerned about the threat of foreign invasion, Stalin emphasized the importance of building up an effective heavy industry to produce modern weapons. But winning the race against capitalism eventually meant aspiring to superiority in all significant social spheres, and sporting success became crucial because of its eminent symbolic value (Keys, 2006). This increasing competitiveness downgraded the 'soft' forms of *fizkul'tura* – physical activities such as gymnastics and dance – as an 'end in itself' or as a means of healthcare. Sport, by contrast, became a matter of prime importance to the state and was seen as every citizen's duty. Under pressure to mobilize the whole country as quickly as possible, there could be no 'sport for sport's sake' (Washburn, 1955/56: 490). Sport became 'serious fun' (Edelman, 1993), a means of physical and mental mass training, social integration and political education. The ideology of 'winning' was transferred from the factory and the front line to the stadium (Brüggemann, 2002: 60). As new-born heroes of the 1930s, the athletes enjoyed equal status with the Stakhanovites, icons of Socialist labour in industry (*udarniki*), air force pilots, or army tank drivers (*tankisty*) (Günther, 1993: 175–79). Popular slogans ('The Red Army – the Real School of Physical Culture', 'Physical Culturists – the Red Army's Reserve'), and martial spectacles such as fencing with carbines with rubber bayonets attached, represented the now undisputed symbiotic alliance between sport and the military (Washburn, 1955/56: 491–92). The so-called GTO plan (*Gotov k trudu i oborone*, or 'Ready for Work and Defence') and an All-Union Athletic Classification System for forty-five recognized sports set standards primarily for citizens aged fourteen to forty (Morton, 1963: 34–39). Supervised by *Komsomol* (Communist Youth League),

Trade Unions and state authorities, millions of people participated in this huge 'socialist competition'. Athletics and winter sports were especially widespread, and team and ball sports such as football, volleyball, basketball and ice hockey, as well as the 'sport of the people', chess, were popular. Amongst the earliest Soviet stars were the Starostin brothers, whose popularity on the football pitch nonetheless did not protect them from the repression of Stalinism (Starostin, 1969, 1986).[6] However, the balance between training the masses (*massovost'*) and producing a sporting elite (*masterstvo*) could be maintained only for a short time.

Gold from the laboratory

In his speech 'Culture and Socialism' (1926), Trotsky adopted a key element of American industrial culture: Fordism. Trotsky understood the conveyor belt, the incarnation of rational factory labour, as the 'highest expression' of 'harmonious-ness' and the 'principle of socialist economy'. Under socialism, he claimed, human nature would be transformed by technology, when the need 'to separate Fordism from Ford and to socialize and purge it', to render it compatible with the Soviet order, had been completed (Trotsky, 1973: 243). Fordism and Taylorism (the rational and measurable maximization of industrial production) can be seen as direct links between Bolshevik theory and Stalinist practice. Stalin's juxtaposition of American efficiency and Russian revolutionary sweep was rooted in Bolshevism from the very beginning (Stites, 1989: 146–55). '*Amerikanizatsiya*' was a metaphor for speedy industrial tempo, high growth and productivity.

Other elements of the Stalinist concept of 'superman in motion' (or all-round *homo sovieticus sportivus*) include 'biomechanics' (in the sphere of body mea-surement and control); 'eurhythmics' (a form of music education pioneered in Switzerland); and Aleksandr Bogdanov's concept of the arts as a medium to affect cognition and emotion (Bogdanov, 1929: 130; Bowlt, 1996). Furthermore, Aleksei Gastev, a proletarian poet who spent many years in industry as a skilled metal worker, dreamt of letting the whole nation sample the benefits of his experimental laboratory of human 'robotics', known as the Central Institute of Labour (1920–38). In this vision of a future Machine Culture, 'the iron demon' of the age would have the 'soul of a man', 'nerves of steel' and 'rails for muscles' (Vaingurt, 2008: 218). In this understanding, the animation of machinery and the mechanization of human beings were seen as opposite poles in a single process. Shaped by modern machinery and military exercises, the 'barbarous' and illiterate peasants and the 'wild' and lazy workers would acquire a new mindset that would stop them from smoking, eating and drinking on the job, and turn them into punctual, efficient, careful and well organized citizens.

The Central Institute of Labour expanded into offices and a network of training centres in which workers were taught to think, act and work with 'iron discipline'. At such places, dozens of men and women trainees in identical costumes received instructions from electronic beeps on a machine. Their 'teacher' was a hammer-machine; a cyclogram photographed their imitational work and recorded their progress (Fülöp-Miller, 1926: plates 171–73; Stites, 1989: 154). Gastev's vision of a 'human machine' culminated in the image of a 'superman' who would master nature, death and time.

'The country of heroes, dreamers, scientists, and scholars', as one popular song of the 1930s put it (Ivanov, 1948: 147), was transformed into a huge laboratory. It comprised more than just large-scale technological projects (*Belomor*, Metro, *Dneprostroi*) (Neutatz, 2001; Gestwa, 2010): under Stalinism the 'scientification' of *all* aspects of life led to highly speculative animal and human experiments. At the intersection of hygiene, eugenics, biology, medicine and physiology, the human body became a limitless interdisciplinary vision (Krementsov, 1997: 782–85; Kojevnikov, 2004). The end product of the scientists', engineers' and revolutionaries' common efforts would be the perfect 'body Soviet' that would produce a constant flow of outstanding cultural and political achievements. This fascination with science is closely reflected in Mikhail Bulgakov's novella *Heart of a Dog*, a Soviet version of *Frankenstein* (Howell, 2006).

The sporting dimensions of Bulgakov's take-off of Soviet Big Science have received little attention and could usefully be set within a broader context. The Bolshevik philosopher and physician Bogdanov, for instance, initiated systematic experiments with blood transfusion, one of which proved deadly for himself in 1928 (Huestis, 2001; Vöhringer, 2006). Others expected new insights into the human constitution to emerge from 'psychotechnique' (*psikhotekhnika*), a branch of applied psychology popular in the 1920s (Vöhringer, 2007). Much better known is the great impact of the behaviourist theories of Ivan P. Pavlov on Soviet sciences and beyond. Usually acknowledged as the founding father of world-leading Soviet research, this eminent physiologist was the first Russian scientist to win the Nobel Prize (in 1904) and mentored numerous scholars and pupils (Rüting, 2002; Todes, 2002). It is obvious that the obscure history of Soviet 'sports medicine' (*sportivnaya meditsina*, a term officially employed, it seems, only in the 1970s) as an independent discipline had its roots within these contexts. By the time it entered international sporting competition at the Winter Olympics in Helsinki in 1952, the Soviet Union already had an integrated, highly centralistic network of sports medical centres, led by the Ministry of Health and drawing on the Academy of Medical Science and the State Committee for Bodily Culture and Sport. Although specialists in injury and rehabilitation, the sports medical experts were in possession of such broad physiological, anatomical and kinetic competence that they could advise athletes and coaches across the disciplines. They were involved in talent spotting and in setting up gender-specific training programmes, which drew – amongst other things – upon 1920s techniques of hygiene. Advances in sports medical research remained off limits for the general public (Katzer, 2008: 217–22).[7]

Iconography of power

The culture of the Stalin period required the reshaping not only of landscapes and cities, but also of the male and female body. Journals, leaflets, newspapers, brochures, books and broadcasting reminded the population of the benefits of physical exercises, cold baths and fresh air. The *Komsomol* and other mass organizations were called upon to mobilize and educate young activists as propagandists for a healthy lifestyle. Their vibrant, muscular and healthy physiques, displayed as examples of a new human species, were cultivated to impress and inspire children in schools and pioneer camps. Socialist realist art played a significant role in glamourizing these idealized, partially undressed bodies. Statues of sportsmen and women decorated the new Moscow subway, and whole stations turned into galleries of heroic bronzes, mosaics and *bas-reliefs* (O'Mahony, 2006: 104–21).

Besides members of the elite who took part in revolutionary festivals, *fizkul'tura* aimed its propaganda at ordinary Soviet citizens, who were subjected to compulsory physical education in schools from 1933 onwards, and exhorted to follow the exercise programmes printed in Soviet newspapers and magazines and, later, to tune into exercise broadcasts on the radio (Ellis, 1998). *Fizkul'turniki* parades were determined to represent the happy and joyous 'land of the Soviets' (Petrone, 2000: 23–39; Rolf, 2006: 167–69). Describing such a parade in Moscow in 1937, the year of the Great Terror, *Pravda* proclaimed, 'It was as if the whole country unfolded in front of the spectators, and they felt that in every corner of the country, no matter how far away, creative work was boiling, amazing human material was springing up whose equal did not exist anywhere else in the world.'[8] From the 1930s, the media interpreted the parades as the Soviet Union *en miniature*. Presenting all regions, nationalities and cultures of the 'fatherland of socialism' as members of a healthy and mighty family, the centre of empire turned into a magnificent image of perfect order (Beissinger, 2006). 'March of the Enthusiasts' (*Marsh entuziastov*), a typical mass song set to music by Isaak Dunaevskii, the most famous 1930s composer of popular songs, praised the gigantic but indivisible land, which stretched across 'steppes and forests' 'from the poles to the tropics'.[9]

Yet as means of identity formation, the parades and mediatized *fizkul'tura* had their limitations. Though effective as rituals of solidarity or contributions to hygiene awareness, gymnastic displays were unable to transmit new roles that were useful outside the boundaries of physical culture itself. Their success lay in their great ability to mobilize extraordinary, festive events. Into the late Soviet period the *Spartakiad* continued to be understood as a symbiosis of mass and high-performance sport, which ideally allowed a leading athlete to emerge from amongst millions of Soviet citizens, who would go on to represent them all at international level.[10] The state project urgently required structures and systems for strengthening self-confidence and shaping individual behaviour within the collective. But precisely this aspect of the *Spartakiad*'s popular appeal seems to have waned consistently from the 1950s onwards. High-performance athletes were no longer incentivized by mass sport, and amateur sportsmen and women, by the same token, gradually lost interest in physical activity due to the privileging of stars, the mediatization of sport, and the growth of a socialist consumer society. The *Gotov k trudu i oborone SSSR* (GTO) sports classification system gave distinction to many athletes but allowed only a few the opportunity to enter the social elite.

Cold War sports

During the first half of the twentieth century, the social dynamics of Russia's urban centres and rural regions changed fundamentally, as they were redefined by radical political decisions that caused turbulent demographic tremors. Initiated by forced collectivization, mass terror and the Second World War, several waves of migrations from villages to towns (and occasionally *vice versa*) shattered identities and social ties. Between 1939 and 1959, around 25 million citizens turned their back on the countryside. Between 1961 and 1980, almost another 20 million followed in the Russian Socialist Federal Soviet Republic (RSFSR) alone (Lovell, 2009: 90). The history of sport mirrored this development as body culture and leisure activities became more than ever an exclusively urban phenomenon. The stubborn campaigns that had tried to bring physical culture to the peasants since the 1920s and 1930s were never successful,[11] just as investment in rural versus urban sports facilities never balanced out. After the war, criticism of the bias towards urban-based structures finally faded. Despite Khrushchev's highly ambitious attempt to urbanize the countryside, the impact of the virgin lands project and the concept of 'agro-towns' was negligible. These missed the train to the Socialist Modern. The collectivized peasantry had no desire to heed any calls for the next huge experiment, which seemed to be no more than another journey into the unknown.

The political leadership's decision to compete with the West in high-performance sport and to advance in the cultural Cold War had a long-term effect on the whole of the sports complex. As a result of the state's massive promotion of elite athletes, sport had no need for the support of a mass sporting infrastructure, especially outside the urban centres. The reality of physical culture in schools, universities, organizations and industrial enterprises rapidly fell behind the official self-image of a properly and fully trained nation. But from the 1950s, the Soviet statistics masked the slipping sporting targets and claimed to be the world's fittest society, with huge numbers of formal participants in union-wide competitions (such as GTO or *Spartakiads*) and physical culture groups (in factories, trade unions and state organizations).[12] In reality, however, a large community of state-funded coaches, advisors, officials and top athletes were towering above the quicksand of mass sport. Formally, the establishment was supposed to function as the nucleus of a nationwide sportive network, but bit by bit this elite lost its clientele. Equally concerned with motivating individuals and groups, children and adults, young and old, men and women, workers, peasants and soldiers to do sport in the morning and in the evening, at work and at home, this huge apparatus habitually claimed to be the motor of a 'society in motion'. As professionals and 'state amateurs', sports officials and stars marked the transformation of the Soviet Union into a modern state the equal of the leading capitalist states. For a time at least, like the Sputnik, modern sport could compensate for the inferior performance of the economy.[13]

But as a significant attribute of Soviet civilization and popular culture, sport remained a predominantly urban matter. It was not until 1974 that new passport legislation provided collective farm workers with the right of free movement within the Soviet Union. Despite this formal right, the majority were condemned to staying in the 'dying villages'. For them, participation in sports lost its connotation as a physical activity and turned into a consumer habit. Until the late 1950s, the rural audience learned about the records of Soviet athletes at Olympic Games, World Championships and other international competitions mainly from the radio. By 1970, television had replaced radio as the dominant national medium, and the higher levels of television watching correlated strongly with a low education level and the marginal status of the agrarian population. In a country expressly committed to the creation of a new culture, not least a 'rational' and 'active' leisure culture, the gap between urban and rural life, and between goals and reality, had increased rapidly since the 1960s. Neither radio nor television could bridge it, however successfully they might otherwise have served as mediators of Soviet norms, attitudes and convictions. As elsewhere in the world, the audiovisual allure of the media seemed to create an all-embracing consumer culture, levelling social differences and uniting ethnic sections of society. However much the broadcasting of sports mega-events may have had an integrating effect on the composition or structure of the audience, the reception was as multiple as the society itself. Mediatized Soviet sport, of course, can be seen as a harmonizing factor. But as a means of changing society, it would have needed more than the development and provision of the technology itself. Some form of active counterpart would have been essential, but it was lacking.

Shaping its distinctive mode in the 1950s and 1960s, the Soviet way of life contained hybrid types of sportive behaviour. Individual elements of this sporting lifestyle derived from the multifaceted inheritance of the pre-war period, and were now supplemented by the symbols of socialist consumer society heralded by Khrushchev and Brezhnev, such as fridges, television sets, washing machines and cars. In this early period of consumerism in the socialist welfare state, new kitchens, the dream of individual mobility, and the sports park took on the importance that the technological race for atomic energy, space travel and arms technology had in the political arena of the Cold War. The battle for cultural and technological superiority had begun most promisingly for the Soviet Union: the sports model that had been maturing over several decades proved itself with immediate and stunning success at the Olympic Games in Helsinki, Melbourne, Rome and Tokyo. In 1956, the luxurious *Luzhniki* sports park with the accompanying Lenin stadium opened in Moscow – a remarkable example of sleek modern architecture after the Stalin era. Parallel to the sensational Sputnik space exploration the following year, the Russian capital projected itself as the cosmopolitan host of a spectacular World Youth Festival with theatre, music and dance (Reid and Crowley, 2000: 9–14; Roth-Ey, 2004; Koivunen, 2009).

While the media presented high-performance sport as a brilliant yet accessible temple of post-war socialism, top athletes vanished from everyday life into the glamorous cosmos of internationalism, tourism and consumerism. As inhabitants of a freshened-up Soviet hall of fame, they appeared as incarnations of success and prosperity. From this point, sport has almost always been a synecdoche for the land of opportunity, a stage for the Soviet dream of global superiority and the incarnation of the body Soviet. Historians, though, need to record the whole story.

For the ordinary urban citizens or the have-nots of the distant countryside, the promise of boundless mobility, material success and a bright future with which the popular press, radio and television regaled audiences had little if any substance in the everyday lives of the majority from the second half of Brezhnev's leadership (Zaporozhets and Krupets, 2008).

The feeling of lost socialist utopia in the 1970s, the exhaustion after decades of enthusiasm, violence and rapid change, and the frustration with the repeated defects of the economic system coincided with the crisis of physical culture (Katzer *et al.*, 2010). Soviet citizens wearied of permanent heroism. In retrospect, the decoupling of high-performance sport from physical culture, the preferential sponsorship of the former and the creeping emaciation of the latter, led to the decay and eventual collapse of the Soviet sports system as a whole. The state's distorted priorities damaged the people's enthusiasm for activity and engagement.[14] The more the gap widened after the Second World War, the more the utopian concepts of the early Soviet period proved illusory.

Legacies

What can we learn about modern sport from the Soviet (Russian) experience? First, it is clear that the requiem for communism was not celebrated in any splendid afterlife of 'Soviet sport'. The Russian experience sheds much light on the place of physical culture and sport in modern society. Further investigation is needed to find out what is more important to the development of sport: political freedom, money, autonomy or social control by state institutions, a democratic and federalist or an authoritarian and centralist structure? Locating the legacy of Soviet sport within the Socialist Modern requires a detailed empirical mapping of institutional networks, social change, centre–periphery connections and international relations. We have to bear in mind that the Russian experience is only one of several in Eastern Europe. Research in this comparative field is still at an early stage (Malz *et al.*, 2007; Wagg and Andrews, 2007). A further open question is whether the Soviet concept of physical culture and sport played any role in relations with the post-colonial world. As far as the Asian periphery of the Soviet Union is concerned, sport always served as a tool to enhance the modernizing mission of socialism in 'backward' regions. But not much is known about the impact Soviet body politics actually had in the process of nation-building at the margins, or on the emancipation of women in patriarchal societies. While debates about the globalization of sport have often focused on the detrimental effects of forsaking regional and traditional games in the name of international development, little is known about national sports cultures under Soviet communism and their stubbornness in the face of centrally organized *Spartakiads* and GTO competitions (Krämer-Mandeau, 1991). Identity evolves not just via global, regional or local symbols and behaviours, but often from a particular mixture of these.[15] The transition of the Soviet Union from a country occupied with its own internal colonization and the subjugation of its peripheries into a world power that sought to extend its civilizing mission to the so-called Third World brought with it questions about the universality, transferability and flexibility of its own sports model. The development and impact of an immense collective force such as the sports complex, acting in a social and economic environment strikingly different from the European West (the birthplace of modern sports), offers an excellent focus and opportunity for comparative analysis.

Non-commercial Soviet sport after the Second World War and under Cold War conditions had an intensifying and increasing effect on the commercialization of global sport. Western sport reacted to the challenge from the East by copying, acquiring and adapting its principles and mechanisms, wherever useful and effective: talent selection, centralization of structures, the bundling of resources, state sponsorship, and promotion by industry and the military.[16] Of course, there was a barely developed market for players, equipment or investors. But the 'supermen' and 'superwomen' of supposedly amateur sport received many privileges and donations as incentives to stay in the USSR and remain loyal to the Socialist state. Not least, the patrimonial system under Brezhnev can be interpreted as a camouflage for the highly differentiated system of (material or financial, not just symbolic) rewards that could be found in other spheres of cultural life, such as literature, music or ballet (Oberender, 2008).

Socialism never came up with a solution for 'sport for the masses' – popular sport. On the contrary, all indicators show that the supply of equipment and facilities (stadiums, swimming pools, sports grounds, halls) to the population was much more advanced in most Western countries than in the Soviet Union (Riordan, 1993: 254). In this respect, there was never a socialist 'sporting society'. From the 1920s, every transformation in the sports sector directly or indirectly strengthened the position of competitive sports and, later, high-performance sport. The gap between *fizkul'tura* (as a synonym for all kinds of mass sport) and elite sport began to widen after 1945, when the Soviet Union decided to participate in the Olympics and World Championships. In place of *homo sovieticus sportivus* (who remained the subject of a utopian project), modern socialist society smoothed the way either for elite athletes or for enthusiasts (fans) watching hockey matches in arenas or on television. (For further details on the latter, see Chapter 2 in this volume.) The vast majority of the rest had to use their talent for improvisation to do sports that did not need facilities, reviving traditional recreations, or to stitch together modern sports kit from patterns published in popular journals. Impressive innovations such as the Park of Culture and Rest (*Park kul'tury i otdykha*) or the *Luzhniki* Sports Park were conceived and constructed, but with a diversionary rationale rather than any transformative vision or goal (Kucher, 2007). These pleasure garden-type sites of more or less active recreation offered citizens of the capital a variety of performance possibilities on outdoor stages – from shooting galleries and roller-coasters to roundabouts – but also sport facilities, such as skating-rinks, tennis-courts and boating lakes. After the Stalinist decades of compulsory mobilization, the 'heroes' of everyday life were looking for the least strenuous activities possible.

Soviet physical culture and sport left a paradoxical legacy. Having started with a holistic concept for shaping a selfless, healthy, strong and optimistic New Mankind, it lost its dynamic social energy by being transformed into a normative set of habits and ritualized body activities. The formative experience of sports in the Stalinist 1930s resulted in a system of competitive values that was not shared by the majority of the population, and produced an exclusive high-performance sports elite enhanced by a huge bureaucratic apparatus. Just like Stakhanovism in heavy industry, the 'piecework' of record-producing Soviet athletes could not be transferred into common property.

Notes

1 Resources were mainly confiscated from pre-Revolutionary sports associations.
2 Cited in Riordan (1977b: 96).
3 The history of this alternative sports culture has been studied in depth only for football (Edelman, 1993) and automobiles (Siegelbaum, 2008). Contemporary Soviet sports journals (such as *Fizkul'tura i sport*, *Fizicheskaya kul'tura* and *Fizkul'tura i socialisticheskoe stroitel'stvo*) reflect the main lines of this controversial – part political-ideological, part scholarly-scientific – debate up to the year of the Great Terror, 1937.
4 'The Sporting March' (*'Sportivnyi marsh'*), a Soviet popular song, put it as follows: 'So your body and soul can be young, / Can be young, can be young – / Don't shrink away from the cold or the heat, / Temper yourself, like steel! / *Fizkul'tura*! Hurrah! / *Fizkul'tura*! Hurrah! / *Fizkul'tura*! Hurrah! Hurrah! / When the hour courses to bash all our enemies, / To drive them from our borders, be prepared! / Left! Right! Don't hang back! Don't be slack!' (A. Ivanov (ed.), (1948), *Pesni sovetskogo naroda*, Leningrad: Gosudarstvennoe Muzykal'noe Izdatel'stvo, 137; translation Atwood and Kelly, 1998: 269).
5 For instance, the slogan 'Will to Victory' in the Bolshevik discourse of the 1920s (Kenez and Shepherd, 1998: 31–33).
6 In general, there are no in-depth studies of the 'sports hero' – of the possible peculiarities of the Soviet cult of the star. But see Soskin (2007) and Vartanian (2001) on two football idols of the post-1945 period, goalkeeper Lev Yashin and striker Eduard Strel'tsov.
7 General decline problems were mentioned in debates about hygiene, healthcare and epidemics. Sports journals (for example *Teoriya i praktika fizicheskoi kul'tury*) regularly reported medical questions of general interest but not the spectacular results of interdisciplinary research. A specialist journal such as the GDR's *Medizin und Sport* did not exist. On the late Soviet Union, see Karpman (1980); Riordan (1987).
8 Pravda, 13 July 1937 (cited in Petrone, 2000: 23).
9 Ivanov (1948: 147; translation Atwood and Kelly, 1998: 271). On the composer Dunaevskii, see Stadelmann (2003).
10 See the bibliographical survey of literature about this ideological construction of common interests of amateur and high-performance sport (Belavenceva, 1956).
11 Sport magazines in the 1920s and early 1930s repeatedly complained about the almost complete lack of interest in physical culture in the countryside. See, for example, Starikov (1922); Gubarev (1928); Zavileiskii (1931).
12 The number of 'collectifs of physical culture' in the RSFSR allegedly increased from 62,000 in 1940 up to more than 190,000 in 1958, and that of 'physical culturists' from 5.3 million to 20.2 million (Samoukov, 1964: 328). After the end of the Soviet Union, the pure statistics for physical culture were scrutinized and compared with data from the medical literature. The latter gave a very different version of events. For instance, at the beginning of the 1980s, the health of schoolchildren and students had deteriorated; 43% of students were suffering from different chronic diseases, and 50% of youths had motor damage; 63% of those examined had been diagnosed with postural damage (Goloshchapov, 2004: 193).
13 On the interrelation of the space race, the Cold War and consumer culture, see Rüthers (2009); Reid and Crowley (2000: 1–24).

14 The 'fallen heroes' of everyday Soviet athleticism were the subject of dozens of ironic poems and songs written and performed by the popular bard of the 1960s and 1970s Vladimir Vysotsky.
15 On the British Empire see Dawson (2006).
16 See Balbier's (2007) study of GDR–FRG sports relations.

References

Atwood, L. and Kelly, C., (1998), 'Programmes for Identity: The "New Man" and the "New Woman"', in C. Kelly and D. Shepherd (eds), *Constructing Russian Culture in the Age of Revolution: 1881–1940*, Oxford: Oxford University Press: 256–90.

Balbier, U. A., (2007), *Kalter Krieg auf der Aschenbahn: Der deutsch-deutsche Sport 1950–1972*, Paderborn: Schöningh.

Beissinger, M. R., (2006), 'Soviet Empire as "Family Resemblance"', *Slavic Review*, 65 (2): 294–303.

Belavenceva, G. N., (1956), '*Shire massovost', vyshe masterstvo sovetskogo sporta! K Spartakiade narodov SSSR: Kratkij rekomendatel'nyi ukazatel' literatury*, Moscow: Ministerstvo kul'tury RSFSR.

Blecking, D. (ed.), (1991), *Die slawische Sokolbewegung: Beiträge zur Geschichte von Sport und Nationalismus in Osteuropa*, Dortmund: Forschungsstelle Ostmitteleuropa.

Bogdanov, A., (1929, repr. 1969), 'Proletariat i iskusstvo', in N. L. Brodskii (ed.), *Literaturnye manifesty: Ot simvolizma k Oktjabriu*, vol. 1, (Moscow), Munich: Wilhelm Fink: 130–31.

Borenstein, E., (2000), *Men without Women: Masculinity and Revolution in Russian Fiction, 1917–1929*, Durham: Duke University Press.

Bowlt, J. E., (1996), 'Body Beautiful: The Search for the Perfect Physique', in J. E. Bowlt and O. Matich (eds), *Laboratory of Dreams: The Russian Avant-Garde and Cultural Experiment*, Stanford: Stanford University Press: 37–58.

Brüggemann, K., (2002), *Von Krieg zu Krieg, von Sieg zu Sieg: Motive des sowjetischen Mythos im Massenlied der 1930er Jahre*, Hamburg: Dr. Kovač.

Dawson, M., (2006), 'Acting Global, Thinking Local: "Liquid Imperialism" and the Multiple Meanings of the 1954 British Empire & Commonwealth Games', *International Journal of the History of Sport*, 23 (1): 3–27.

Edelman, R., (1993), *Serious Fun: A History of Spectator Sports in the U.S.S.R.*, New York: Oxford University Press.

Ellis, F., (1998), 'The Media as Social Engineer', in C. Kelly and D. Shepherd (eds), *Russian Cultural Studies: An Introduction*, Oxford: Oxford University Press: 192–222.

Fitzpatrick, S., (2002), *Education and Social Mobility in the Soviet Union, 1921–34*, Cambridge: Cambridge University Press.

Fülöp-Miller, R., (1926), *Geist und Gesicht des Bolschewismus: Darstellung und Kritik des kulturellen Lebens in Sowjet-Russland*, Zurich: Amalthea.

Gestwa, K., (2010), *Die Stalinschen Großbauten des Kommunismus: Sowjetische Technik- und Umweltgeschichte, 1948–1967*, Munich: Oldenbourg.

Goloshchapov, B. R., (2004), *Istoriia fizicheskoi kul'tury i sporta: Uchebnoe posobie dlia studentov vysshikh uchebnykh zavedenii*, Moscow: Izdatel'skii centr Akademiia.

Goscilo, H. and Lanoux, A. (eds), (2006), *Gender and National Identity in Twentieth-Century Russian Culture*, DeKalb: Northern Illinois University Press.

Gounot, A., (1998), 'Between Revolutionary Demands and Diplomatic Necessity: The Uneasy Relationship between Soviet Sport and Worker and Bourgeois Sport in Europe from 1920 to 1937', in P. Arnaud and J. Riordan (eds), *Sport and International Politics: The Impact of Fascism and Communism on Sport*, London: Spon: 184–209.

Graham, L. R., (1998), *What Have We Learned About Science and Technology from the Russian Experience?* Stanford: University Press.

Gubarev, A., (1928), 'Fizkul'tura – v derevniu!', *Fizkul'tura i sport*, 13, 31 March: 1.

Günther, H., (1993), *Der sozialistische Übermensch – Maksim Gor'kij und der sowjetische Heldenmythos*, Stuttgart: Metzler.

Halfin, I., (2007), *Intimite Enemies: Demonizing the Bolshevik Opposition, 1918–1928*, Pittsburgh: University Press.

Heeke, M., (2003), *Reisen zu den Sowjets: Der ausländische Tourismus in Rußland 1921–1941*, Münster: LIT.

Holmes, L. E., (1991), *The Kremlin and the Schoolhouse: Reforming Education in Soviet Russia, 1917–1931*, Bloomington: Indiana University Press.

Howell, Y., (2006), 'Eugenics, Rejuvenation, and Bulgakov's Journey into the Heart of Dogness', *Slavic Review*, 65 (3): 544–62.

Huestis, D. W. (ed.), (2001), *Alexander Bogdanov: The Struggle for Viability: Collectivism Through Blood Exchange*, Tucson: Xlibris Corporation.

Ivanov, A. (ed.), (1948), *Pesni sovetskogo naroda*, Leningrad: Gosudarstvennoe muzykal'noe izdatel'stvo.

Karpman, V. L., (1980), *Sportivnaya meditsina*, Moscow: Fizkul'tura i Sport.

Katzer, N., (2008), 'Am Rande der Vollkommenheit: Aspekte einer Geschichte sowjetischer Körperoptimierung', in K. Latzel and L. Niethammer (eds), *Hormone und Hochleistung: Doping in Ost und West*, Cologne: Böhlau: 205–30.

Katzer, N., Budy, S., Köhring, A. and Zeller, M. (eds), (2010), *Euphoria and Exhaustion: Modern Sport in Soviet Culture and Society*, Frankfurt am Main: Campus.

Kenez, P. and Shepherd, D., (1998), '"Revolutionary" Models for High Literature: Resisting Poetics', in C. Kelly and D. Shepherd (eds), *Russian Cultural Studies: An Introduction*, Oxford: Oxford University Press: 21–55.

Keys, B. J., (2006), *Globalizing Sport: National Rivalry and International Community in the 1930s*, Cambridge, MA: Harvard University Press.

Koivunen, P., (2009), 'The 1957 Moscow Youth Festival: Propagating a New, Peaceful Image of the Soviet Union', in M. Ilic and J. Smith (eds), *Soviet State and Society Under Nikita Khrushchev*, London: Routledge: 46–65.

Kojevnikov, A., (2004), *Stalin's Great Science: The Times and Adventures of Soviet Physicists*, London: Imperial College Press.

Krämer-Mandeau, W., (1991), 'Regionale Spiele und Sportarten auf dem Gebiet der ehemaligen Sowjetunion', *Stadion: Internationale Zeitschrift für Geschichte des Sports*, 17 (2): 245–77.

Krementsov, N., (1997), 'Russian Science in the Twentieth Century', in J. Krige and D. Pestre (eds), *Science in Twentieth Century*, Amsterdam: Harwood: 777–94.

Krüger, M., (1996), *Körperkultur und Nationsbildung: Die Geschichte des Turnens in der Reichsgründungsära – eine Detailstudie über die Deutschen*, Schorndorf: Hofmann.

Kucher, K., (2007), *Der Gorki-Park: Freizeitkultur im Stalinismus 1928–1941*, Cologne: Böhlau.

Lovell, S., (2009), *The Soviet Union: A Very Short Introduction*, Oxford: Oxford University Press.

McReynolds, L., (2003), *Russia at Play: Leisure Activities at the End of the Tsarist Era*, Ithaca: Cornell University Press.

Makoveeva, I., (2002), 'Soviet Sports as a Cultural Phenomenon: Body and/or Intellect', *Studies in Slavic Cultures*, 3 (July): 9–32.

Malz, A., Rohdewald, S. and Wiederkehr, S., (2007), *Sport zwischen Ost und West: Beiträge zur Sportgeschichte Osteuropas im 19. und 20. Jahrhundert*, Osnabrück: fibre.

Morton, H. W., (1963), *Medaillen nach Plan: Der Sowjetsport*, Cologne: Wissenschaft und Politik.

Neutatz, D., (2001), *Die Moskauer Metro: Von den ersten Plänen bis zur Großbaustelle des Stalinismus (1897–1935)*, Cologne: Böhlau.

O'Mahony, M., (2006), *Sport in the USSR: Physical Culture – Visual Culture*, London: Reaktion Books.

Oberender, A., (2008), 'Die Partei der Patrone und Klienten: Formen personaler Herrschaft unter Leonid Brezhnev', in A. Schuhmann (ed.), *Vernetzte Improvisationen: Gesellschaftliche Subsysteme in Ostmitteleuropa und in der DDR*, Cologne: Böhlau: 57–76.

Petrone, K., (2000), *Life Has Become More Joyous, Comrades: Celebrations in the Time of Stalin*, Bloomington: Indiana University Press.

Prozumenshchikov, M. Yu., (2004), *Bol'shoi sport i bol'shaya politika*, Moscow: ROSSPEN.

Read, J., (1996), 'Physical Culture and Sport in the Early Soviet Period', *Australian Slavonic and East European Studies*, 10 (1): 59–84.

Reid, S. E. and Crowley, D. (eds.), (2000), *Style and Socialism: Modernity and Material Culture in Post-War Eastern Europe*, Oxford: Berg.

Riordan, J., (1977a), 'Pyotr Franzevich Lesgaft (1837–1909): The Founder of Russian Physical Education', *Journal of Sport History*, 4 (2): 229–41.

——, (1977b), *Sport in Soviet Society: Development of Sport and Physical Education in Russia and the U.S.S.R*, London: Cambridge University Press.

——, (1987), 'Sports Medicine in the Soviet Union and German Democratic Republic', *Social Science & Medicine*, 25 (1): 19–26.

——, (1993), 'Rewriting Soviet Sports History', *Journal of Sports History*, 20 (3): 247–58.

Rolf, M., (2006), *Das sowjetische Massenfest*, Hamburg: Hamburger Edition.

Roth-Ey, K., (2004), '"Loose Girls" on the Loose? Sex, Propaganda and the 1957 Youth Festival', in M. Ilic, S. Reid and L. Attwood (eds), *Women in the Khrushchev Era*, Basingstoke: Palgrave: 75–95.

Ruffini, M. and Sivulka, J., (2005), 'Die historische Entwicklung der Sokolbewegung in Böhmen und Mähren im 19. und in der ersten Hälfte des 20. Jahrhunderts in Bezug auf das Deutsche Turnen', PhD thesis, Bremen.

Rüthers, M., (2009), 'Kindheit, Kosmos und Konsum in sowjetischen Bildwelten der 1960er Jahre: Zur Herstellung von Zukunftsoptimismus', *Historische Anthropologie*, 17 (1): 56–74.

Rüting, T., (2002), *Pavlov und der neue Mensch: Diskurse über Disziplinierung in Sowjetrussland*, Munich: Oldenbourg.

Samoukov, F. I. (ed.), (1964), *Istoriya fizicheskoi kul'tury*, Moscow: Fizkul'tura i sport.

Siegelbaum, L. H., (2008), *Cars for Comrades: The Life of the Soviet Automobile*, Ithaca: Cornell University Press.

Soskin, A. M., (2007), *Lev Yashin: Za kulisami slavy*, Moscow: Algoritm.

Stadelmann, M., (2003), *Isaak Dunaevskij – Sänger des Volkes: Eine Karriere unter Stalin*, Cologne: Böhlau.

Starikov, V., (1922), 'Sport i derevnia', *Fizicheskaia kul'tura*, 4–5 (August): 5–6.

Starks, T., (2008), *The Body Soviet: Propaganda, Hygiene, and the Revolutionary State*, Madison: University of Wisconsin Press.

Starostin, N. A., (1969), *Zvezdy bol'shogo futbola*, Moscow: Fizkul'tura i sport.

——, (1986), *Moi futbol'nye gody*, Moscow: Izdatel'stvo Pravda.

Stites, R., (1989), *Revolutionary Dreams: Utopian Vision and Experimental Life in the Russian Revolution*, New York: Oxford University Press.

Todes, D. P., (2002), *Pavlov's Physiology Factory: Experiment, Interpretation, Laboratory Enterprise*, Baltimore: Johns Hopkins University Press.

Trotsky, L., (1973), *Problems of Everyday Life*, New York: Pathfinder Press.

Vaingurt, J., (2008), 'Poetry of Labor and Labor of Poetry: The Universal Language of Alexei Gastev's Biomechanics', *The Russian Review*, 67 (2): 209–29.

Vartanian, A. T., (2001), *Eduard Strel'tsov: Nasil'nik ili zhertva?* Moscow: Terra Sport.

Vöhringer, M., (2006), 'Blut und Proletkult: Alexander Bogdanovs Arbeit am Allgemeinen', in M. Hagner and M. D. Laubichler (eds), *Der Hochsitz des Wissens: Das Allgemeine als wissenschaftlicher Wert*, Zurich: Diaphanes, 291–313.

——, (2007), *Avantgarde und Psychotechnik: Wissenschaft, Kunst und Technik der Wahrnehmungsexperimente in der frühen Sowjetunion*, Göttingen: Wallstein.

Wagg, S. and Andrews, D. L. (eds), (2007), *East Plays West: Sport and the Cold War*, London: Routledge.

Washburn, J. N., (1955/56), 'Sport as a Soviet Tool', *Foreign Affairs*, 34 (1–4): 490–99.

Zaporozhets, O. and Krupets, Ya., (2008), 'Sovetskii potrebitel' i reglamentirovannaya publichnost': novye ideologemy i povsednevnost' obshchepita konca 50-kh', in E. R. Yarskaya-Smirnova and P. V. Romanov (eds), *Sovetskaya sotsial'naya politika: stseny i deistvuyushchie litsa, 1940–1985*, Moscow: Variant: 315–36.

Zavileiskii, F., (1931), 'Vnimanie derevne', *Fizkul'taktivist*, 2 (February): 5–6.

Zlydneva, N. V. (ed.), (2005), *Telesnyi kod v slavianskikh kul'turakh*, Moscow: Institut slavianovedeniia RAN.

2 East beats West

Ice hockey and the Cold War

John Soares

The dollar figure was astonishing. In September 1972, *two* National Hockey League (NHL) clubs – the Minnesota North Stars and Toronto Maple Leafs – were talking about paying a whopping $1,000,000 for the services of Soviet star Valerii Kharlamov (Anon., 1972a, 1972b). The NHL was the top North American professional hockey league, with teams in the United States and Canada. Just a couple of years earlier, some of its top players earned as little as $12,000–15,000 per season. In 1972, the emergence of the rival World Hockey Association (WHA) was pushing salaries sharply upward, and the highest-paid NHL stars commanded annual salaries of $200,000 (Eskenazi, 1972b), but Bobby Hull was the only hockey player who had received the kind of money being discussed for Kharlamov.

The WHA's Winnipeg club had paid Hull a million-dollar signing bonus to try to purchase credibility for its new league (Eskenazi, 1972a). Hull was arguably the greatest player in the game, a 33-year-old superstar with many productive years left who already had tallied more than 600 career goals. He had been the NHL's leading active goal scorer and ranked second all-time in league history. Kharlamov, by contrast, had by that time played only a couple of games against NHL competition. He was part of the Soviet national team then playing a squad of NHL all-stars in the 'Summit Series', a historic eight-game clash that began on 2 September 1972.

Heading into the Summit Series, most Canadians had expected Team Canada would easily handle the Soviets. Pre-series scouting reports had claimed only one Russian might 'possibly' be good enough for the NHL (Davis, 1972). But the Soviets stunned the Canadians, 7–3, in Game One, and posted three wins and a tie in the first five games. Canada staged an epic rally, winning the last three games in Moscow to claim victory in the Series, but hockey had changed forever. As the official Soviet news agency put it, the Summit Series had ended 'the myth of invincibility of the best Canadian professionals' (Anon., 1972c). Forced to reassess the quality of Soviet players, NHL executives went from dismissing them to offering unbelievable sums for one: at the same time as Toronto's owner said he would pay $1,000,000 for Kharlamov, he professed that he could not 'afford to pay' his incumbent star $150,000.

The skill of the Soviet players should not have come as such a surprise. Despite hockey's Canadian origins, the game took root in Europe early on. By 1910, the forerunner to the International Ice Hockey Federation (IIHF) was conducting

European championships. Bohemia won European titles while part of the Austro-Hungarian Empire, and independent Czechoslovakia continued that tradition. Latvia participated in the European championships in 1932, decades before Russia or the USSR. Belgium, Great Britain and Spain regularly competed in the 1910s and 1920s, as did frequent post-1950 participants Austria, Germany, Italy, France, Poland, Sweden and Switzerland. Still, Canadian teams usually dominated at the Olympics and world championships, first held in 1920 and regular events beginning in 1930. Only three times before 1954 did the Canadians fail to capture the top prize when competing at a world or Olympic tournament. Not only was Canada the strongest democracy in IIHF tournaments into the 1960s, and the capitalist power against which the Soviets measured themselves, but in most years from 1930 through 1991 world tournaments doubled as European championships, with games against Canada counting in determining the final standings of European nations (Diamond, 2000: 496–98).

Not only was Canada historically dominant in amateur hockey, it invented the NHL. The league was organized in 1917 entirely in Canada; even after it expanded to US cities in 1924, the players remained almost entirely Canadian into the 1970s. For decades, the NHL was unchallenged as the premier professional hockey league, but beginning in 1972 the WHA began play with the intention of joining the NHL at the pinnacle of professional hockey. Bobby Hull was the most famous defector, but only one of a number of established NHL stars who jumped to the WHA. Despite this, the WHA never won recognition as the NHL's equal, and in the seven years of its existence it was mostly seen – often unfairly – as a combination of a few overpriced stars and a lot of borderline professionals not good enough to play in the NHL. Throughout the 1970s, even with the challenge from the WHA, the NHL was still the premier professional hockey league.

As the Summit Series opened, NHL officials remained convinced that the best Canadian players were far superior to Russians, even though the USSR had won every Olympic and world tournament from 1963 through the 1972 Olympics. So many Canadians were playing pro hockey and ineligible for these amateur events that the Soviets were defeating squads no better than Canada's thirty-first-best (Hay, 1970: 12); the Europeans they beat played a finesse style considered too 'soft' for the NHL. Surely, domination of that calibre of competition gave little indication that the Soviets could match the best of Canada's professionals.

Pre-Series predictions of a Canadian sweep were easy to find; the most pessimistic Canadians seemed to expect Canada would win six games. Noted columnist Dick Beddoes famously promised to eat his column if Canada did not win 8–0 (Anon., 1972f). A report in Canada's national newspaper, the *Globe & Mail*, even claimed '[o]bservers of international hockey believe that this Russian team is a team in decay' because its ageing stars had broken their string of championships by losing the 1972 world title to Czechoslovakia (Beddoes, 1972b). So little was thought of Soviet hockey that copies of a book about the programme by its architect, Anatolii Tarasov, were selling for a mere 66 cents (down from the cover price of $4.95) on bargain shelves at Toronto area bookstores that summer. Neither Canadian coach bothered to read the book before the series (Proudfoot, 1972).

The Summit Series was the first meeting between Canada's best pros and the top Soviets, but these antagonists met in other competitions for the remainder of the Cold War, including mid-season tours of NHL cities by Soviet elite league clubs, the 1979 Challenge Cup series between the NHL all-stars and the Soviet national team, and the Canada Cup tournaments held periodically beginning in 1976 that included professionals from Canada and the United States, Soviet and Czechoslovakian national teams, and squads of the best players from Sweden and Finland or West Germany – the best players from the world's hockey-playing countries.[1] Even the WHA got in on the act, with contests against European national teams and its own eight-game series with the Soviets in 1974. When the Soviets met Canada's best, they usually performed very well. The Russians actually outscored the Canadians despite losing the Summit Series, easily beat the WHA all-stars in 1974, and usually won most of the games when their teams toured North America. In addition, the USSR humiliated the NHL all-stars in the 1979 Challenge Cup series and won the 1981 Canada Cup.

The Soviets' obvious hockey skill left NHL officials fantasizing about signing Russians, even though none came to the league before 1989 (Janofsky, 1989). In addition to the million-dollar dreams about Kharlamov, during the Summit Series Toronto's 43-year-old goaltending legend Jacques Plante hoped his team might sign Vladislav Tretiak to share goaltending duties (Anon., 1972e). After returning to the Boston Bruins, Team Canada coach Harry Sinden unsuccessfully sought an official 'cultural exchange' in which an American artist or singer would visit the USSR and the Bruins would get Soviet winger Aleksandr Yakushev (Mulvoy, 1974; Dunnell, 1989; Anon., 2005). In 1983, the Montreal Canadiens secured the rights to Tretiak in the hope that the Kremlin might permit him to spend the twilight of his career with them (Swift, 1983).

But while Soviet players were not on NHL rosters before 1989, some North American coaches copied elements of the Soviet style. More importantly, expansion in the NHL and the WHA's desperate need for players and credibility opened opportunities for other European stars. In 1982, the *New York Times'* Robin Herman wrote that while 'ten years [earlier] there were no European players at all' in the NHL, '[i]n the past five years, more than 50 hockey players from Czechoslovakia, Sweden, Finland, Germany and Switzerland' had joined league teams. With the influx of European players came more European tactics. Even though NHL ice surfaces were (and most still are) smaller than those in Europe, and the smaller ice surface combined with rules differences to promote more physical play, some NHL and WHA teams employed more of the speed, puck possession and precision passing common in Europe.

This infusion of European players and tactics was important because it made hockey the most globalized, and Europeanized, of the major professional sports in the United States during the 1970s. Although the National Basketball Association has seen a pronounced European influence since the 1990s, this effect did not take place before rule changes in the late 1980s permitted professionals at the Olympics; previously, the NBA was composed almost entirely of American players. Europeans to this day have had little impact in major league baseball aside from the stellar pitching career (1970–92) of the Netherlands' Bert Blyleven. American football began to employ 'soccer-style' kickers in the 1960s, but so few Europeans succeeded in the professional American game in the 1970s that those who did stood out, like Hungarian émigrés Pete and Charlie Gogolak, Cypriot Garo Yepremian, Norwegian Jan Stenerud, and Englishman John Smith. Only the North American Soccer League could compete with hockey when it came to globalization in the 1970s, but the sport Americans called 'soccer' differed markedly from other US professional sports: the obvious inferiority of the US game meant European footballers such as Giorgio Chinaglia and Franz Beckenbauer never faced the prejudice and scepticism confronting their counterparts at the hockey rink.

During the 1970s, European players transformed hockey from a virtual closed shop for Canadian talent into a global enterprise. This development was encouraged by the distinctively communist success of Soviet hockey, and by the capitalist struggles of Canadian hockey that were further complicated by Canadian–American interaction. NHL expansion and the WHA–NHL rivalry created opportunities for highly skilled Czech, Slovak, Swedish and Finnish players in the 1970s, who in turn had an impact in North America out of proportion to their numbers.

The USSR and the triumph of 'collective hockey'

After the Second World War, Kremlin officials shed their pre-war vision of the Olympics as a bourgeois diversion and embraced participation as an opportunity to defeat the capitalists and imperialists (Parks, 2007). Consistent with these aims, the Soviets began to field a national team in ice hockey in 1947, and debuted at the world tournament in 1954. The Soviets had the good fortune to find Anatolii Tarasov, a Russian patriot and communist true believer, who became the architect of their programme. Tarasov drove the establishment of a distinctively Soviet style of hockey that sought to apply in practice the principles of communism. Starting a new programme in a sport in which there was no established Russian tradition (although the Russians had played bandy), emphasizing team play over individual skill, benefiting from prominent involvement by army and secret police clubs, and including communist ideological training as part of the programme, the Soviets produced a phenomenally successful approach to 'collective hockey'.[2]

Tarasov knew he was trying to beat the Canadians; to offset their superior individual skills, his teams emphasized passing, puck possession, and selectivity in taking shots only when there was a good chance of scoring. Soviet players were reluctant to engage in 'rough play' and risk penalties, which they saw as cowardly: the penalized player hurt the team by subjecting it to a manpower disadvantage, and left his comrades to face the consequences of his irresponsible actions. This contrasted markedly with the Canadian approach. While there were exceptions, especially among French Canadians, whose style resembled the Europeans, Canadians tended to place greater responsibility for offence on the individual with the puck; often surrendered the puck expecting to use physical play to regain possession in better scoring position; and took frequent shots hoping to score on deflections or rebounds. Canadians often saw penalties as evidence of praiseworthy aggressiveness.

In constructing their national programme, the Soviets benefited from the structure of their elite league and international sports officials' laxity in defining 'amateurism'. In the USSR, elite athletes were always classified as army officers, students, workers, or in some other profession. They could train full-time for eleven months each year, receive compensation and perks among the most lavish in the Soviet system, and still claim to be amateur and, therefore, eligible for the Olympics and world hockey championships. (In fairness, the hockey nations of Europe all found some way to keep their best players officially classified as amateurs; Hay, 1970: 5.) The best elite league players skated for Moscow-based clubs, led by TsSKA (Central Army) and Dinamo (the secret police). In some cases, national team players skated with their national team line-mates year round. The league schedule was built around major international competitions – Olympics, world championships and, after 1972, opportunities to meet Canadian professionals – so that the national team had ample time to practice and prepare as a unit before those events.

The USSR won the title at its first world tournament in 1954 and took gold at its Olympic debut in 1956. But while they were always in contention at world and Olympic tournaments and frequently won medals, the Soviets did not claim another top prize until 1963. That year began a historic run which was largely the result of Tarasov's adoption of a revolutionary approach to offence. In traditional North American hockey thinking, the five skaters on a team are broken into two defence-men and three forwards. Trying to improve Soviet offence, Tarasov borrowed tactics from Soviet football and deployed one defence-man, two halfbacks and two forwards to encourage attacks 'in depth'.

This system was stunningly successful. From 1963 through 1990, the Soviets won six of seven Olympic gold medals, and twenty of twenty-five world championships.[3] Where they didn't claim the top prize, the Soviets won silver in the 1980 Olympics, and they posted three second-place finishes and two third-place finishes in world tournaments. And they had considerable success in their games with the best Canadian pros, starting with the Summit Series. Given the factors that went into its rise, Soviet hockey's accomplishments were a distinctive communist achievement.

Canadian hockey: capitalist disappointments and American complications

Canada did not have the ideological coherence in its hockey programme that Tarasov developed in the Soviet system, but, in the way it operated, Canadian hockey's shortcomings were effectively capitalist failings, even though Canada was able to retain its domination for almost a decade after the Soviets arrived. Canada boycotted the 1957 world championships in Moscow to protest the Soviet invasion of Hungary, but Canadian teams won world titles in 1955, 1958, 1959 and 1961, and finished second to the United States in 1960 only because of the heroic goaltending of American Jack McCartan. But beginning in 1963, Canada became an IIHF also-ran. Canada's only Olympic hockey medal for the rest of the Cold War was a bronze in 1968; it did not win another world championship until 1994.[4]

The biggest difficulty facing Canadians in IIHF competitions was the openness of their professionalism: it was inconceivable that a free, open society like Canada could engage in the brazen hypocrisy of the USSR and other communist countries in passing off its best athletes as amateurs. Moreover, its tradition and public embrace of professional hockey meant Canada could not replicate the more subtle inconsistencies of other European hockey powers such as Sweden. The best Swedish players were nominally amateur because they played for company teams, and had real jobs with their companies even though their position and their compensation were tied to their on-ice performance. More importantly, Canadian hockey was structured to produce players for the NHL. The real purpose of junior hockey, played by boys under the age of twenty, was to determine which players would become good enough for the NHL. Under the regulations in place into the 1960s, Canadian players could be bound to an NHL organization as early as age fourteen (Brunt, 2007: 53).

For decades, the Canadians' skill level had been so high that Canada could win world or Olympic tournaments by sending its top (or one of its top) 'senior amateur' teams, composed of players over twenty who were not good enough for the NHL or a minor professional league. They usually won, despite playing on the larger ice surface under rules less conducive to the Canadian style of play. But that changed, beginning at the 1962 world championships, where Canada finished second despite a boycott by the USSR and Czechoslovakia.[5] In 1963, Canada failed to win any kind of medal at the world tournament, languishing behind the USSR, Czechoslovakia and Sweden. Starting in 1963–64, Canadian amateur hockey officials built an actual national team that would have top amateurs practising and training together for much of the year, playing exhibitions as a team, then representing Canada at world or Olympic tournaments. Despite these efforts, the Canadian national team produced few world tournament medals, winning only bronze in 1966, 1967 and 1968.

In many ways, though, the national team was hobbled by the Canadian commit-ment to professional hockey.[6] NHL clubs chose not to embrace the talent develop-ment possibilities of the national team, nor did they encourage it for patriotic reasons. Instead, NHL clubs preferred to keep prospects within their organization, on junior or minor professional teams. And NHL clubs were unhelpful in other ways. When the national team sought the loan of Montreal Junior Canadiens scoring sensation Yvan Cournoyer just for the 1964 Olympics, the Junior Canadiens' parent club turned down the request. An agreement with an NHL farm league, the Central Professional Hockey League (CPHL), was cancelled after the national team dominated exhibition play against CPHL teams for a couple of seasons (Conacher, 1970: 33, 121–22).

There was little reason for many Canadian hockey officials to care about amateur hockey because they hoped the IIHF would revise its rules to permit 'open' world tournaments. This was one of the issues promoted by Hockey Canada, a quasi-governmental body formed in the late 1960s. Another of its main goals was to improve Canadian performances in international hockey: government officials explicitly blamed poor hockey performances for hurting 'our national image, especially in Europe'. Hockey Canada also wanted to address concerns arising from the increasing involvement of US interests in the NHL (Anon., 1969b).

In seeking to open the competition at prestigious tournaments previously limited to amateurs, Canadian hockey officials were in keeping with the spirit of the times: in 1968, the previously all-amateur Wimbledon and French tennis championships moved to open formats. The Canadians were confident that even minor professional players would be strong enough to tilt world hockey tournaments in Canada's favour. Heading into the 1970 world championships, the Canadians had secured an IIHF agreement permitting nine minor professionals to join the Canadian team (Macintosh and Greenhorn, 1993: 103–6). But International Olympic Committee (IOC) president Avery Brundage responded by saying 'the fact that the IIHF has opened its World Championship as well as other tournaments to professional players, will no doubt affect the Olympic eligibility of all participating teams' (Brundage, 1969). Comments from the IOC head threatening the Olympic eligibility of players convinced the Europeans to back away from their earlier agreement, and the 1970 world tournament proceeded without Canada and its professionals. However, Brundage recognized the inconsistent application of amateurism and thought it 'ridiculous' that the Canadians were not permitted to compete while the Russians, Swedes and others were (Brundage, 1970). Either way, Brundage thought hockey was too commercialized to be genuinely amateur; he preferred to see the Winter Olympics end, and Olympic hockey with them.

Hockey Canada would continue to lobby for the inclusion of professionals in IIHF world tournaments, which would eventually happen in 1977. Canada would not participate in world championship hockey again until then, and it skipped Olympic hockey until 1980. Even when it returned to world tournaments with professionals, these players were not necessarily the country's best, as world tournaments overlapped with NHL playoffs that kept the best players with their clubs. Even with professionals available, Canada's world tournament entries finished fourth in 1977 and 1979 and third in 1978. In the remaining Cold War years, Canada finished as high as second at the world championships, but often ended third or fourth and never regained the world title during the Cold War. When Canadian amateurs returned to Olympic hockey, they finished a disappointing sixth at Lake Placid, and fourth in the subsequent Cold War Olympics at Sarajevo and Calgary (Diamond, 2000: 494–95, 498).

Complicating matters was the growing influence of American interests in the NHL. Throughout its history, almost all of the league's players had been Canadian and the teams in Canada were very successful. During the era of the so-called 'original six' teams, from 1942–43 to 1966–67, the two teams based in Canada and the team located in the border city of Detroit – which had a substantial following among Canadians living in south-western Ontario – dominated league play. Montreal won ten Stanley Cups as league champions during these years, Toronto nine, and Detroit five. The other teams in US cities – Boston, New York and Chicago – claimed just one Cup, won by Chicago in 1961 (Diamond, 2000: 120).

But this began to change in the mid-1960s. Expansion added six teams for the 1967–68 season, all located in the United States. By 1974–75, the league had expanded to eighteen teams, fifteen of which were in the United States; Vancouver was the only Canadian addition. Teams were established in US locations with little tradition or popular interest in the game, such as California, Atlanta and Washington. Canadian-based teams also became relatively weaker, as Toronto (and Detroit) declined while New York and Chicago became stronger and Boston and Philadelphia won multiple Stanley Cups. Canadians worried about the growing influence of American owners, about efforts to appeal to Americans who knew nothing about the game, about expansion depleting the talent level, and about American money influencing decisions – for the worst – about Canada's national game. This was best exemplified leading up to the Summit Series, when NHL owners agreed to let their players compete only if the roster were limited to NHL players – thus keeping Bobby Hull off the team because he had committed the 'treason' of leaving an NHL team in Chicago, USA, to join a WHA club in Winnipeg, Canada (Anon., 1972d). Columnist Beddoes (1972a) was so upset that Hull had been 'blackballed by the US imperialists manipulating Hockey Canada' that he referred to Team Canada throughout the series as 'Team US NHL'.

It should be emphasized that while Canadians were worried about American owners, they were not worried about American players. With expansion, and especially with the rise of the WHA, more American players made it into the top ranks of professional hockey. But even with an increasing number of American players – and a European invasion – Canadians still owned the overwhelming majority of NHL roster spots in the 1970s and beyond. Even though some US players became important contributors to their teams – Robbie Ftorek becoming the first American named most valuable player in the WHA or the NHL when he won the WHA honour in 1977 (Herman, 1977) – the United States did not produce top-calibre NHL stars until the 1990s. Heading into the inaugural Canada Cup, a major Canadian newspaper reported that '[n]ot one member of the 29-man US team could make the Team Canada squad [. . .] Some likely would ride the bench for the Washington Capitals', an expansion team that been the NHL's worst in the two previous seasons (Martin, 1976). When Canada met the United States, the Canadians won despite a lacklustre performance that left their star Serge Savard saying, 'It was a good thing we were playing the US tonight and not someone stronger. We would have been in trouble' (Ramsay, 1976a). The Americans, for their part, were pleased by the close game despite the loss, believing they had 'proved something to' the Canadians (Gammons, 1976: 48).

Not only did the WHA help increase the number of American players in pro hockey during its existence from 1972–73 to 1978–79, it also did a great deal to globalize hockey. It signed European stars, scheduled exhibition matches against European teams, and even counted games against Soviet all-star and Czechoslovakian and Finnish national teams in league standings (Diamond, 2000: 426–27). Czechoslovakian players were among this wave of invaders, despite their homeland's communist regime.

The Czechoslovakian challenge

Before it was a communist dictatorship, even before it was independent from Austria-Hungary, hockey players from Czechoslovakia were among Europe's best. In 1949, Czechoslovakia became the first continental European power ever to win an IIHF tournament in which Canada participated. That 1949 title was the second in three years, sandwiched around a silver-medal finish in 1948. But then the communist regime dealt the programme a major setback, wrongly arresting and imprisoning eleven players for treason and espionage, and fuelling rumours that Prague had deliberately sabotaged its own national hockey programme to smooth Soviet entry into IIHF competition (Anon., 2000). Only once in the next fifteen years did Czechoslovakia finish higher than third in a world tournament.

By the mid-1960s, though, Czechoslovakian hockey was back. Czechoslovakia finished second to the Russians at the 1965 and 1966 world championships, and beat the Soviets at the 1968 Olympics and then twice more at the 1969 world championships (despite finishing behind them both years), posting an astonishing three straight wins against the Soviets in tournaments at the pinnacle of world amateur hockey. Of course, Czechoslovakian teams playing against the USSR had added motivation in the wake of the Soviet invasion in August 1968 and the further crackdown by communist hardliners following the riotous celebrations after the second Czechoslovakian win at the 1969 world tournament.[7] Czechoslovakia claimed silver medals behind the USSR at the world championships in 1971, 1974, 1975, 1978 and 1979. It broke the USSR's string of world titles in 1972, and by 1976–77 looked like it might surpass the USSR as a hockey power. The Soviets needed a heroic rally in the final five minutes against Czechoslovakia to escape with the 1976 Olympic gold medal. Czechoslovakia claimed both the 1976 and 1977 world championships, becoming the first nation other than Canada or the USSR to win consecutive world titles. During the inaugural Canada Cup tournament in September 1976, it beat out an experimental Soviet squad and finished second to a Canadian team many consider the finest ever assembled. More impressively, Czechoslovakia was the only team to win a game over Canada during that tournament (Diamond, 2000: 488–89, 506; Brunt, 2007: 269).

With their international success, some Czechoslovakian players became well known in North America for their exploits. For example, goaltender Vladimir Dzurilla, who at the 1969 world championships earned the distinction of being the first goaltender since 1955 to shut out the Soviets in a world tournament, impressed Canadians by keeping a clean sheet against their great team during the 1976 Canada Cup (Anon., 1969a; Ramsay, 1976b). Under the circumstances, NHL and WHA teams sought Czechoslovakian stars, and sometimes received Prague's cooperation when the players in question were over the age of thirty. Czechoslovakia's Jaroslav Jirik was the first from the communist bloc to sign with the NHL, joining St Louis with Prague's blessing after competing in six world championships and three Olympics, and leading the Czechoslovakian league in goals in 1968–69. Yet he spent most of the 1969–70 season toiling for St Louis' minor pro farm team in Kansas City. He played only three games in the NHL without tallying a single point, and returned to ZKL Brno in Czechoslovakia after the season (Diamond, 2000: 1226).

While Jirik had been a disappointment, his countrymen had more success. Not all of them came with permission, though. Vaclav Nedomansky led the Czechoslovakian league in goals five times before joining the WHA's Toronto Toros in 1974. At the time, the leading US sports magazine proclaimed him 'the most famous athlete' to flee the Eastern bloc since 1956 (Mulvoy, 1974: 52). In a sport in which 50 goals in a season was the recognized mark of offensive greatness, Nedomansky became a 50-goal scorer in the WHA before he was traded to the NHL club in Detroit. In his first full season with the Red Wings, he led the team in scoring, was the team's most valuable player, and became only the twentieth player in NHL history to tally thirty goals in a season (Diamond, 2000: 1464; Anon., 1980).

Still, obtaining players from Czechoslovakia could be a difficult task. When encouraged by his brother, who had defected to Canada, Dzurilla was denied permission to join the Winnipeg Jets in 1972 (Davis, 1976a). It was even more problematic when North Americans sought younger players whom Prague wanted to play on the national team. After Peter and Marion Stastny defected to the Quebec Nordiques in 1980, the Quebec team president said 'Had I known the dangers, had I known that I would be risking my life, I never would have encouraged the defection' (Quinn, 1980: 43). Under these circumstances, it was unsurprising that Czech and Slovak players did not enter professional hockey in the same numbers as the Swedes and Finns who began appearing in the WHA and NHL in the 1970s.

From 'chicken Swedes' to perennial all-stars

It was not politics but Canadian perceptions of their softness that challenged Swedish players. Although the phrase 'chicken Swede' became a standard denigration among NHL players and officials,[8] Sweden displaced Canada as the most powerful democracy in IIHF hockey in the 1960s, winning the world title in 1962, finishing second to the USSR in 1963, 1964, 1967, 1969 and 1970, and frequently medalling for the remainder of the Cold War even after Czechoslovakia established itself as the Soviets' closest competition. Challenging Canadian perceptions of Swedish softness was the stellar NHL career of Borje Salming, who joined Toronto in 1973 and became a perennial all-star during a career that lasted until 1989–90.

Perhaps as important to the Swedish invasion was the role played by the WHA's Winnipeg Jets. In part because of a fortunate confluence of events, including desperation for talent to support superstar Hull, a Winnipeg doctor who had spent a research year in Stockholm and a team official whose friendship with a travel agent secured cheap flights undertook scouting trips to Scandinavia. As a result, the Jets became particularly successful in drawing European players, beginning in 1974 with Swedes Anders Hedberg, Ulf Nilsson and Lars-Eric Sjoberg, and Finns Veli-Pekka Ketola and Heikki Riihiranta (Willes, 2004: 173–78). Hedberg and Nilsson joined Hull on the 'Hot Line', a combination that produced dazzling offensive numbers. Hull and Hedberg routinely scored 50 or more goals per season and each notched 70 once. Nilsson often compiled 85 or more assists per year. All three players usually tallied above 100 points in a season, with Hull reaching as high as 142, Hedberg hitting 131 and Nilsson ordinarily coming in over 120. Hedberg and Nilsson were so successful in the WHA that after the 1977–78 season, the New York Rangers lured them to the NHL with lucrative contracts; in their first season in New York they helped the Rangers reach the Stanley Cup finals (Diamond, 2000: 1167, 1207, 1475).

The importance of Swedish participation in North American hockey became particularly clear at a couple of international tournaments in 1976. At the inaugural Canada Cup, six Winnipeg Jets played for Sweden (Anon., 1976a); all told, nine Jets played for three different nations (Anon., 1976b). That December, the Jets became the first Canadian professional team to play in Moscow's prestigious Izvestiia Cup. They were referred to in the Soviet media as 'Team Kanada', but their roster featured eight Swedes (Davis, 1976c) and several Finns (Davis, 1976b). Heading into the tournament, Jets players expected difficult games against the Soviet and Czechoslovakian national teams but were confident they would beat Sweden and Finland; as one player said, 'After all, we have the best of Sweden and Finland' (Davis, 1976b). In a surprising twist, the Jets suffered a disappointing tie in their game against Sweden because '[i]nstead of playing the style of hockey that repeatedly wins for them, they tried to break the will of the Swedes by intimidation' – unsuccessfully attempting against Sweden what less skillful WHA clubs ordinarily tried in league games against them (Davis 1976c).

The Jets' performance in the Izvestiia Cup proved to be a controversial disappointment. Close losses to the USSR and Czechoslovakia, together with the tie against Sweden and a lone win over Finland, earned Winnipeg a fourth-place finish in the five-team field. In a demonstration of capitalist problems in professional hockey, five WHA clubs had rejected Winnipeg's request for the loan of specific individual players for the tournament (Korobanik, 1976): even though Winnipeg's performance reflected on the league's credibility, individual clubs put their own interests first. The Jets' poor Izvestiia Cup performance brought complaints that it had offset Canadian success in the Canada Cup, best exemplified in one official's comment that the '[t]he Russians have gained a lot of political advantage from this foolishness' of 'sending a second-rate team to a high-calibre tournament' (Anon., 1976c).

Still, in historical terms, the Winnipeg Jets' appearance in the Moscow tournament, like the number of Swedes and Finns on Winnipeg's roster, was a testament to the Europeanization of North American professional hockey. And the Jets' influence extended into the NHL in the 1980s. After the Edmonton Oilers became one of the four surviving WHA teams that merged into the NHL, coach Glen Sather 'patterned the Oilers after the WHA Winnipeg Jets who surrounded Bobby Hull with speedy, talented Swedes like Anders Hebderg, Ulf Nilsson, [and] Lars-Eric Sjoberg' (Korobanik, 2000). Sather's European-influenced approach, deployed by legendary Canadian players like Wayne Gretzky, Mark Messier and Paul Coffey, and Finnish scoring sensation Jari Kurri, brought Edmonton five Stanley Cups in seven seasons from 1984 through 1990.

Conclusion

By February 1977, the success of Soviet and Czechoslovakian teams and that of individual Swedes, Finns, Czechs and Slovaks in North America had fuelled the globalization and Europeanization of hockey to the point that the *New York Times'* highly respected sports columnist Dave Anderson called for the transformation of the NHL into the World Hockey League. With two of the eighteen NHL franchises and much of the WHA struggling economically, Anderson (1977) argued that the sixteen strong NHL franchises should join with four WHA clubs and add ten teams from European cities to create a thirty-team World League. Anderson proposed the inclusion of two Moscow teams in addition to clubs from Leningrad, Helsinki, Belgrade, Prague, Stockholm, Oslo, Warsaw and West Berlin. In making this appeal, he contended that among the major US sports '[h]ockey is the only sport ready for expansion on an international basis' and that 'now hockey is as popular and as significant in Europe as it is in Canada and the United States'. It was important that Anderson proposed the inclusion of cities not only in the USSR, Sweden, Finland and Czechoslovakia, but also in other European countries with their own long traditions of domestic league play and Olympic participation: Germany, Poland, Yugoslavia and Norway.

The term 'globalization' was not in currency at the time, but this was the situation Anderson had correctly diagnosed. Europeans had transformed – globalized – the highest levels of hockey. The best Europeans were competitive with the best professionals playing in the United States and Canada. Soviet strength in the 1972 Summit Series, combined with the need for players because of NHL expansion and the new WHA, helped to make hockey the first – and for a time, the only – major US professional sport to move beyond a local talent base and utilize once-disparaged European players. A sport that for years was an almost entirely Canadian enterprise, even when clubs were located in the United States, had proven to be ahead of its counterparts in this noteworthy respect.

Notes

1   Canada Cup tournaments were held in 1976, 1981, 1984, 1987 and 1991; in 1996 the tournament became the World Cup of Hockey (Diamond, 2000: 504, 506–7).
2   Information about the Soviet hockey programme in this chapter derived from a reading of Tarasov (1972), Bauman (1988) and Edelman (1993; 2009).
3   Information about the final standings at Olympic and World Championship hockey can be found in Diamond (2000: 493–99).
4   Through 1968, Olympic tournaments doubled as the world championships; in 1972 and 1976 separate world championships were held, and in 1980, 1984 and 1988 there were no recognized world tournaments, only the Olympics.
5   The USSR and Czechoslovakia boycotted the 1962 world championships because the restrictions on East German travel imposed by the Western allies in response to the Berlin Wall prevented East Germany from participating (Soares, 2009).
6   For a quick introduction to the Canadian National Team, see Mott (1998: 434–38). Dr Mott is not only a professional historian at Brandon University in Manitoba, Canada, but a former member of the Canadian National Team; he also played in the NHL and in Sweden and had a brief stint in the WHA with the Winnipeg Jets (Diamond, 2000: 1447).

7   Adding further fuel to Czechoslovakian discontent with the Soviets was their belief the riotous portion of the 1969 post-victory hockey celebrations were actually staged by agents of the Czech secret police, acting under orders from their Soviet overlords in order to justify a crackdown (Dubcek, 1993: 236–37; Skoug, 1999: 225–30).

8   The phrase 'chicken Swede' became such a part of the North American hockey lexicon that a search for that exact phrase on the LexisNexis® Academic database of the News, All (English, Full Text) library on 10 February 2010 found 275 stories.

References

Anderson, D., (1977), 'It's time for a World Hockey League', *New York Times*, 3 February: 52.

Anon., (1969a), 'Czechs win hate match, refuse to shake hands with Russian losers', *Globe & Mail* (Toronto), 22 March: 1.

Anon., (1969b), 'The Meeting of Hockey Canada, Winnipeg, Manitoba', From the office of the Minister of National Health and Welfare, for release 3:30 pm EST, 18 November, in *Avery Brundage Collection*, University of Illinois, Urbana-Champaign, IL, box 119, file: Canada NOC, Canadian Olympic Association 1968–69.

Anon., (1972a), '$1 million Bush bid', *Globe & Mail* (Toronto), 9 September: 38.

Anon., (1972b), 'Ballard says Kharlamov worth $1 million', *Globe & Mail* (Toronto), 4 September: S11.

Anon., (1972c), 'Canada mourns hockey myth', *Globe & Mail* (Toronto), 4 September: 1.

Anon., (1972d), 'Canada will hold the coats', *Globe & Mail* (Toronto), 14 July: unnumbered page.

Anon., (1972e), 'Plante advocates Leafs buy Tretiak to replace Parent', *Globe & Mail* (Toronto), 6 September: 32.

Anon., (1972f), 'The Russians have come. . .', *Globe & Mail* (Toronto), 4 September: unnumbered page.

Anon., (1976a), 'Swedish camp opens with Widing absent', *Globe & Mail* (Toronto), 11 August: S3.

Anon., (1976b), 'Will be divided', *Winnipeg Free Press*, 4 August: 62.

Anon., (1976c), 'Winnipeg's participation "senseless" says Eagle', *Winnipeg Free Press*, 20 December: 51.

Anon., (1979), *Detroit Red Wings 1979–80 Factbook*, Detroit: Detroit Red Wings.

Anon., (2000), 'Worst Wrong Done To Czechoslovak Hockey Fifty Years Ago', Czech News Agency, 10 March, available via LexisNexis®.

Anon., (2005), 'From Russia, Almost', *Calgary Sun*, 8 June: 57.

Bauman, R., (1988), 'The Central Army Sports Club (TsSKA): Forging a Military Tradition in Soviet Ice Hockey', *Journal of Sport History*, 15 (2): 151–66.

Beddoes, D., (1972a), 'By Dick Beddoes', *Globe & Mail* (Toronto), 10 August: 36.

——, (1972b), 'Russian hockey team has an aggregate sameness, including red helmets', *Globe & Mail* (Toronto), 1 September: 36.

Brundage, A., (1969), 'Letter to International Ice Hockey Federation, 11 December', *Avery Brundage Collection*, University of Illinois, Urbana-Champaign, IL, box 119, file: Canadian NOC/Canadian Olympic Association 1968–69.

——, (1970), 'Letter to Severin Lovenskiold, 2 April', *Avery Brundage Collection*, University of Illinois, Urbana-Champaign, IL, box 216, file: Ice Hockey 1970–72 (Severin Lovenskiold).

Brunt, S., (2007), *Searching for Bobby Orr*, Toronto: Triumph Books.

Conacher, B., (1970), *Hockey in Canada: The Way It Is!*, Toronto: Gateway Press.

Davis, R., (1972), 'Canadians were thud and blunder', *Winnipeg Free Press*, 5 September: 1A.

——, (1976a), 'Dzurilla chills Canadians', *Winnipeg Free Press*, 10 September: 47.

——, (1976b), 'WHA reps don't share Powers' opinion', *Winnipeg Free Press*, 10 December: 60.

——, (1976c), 'Jets Out of Character Against Sweden', *Winnipeg Free Press*, 18 December: 65.

Diamond, D. (ed.), (2000), *Total Hockey*, 2nd edn, Kingston, NY: Total Sports Publishing.

Dubcek, A., (1993), *Hope Dies Last: The Autobiography of Alexander Dubcek*, edited and translated by Jiri Hochman, New York: Kodansha International.

Dunnell, M., (1989), 'Sinden only wanted one Soviet', *Toronto Star*, 31 December: G1.

Edelman, R., (1993), *Serious Fun: A History of Spectator Sports in the USSR*, New York: Oxford University Press.

——, (2009), *Spartak Moscow: A History of the People's Team in the Workers' State*, Ithaca: Cornell University Press.

Eskenazi, G., (1972a), 'Bobby Hull shifts hockey leagues for $2.5-million', *New York Times*, 28 June: 1.

——, (1972b), 'Rangers spur dollar war; give Park $200,000 pact', *New York Times*, 20 July: 19.

Gammons, P., (1976), 'Canceling a bunch of good Czechs', *Sports Illustrated*, 27 September: 48–49.

Hay, C., (1970), 'Address by Charles Hay, President, Hockey Canada to the Calgary Chamber of Commerce, 4 March', *Avery Brundage Collection*, University of Illinois, Urbana-Champaign, IL, box 119, file: Canada – 1970 World Ice Hockey Championships.

Herman, R., (1977), 'American-born Ftorek stars in dimming WHA', *New York Times*, 29 May: 132.

——, (1982), 'Europe's icemen cometh', *New York Times Magazine*, 3 January: 19, 30, 32, 35, 36, 46.

Janofsky, M., (1989), 'Few answers on defection', *New York Times*, 7 May: S4.

Korobanik, J., (1976), 'Jets, in name only, get set for Moscow', *Winnipeg Free Press*, 9 December: 81.

——, (2000), 'Brash, arrogant . . . and a winner: Love him or hate him, Glen Sather was the architect of one of the most successful franchises of the last 20 years', *Edmonton Journal*, 20 May: D1.

Macintosh, D. and Greenhorn, D., (1993), 'Hockey diplomacy and Canadian foreign policy', *Journal of Canadian Studies*, 28 (2): 96–112.

Martin, L., (1976), 'A storm warning for Team USA', *Globe & Mail* (Toronto), 13 August: 26.

Mott, M., (1998), 'The Canadian National Team, 1963 to 1970', in D. Diamond (ed.), *Total Hockey*, Kingston, NY: Total Sports Publishing: 434–38.

Mulvoy, M., (1974), 'Check and double-Czech', *Sports Illustrated*, 29 July: 52.

Parks, J., (2007), 'Verbal gymnastics: sports, bureaucracy and the Soviet Union's entry into the Olympic Games, 1946–52' in S. Wagg and D. Andrews (eds), *East Plays West: Sport and the Cold War*, London: Routledge: 27–44.

Proudfoot, D., (1972), 'Tarasov's hockey book helps to make masters of pupils', *Globe & Mail* (Toronto), 11 September: S10.

Quinn, H. (1980), 'Cloaks, daggers and a moonlit border run', *Maclean's*, 29 September: 43–44.

Ramsay, D., (1976a), 'US goalie sharp, Canada pressed in 4–2 win', *Globe & Mail* (Toronto), 6 September: Sports Section: 1.
——, (1976b), 'Goaltenders shine as Czechs beat Canada', *Globe & Mail* (Toronto), 10 September: 32.
Skoug, K., (1999), *Czechoslovakia's Lost Fight for Freedom, 1967–1969: An American Embassy Perspective*, Westport: Praeger.
Soares, J., (2009), 'Boycotts, Brotherhood and More: International Hockey From Moscow to Colorado Springs via Squaw Valley', in J. Dopp and R. Harrison (eds), *Now Is The Winter: Thinking About Hockey*, Hamilton: Wolsak & Wynn: 97–111.
Swift, E. M., (1983), 'An Army man to the core', *Sports Illustrated*, 14 November: 38–46.
Tarasov, A., (1972), *Road to Olympus*, Toronto: Pocket Books.
Willes, E., (2004), *The Rebel League: The Short and Unruly Life of the World Hockey Association*, Toronto: McClelland and Stewart.

3 Communism, youth and sport

The 1973 World Youth Festival in East Berlin[1]

Kay Schiller

Introduction

The Xth *Weltfestspiele der Jugend und Studenten* (World Youth Festival, WYF) took place in East Berlin over nine days from 28 July to 5 August 1973. They brought together more than 20,000 foreign participants, 3000 delegates from the German Democratic Republic (GDR), 40,000 East Berlin youth and around 330,000 East German 'organized mass participants', young people from all over the GDR who came to Berlin to attend one or more Festival events (Rossow, 1999: 257). According to Maurice Roche's definition, the WYF was clearly a 'mega-event'. It qualified as a large-scale cultural event with 'a dramatic character, mass popular appeal and international significance' (Roche, 2000: 1). Remembered by many domestic and foreign visitors in glowing colours, it left its mark on the popular memory of the GDR as one of the few occasions during which GDR citizens, especially the young, overwhelmingly displayed a positive attitude towards their state.

This chapter discusses the institutional as well as the national context in which the 1973 WYF took place, since, as Roche notes, 'the staging of international mega-events [. . .] remains important in the "story of a country", a people, a nation. They [. . .] represent key occasions in which nations [. . .] construct and present images of themselves for recognition in relation to other nations and "in the eyes of the world"' (Roche, 2000: 6). Linked to this, the 1973 WYF will then be located in the wider history of festival culture in the Eastern bloc. Particular attention will be paid to the reasons for the Festival's favourable reception amongst the audience for which it was primarily intended: the youth of the GDR.

The final part of this chapter is dedicated to the role of sport during the Festival. While the WYF was not primarily a sports event, but rather a political and cultural festival with particular emphasis on popular music and political discussion, sport was nevertheless an important ingredient of the Festival. There were several reasons for this. First, the East Berlin WYF was part of socialist festival culture since the 1920s, in which sports had always played an important role. Within that broader tradition, the 1973 event was shaped more specifically by sports events in the GDR, the Children and Youth *Spartakiads* held since 1964 and the Leipzig German Gymnastics and Sports Festivals (*Deutsche Turn- und Sportfeste*) since the 1950s. The latter were 'mega-events' (albeit national ones) in their own right, attracting tens of thousands of participants and spectators into the city's *Zentralstadion*. They provided a template for the holding of mass sports events involving competitions, displays and amateur 'sports shows' (*Sportschauen*), which could be recycled in 1973. The primary role of these was to emphasize the population's conformity with the aims of the Festival and regime and to stress sport's prominent place in GDR politics and ideology – a strategy with which the regime was largely successful. However, this chapter argues that the mass sports events were also appropriated by participants for their personal enjoyment and as an affirmation of their spontaneity and individuality or *Eigen-Sinn* (Lüdtke, 1985). This is to say that participants attached other, or additional, meanings to them than simply those provided by the regime (Lindenberger, 1999: 24). Finally, on the basis of the semiotic similarities between the two events and the general trends in the relationship between the two German states, it is evident that the WYF of 1973 was also clearly influenced by the holding of a mega-event in West Germany a year earlier: the Munich Olympic Games.

Contexts

World Federation of Democratic Youth

The first requirement here is to understand the institutional context of the 1973 WYF as well as the particular moment in the history of the GDR in which it was situated. The Festival took place under the auspices of the World Federation of Democratic Youth (WFDY), an international non-governmental organization, which awarded its world youth festivals on a multi-annual basis to a host city and, along with the agencies, institutions and officials of the host country, was also involved in its implementation and organization.

The WFDY was founded in 1945 in the immediate aftermath of the Second World War. This influenced its pacifist agenda and helps explain the WYF slogan: 'For Anti-imperialist Solidarity, Peace and Friendship'. While originally bringing together youth organizations of different political convictions and ideological orientations, the WFDY was quickly dominated and controlled by communist youth organizations from the Eastern bloc under the leadership of the *Komsomol*, the youth wing of the Soviet Communist Party. It was, in effect, the successor to the Moscow-led Communist Youth International, which had been dissolved in 1943 along with *Cominform* (Bresslein, 1973). The world youth festivals served as regular propaganda events to foster and demonstrate the international solidarity of communist youth. Given the cost of these mega-events, which often exceeded the Olympics in terms of participant numbers – for example, 23,000 delegates in the 1973 WYF compared with some 14,000 athletes and officials at the 1972 Munich Olympics – these socialist festivals also required extensive sponsorship by the host nation. The necessity felt by Moscow to carefully monitor the ideological messages these festivals sent out to international and domestic audiences meant that during the Cold War they took place in Eastern bloc capitals or in the capitals of two (semi)-neutral states (Vienna and Helsinki in 1959 and 1962, respectively).

The GDR: a safe choice

East Berlin hosted the third WYF in 1951 and was awarded it again in 1973. There were several reasons for this. First, on account of the vocal presence of '1968' Maoist and independent leftists, who were as critical of Eastern bloc 'socialism' as of Western capitalism, the 1968 Sofia WYF was a public relations disaster. The local police barely managed to keep the event under control and used excessive violence to put an end to an unauthorized anti-Vietnam war demonstration at the US embassy. The Western press sided with the extra-parliamentary left and was scathing in its criticism (Wesenberg, 2007: 10). In comparison with Bulgaria or with other Eastern European states such as Czechoslovakia and Poland, which had both been through recent political upheavals, the GDR seemed a safe choice. It was the richest of all Eastern bloc countries and could shoulder the expenditure. The East German state seemed a paragon of socialist virtue and reliability, a country where what little popular discontent existed was largely channelled into a culture of complaint (*Eingaben*) rather than a culture of public protest (Fulbrook, 2005: 269–88).

Two years earlier, the GDR had experienced a Moscow-enforced change in leadership from Walter Ulbricht to Erich Honecker. As opposed to his predecessor, Honecker toed the Moscow line in relation to Willy Brandt's *Ostpolitik* and, more generally, in terms of détente with the West (Sarotte, 2001: 109–11). As a co-founder and chair of the Free German Youth (*Freie Deutsche Jugend*, FDJ) from 1946 to 1955, Honecker had also been instrumental in organizing the previous WYF in East Berlin.

Honecker's priorities

Acting from a position of relative strength, Honecker felt the WYF was an opportunity to put on a political and cultural propaganda display. He used it to articulate and propagate the policy priorities under his leadership and to emphasize recent GDR political successes and those of socialism in general, such as the recent American defeat in Vietnam. The WYF took place only months after the Basic Treaty between the two German states was ratified by the West German parliament and provided a good opportunity to celebrate the increasing diplomatic recognition of the GDR. In the first six months of 1973, a total of fifteen new states recognized East Germany under international law. In February, Britain and France, both of which were represented by Festival delegations, opened diplomatic relations with the GDR. Soon after the Festival, the two German states joined the United Nations (18 September). Despite some belligerent rhetoric from 'progressive forces' involved in anti-imperialist struggles in the 'third world', ranging from support for Frelimo in Mozambique to the Vietcong, the Festival also expressed the GDR's continued commitment to détente between the two Cold War blocs.

In terms of domestic priorities, this was an occasion to deliver on two promises made by Honecker when he had taken over. First, the WYF was an occasion to publicize, and add some substance to, 'consumer socialism', the Politburo's new 'main task' of improving the people's standard of living under the slogan 'unity of economic and social policy', set out by the VIIIth Congress of the Socialist Unity Party of Germany (*Sozialistische Einheitspartei Deutschlands*, SED) in June 1971 in order to prevent a repetition of the Prague Spring in the GDR. Many of the Festival events were scheduled to take place against the background of newly built, prefabricated concrete-slab buildings (*Plattenbauten*) in the city centre, images of which were broadcast non-stop by GDR television during the Festival. Food that was normally difficult to find or unavailable in the GDR's 'shortage economy', such as bananas, oranges and water melons, filled windows of Berlin stores and were available in abundance for the nine days of the Festival. Secondly, this was an occasion to show that the 'no taboos' cultural policy had been meant seriously. The change of leadership two years earlier, welcomed by contemporary popular opinion as a 'second awakening', heralded a cultural thaw which the Festival promoted and embodied (Madarász, 2003: 22). However, despite the thaw, singer/songwriter Wolf Biermann was still not welcome at the Festival, and his application to take part in the Political Songs section with his newly composed (and now classic) song about 'Commandante Che Guevara' was rejected. While generally the cultural thaw lasted longer than the sudden appearance of fresh fruit in the shops, it came to a definitive end in 1976, when Biermann was forcibly expatriated after a concert he gave in West Germany.

Finally, the Berlin WYF was also an occasion to show the world that despite Western anti-communist propaganda East Berlin was the capital of an open and tolerant (*weltoffen*) country (Wesenberg, 2007: 10). To bring this about, many of the familiar rituals and structures associated with communist festivals were diluted and dissolved into a more carnival-like atmosphere. Arguably, this rejection of discipline, collectivism, conformity and subordination which characterized the WYF was meant to show that the GDR was a friendly and relaxed society, equal if not superior to its West German rival and to Western societies in general. Along with other cultural forms, sport also played its part in this short-lived celebration of more informal styles of behaviour and social relations more commonly associated with the capitalist West.

Communist festival culture

Recent scholarly literature on festivals and political power has moved beyond the familiar idea, which was derived from an analysis of the mass spectacles of National Socialism, that festivals were restricted to dictatorial regimes seeking to manipulate and to mobilize the masses through propaganda, the aestheticizing of politics and the creation of 'beautiful images' (*schöner Schein*) (Reichel, 1992). Paulmann (2000) and Rolf (2006: 44–45) have convincingly argued that mass festivals and spectacles are not the preserve of revolutionary regimes or modern dictatorships, but that all political regimes – monarchies, democracies and dictatorships alike – rely on pomp and splendour, including mass spectacles, a continuous 'self-staging' (*Selbstinszenierung*), to achieve legitimacy and to demonstrate authority. In democratic regimes, festivals are of secondary importance because there are other symbols, rituals and political practices that provide legitimacy, such as elections or constitutions. However, this kind of collective display was central to communist dictatorships in order to communicate their aesthetic and ethical vision of the 'new man', which the regimes aimed to create.

While in democracies the organization of such mass events tended to be left to administrative elites without much political interference (Schiller and Young, 2010: 222), communist festivals were a matter for the political leadership of the country. Although the GDR's mass youth organization, the FDJ, played the leading role in organizing the WYF, the Festival got its overall steer from the very top of the party-state, with Honecker himself chairing the GDR preparatory committee (*Nationales Vorbereitungskomitee*).[2]

In her analysis of the German Gymnastics and Sports Festivals in Leipzig in the 1950s, historian Molly Wilkinson Johnson emphasizes the central role Ulbricht played in arranging such spectacles. Not only did he set the tone in his official opening speech and encourage mass sports with his slogan 'Everyone in every place should practice sport once every week' (*Jedermann an jedem Ort, jede Woche einmal Sport*); he also 'gave direct input into the choreography of the synchronized exercises that comprised the Sports Display' (Wilkinson Johnson, 2008: 143). In keeping with the Stalin era's cult of personality, Ulbricht used these festive spectacles to emphasize the subordination of the GDR's citizens to his will as the country's communist leader. The hierarchical relationship between the people and the leadership had been all too evident in the custom of festival participants parading past a tribune filled with party bigwigs. Famously, the Leipzig arena which seated some 100,000 spectators also had a special stand, where thousands of participants displayed slogans in full view of Ulbricht, holding up coloured flags on command that spelled out words and phrases like 'Friendship' or 'FDJ – Fighting Reserve of the Party' (Wilkinson Johnson, 2008: 134, 145).

While dissociating himself from his predecessor by emphasizing his own role as a party functionary subordinate to the collective will, even Honecker could not do without using VIP tribunes during the opening ceremony and on Karl-Marx-Allee, where parades were held during the Festival (Betts, 2008: 165). Tellingly, however, in contrast to the 1950s and 1960s, the distance between ordinary participants on the one hand, and the party elite and guests of honour on the other, was visibly reduced in the Stadium of World Youth. The 70,000-spectator Walter-Ulbricht-Stadion in Chausseestrasse, not far from the Berlin Wall, purpose-built for the 1951 WYF and fallen into disrepair thereafter, had been renovated and renamed in the run-up to 1973. The step-by-step eradication of the memory and image of the previous leader from public discourse, of which this was part, was a kind of symbolic death. In fact, Ulbricht, by then a frail old man, died during the Festival. This went largely unnoticed by participants, and the Festival programme was not interrupted (Betts, 2008: 163). The new informality allowed participants to get quite close to special Festival guests such as the first woman cosmonaut, Valentina Tereschkowa, the Palestine Liberation Organization (PLO) leader Yasser Arafat, or, most promi-nently, Black Panther activist Angela Davis, and feel a connection to them. Davis, recently released from a US prison after her acquittal from a trumped-up murder charge, was especially popular with participants (Wierling, 2006: 37). With her 'Afro' hairstyle and her clenched-fist salute, she 'single-handedly managed to inject dignity and coolness to the world-wide movement for socialism, human rights and an end to war' (Fenemore, 2007: 206).

Other Stalin-era traditions, however, continued unchanged. Just as in previous mass spectacles, this event was also used to exclude and marginalize real and presumed 'enemies of socialism'. From 1972 onwards, 30,000 mostly young people were screened by the East German Ministry of State Security, with the number of work camp inmates increasing dramatically. In the first six months of 1973 alone, there were 6635 prosecutions under section 249 of the GDR penal code for 'anti-social behaviour', more than half of which happened in the week before the Festival. 'Anti-social behaviour', a very loosely defined criminal offence, was punishable with fines, court orders, 'work education' (a euphemism for forced labour), or up to two years imprisonment. In the event, 604 people were interned in psychiatric hospitals, almost 1000 in special youth work education facilities (*Jugendwerkhöfe*), and 1473 in special children's homes. In order to make any disruptions of the Festival impossible, access to Berlin was heavily regulated, so that only Festival participants and young people with relatives in Berlin could enter the city (Ohse, 2003: 351–52).

In order to make sure that the event did not veer off the desired course of staged informality and, as we shall see, to secure it against a terrorist attack like that experienced at the Munich Olympics in the previous year, 20,000 Festival personnel were joined by some 60,000 security staff. This included 20,000 VoPo (*Volkspolizei*) policemen; troops of the National People's Army (*Nationale Volksarmee*, NVA) and the misleadingly named paramilitary Society for Sports and Technology (*Gesellschaft für Sport und Technik*, GST); and 27,000 Stasi men in various guises, from uniformed troops of the Ministry of State Security's own military regiment (*Wachregiment Feliks Dzierzynski*) to state operatives disguised in FDJ blue shirts, comprising half of the entire Stasi at the time (Ochs, 2003: 983). This made the 1973 Festival not only the largest Stasi operation ever, but with one member of the security forces for every three participants and guests, also the best protected mass event in modern German history.

Youth

In her 2003 study of the Honecker era, historian Jeanette Madarász has stressed the peculiar importance attached to young people as representatives of the future of socialism. Hence the slogan 'he who has the Youth, owns the future' (*Wer die Jugend hat, der besitzt die Zukunft*) (Madarász, 2003: 32). This meant that from the 1970s onwards, GDR youth found itself in a position of privilege on the one hand and constant surveillance and control on the other (Madarász, 2003: 15). While previously the regime had taken an authoritarian approach to youth policy, under Honecker's leadership the picture changed. Honecker had built his early career on opposition to reform. Now, however, the emphasis shifted towards propaganda extolling young people and their role in the political struggle and positive measures to encourage community spirit, a sense of integration into the GDR, active citizenship and the creation of the 'elusive socialist personality' amongst the young (Madarász, 2003: 36; Fulbrook, 2005: 131). By the mid-1970s, the socialist personality was officially defined as:

> an all-round, well-developed personality, who has a comprehensive command of political, specialist and general knowledge, possesses a firm class outlook rooted in the Marxist–Leninist world-view, is notable for excellent mental, physical and moral qualities, is thoroughly imbued with collective thoughts and deeds, and actively, consciously and creatively contributes to the shaping of socialism.
>
> (Fulbrook, 2005: 115)

However, alongside this positive acknowledgment of the role of youth for the present and future of 'real-existing socialism', no other group in GDR society was subject to such direct and constant state control. Young people, upon whom the future of the regime was seen to rest, were perceived as vulnerable and easily led astray by the lure of capitalist consumerism.

The WYF is a perfect illustration of emphases on both the participatory and the controlling aspects of SED youth policy. On the one hand, the party-state staged a mega-event for and by youth, used its propaganda arsenal to emphasize this group's importance for international friendship, peace and solidarity, catered to youth's interests and desires from music to sports and relied on its mass participation. On the other hand, the numbers of those excluded as a preventative measure and the army of Stasi operatives and other monitors suggest that the socialist authorities did their utmost to control the event. This was partly on account of the presence of foreign visitors, particularly those from the capitalist West, including 800 from the Federal Republic who spoke the same language but did not necessarily share the same socialist beliefs. East German youth could have been easily led astray.

There can be no doubt that the Xth WYF would not have proved such a success, had it not been for the willingness of East German youth either to participate in the Festival programme in one form or another, or to join the tens of thousands who simply attended its events. This chimes in with the general willingness of young people to become absorbed into, and influenced by, the FDJ. While it would be wrong to assume that FDJ membership numbers received a massive boost from the Festival alone, the party's changed direction in youth policy as a whole led to an increase in membership from 1.7 million in 1969/70 to 2 million in 1973/74 (Ohse, 2003: 345). These numbers continued to rise slightly from the later 1960s to the 1980s. In line with her interpretation of the GDR as a 'participatory dictatorship', whereby GDR citizens over the years increasingly participated in and benefited from the communist system, Fulbrook has emphasized that 'for most of the Honecker period, at least formal (if not active) membership [of the FDJ] encompassed between two thirds and four fifths' of young people aged between 14 and 25 (Fulbrook, 2005: 128).

What actually motivated youth to participate or attend is harder to determine. Certainly, the active encouragement and support by the authorities of westernized pop and rock music (rather than its mere toleration), and its massive presence in the Festival programme, surely played a major role in attracting young people. This was the heyday for East German rock groups such as the Klaus-Renft-Combo and the Puhdys, who were joined on this occasion by West German socialist rockers Floh de Cologne. But other musical tastes were also catered for by the GDR's own pop star Frank Schöbel, who sang the 'pacifist' Festival hit '*Wer die Erde liebt*' ('Those who Love the Earth'), by members of the GDR's 'singing movement' (*Singebewegung*), as well as left-wing singer-songwriters from the West such as Franz Josef Degenhardt and the 'red Elvis' Dean Reed (Wesenberg, 2007: 13–15).

Moreover, it is clear that despite the best efforts of the authorities a festival of this size could not be totally controlled. Whilst the idea of the WYF as a 'red Woodstock' is clearly an exaggeration, the Festival nevertheless created spaces outside the reach of the state and mainstream society for young people to express their individuality and independence by appropriating the event for their own purposes. Examples of this range from creative ways of wearing the ubiquitous blue FDJ blouse and shirt, to impromptu music-and-dance sessions; from the exchange of addresses and autographs (which became something of a festival sport), to spontaneous, heated and uncontrolled political discussions all over the centre of East Berlin (Rossow, 1999: 258; Wesenberg, 2007: 31–33). Moreover, participants and visiting youth could freely enjoy themselves on a long 'Dance Street' (*Tanzstraße*) that led from the centre of East Berlin all the way up to the Prenzlauer Berg. In the same spirit of enjoyment, the Festival film marking the occasion 'shows Honecker distributing large flagpoles to slim, long-legged blondes with FDJ shirts and mini-skirts. [. . .] Elsewhere delegates of all races and peoples can be seen flirting and cavorting to a soundtrack provided by [. . .] Floh de Cologne. One gangly FDJler can be seen evidently enjoying a kissing game with a giggling *señorita* from South America' (Fenemore, 2007: 206).

With the summer weather playing its part, closer international encounters on the lawns of East Berlin parks were the order of day – and the night – leading to jokes about World Youth Festival being a euphemism for the World Bed Festival. Local gossip in East Berlin claimed that a significant number of WYF children (*Weltfestivalskinder*) – often of mixed race – were conceived in the summer of 1973.

Partly because of this new informality and the associated relaxation of moral and social norms for the duration of the Festival – even East Berlin's main square Alexanderplatz became somewhere to spend entire nights in the company of new international friends – the memory of the WYF was overwhelmingly positive. This not only applied to the foreign visitors, whom the regime wished to impress so that they returned home with a good impression of the GDR; it also applied to East German youth, many of whom can still warmly recall the experience (Langelüddecke, 2003: 991). The Festival summer of '73 lives on as a marker which those from the former East Germany sometimes still use to tell their own life histories of the GDR (Roche, 2000: 5).

Of course, even at the time, as soon as life had reverted back to normal at the end of the Festival, critical voices spoke of 'window dressing' (*Schaufenster-veranstaltung*) (Rossow, 1999: 273; Ohse, 2003: 356). Eyewitness and historian Stefan Wolle called the Festival, in retrospect, a Potemkin's village (Wolle, 1998: 163), while Wesenberg's observation that 'the light of the WYF shone especially bright because it was so much darker before and after' has a ring of truth (Wesenberg, 2007: 52). The Festival was a sudden splash of colour in the otherwise dismal grey of East German daily life. There were other such moments in the early 1970s. For example, the 1973 DEFA film *The Legend of Paul and Paula* – based on a script by Ulrich Plenzdorf with GDR stars Winfried Glatzeder and Angelika Domröse in the title roles, and opening with the tearing down of dilapidated East Berlin housing stock to create space for Honecker's public housing programme, accompanied by a pop soundtrack of a Puhdys song – expresses an optimistic and exuberant mood akin to the attitudes and spirit manifest in the WYF.

Arguably, some of the individualism and mildly subversive spirit of the WYF outlasted the event itself. Cultural anthropologist Ina Merkel, a participant at the Festival, suggests that the presence of foreigners had 'a very euphoric (*euphorisierend*) effect on GDR citizens'; this was especially due to those involved in liberation struggles against colonialism in Africa and Asia, who 'embodied the pathos of revolution, of rebelliousness and resistance' (Merkel, 2003). Whilst it is misleading to draw any direct connections between this moment of *Eigen-Sinn* and the ultimate demise of the GDR a quarter of a century later (Palmowski, 2002: 501), these nine days of youthful fun and freedom accumulated and stored in the experiences of young people may have influenced popular attitudes long after the event.

Sport

What part did sport play in the Xth WYF? The Festival coverage in the party newspaper *Neues Deutschland* (ND) would suggest that apart from the opening ceremony sport was virtually non-existent at the event (ND, 29/7/1973: 1–5). However, leafing through the pages of the popular East German daily sports newspaper *Deutsches Sportecho* (DSE) gives the opposite impression. According to the mouthpiece of the East German Sports Association (*Deutsche Turn- und Sportbund*, DTSB), which in the 1970s and 1980s had a print-run of up to 185,000 copies, the WYF was a nine-day sports event rather than a political and cultural festival. This began well before the event itself with a series on sport at previous world festivals under the title 'The Festival Flower Blossoms' (*'Die Festivalblume blüht'*). Not surprisingly, given that the DTSB had been entrusted with organizing the sports programme, from 28 July to 5 August the paper reserved its first five pages for extensive coverage of the sports events taking place as part of the Festival.

These sports events, however, had a rather different and unusual atmosphere, the venues 'falling into line with the colourful image of this meeting of youth and students' (DSE, 3/8/1973: 5). Sport, in other words, was enlisted to spread the wider ideological message of the Festival and in this sense conforms to Edelman's observations on Soviet multi-sports events:

[W]hen so many games were played at once, the dominant discourse was about the coming together of athletes [. . .] in festivals of youth, dynamism, and optimism. Over the course of several decades, it would prove far easier for the state to ascribe a changing series of meanings, lessons, and signs to spartakiads, and later, Olympiads, than to competitions in a single sport, in which the game itself was the thing.

(Edelman, 1993: 39)

On this occasion, sport was used primarily as a propaganda instrument to underline and dramatize the ubiquitous festival message of socialist friendship, solidarity and peace. Accordingly, Rudi Hellmann, head of the sport bureau at the party's central committee, emphasized in his first assessment after the event that the sports programme had provided 'a vivid impression of the capabilities, close attachment to the people (*Volksverbundenheit*), expressive powers and beauty of socialist body culture and supported the political aim of the Festival "For anti-imperialist solidarity, peace and friendship"' (Hellmann, 1973).

This began with some of the ceremonial aspects of the Festival, which, like the Children and Youth *Spartakiads* that the GDR used for spotting its future high-performance athletes, imitated Olympic ritual. Not only did the five-hour opening ceremony take place in the Stadium of World Youth, but the foreign delegations marched into the stadium following their national flag, sometimes borne aloft by Olympic gold medallists such as Teofilo Stevenson, the Cuban heavyweight, and Alexander Medved, the Russian three-time Olympic wrestling champion. Afterwards a ceremonial flame was lit by Wolfgang Nordwig, the pole vault gold medallist at the 1972 Munich Olympics, dressed in white sportswear, followed by the release of a flock of doves into the sky as a symbol of peace (DSE, 30/7/1973: 2).

Moreover, the organizers held a number of international sports competitions, including football and volleyball tournaments between amateur members of several delegations for the title of festival champion.[3] A high-quality athletics meeting and a gymnastics display in the Dynamo Berlin gym brought together seven Olympic gold medallists.[4] Despite the quality of the competitors, these events were intended to stress international camaraderie and friendship rather than sporting rivalry. In Hellmann's words, they 'demonstrated the mass impact of sports during the World Youth Festival and contributed to varied and sophisticated leisure activities' (Hellmann, 1973). Other examples of sporting fraternity included the Italian delegation's football team from the communist town of Reggio Emilia, which played several friendlies against local East Berlin teams. There were demonstrations of different national sports such as the Polish sport of 'ringo', played with a rubber ring which has to be thrown across a net and caught; Japanese Kendo, Indian Kabaddi and Cuban baseball. The most prominent sports event was an international cross-country run to celebrate the building of socialism in Vietnam after the defeat of the US forces, in which some 36,000 recreational athletes participated under the banner 'The Solidarity Continues!' (*'Die Solidarität geht weiter!'*) (DSE, 30/7/1973: 3).

These activities harked back to an earlier period of Soviet-inspired class-based body culture, during which Western bourgeois individualism and record-seeking were eschewed in favour of proletarian collectivism and revolutionary agitation (Keys, 2006: 159). Despite the fact that the Soviets gave up their opposition to 'bourgeois sports' as early as the 1930s, *fizkultura* in this sense continued to exist side by side with its individualist, performance-oriented variety in socialist body culture and became part of the heritage and standard repertoire of communist festivals. However counter-intuitive this seems in view of the well known obsession with results-oriented high-performance athleticism in East Germany, the focus on collectivism and solidarity was also typical of the early 1970s, when the GDR was in a position of relative economic and political strength and was able to extend the hand of friendship and support to other smaller, poorer or less successful socialist nations. Sport was part of this process, from sending coaches to 'third world' countries to educating their sports students at the German Sports College in Leipzig.

This support also extended into the realm of sports politics. During the 1973 WYF, for example, the GDR, following the Soviet line, demanded the democratization of the International Olympic Committee (IOC). In preparation for the forthcoming IOC Congress in Varna, Bulgaria, high-ranking East German sport officials expressed their solidarity with 'third world' aspirations for equal representation on the self-selecting IOC (DSE: 5/8/1973: 8; see also Schiller and Young, 2010: 15). Related to this were round-table talks in a well frequented International Club of Sports on how to imitate East Germany's athletic successes at elite level. This naturally stayed well clear of discussing performance-enhancing drugs and equally remained silent on the system of talent-spotting and intensive coaching in East Germany's special sport schools for talented children, whose existence was treated like a state secret (Wiese, 2007). As DTSB Chairman Manfred Ewald put it in his speech on the occasion, '25 Years of Socialist Body Culture in the GDR': 'There is no sport miracle in the GDR.' Rather, the country's successes at Olympics and world championships were the 'result of a normal, planned development, because body culture (*Körperkultur*) and sports were on an equal footing with other elements of socialist society. They were an integral part of national culture and an essential element in the education and moulding of socialist personalities' (DSE, 3/8/1973: 8).

The presence of elite athletes may have suggested that the WYF was meant to increase East Germany's influence in the politics of sports and build collective pride through the achievements of its sporting heroes, whose ideological role was to help shape the socialist personality (Rossade, 1987: 74–76). While this is a valid point, as autograph sessions with 100 prominent athletes pulled in large crowds (Hellmann, 1973), an additional focus lay elsewhere. The presence of world record-holders and Olympic gold medallists, such as the boxer Manfred Wolke and the cycling star Gustav-Adolf 'Täve' Schur, who sat on the organizing committee, was meant to show that there was a close and harmonious relationship between mass and elite sports. This, however, was no longer true. After the historic *Leistungssportbeschluß* of 1969, the state decided to dedicate the vast majority of its funds to elite sport to the detriment of amateur athletes (Teichler, 2002: 567).

This division deepened during the 1970s and 1980s, with the leadership placing increasing priority on gaining Olympic gold medals at the expense of the proper provision of sports facilities and sports equipment for the wider population (Braun, 2009: 417).

Not much of this was evident at the time. The renovated Stadium of World Youth, for example, was hailed as a 'paradise of health' (*Paradies der Gesundheit*), which after the Festival would be used both by the sports science students of Humboldt University and also for *Volkssport* (DSE, 12/6/1973: 2). Ewald in turn claimed that a 'not insignificant part of the national income was spent on the general population's body culture (*Volkskörperkultur*)' (DSE, 6/8/1973: 4). In one of the rare attacks on sports in the capitalist West during the Festival, the Italian education system was criticized for doing too little against 'physical illiteracy' (*Analphabetismus des Bewegungsapparates*) (DSE, 31/7/1973: 4). However, despite the emphasis on mass sports participation in July 1973, over time the GDR came to lag seriously behind countries in the West in terms of both facilities and membership of sports clubs. By 1983, the GDR had 886 swimming pools compared with 3400 in West Germany. While in the months before the Festival the DTSB used the forthcoming event for a successful recruitment drive, increasing its membership numbers by 60,000 to 2.4 million in 1973, by 1983 only 3.3 million East Germans belonged to sports clubs compared with 18.4 million in the West (DSE, 24/7/1973: 2; 25/7/1973: 8). Even taking the different population sizes into account, with roughly three times as many West Germans as East Germans, the differences were striking and easy to see (Fulbrook, 2005: 80).

In its emphasis on mass sports, the WYF followed the example of the German Gymnastics and Sports Festivals in Leipzig, which had last taken place in 1969. In the 1970s there would be only one such festival, held in 1977, rather than the usual two or three per decade. Given its stress on participation, the Berlin WYF in 1973 might be seen as a replacement for the Leipzig event on this occasion. The Leipzig festivals provided a template for mass sports events which were used by the WYF. A striking example of this was the 'Festival Mile', which was run by hundreds of thousands of East German men and women (DSE, 31/7/1973: 5); another case in point is the 'Mass Sports Pennant' (*Volkssportwimpel*), given out to some 70,000 East German and 3000 foreign recreational athletes (Hellmann, 1973), who had to run the mile and perform three additional prescribed exercises during the nine days of the Festival. The demonstrations of acrobatics and syn-chronized group displays by gymnasts, which were put on at the opening ceremony, during a large sports event on the last day of the Festival and at the main Festival parade on Karl-Marx-Allee, all drew on the Leipzig precedent. During the opening ceremony alone, no fewer than 3500 young GDR athletes, including a large contingent of young DTSB members, sport science students and more than 1000 eight-to-nine year-olds, fulfilled their 'Festival obligation' (*Festivalsauftrag*), showing off their gymnastics skills by performing very difficult and occasionally dangerous exercises (DSE, 18/7/1973: 2; 26/7/1973: 2). In Hellmann's assessment 'they confirmed their political commitment through the exemplary quality and impressive originality of their performances' (Hellmann, 1973).

While the presence of such elements could be construed as evidence of the continuing stress on discipline, conformity and subordination, rather than for individualism and the loosening of hierarchical control, this would be overly reductionist. The sports press certainly suggested that in addition to international socialist friendship, the solidarity of elite and mass sport and the health benefits of exercise, sport was mostly about *joie de vivre*, fun and laughter, playing and joking, youthful optimism and enthusiasm. Whatever the actual differences between play and sport on the one hand, and dance and music on the other, these were overlooked in the reporting of the Festival, which tended to elide various forms of popular culture. This was particularly noticeable in the coverage of the Festival in *Deutsches Sportecho,* in which page five was always reserved for a kaleidoscope of photographic festival impressions. Sport did not always have to be taken too seriously. On 2 August, for instance, the paper reported an event in the Karl-Friedrich-Friesen open-air swimming stadium in East Berlin, which due to some 8000 visitors was bursting at the seams. Among other activities, famous athletes including Renate Stecher, the 1972 100- and 200-metre gold medallist, who had just broken the world records over both distances, joined in a jocular competition in which surfboards in the shape of the five-petal Festival flower, manned by plastic animals and toys, were pulled across the pool.

The individual motivation to attend and enjoy such events as a spectator, or to run the 'Festival Mile', or to participate in a friendly athletic competition with a foreign visitor, is difficult to pin down. It may, of course, have resulted partly from propaganda and even have included an element of coercion. Yet there can be no doubt that, as in all sports events, the joy of being swept up in the action probably also played a very important role and allowed participants to attach other, or additional, meaning to these activities than that provided by the regime. Beyond the political, cultural and social contexts in which it is located, sport also occupies a realm of its own, which can provide a space for individual freedom and self-expression (Schiller and Young, 2009: 319).

West to East?

Whereas most of what was on show at the 1973 WYF was part of the repertoire of socialist festival culture, it is plausible to suggest that contemporary mega-events in the West also played a role in shaping it. The ritualistic elements borrowed from Olympic opening ceremonies have already been mentioned. But given that the previous Olympic Games before the 1973 WYF took place so close in time and space to East Germany, it would hardly be surprising if the Munich event had a direct impact on the one held less than a year later in Berlin. As Klessmann has suggested, the Federal Republic and GDR constantly found themselves in an asymmetrical relationship of demarcation and interconnection throughout the Cold War. West Germany, larger, wealthier and more powerful than its eastern counterpart – the 'secret comparison society' (Jessen, 1995) – was always more important to East Germany than East Germany was to the Federal Republic (Klessmann, 2001). Accordingly, every political decision in the GDR has to be understood to some extent as a reaction to decisions taken in the Federal Republic. As historian Michael Lemke has aptly put it, Bonn always occupied a seat at the conference table of the SED Politburo as a 'silent guest' (Lemke, 1999: 102).

While one must be careful not to overstate this point for lack of documentary evidence, it is difficult to deny that, on the level of visual appearances, similarities abound between Munich '72 and East Berlin '73. Although these may be explained partly by the general trends of 1970s design, which transcended Cold War borders in a kind of 'aesthetic détente', the emphasis on colour in the iconography of both events, the use of standardized interchangeable design elements, as well as a poster series and what looked like an imitation of the system of pictograms for visitors' orientation created by Otl Aicher for the 1972 Olympics, suggest there was a close relationship (Steineckert and Walther, 1974: 151; see also Schiller and Young, 2010: 98–102). Peter Brügge of the Hamburg magazine *Der Spiegel* certainly thought that the WYF competed with Munich, calling it 'the red Olympiad' (Brügge, 1973: 47).

Not surprisingly, those who designed the East Berlin event, among them 'state artist' Walter Womacka, one of the foremost representatives of socialist realism, wanted to create a positive psychological climate and directly influence the mood of participants and audiences. Similarly to their West German counterparts, the East German intention was to emphasize the 'youthful and optimistic (*jugendlichoptimistisch*) atmosphere' of the event (Womacka, 1973). In fact, this aspect was more evident in Berlin in 1973 than in Munich 1972, where funding for the festive decoration of the city was very limited. In East Berlin no expense was spared. This consisted of *Sichtagitation*, large placards with propaganda slogans and other forms of visual display, most prominently the beautification of the centre by way of decorating newly built high-rise *Plattenbauten* and city squares with huge, red stars and multi-coloured, five-petal flowers – the Festival emblem, which was itself an imitation of the five Olympic rings (Steineckert and Walther, 1974: 63; Wesenberg, 2007: 15).

The direct influence of Munich on East Berlin is backed up with documentary evidence when it comes to the question of security. East Germany's security forces did their utmost not to fall into the same traps as their Western counterparts a year earlier (Wesenberg, 2007: 21). Most importantly, in order to avoid a repetition of the terrorist outrage, Stasi operatives received special training in urban combat, with State Security Minister Erich Mielke issuing explicit instructions on how to deal with hostage situations. Foreign Festival guests and delegations were protected by heavily armed and disguised Stasi bodyguards. At the same time, to avoid compromising the joyous image of the event and to permit the GDR to appear in as positive and peace-loving a light as its West German neighbour, these weapons were carefully concealed from view (see also Ochs, 2003: 985). All Palestinians in the GDR, including fifty who had taken up residence in East Germany after the Munich events, were put under increased surveillance.[5] As intelligence suggested that Black September, the Al-Fatah splinter group responsible for the Munich massacre, also wanted to target the WYF, the invitation extended to Al-Fatah and PLO leader Yasser Arafat to join the other prominent guests of the Festival was probably based on more than mere 'anti-imperialist solidarity'.

Conclusion

The Xth WYF in East Berlin was not primarily a sports event. Nevertheless, sport and sporting events played an important role in it. There were several reasons for this. First, it is clear that sport's role was primarily to emphasize the population's acceptance of the Festival's wider ideological message of socialist friendship, solidarity and peace, and political support for socialist regimes. Second, the legacy of Eastern bloc festivals more generally, and especially the Leipzig German Gymnastics and Sports Festivals, were highly significant as templates for the mass participation aspects of the 1973 sports events. Third, the influence of Olympic ritual, and of the 1972 Games in particular, on the image and appearance of the Festival must be taken into account. Finally, however, there is the alternative popular narrative, which emphasises the way in which the Festival was appropriated from below by its participants for their personal enjoyment and as an expression of their spontaneity and individuality.

Notes

1   My thanks go to Sylvia Drebinger for her research assistance and to Lawrence Black, Sarah Davies and the editors of the book and series for their critical comments and useful suggestions.
2   While it is impossible to discuss this point in depth here, it would be wrong to assume that the SED leadership had total control over the entire 'discourse of celebration'. Not only were different GDR agencies, institutions and officials with different opinions and interests involved, but also the national preparatory committees representing youth organizations from participating countries, as well as the international preparatory committee headed by Dominique Vidal, a young French communist and writer (Petrone, 2000: 4; Rolf, 2006: 48–49).
3   Won by Czechoslovakia and France, respectively.
4   These were Wolfgang Thüne (GDR), Andrzej Szajna (Poland), Sawao Kato, Shigeru Kasamatsu and Eizo Kenmotsu (Japan), and Viktor Klimenko and Ludmilla Tourischeva (Soviet Union); see *Deutsches Sportecho*, 6 August 1973: 5.
5   Regarding the security measures, see especially the following files in the *Bundesbehörde für die Stasi-Unterlagen*, Berlin: MfS-BdL-Dok. 1802: Mielke, Befehl Nr. 13/73, 18 April 1973; AS 432/73, Bd.1b: AG AF, Konzeption, 18 June 1973, especially pp. 132, 145, and AS 432/73, Bd.2: AG AF, Bericht, 25 July 1973, pp. 153–54.

References

Anon., (1973a), *Deutsches Sportecho* (East Berlin), May–August.

Anon., (1973b), *Neues Deutschland* (East Berlin), July–August.

Betts, P., (2008), 'When Cold Warriors Die: The State Funerals of Konrad Adenauer and Walter Ulbricht,' in A. Confino, P. Betts and D. Schumann (eds), *Between Mass Death and Individual Loss: The Place of the Dead in Twentieth-Century Germany*, New York: Berghahn: 151–76.

Braun, J., (2009), 'The People's Sport? Popular Sport and Fans in the Later Years of the German Democratic Republic', *German History*, 27 (3): 414–28.

Bresslein, E., (1973), *Drushba! Freundschaft? Von der Kommunistischen Jugendinternationale zu den Weltjugendfestspielen*, Frankfurt a. M.: Fischer Taschenbuch Verlag.

Brügge, P. (1973), 'Lesen Sie mal Marx, Herr Dutschke', *Der Spiegel* 32, 6 August 1973: 47–49.

Edelman, R., (1993), *Serious Fun: A History of Spectator Sport in the USSR*, New York and Oxford: Oxford University Press.

Fenemore, M., (2007), *Sex, Thugs and Rock 'N' Roll: Teenage Rebels in Cold-War East Germany*, New York: Berghahn.

Fulbrook, M., (2005), *The People's State: East German Society from Hitler to Honecker*, New Haven and London: Yale University Press.

Jessen, R., (1995), 'Die Gesellschaft im Staatssozialismus. Probleme einer Sozialgeschichte der DDR', *Geschichte und Gesellschaft*, 21 (1): 96–110.

Hellmann, R., (1973) 'Sportprogramm X. Weltfestspiele', *Stiftung Archiv der Parteien und Massenorganisationen der DDR*, Berlin: DY30/IV B2/18/15.

Keys, B.J., (2006), *Globalizing Sport: National Rivalry and International Community in the 1930s*, Cambridge, Mass.: Harvard University Press.

Klessmann, C., (2001), 'Introduction', in C. Klessmann (ed.), *The Divided Past: Rewriting Post-War German History*, Oxford: Berg: 1–10.

Langelüddecke, I., (2003), 'Ostalgie oder Aufarbeitung? Bericht über "Heldinnen, Bands und Klassenbrüder – Weltfestspiele '73"', *Deutschland-Archiv*, 36 (6): 991–94.

Lemke, M., (1999), 'Foreign Influences on the Dictatorial Development of the GDR, 1949–55,' in K. H. Jarausch (ed.), *Dictatorship as Experience: Towards a Socio-Cultural History of the GDR*, New York: Berghahn: 91–108.

Lindenberger, T., (1999), *Herrschaft und Eigen-Sinn in der Diktatur. Studien zur Gesellschaftsgeschichte der DDR*, Cologne, Weimar, Vienna: Böhlau.

Lüdtke, A., (1985), (ed.), *The History of Everyday Life: Reconstructing Historical Experiences and Ways of Life*, Princeton: Princeton University Press.

Madarász, J. Z., (2003), *Conflict and Compromise in East Germany, 1971–1989: A Precarious Stability*, Basingstoke: Palgrave Macmillan.

Merkel, I., (2003), 'Hinterher war alles beim Alten,' video interview with Ina Merkel, *Spezial: Weltfestspiele 73*, Bundeszentrale für politische Bildung, www.bpb.de/themen/ CQPRCM,0,Hinterher_war_alles_beim_Alten.html

Ochs, C., (2003), 'Aktion "Banner": operativer Einsatz, Taktik und Strategie des MfS während der X. Weltfestspiele 1973', *Deutschland-Archiv*, 36 (6): 981–90.

Ohse, M.-D., (2003), *Jugend nach dem Mauerbau. Anpassung, Protest und Eigensinn (DDR 1961–1974)*, Berlin: Christoph Links Verlag.

Palmowski, J., (2002), 'Between Conformity and Eigen-Sinn: New Approaches to GDR History', *German History*, 20 (4): 494–502.

Paulmann, J., (2000), *Pomp und Politik: Monarchenbegegnungen in Europa zwischen Ancien Régime und Erstem Weltkrieg*, Paderborn: Fedinand Schöningh Verlag.

Petrone, K., (2000), *Life Has Become More Joyous, Comrades: Celebrations in the Time of Stalin*, Bloomington: Indiana University Press.

Reichel, P., (1992), *Der schöne Schein des Dritten Reiches. Faszination und Gewalt des Faschismus*, Munich and Vienna: Carl Hanser Verlag.

Roche, M., (2000), *Mega-events and Modernity: Olympics and Expos in the Growth of Global Culture*, London: Routledge.

Rolf, M., (2006), 'Die Feste der Macht und die Macht der Feste: Fest und Diktatur – zur Einleitung', *Journal of Modern European History*, 3 (1): 39–59.

Rossade, W., (1987), *Sport und Kultur in der DDR: Sportpolitisches Konzept und weiter Kulturbegriff in Ideologie und Praxis der SED*, Munich: Tuduv-Verlags-Gesellschaft.

Rossow, I., (1999), '"Rote Ohren, roter Mohn, sommerheiße Diskussion": die X. Weltfestspiele der Jugend und Studenten 1973 als Möglichkeit vielfältiger Begegnung', in Dokumentationszentrum Alltagskultur der DDR e.V. (ed.), *Fortschritt, Norm und Eigensinn: Erkundungen im Alltag der DDR*, Berlin: Christoph Links Verlag: 251–75.

Sarotte, M. E., (2001), *Dealing with the Devil: East Germany, Détente, and Ostpolitik, 1969–1973*, Chapel Hill and London: University of North Carolina Press.

Schiller, K. and Young, C., (2009), 'The History and Historiography of Sport in Germany', *German History*, 27 (3): 313–30.

——, (2010), *The 1972 Munich Olympics and the Making of Modern Germany*, Berkeley and Los Angeles: University of California Press.

Steineckert, G. and Walther, J., (1974), *Neun-Tage-Buch. Die X. Weltfestspiele in Berlin: Erlebnisse, Berichte, Dokumente*, East Berlin: Verlag Neues Leben.

Teichler, H. J., (2002), *Die Sportbeschlüsse des Politbüros: Eine Studie zum Verhältnis von SED und Sport mit einem Gesamtverzeichnis und einer Dokumentation ausgewählter Beschlüsse,* Cologne: Sport und Buch Strauß.

Wesenberg, D., (2007), *Die X. Weltfestspiele der Jugend und Studenten 1973 in Ost-Berlin: unter "operativer Kontrolle"*, Erfurt: Landeszentrale für politische Bildung.

Wierling, D., (2006), 'Amerikabilder in der DDR', in U. A. Balbier and C. Rösch (eds) *Umworbener Klassenfeind: das Verhältnis der DDR zu den USA,* Berlin: Christoph Links Verlag: 32–38.

Wiese, R., (2007), 'Staatsgeheimnis Sport – Die Abschottung des Leistungssportsystems der DDR', *Historical Social Research*, 32 (1): 154–71.

Wilkinson Johnson, M., (2008), *Training Socialist Citizens: Sports and the State in East Germany*, Leiden and Boston: Brill.

Wolle, S., (1998), *Die heile Welt der Diktatur: Alltag und Herrschaft in der DDR 1971–1989*, Berlin: Christoph Links Verlag.

Womacka, W., (1973), Interview with Walter Womacka, in *Neue Berliner Illustrierte*, 26 July 1973.

4 Resurrecting the nation[1]

The evolution of French sports policy from de Gaulle to Mitterrand

Lindsay Sarah Krasnoff

Introduction

'Sport has become an element of international life', wrote the French Secretary of State for Youth and Sport, J.P. Soisson, in December 1977, 'amplified by mass communication [. . .] [it] is a factor in establishing the influence of a country.'[2] Under the Fifth Republic, France took this lesson to heart, and for Charles de Gaulle and subsequent presidents it became an affair of state. The standards and achievements of French sport were discussed not only in the sporting media but in parliament and at the *Elysée* itself. The long-standing French tradition of state intervention (*l'État gestionnaire*) created a distinctive sports configuration within the wider world of liberal democracy. From the 1960s to the 1980s, French sport moved incrementally to a position between the 'big state' Soviet model and the liberal capitalist 'small state' model of Britain and the United States, where the running of sport was largely left in the hands of the relevant national bodies and civil associations for each sport, as well as the university sports programmes in the United States. In the third quarter of the century – coinciding with the consolidation of the Cold War and the creation of a media-driven global sports system with the Olympic Games and the FIFA World Cup at its apex – France created a 'middle way'. The strong Gaullist state established 'a large degree of consensus as regards the proper role of *l'Etat gestionnaire*, with the principle of cooperation between the public and the private sectors now enshrined as the model for French sports administration' (Dine, 1998: 311). Although the government, alongside the national sports federations, was charged with the production of elite athletes to represent the nation in international competition, private clubs were increasingly required by the state to play an integral part in the production and training of elite athletes and players.

This pattern of state involvement without full state control had begun between the wars with the promotion of popular sport by the socialist Popular Front government of 1936–38. It was, however, taken up with much greater enthusiasm by the right-wing Vichy regime, which published a 'Sports charter' in December 1940, setting out the role of the state in revitalizing French youth through sport and appointing Jean Borotora, the famous 'bounding Basque' of Wimbledon fame, as its first minister of sport (Gay-Lescot, 1991: 9). Although the Fourth Republic

(1944–58) utterly repudiated the politics of Vichy, there was no purge of the sporting 'collaborators' of the kind seen in other areas of French life. Hence the state's role in sport remained relatively unchanged, but with a lower profile and a less strident emphasis on the militaristic and nationalistic role of sport for French youth. With the collapse of the Fourth Republic in 1958 and the creation by de Gaulle of the Fifth Republic, with its emphasis on a stronger state and greater international influence for France, sport once more came to the fore as a key element in state policy. Sport – and the prestige that was seen to go with it – was too important to be left to sportsmen and women.

Cold War sport is typically conceived within an East–West ideological context, with a focus upon the Soviet Union, the German Democratic Republic (GDR), and the United States. Yet the nuclear reality of the Cold War world induced smaller countries with fewer military, demographic and economic resources to seek out alternative ways to achieve international prestige. Sport provided new opportunities for nations to gain power and influence abroad. Although France had an international reputation as a centre of artistic and intellectual culture as well as the home of fashion and gastronomy, under the Fifth Republic the Gaullist emphasis swung towards more strenuous expressions of greatness. This 'soft power' might be acquired by athletes winning medals at major international athletic competitions, such as the Olympic Games, and could be used to display the strength and prowess of a nation, as the medal-hunting of the Soviet Union and the United States revealed. These victorious images were broadcast to an ever-increasing global audience as the technology of television and satellite broadcasting was rapidly transformed after 1960. Only 9% of French households had a television in 1958, but this figure rose to 42% in 1965, with saturation coverage by the 1970s. This media revolution altered the sporting landscape. In conjunction with the rapid post-colonial proliferation of new *Fédération Internationale de Football Association* (FIFA) members, by 1966 another event joined the quadrennial Olympics as one of the more important and powerful competitions for Cold War sports power: the football World Cup. Taking top honours in this event, a sport in which neither the Soviet Union nor the United States historically excelled, provided a different way for nations to set themselves apart from the political–military alliance of the bipolar world.

As Patrick Mignon (1998) has noted, history interpreted through a nation's athletic narrative reflects that state's values, characteristics and ideals; class divisions and tensions; and sense of community. Sport is also an important agent in creating a sense of unity and thus of forging identity. Team sports, in particular, cultivate the characteristics of heroism and unity (Mangan, 2003: 1) and reinforce the concept of courage, a trait that, along with heroism, was considered a crucial part of French masculinity prior to 1945 (Nye, 1993: 220). Moreover, sports are a good way to view assimilation historically within the context of a republican tradition (Bromberger, 1998), for it marries them to a collective identity. In wearing the national team uniform, which reflected the colours and symbolism of the nation, a citizen could feel a full part of France. Emerging from the aftermath of the Second World War and two bloody colonial wars, and coping with increased immigration, by 1958 France was in desperate need of a single, coherent national identity. Sport was enlisted in this national project.

After 1960, the French Fifth Republic led its Western European neighbours in its commitment to elite sport. Whether through the devotion of state resources to training athletes (youth and adult alike), the institutionalisation of sport via national legislation, the construction of new sports facilities, or the creation of a national sports culture, France sought to harness sport for the benefit of the state. The sports policies and programmes were important ways for the French to regain their sense of honour and prestige both domestically and abroad. In short, France used sport to relaunch itself as a rejuvenated nation that relied on rationalized athletic development to produce elite athletes, ideal citizens who would win international sporting events and titles.

However, external recognition was not the only driver of French sports policy. A combination of demographic, economic and cultural forces created a 'youth problem' of disaffection and rebelliousness in the 1960s throughout advanced Western societies.[3] Sport was seen as an antidote to the '*blousons noirs*' or 'hooligan/biker' phenomenon of the late 1950s, which was given a new twist in the 1960s by the rapid expansion of a rigidly state-controlled higher education system. When combined with the direct-action traditions of the French left, in May 1968 this produced a more dramatic challenge to state power in France than was seen anywhere else. As the government tried different methods to remedy this predicament, it became clear that sport was to be part of the solution, providing both discipline and role models for young men. In the 1970s, sport was to become a tool to assimilate youth into society and an antidote to the legacy of 1968. Youth programmes fostered this new sense of self as part of the athletic development process, and also served to assimilate immigrants into society and confer French identity and legitimacy. Once such training systems began to produce quality athletes who won major awards, beginning in the 1980s, the export of these sports models was a way to maintain ties to former colonies following decolonization.

The Gaullist revolution

General Charles de Gaulle, the exiled wartime leader and symbol of French military and political resolve, returned to power in 1958 amidst the threat of an army revolt and civil war over Algeria. The new form of government that he instituted, the Fifth Republic, was one in which the executive arm of the Republic was strengthened in order to take a more strongly interventionist role in the political, economic and social lives of its citizens. Under his leadership, France continued its strong post-war economic boom, came to terms with decolonization, absorbed an unprecedented number of immigrants and tried to integrate the post-war baby-boom generation. De Gaulle recognized the political value of sport and wanted France to rise to the challenge, rebuilding the mythical glory of the state through the sporting successes of its athletes. As early as 1934, when he was a rising star of the French army, he had written in praise of 'the twentieth century's immense investment of energy and pride in physical effort and competition' (Dietschy and Clastres, 2009: 168).

He wanted to create a third, alternative path to that of the United States or the Soviet Union, one that other countries, such as those of the 'Third World', could adhere to. Winning international athletic competitions was one way to demonstrate to these Third World powers that France had the vitality to successfully negotiate the path between Washington and Moscow.

The desire for a crypto-Napoleonic '*gloire*' was combined with the domestic requirement to meet expectations and provide a framework of discipline for the baby boomers. The population of France increased from 40.5 million in 1946 to 49.7 million in 1968 and 52.6 million by 1975.[4] Some of this was due to immigration, but the populace also expanded because of lower mortality rates and significantly higher birth rates. The baby boomers were the first generation of the twentieth century to be acculturated by non-French influences, and youths idolized American and British icons and trends. The growing frequency of speaking in English, and the popularity of blue jeans and rock 'n' roll were perceived by Gaullists as an assault on French society and culture. This sense of anxiety manifested itself in several ways: from the state's establishment of programmes abroad to promote the French language and arts, to instituting quotas on English language films and television programmes, and fostering a newly invigorated national sporting culture around the idea of '*La France qui gagne*' ('the France that wins'). By following the proscribed rules of a given game, the young learned to abide by and respect authority. Given the dramatic social and economic changes that occurred during this era, the concepts of community, citizenship, meritocracy and teamwork were viewed as increasingly important attributes in order to provide a stable foundation to a rapidly changing society.

Maurice Herzog was de Gaulle's chosen instrument to revitalize the nation through sport. Herzog was a national hero, a mountaineer, conqueror of Anapurna in 1950, who had written a hugely successful book about his exploits, and been elected President of the Club Alpin in 1952 and member of the *Haut Comité à la Jeunesse* in 1955. He was a meritocrat, who worked as a manager in private industry as well as for the state. De Gaulle made him High Commissioner for Youth and Sport in 1958, and then Secretary of State for Youth and Sport in 1963, with a substantial budget to promote elite excellence and mass participation. The nation's inability to gain athletic acclaim was perceived as parading its inadequacies in public, displaying a nation in decay, an old and stagnant France rather than a dynamic 'new France'. When taken in the larger context of the changes and adjustments to France's international and domestic problems of the 1960s, the 'sports crisis' became important to the French national psyche and self-perception.

The Fourth Republic had acknowledged the Cold War reality that it was middle-of-the-road in many pursuits, such as finance, science, economy, commerce, industry, aeronautics and the military. It pointed out that the country's 1956 Olympic finish (eleventh place) was in accordance with the performance of France in these other areas.[5] This, however, would not do for de Gaulle, for whom mediocrity was not an option. France was now obligated to rise up and climb the ladder of world rankings: 'The best [youths] must be taken in hand to prove the continuity of the French vigour and its rebirth in international competitions.'[6]

The government focused on sports at which it felt it already excelled, specifically fencing and basketball, also noting that 'for the principle of honour, give emphasis to the two major Olympic sports: track and field, and swimming'.[7] Yet, despite concentrating resources, the 1960 Rome Olympics were disastrous. In terms of the overall medal count, France finished twenty-fifth out of eighty-three nations, garnering a paltry two silver and three bronze medals.[8] The nation and de Gaulle were stunned and humiliated that Pakistan, Norway, Ethiopia, Japan, Turkey and New Zealand finished higher in the overall medal count. It was not just the French who were reading or viewing these disappointments, it was the entire world. The 1960 Games were the first to be broadcast live to a global audience of significant size. French decay and decline, as expressed through its inability to garner many medals, was showcased to the world on television and described in the press as 'a grand melancholy [that] grips us'.[9] The 1960 Rome Olympic Games were watched with mounting anger and shame by de Gaulle. The impact was significant and the fallout immediate. De Gaulle was enraged. He had pledged a resurgent, rejuvenated France that would carve out a niche in the Cold War world.

Jean-Emile Mazer highlighted the significance of the Rome games in that 'this was, for the first time, a flagrant contradiction between the discourse of General de Gaulle and the objective results that the world saw on television'.[10] In the public and governmental debates that followed in September 1960, the French identified four areas that explained their poor display: the lack of a national sports culture; a youth uninterested in sport; the absence of a state structure to support sports; and the print media. Rome 1960 provoked France to formulate a sports policy that would mobilize the nation's youth to obtain better results. The establishment of a stronger national sports culture to encourage greater athletic participation was a main goal (Lipsyte, 1965). As Michel Clare (1960) noted in *L'Équipe*, 'by itself sport does not have a chance of being accepted by us because of our absence of sporting mentality'. France sought to improve the nation's attitude toward sports by incorporating sport into the youth culture to create an environment that encouraged athletic competition. Shortly after coming to power, Herzog had reinforced the role of sport in schools, making it obligatory in the baccalaureat. He harangued doubtful parents who thought their children should be studying by stressing that sport was a means of education. He played down the principle of excellence at any cost in favour of promoting as wide a degree of participation as possible. Sport, he argued, could help reduce the numbers of juvenile delinquents, create stronger morals, fill leisure time and form character – all elements identified with the concurrent 'youth crisis' (Ministry of Justice, 1968: xii).

An important component of state funding for athletics in the 1960s was the commitment to building new facilities and fields to encourage greater athletic participation and competition. Funds allotted to the High Commission of Youth and Sports' budget increased with each subsequent year (French Embassy in the USA, 1965: 4). The achievements of the 1960s in terms of provision of facilities were remarkable. A five-year budget was set in 1961 to run in three phases for fifteen years. The number of physical education teachers more than doubled to over 15,000 between 1958 and 1968. By the early 1970s, the sporting landscape had been transformed, with 2600 swimming pools plus 11,000 covered and 49,000 uncovered sports facilities. Due to the new government initiative to provide facilities, and fuelled by economic prosperity and social mobility, participation in sport grew steadily by about 2 million every five years, from 4 million in 1966 to around 10 million in 1982. There were some exceptional successes. Judo, for example, grew in popularity from around 30,000 participants in 1957 to 380,000 in 1978, with French women winning four world championships medals in 1982. Tennis was a striking beneficiary of improved state-subsidized facilities and a closer working relationship between the French government and the French Tennis Federation, purged of the old guard and headed by the reforming Philippe Chatrier, whose declared aim was to democratize tennis. In 1965 there were 100,000 registered tennis players in France; this figure rose to 400,000 in 1976 and to 1.2 million by 1983. Skiing also boomed in the 1960s with support from Herzog, who provided '*bourses de neige*' to encourage wider access to winter sports. The number of registered footballers doubled from 500,000 to a million between 1965 and 1975 (Dietschy and Clastres, 2009: 176–77).

The de Gaulle government recognised the need to encourage greater athletic participation and to improve elite performance, following the Coubertin dictum that the elite would inspire the masses. Many sports were costly to practice, so the High Commission (later Ministry) of Youth and Sport provided equipment to make training for competitions more accessible, and created financial subsidies to assist athletic training. The goal was to never again be outside the top tier (top five) at the Olympics, and to build upon the 1958 national football team's third-place finish at the World Cup.[11] The government turned to the national sports federations in France for help. It was hoped that, with combined efforts and finances, French athletes could be groomed using the most modern materials and methods available.

De Gaulle took a personal interest in the achievements of leading French sportsmen and women whose performances he followed on television. He told Michel Jazy 'you ran a fine 5000 metres on Saturday, I saw it on television' and to Jean-Claude Killy, who was to win three gold medals in skiing at the Grenoble Winter Olympics, he confided 'unfortunately I only know you through television; one day I would like to see you in action in the flesh' (Dietschy and Clastres, 2009: 168). This kind of encouragement of leading performers, who were regularly invited to the *Elysée*, was complemented by a more formal processes of awarding the *legion d'honneur* to France's best sportsmen and women. During Herzog's period in office, no fewer than twenty-one sporting figures were awarded the *legion d'honneur*, which had rarely been given to sportsmen or women before that time. Eric Tabarly, who had triumphed in single-handed transatlantic yacht racing and been actively supported by the French navy, was an early beneficiary of the new dispensation. When Francois Missoffe replaced Herzog as Minister of Sport in 1966, the award of state honours for sport was raised to a new level, with the President himself presenting 'the red ribbon'. De Gaulle made a short speech in which he praised the recipients for their contribution to the nation: 'each time you take part, you extend French influence', adding that 'champions by their continued efforts set an example and by their results contribute to the heritage of the whole country [. . .]

which the government should recognise and reward' (Dietschy and Clastres, 2009: 172). Amongst the first to be honoured in this way were five time winner of the *Tour de France*, Jacques Anqueteil, and the Olympic athletes, Michel Jazy and Jocelyn Delecour, followed by the captain of the French rugby union side (de Gaulle's favourite sport).

The issue of state financial support for athletes was contentious in the 1960s because, it was argued, monetary payment to elite athletes would cripple the notion of amateurism enshrined in Pierre de Coubertin's Olympic concept. Herzog supported the idea that the state should subsidize the athlete, especially the elite athlete, 'just as it gives money to the scholar' (Lipsyte, 1965: 51). However, France shied away from total state subsidy of elite athletes on the lines of the Eastern Bloc (*ibid.*). This was partly attributable to the debate surrounding amateurism and professionalism. In a series of three articles that sought to address whether sport could be considered an actual profession, *Le Monde* took the view that amateurism meant that one should not receive stipends from anyone (Legris, 1967: 1). The Gaullist tradition owed much to the ideals of de Coubertin, whom the General admired, but this also conflicted with the need to compete successfully at the highest level. Matters came to a head when France hosted the Winter Olympics at Grenoble in 1968. Vast sums were spent on preparing the infrastructure and ensuring cameras were there to record French triumphs. With his three golds in skiing, Jean-Claude Killy was the French hero of the Games, but his participation had been questioned prior to the event on the grounds of commercial contracts with ski manufacturers. This required ministerial attention and finally de Gaulle's personal intervention with Avery Brundage, the President of the International Olympic Committee.

Throughout the 1960s, French recognition that it had to build a national sports programme to display power abroad remained constant, or even increased in terms of overall importance and concern. *Le Monde* ran a front-page story on 8 August 1967, which noted the growing importance of sport as a means of exercising influence in third world countries, an attractive aspect for a country that had recently decolonized:

> The triumphs and the prestige that accompanies [sport] lead to concrete results. France is victorious? The countries of the Third World will appeal to French coaches, providing an advantage in the area of cooperation.
>
> (Legris, 1967: 1)

As Legris observed, many governments, especially the new African governments, started to adopt European sports training programmes and modelled their sports ministries and plans after those found in Europe. For France, to be viewed as an athletically victorious nation could enable it to keep a certain degree of influence and respect from its former African colonies.

The sports policies enacted after 1960 began to increase athletic participation by mid-decade. Yet the sports remedies, and the controversy they created around the debate over amateur and state athletes, did not produce immediate changes in the way the French perceived sport. The continued lack of athletic success at the international levels spurred on the French government to rethink once again how it embraced and promoted sport.

Rectifying the sports crisis, 1973–92

During the 1970s, the general thrust of Gaullist policy was broadly followed under Valery Giscard d'Estaing, and the historic socialist victory of François Mitterrand in 1981 generally endorsed and continued the state-led structure of French sport. However, over the course of the two decades there was a stronger emphasis on promoting excellence through institutional means rather than relying on patriotic rhetoric. The attempt to impose a French sporting presence on the world proved futile in terms of the production of gold-medal performances in global and European competitions. The French took seventeenth place in the overall medal count of the Munich 1972 Summer Games, and sixteenth at the 1972 Winter Games in Sapporo. Its football team did not qualify for the 1970 or 1974 World Cup. The men's basketball team failed to qualify for the basketball World Championships of 1967 and 1970 and did not qualify again for the World Championship until 1986, when they placed thirteenth overall. The post-war economic boom came to a close and French prosperity and modernization seemingly stagnated. Moreover, the pressure to fix the sports crisis mounted. In the 1970s, when China's use of ping-pong diplomacy began to alter international attitudes and policy, and East Germany rose to the forefront of sports (such as swimming) through its sports schools and doping programmes, the incentive to attain athletic victory grew.

France took to new tactics to rectify the performance 'crisis'. New legislation was enacted to legitimize sport institutionally and give it more state sponsorship. Youth sports development programmes were launched to identify and train the nation's future elite athletes. These measures, in turn, began to create a genuine sport culture that began to produce results (and also, seemingly, to solve the youth crisis of the 1960s). These trends were influenced by the changing way that sport was transmitted to the public on television, which transformed sport in France from a leisure activity into a form of public entertainment. Thus sporting success combined with the new format for transmitting sport through the media to allow the Fifth Republic to do what it had failed to do in the 1960s: to project power abroad and domestically through elite athletes who won major international competitions.

The first part of the answer was government legislation to grant further official legitimacy to sports. Named after then Minister of Youth and Sport, Pierre Mazeaud, the October 1975 Mazeaud Law gave an official voice and national backing to the preparation of elite athletes. It provided social and financial assistance to elite athletes on the basis that 'the development of the practice of sport and physical activities is a fundamental element of culture, which constitutes a national obligation' (French Government, 1975). This was the first time that the French state acknowledged that sport, as distinct from physical education, was an integral part of French education and culture.[12] Furthermore, in the promise of state support for sports development, the government pledged itself to a remarkable new route, one previously undertaken only by the Eastern European communist regimes, in making sport a crucial element of national policy and funding.

The law created the National Institute of Sport and Physical Education (*Institut National d'Éducation Physique et du Sport*, INSEP), with a mission to conduct scientific research that could be applied to pedagogical, medical and technical material. This translated into the introduction of medical science to state-sponsored athletic development, a growing trend during the Cold War era. INSEP was to train elite youth athletes to serve the state in international competitions through a cadre of professional coaches, teachers and other personnel. Located on the outskirts of Paris in the Bois de Vincennes, INSEP was where the top youth prospects in all the Olympic sports except football were to live and train to form the nation's elite tier of athletes.[13] It was an elite athletic academy on a vast scale, which replaced the former institution on the same site whose role had been mainly to train physical education teachers.

To aid the identification, recruitment and training of young athletes with athletic potential, the National Committee for Elite Sport (*Comité National du Sport de Haut Niveau*, CNSHN) was created on 10 October 1978.[14] The CNSHN was responsible for drawing up lists of the nation's premier athletes according to their age and ability: Youths, Seniors, Elite and Reconversion. These lists were created in conjunction with each sport federation's National Technical Director, and were modified each year so that the government could keep track of various athletes, sports disciplines, major competitions and results.

The Mazeaud Law was important in that it set out for the first time a full national sports policy. As noted by Benjamin Louche of the Ministry of Youth and Sport, 'the Mazeaud Law was the first to lay down the basic essence of elite sport and how to fund it.'[15] This was a significant development in a country that during the 1960s felt it was in the throes of a sports crisis. That the French enacted national legislation to train young athletes spoke volumes about how sensitive they were to the continued lack of athletic success and their desire to regain influence through the soft power of sports.

The establishment of a strong state–sport relationship made France distinctive amongst the Western European powers of the time (Riordan and Krüger, 2003). While the West German regime had state-funded elite athletic programmes, it only directly financed athletes selected to represent the country on the international stage, the actual national squad (Cadre A), in an effort to shy away from what some considered the totalitarian nature of state-sponsored elite athletics. In Italy, elite sport was run by the National Italian Olympic Committee (*Comitato Olimpico Nazionale Italiano*, CONI), an organ of the state, but financed through the national sports lottery, *Totocalcio*. In the Italian case, CONI's ability to finance sport independently of the government enabled elite Italian sport to evade any direct ties or obligations to politics. In Britain, there was an increased push for greater government involvement with the setting up of the Sports Council in the 1960s, but little sense that elite performance on the world stage was ultimately the responsibility of government (Hill, 2002: 154). Hence, despite the creation of a British Sports Minister in 1966, the relationship between the state and sport in

Britain in the 1970s and 1980s was much less close than it was in France, with school sports facilities sold off during the Thatcher years.

Ludovic DeBru of the French Football Federation's National Technical Direction bureau noted that 'the law of 1975 had a big, big impact' upon the trajectory of French sport.[16] The Mazeaud Law stoked the popularity of sport and fostered a culture of youth athletics that, by the early 1980s, began to produce talented players who started to win international athletic honour for the country. Moreover, it began to allocate greater funding for youth and sports initiatives, increasing the Youth and Sport budget from just over 1 billion francs in 1970 to 3.5 billion by 1980 (Nys, 1984: 1). With subsequent increases in the funding allocated for sport, France was the big spender of West European sport.

The sea-change in French politics in 1981 with the election of socialist François Mitterrand and the subsequent socialist–communist coalition had little impact on the distinctive French approach to sport. The priorities remained the same, but the method of achieving them was revised. In 1984, Mazeaud's successor as Minister of Youth and Sport, Edwige Avice, reinforced and expanded the Mazeaud Law.[17] Her main goal was to liberalize the athletic system, to make it more like the American one, in which youth athletic development was an integral part of education.[18] On 16 July 1984, the French legislature passed the Avice Law (Law Number 84–610), which further codified athletic development within France. The Avice Law served to ensure that the practice and promotion of sport was grounded in the attempt to ensure a healthy population (French Government, 1984: Article 1). It established a national commission of elite sport, which was made up of representatives from the state, the National Committee of French Olympics, and of French sport, with additional advice provided by interested sports federations. This body, which became the Bureau of Elite Sport, was responsible for overseeing the development of the nation's elite athletes within the educational system (French Government, 1984: Article 27).

The Avice Law sought to transfer more power from the sports federations to the government, which according to Avice was highly desirable.[19] It also tried to switch to a more American style of financing sport. Previously, French athletics relied almost exclusively upon public funding. In creating the new law, Avice tried to bring the funding of French sport more in line with the American system, to incorporate a greater involvement of private enterprise to sponsor the nation's athletic initiatives.[20] In this regard, she pointed to the 1984 Los Angeles Summer Olympics as being 'very influential'.[21] Ironically, it was a socialist government that departed from the pure tradition of state intervention in favour of a neoliberal model.

The shift towards a more Americanized system may have been reflective of the increased emphasis on winning international sports competitions during the 1980s, at the height of the Cold War's sports diplomacy. Through liberalizing some of the state's control of sport, it was felt that better results could be obtained. Both the Mazeaud and Avice Laws helped to provide French youth with an avenue for pursuing sport in conjunction with their academic studies, and thus succeeded in conferring legitimacy to sport.

Codifying sports helped garner support for the 1973 launch of two new youth sports programmes designed to produce better youth athletes. One of these programmes was the government-run sport-study section (*section sport-étude*, SSE); the other was the football *centre de formation*, financed and administered privately through the professional clubs. Although the SSE and the *centre de formation* shared the same goal, to allow young athletes to improve and refine their athletic skills under the supervision of specialized coaches, they were originally quite different. Run within the national education system, the SSE focused primarily on academic matters. The *centre de formation*, on the other hand, initially focused on athletic performance. As the 1970s and 1980s progressed, the SSE and *centre de formation* structures evolved. The SSE increasingly emphasized athletics, and by 1984 fed elite youth athletes into the regional and national sports programmes. By the same point in time, the *centres de formation* adopted a greater emphasis on educational achievement.

Eventually, the *centre de formation* transformed itself into a mini-boarding school for elite youth football players, while the SSE programmes also evolved into similar entities for elite youth athletes of other sports. Both structures sought to school, socialize and train gifted athletes, and to imprint upon their young charges the importance of community and citizenship. Although a privately run enterprise, by the late 1980s and early 1990s the *centre de formation* had become the preferred model for combining youth sports training and scholastic education to produce socialized young citizens who won major athletic honours for France. Although these structures were successful in terms of producing better athletic results, and seemingly at integrating youth into society, the question emerged as to who gained from such structures. This was particularly the case when contemplating the position of young players at the *centres de formation*, who often found themselves signing contracts with draconian labour restrictions.

The youth sports programmes were also a means to help assimilate immigrant youth into the republican fabric of the nation. According to Dr Joel Costes, a long-serving doctor for the football *centre de formation* of Olympique de Marseille (OM), sport was an essential element in the assimilation of the newer immigrants from Africa. One of the critical services provided to youths of immigrant extraction who entered youth sports programmes at OM was that they were taught the basics of hygiene and sanitation, as well as the meaning of citizenship and belonging to a team.[22]

The SSEs and *centres de formation* reflected the close association of youth and sport, the most striking initiative of its kind since the Vichy Regime. Yet, as the Mazeaud Law claimed, sport was a valuable cultural element, one that the state was responsible to teach and develop, and this distanced youth sports programmes from the taint of Vichy (French Government, 1975). It was also responsible for helping to foster a national sports culture that valued athletics as an integral part of education. The successes of the youth sports training programmes and sports legislation took hold, and by the late 1970s and early 1980s they began to produce results.

At the 1984 Summer Olympic Games in Los Angeles, France took home twenty-nine medals, the most it had garnered at the Summer Games since 1948 (IOC,

2010a). Although this could be attributable to the Soviet boycott of the Olympics, nineteen medals were won at the 1988 Summer Games in Seoul, a significant increase over the numbers won at Summer Olympics in the 1960s and 1970s. At the 1992 Barcelona Games, France took home thirty-eight medals. France was placed in the top ten of overall medal counts at these three Games.

Within the realm of football, a generation of young players emerged to take France to the 1978 World Cup in Argentina. This group, often referred to as the Platini generation, matured and won fourth place in the 1982 World Cup in Spain. Two years later, the French national team won the European Championship, while the Olympic team celebrated their first-ever gold medal at the Los Angeles Summer Games. A third-place finish at the 1986 Mexico World Cup followed these triumphs. Such results translated into sports becoming part of youth culture, especially for boys, and the number of licensed players increased.[23] Moreover, increasingly, more youths saw their national athletes competing on television. As Gérard Precheur, a former football player and now a coach at the national football training centre for girls at Clairefontaine, noted: 'more and more of society was interested [in sport] thanks to television'.[24]

Moreover, throughout the 1980s, televised broadcasts and the new financial incentives for sports were enticing to youths of immigrant extraction. The inducement to become an elite athlete encouraged immigrant youths to emulate their sports heroes while climbing the socio-economic ladder. As athletes, especially footballers, were increasingly drawn from this immigrant population, their televised performances conferred a 'Frenchness' on them in the eyes of the public. It was one of the strongest elements in forging national identity in the late twentieth century (Gabaston and Leconte, 2000: 22). This was also true of sport at the youth level. As *Agence France Presse* journalist Eric Lagneau noted, 'the youth of modest backgrounds, notably in the suburbs [the housing estates ringing the big cities], where there is little in the way of social mobility, all these youths think they can get success through football'.[25]

Television had one of the greatest impacts on sport in France. Its growth accelerated throughout the 1960s and 1970s, but it was the 1980s that revolutionized television and, subsequently, sport. Until the mid-1980s, the government owned and ran the country's three television channels, *Télévision Française 1* (TF1), *Antenne 2* (A2) and *France Régions 3*. The Fifth Republic deemed television an educative tool, thus focusing much of its budget for educational programming. Although each station broadcast sports, they were limited by meagre financial incentives to offer sports federations in exchange for transmitting competitions. Additionally, sports programming was not cheap. As the technology used to broadcast sports events grew more sophisticated and required more equipment, technicians and sportscasters, the costs for televising sports competitions began to escalate.

In 1984, *Canal Plus* launched France's first private television network, a paid subscription channel, thus ending the government's monopoly of television broadcasting. A commercial enterprise bolstered by the money of its subscribers, *Canal Plus* had the deep coffers needed to induce sports federations – particularly the FFF – to allow live transmission of their competitions. It could also invest in state-of-the-art broadcast technology to keep pace with the continuing revolution in media consumership. *Canal Plus* changed forever how the French public viewed, interacted with, and consumed sports. These changes reverberated from the elite to the recreational levels, from adult athletes to the youth. Television and its evolution during the 1973–92 period ensured that French sport was firmly entrenched in society, aided in cultivating a national sports culture, infused money into the sports system, and made athletics a component of youth culture. Lastly, television helped to lay the foundations for the phenomenon of the celebrity athletes who many youths viewed as sports heroes, for, as Mazeaud noted, 'when a country does not have any champions, it suffers a real disaffection for sport' (Mazeaud, 1980: 92). The revolution of media during this period was important for creating an athletic culture in France.

While the generation of 1968 had been influenced by an internationlist outlook, the French youth sports programmes of the 1970s and 1980s served to counteract part of the legacy of this generation and helped to reassert French identity amongst its young players. Thus, the *centres de formation* and SSE, in creating a new generation of elite athletes, served to reverse the 1960s trend towards cultural internationalism. This was illustrated by the Platini generation of footballers, who regained French prestige and honour by making French football a major contender on the international arena during the 1980s. Televised images of their successes from 1982–86 reinforced and helped to reinvent French identity: that of an athletic, victorious nation.

Conclusion

The role of the French state in elite sport during the Cold War was reflective of the nation's Cold War history. The Fifth Republic was not the only regime that sought to utilize sport during the Cold War. However, the French example was unique in that it attempted to create an alternative sports model from the Eastern Bloc and United States models. Elite sport, especially at the youth level, was a means to adopt and adjust to the new realities of the post-1945 world. The youth and sports crises of the 1960s helped to shape public and government support for youth and sports programmes. The problem of the large youth demographic; the way it challenged the traditional social and institutional norms of the nation; and the forms of popular culture that developed during the period helped to compound the sense of a youth crisis. To ease these domestic pressures, French officials used sport as a tool to shape youth, instil republican ideals, and reinforce meritocracy and democracy.

The French turned their attention to sport in order to establish a new image of the nation, one that was youthful, victorious and influential. With the expansion of television during the 1960s, international impressions of a nation's athletic victories or defeats had new resonance. As television broadcasts became integral athletic components during the 1970s and 1980s, images of teams and athletes competing for the nation had a powerful impact and reinforced national identity. In a globalizing world, the French youth sports programmes helped to reassert French identity amongst young players, trying to counteract the trend of the transnational youth culture that was produced during the 1960s. As France began to produce winning teams and internationally recognized athletes such as Michel Platini, televised images reinforced and helped to invent a French identity, which could assimilate immigrant youth into the wider social fabric and serve as a way to legitimize their Frenchness.

In early 1979, Secretary of State for Youth and Sport Paul Dijoud noted that the main objective for French sport was 'to make France a grand sports nation that will permit it to take one of the premier places in international competitions'.[26] Whether it succeeded in doing so is debatable. However, the story of French sport policies during the Cold War is indicative of how countries without superpower status tried to harness sport for their own uses and, in the French case, to present to the world a new, rejuvenated and revived image of the nation.

Notes

1 All views expressed are those of the author and do not represent those of the US Department of State. Information presented here is based on publicly available declassified sources.
2 J.P. Soisson replaced Mazeaud as head of Youth and Sports in 1976. 'Letter of 13 December 1977', from the Secretary of State for Youth and Sport to Monsieur le Ministre [recipient unclear] on the subject of 'Elements for the communication of sport in the Council of Ministers', Center for Contemporary Archives, Instalment 19840019, Article 9, 'Studies on Sport'.
3 For the purposes of this study, the term 'youth' refers to those aged fourteen to twenty-five.
4 Institut national de la statistique et des études économiques (INSEE), 'Population en France métropolitaine depuis 1851,' www.insee.fr/fr/themes/tableau.asp?ref_id=NAT non02145
5 'Notes for the Director General of Youth and Sport on the Preparation for the 1960 Olympic Games', Center for Contemporary Archives, Instalment 19780586, Article 100, 'Rome Olympic Games of 1960'.
6 *Ibid.*
7 The report noted that French fencers and basketball players were already quite good, but that 'fencing is the most intelligent individual sport'; that 'basketball is the most intelligent team sport'; and that the French could excel at 'intelligent' sports because 'we produce intelligent athletes' (*ibid.*).
8 The French athletes won their medals in equestrian and rowing events.
9 Gaston Meyer, 'L'Allemagne a menace les deux "grands" mais la France n'est nulle part!', *Sport et Vie*, October 1960: 6, Center for Contemporary Archives, Instalment 19780586, Article 100, 'Rome Olympic Games 1960'.
10 Jean-Emile Mazer, interview with the author, Paris, France, 13 April 2006.
11 *Ibid.*
12 Since the rise of modern sports in the nineteenth century, the French state showed a proclivity to favour physical education (gymnastics, calisthenics) over sports or sportive education, which included team sports but also individual sports such as skiing, swimming and cycling.
13 Elite youth footballers were corralled into the National Institute of Football (*Institut National de Football*, INF) of the French Football Federation (*Fédération Française*

de Football, FFF). The INF opened in 1972 and, despite being run by the FFF rather than the government, strove for the same goals as INSEP. Originally located in Vichy, the INF moved to Clairefontaine in 1986, where today it remains the centre of French football.

14 Benjamin Louche, 'Le sport de haut niveau,' email to the author, June 2007.
15 *Ibid.*
16 Ludovic DeBru, interview with the author, Paris, France, June 2007.
17 Edwige Avice, interview with the author, Paris, France, 28 June 2007.
18 *Ibid.*
19 *Ibid.*
20 *Ibid.*
21 The 1984 Los Angeles Olympics were the first financed by a combination of public and private funding (*ibid.*; IOC, 2010b).
22 Joel Costes, interview with the author, Marseille, France, June 2007.
23 Licences were the standard measure of a given sport's popularity and were often the barometer for the amount of government subsidies given to a particular club or sports association.
24 Gérard Precheur, interview with the author, Clairefontaine, France, June 2007.
25 Eric Lagneau, email correspondence with the author, March 2002.
26 'Measures taken by M. Dijoud, Secretary of State for Youth and Sport', 22 March 1978, Center for Contemporary Archives, Instalment 19840019, Article 9, 'Studies on Sport'.

References

Bromberger, C., (1998), *Football: la bagatelle la plus sérieuse du monde*, Paris: Bayard.

Clare, M., (1960), 'Le sport est le parent pauvre du haut-commissariat aux sports', *L'Équipe*, 22 September: 11.

Dietschy, P. and Clastres, P., (2009), *Sport, société et culture en France du XIXe siècle à nos jours*, Paris: Hachette.

Dine, P., (1998), 'Sport and the State in contemporary France: from la Charte des Sports to decentralisation', *Modern and Contemporary France*, 6 (3): 301–11.

French Embassy in the USA, (1965), 'France and the Rising Generation', New York: French Embassy Press and Information Service.

French Government, (1975), 'Relative au Développement de l'Éducation Physique et du Sport', 'Mazeaud Law', Law Number 75–988 of 29 October 1975 (*Journal Officiel de la République Française*, 30 October: 11180).

——, (1984), 'Relative à l'Organisation et à la Promotion des Activités Physiques et Sportives', 'Avice Law', Law Number 84–610 of 16 July 1984 (*Journal Officiel de la République Française*, 17 July 1984: 2288).

Gabaston, P. and Leconte, B., (2000), *Sports et television: regards croisés*, Paris: l'Harmattan.

Gay-Lescot, J.-L., (1991), *Sport et Eductation sous Vichy, 1940–1944*, Lyon: PU de Lyon.

Hill, J., (2002), *Sport, Leisure and Culture in Twentieth Century Britain*, New York: Palgrave.

IOC, (2010a) 'Olympic Medals: Summer Games', International Olympic Committee, www.olympic.org/france

——, (2010b) 'Los Angeles: 1984', www.olympic.org/los-angeles-1984-summer-olympics

Legris, M., (1967), 'Le sport peut-il être un métier? Competitions sportives et competition politique', *Le Monde*, 8 August: 1.

Lipsyte, R., (1965), 'Sports Chief Finds French Apathetic', *New York Times*, 15 June: 51.

Mangan, J. A. (ed.), (2003), *Militarism, Sport, Europe: War Without Weapons*, Portland, OR: Frank Cass.

Mazeaud, P., (1980), *Sport et Liberté*, Paris: Denoël.

Mignon, P., (1998), *La Passion du football*, Paris: Odile Jacob.

Ministry of Justice, (1968), *Le Role de l'Éducation Physique et Sportive dans le Traitement des Delinquents*, Paris: Ministry of Justice.

Nye, R.A., (1993), *Masculinity and Male Codes of Honour in Modern France*, New York: Oxford University Press.

Nys, J.-F., (1984), *Les Subventions municipales aux clubs de football: une analyse économique*, Limoges: A. Bonpoint.

Riordan, J. and Krüger, A. (eds), (2003), *European Cultures in Sport: Examining the Nations and Regions*, Portland, OR: Intellect Books.

5 Bikila's aria

The 1960 Rome Olympics

Simon Martin

Supported by the Rome Commune (City Council) and Alcide De Gasperi's Christian Democrat government, the Italian Olympic Committee (*Comitato Olimpico Nazionale Italiano*, CONI) began preparing its bid to host the Games in 1950, less than seven years after the fall of Fascism. The dream became a reality on 15 June 1955, when the fifty-five members of the International Olympic Committee (IOC) selected Rome as the host city for the 1960 Games. Italy was on the cusp of an economic boom that would be in full, decadent and joyous cry by the time of the Games, and attracting tourism and foreign currency and repatriating goodwill further underlined the success and speed with which democracy had been restored to the former dictatorship.[1] With the nation's re-entry into the international diplomatic community signalled by a series of key events, most notably its membership of the United Nations in 1955, the awarding and hosting of the Olympic Games was further confirmation and reward.

A great national project within a global event, the Games exposed changes in Italian society and identity, revealing how Italy's elite wanted the country to be seen as an important and progressive actor in the international arena, rather than one undergoing transition or economic decline. A high-profile opportunity to demonstrate democratic Italy's great leap forwards and to rebrand the country, hosting the Games of the XII Olympiad demanded significant renovation of existing buildings and the construction of new facilities and infrastructure. Yet what appeared to be a sparkling new era of innovative Italian design and engineering left a deep imprint upon the city that irreparably directed its future urban development. Far from stimulating Rome's urban regeneration, it was a traumatic missed opportunity that underlined the powerlessness of the planners in the face of rampant speculation.

The Rome Olympics were also a pivotal moment for the IOC. The first to be broadcast live, they were also the first to take place outside the post-war austerity era. Contextualized by the Cold War, however, their politicization was intensified by Italy's strategic border with Communist Yugoslavia and its sharply polarized politics. Somewhat remarkably, given their enormous local, national and international importance, the Rome Games have received less attention than other competitions, with David Maraniss' recent work providing the most illuminating account (Maraniss, 2008). The fiftieth anniversary of the Games, in 2010, and the city's candidacy to host the 2020 event have provided timely reasons to take stock of one of sport's significant contributions to the development of Republican Italy.

The Sack of Rome

The Catholic Church's 1950 Jubilee saw the beginning of a period of unbridled construction and building speculation, commonly known as the 'Sack of Rome', which changed the capital forever. The decade's parentheses were closed by the 1960 Rome Olympics which, rather than regenerating and re-projecting the city, redirected and restricted its future urban development. As Tim Kirk proposed in his architectural study of the city: 'For the same reasons that Mayor Ernesto Nathan had turned down the idea of hosting the Olympics in 1908 – encouraging real-estate speculation – Mayor Salvatore Rebecchini of the Christian Democrat party accepted' (Kirk, 2005: 196–97). Despite this, Rome 1960 still represented a new era in terms of the Olympic movement's impact upon host cities. With the emphasis principally upon the Games' efficient organization with very limited budgets, from 1960 onwards the event increasingly stimulated huge regeneration projects.

Rome's development in the 1950s was still governed by the demands of the 1931 Regulatory Plan. Frequently contravened by Fascism's monumental projects, this was further altered by the regime's construction of the EUR '42 district (Rossi, 2003: 150–54), which encouraged the city's expansion towards the sea 'on a wave of imperial rhetoric more than meditated strategy' as Fascism sought to connect its capital with its Empire (Avarello, 1999: 165).[2] Although ideologically driven, this southerly expansion was included in a proposed modernization of the Regulatory Plan, in 1958, which also proposed the development of Rome's impoverished eastern periphery. Not only did the Olympic construction programme undermine this, it also intensified existing land and building speculation in the already packed northern and western quarters.

The most significant decision in planning for Rome 1960 was the unusual move to create two Olympic centres: one in the north (at the Foro Italico) and another in the south (in the EUR zone). There were two logical alternatives: (a) the use and expansion of the existing facilities solely in the north of Rome; or (b) the development of new facilities in the poorly equipped east of the city. Contributing to the area's regeneration and industrialization, this would also have left a legacy of sports facilities in an area that previously lacked them (Insolera, 1962: 243). Yet, with CONI's focus upon elite rather than mass sport,[3] this golden opportunity to improve drastically low participation levels had little appeal. More importantly, as Arrigo Benedetti's *L'Espresso* editorial argued:

> If it had been limited to this, the huge real-estate deal would have been miss-ing. Here is why the extravagant idea of building a second sporting centre was born, exactly at the opposite and furthest point away: in the EUR zone, on the road to Ostia, fifteen kilometres from the Foro Italico, with all of Rome in between.
>
> (Benedetti, 1960: 1)

The use of the Foro Italico and EUR sites was controversial, partly because these were Rome's largest and most easily identifiable Fascist-built zones, but primarily due to the need for a road to connect them. Totally undermining the city's proposed eastern development, the decision paved the way for the construction of the Via Olimpica.

The Holy Highway and the road to hell

The Via Olimpica was one of a number of important changes in the road network, which included the construction of the Corso Francia and its viaducts (1958–60) that crossed the river between the northern Olympic site and the Village, plus four underpasses along either side of the Tiber embankments that made up the first section of a somewhat inconceivable inner-city highway. Part of 'a definitive structure for our city', this 'grandiose project' (G. R., 1960: 4) was, according to the Christian Democrat daily *Il Popolo*, designed to bring the 'feel of America to Rome' (Silvestri, 1960a: 5). The idea was castigated by the journalist and father of Italian environmentalism Antonio Cederna: 'What counts most is that for a futile aim like the Olympics these works together with others [. . .] conducted outside of the Regulatory Plan and in contempt for the elementary norms of reasonable urban planning, marked truly a decisive turn for Rome' (Cederna, 1965: 59).

Built along the western flank of the city, the Via Olimpica connected the northern Foro Italico site with EUR's venues in the south.[4] Conceived as a fast-flowing highway, in reality it was disjointed and stitched together from existing and new streets, one of which slashed a huge gash through one of Rome's great public parks, the Villa Doria Pamphili. Despite *Il Popolo*'s celebration of the Via Olimpica's road test that apparently 'took place in a "crescendo" of euphoria and enthusiasm' (S. B., 1960: 2), the road was so incapable of dealing with the traffic that its use during the event was restricted to athletes and accredited journalists (De Santis, 1960a: 7).

Much of the land required to build it was owned by the General Estate Agency (*Società Generale Immobiliare*, SGI), whose major shareholder was the Vatican. FIAT and the cement producer Italcementi were two of the many other shareholding companies whose interests were rooted in urban development. The road, according to Cederna, had one precise purpose: 'to increase the value of land in the northern and western arc of Rome and thus to overturn every reasonable perspective for the Regulatory Plan' (Cederna, 1960b: 13). Cederna was supported by *L'Espresso*'s editor (Benedetti, 1960: 1) in 1960, and Pier Ostilio Rossi in his architectural guide to Rome, some forty plus years later:

> If you also bear in mind that in 1960 the sites for two bridges in the north of the city were also opened [. . .] you can easily conclude that while the 'Council's Plan' repeated the need to move the city's gravitational centre towards the east and south-east, the entire infrastructure built on the basis of its provisions [. . .] actually overturned this scheme. In the second half of the

Sixties, in fact, these streets and bridges constituted an important supportive element for the city's development towards the north and west.

(Rossi, 2003: 204)

An alleged carve-up to the exclusive advantage of the religious proprietors of adjacent land, the value of which rose by 150% in ten years, 'paradise-street' (Cederna, 1960b: 13) made the Vatican the clear Olympic winner, according to the Communist daily *L'Unità* (Perria, 1960a: 3). It was supported by *L'Espresso*'s inquiry 'to establish a list of properties crossed by the Via Olimpica [. . .] We are able to say now that the list is reduced to a rosary of pious institutions of nuns and brothers' (Benedetti, 1960: 1).

The SGI's simple and profitable strategy was to acquire land across Rome and build a small plot of apartments at the furthest point. Forcing the council to bring water and infrastructure, this raised the value of the intervening, undeveloped land, which was then sold on to smaller builders at a significant profit. 'Thus, the big builders sell [the land] and leave construction to the smaller ones' (Cancogni, 1960: 3), which created a boom in land and housing prices and promoted the city's concentric development (Telesca, 2006: 61).

Due to its holding considerable acres of land in Rome's eastern periphery, there was good reason for the SGI to support its Olympic development there, rather than in its significant portfolio in the north-western, luxury housing district of Vigna-Clara. While it should have provided the perfect pretext to launch a new wave of building speculation in the area's still undeveloped zones (Cederna, 1960b: 13), Rome 1960 and the Via Olimpica instead restarted the concentric development of the city that significantly reduced its expansion to the east, where regeneration was most needed (Insolera, 1962: 233).[5] The whole process was, according to Cederna, a direct and deliberate choice by the city's ruling class to:

> [. . .] keep the outcasts, immigrants, second class citizens away from middle class and 'Sacred' Rome [. . .] They keep land prices artificially high and thus make it impossible to resolve [. . .] the housing problem: for as many slums as they knock down, even worse zones of speculation rise in their place and even more slums will be born even further away.

(Cederna, 1960a: 13)

Besides the immediate speculation in the city's north-west, the decision to build an Olympic sister-site in the south of the capital also indicated the council's future vision: the 'fattening up of EUR' and the 'pushing of Rome to the sea, towards other areas that were dear to the city's owners' (Cederna, 1960b: 13). Augmenting existing speculation, it condemned the city's poorest zones to dereliction. Thus, while the Games appeared a national celebration of Italy's rise from the ashes of Fascism and war, its reconstruction and modernization, beneath the glitz and glamour everyday life saw little improvement:

> The Olympic atmosphere, the road works completed for the Games, the magnificence of the new sport facilities etc, should not be enough for foreign

and Italian tourists to [. . .] forget to visit the real Rome, that of the villages, the slums and the 'working class' zones; the Rome of unauthorised buildings, of caves and of second class citizens: rotten, exhausted Rome where [. . .] around half a million people live [. . .] in the great eastern arc from the Salaria road in the north to the Appia Antica in the south.

(Cederna, 1960a: 13)

Homes for heroes and political playgrounds

A tiny percentage of Rome's poor would be housed after the Games in the low-income housing provided by the Olympic Village's 1350 apartments. Naturally, *Il Popolo* didn't stint in its celebration of yet another Christian Democrat urban planning and architectural achievement (Silvestri, 1960b: 5).[6] Constructed on the former Parioli field on the east side of the Tiber, the area had been designated as parkland until 1950, when its use was changed to accommodate sports facilities, offices and housing, as the city's population exploded with immigrants seeking work in the economic boom.

Although costs rose dramatically, Rome gained a rejuvenated sporting infra-structure that was financed directly by CONI with profits from its weekly football pools betting scheme *Totocalcio*. 'A miracle of sporting passion?' asked the Communist daily *L'Unità* rhetorically. 'Not exactly. Rich and poor Italians have given their weekly contributions in filling in the coupon. Stadiums, swimming pools, gymnasia and velodromes have risen from the hopes and dreams of the people' (Anon., 1960c: 3). Central government financed the necessary road and rail developments plus the majority of the Village, while the Commune granted land either free or at extremely discounted rates, and improved local transport. Construction of the already planned Fiumicino airport was hastened, but not quickly enough to be fully operational until after the Games were concluded. Indicative of the disconnected planning exposed by the Olympics was the lack of any direct road or rail connection to the city. While it was ridiculous enough that the required motorway was not completed until eight years after the Games, only a few months prior to Fiumicino's inauguration, road improvements to Rome's now secondary Ciampino airport were finally finished.

***

When the Games were awarded in 1955, Rome's only significant sports facility was the former Cypress Stadium, which had become the Olympic Stadium in 1953. In a clear attempt to convince the world of Italy's commitment and capacity to deliver, work on its redevelopment began as early as 1950. With the bid secured, the 55,000 capacity Stadio Flaminio rose alongside the new 5000-seater indoor Palazzetto dello Sport. On the EUR site a swimming pool, the main indoor arena, the 16,000 capacity Palazzo dello Sport, and the velodrome were also built.[7]

In addition to these new buildings, some events were also held in ancient Roman structures. Gymnasts performed in the Baths of the Emperor Caracalla, Greco-Roman wrestlers grappled under the arches of Maxentius' Temple, while one marathon runner danced a jig of joy and others collapsed at the race's finish under the Arch of Constantine, close to the Colosseum and the Forum. Emphasizing the continuity between the ancient past and the present, the Organizing Committee was unable to ignore Fascism's sport zone at the Foro Italico (formerly Foro Mussolini) and its extensive demolition and rebuilding programme, which had stamped its identity on the city. While many axes, *fasces* and insignia had been chipped away, nowhere in the capital was the regime's politicization of buildings and public space more evident than at the competition's two sites, the Foro Italico and EUR. Overtly political, they demanded, and ignited, a problematic reckoning with the past.

In July, only weeks before the Games began, Fernando Tambroni's controversial administration collapsed when its Neo-Fascist *Movimento Sociale Italiano* (MSI) coalition allies withdrew their support in protest at the banning of a conference they had provocatively planned for Genoa, a red, Resistance city which had suffered terribly in the war. Following the appointment of Amintore Fanfani's new, more leftward-looking government on 22 July, what should have been the ultimate sedative, the opening of the Games, scratched at Italy's wound that would not heal.

The focus of the controversy was the Via dell'Impero (Empire way), the main Foro Italico thoroughfare. Leading from the imposing 'Mussolini' engraved obelisk to the Olympic stadium, it was paved with ancient-style mosaics of Fascist sports-men and slogans, and flanked by huge blocks of travertine stone etched with key moments in the regime's history. Such imagery, in what was to be the first live, global television broadcast of an Olympic Games, caused fierce parliamentary debate as left-wing politicians were afraid of offending athletes and visitors or giving the impression that there was still support in Italy for Mussolini; which, of course, there was. Most contentious of all was the lack of any mention or symbol of the Republic, which had completed the construction of the zone in preparation for the Games. Raising the issue in parliament, in November 1959, deputies asked the Ministers for the Interior and Tourism if:

> [. . .] they considered it opportune, on the occasion of the Rome Olympics and considering the pacifist international solidarity of the great event, to remove from the Foro Italico, the inscriptions to the apologetic memory of a past that the Italian people and the democratic conscience of the world had condemned; writings that could be considered by guests as a glorification expressed by our country.
>
> (Camera dei Deputati, 1959: 10612)

The Ministers' justification for leaving the zone untouched was persuasive: 'We [. . .] consider that Italian democracy will demonstrate great seriousness let alone belief in itself if, rather than being merciless against those stones and [. . .] mosaics, it leaves them [. . .] in testimony of the past' (Camera dei Deputati, 1959: 10616). Potentially demonstrating a bold confidence in the new democracy, it nonetheless served Tambroni's administration's needs. As the Socialist deputy Oreste Lizzadri had argued: the government's primary concern was 'not to upset the "Missini" who

[. . .] represent the indispensable element for [its] permanence in power' (Camera dei Deputati, 1959: 10612).[8]

As the Games approached, however, pressure grew on Fanfani's new government to at least cover up the unpleasant past. As *L'Unità* argued: 'When the champions and tourists step foot in the great sporting complex, they will get a punch in the eye. They will think they've gone back twenty years or, worse still, have found themselves in a very strange country where an infamous past of crimes and unceasing mourning and misery is held [. . .] in the greatest honour' (Anon., 1960e: 1). Besides the Fascist tablets and the 264 references to the Duce, it was the celebration of pre-Fascist events, such as the First World War victory at Vittorio Veneto which was appropriated as a Fascist success (Camera dei Deputati, 1959: 10612–13), plus the post-war addition of further stones celebrating the Liberation, the formation of the Republic and the Constitution, which most offended. The inclusion of tablets celebrating pre- and post-Fascist history was, according to *L'Unità*: 'a gross and vulgar cover-up that aggravated the scandal instead of putting an end to it, giving the impression of a desire to confirm a sort of monstrous "continuity" between Fascist and democratic Italy' (Anon., 1960f: 1).

The paper's demand that Mussolini's name be cut from the obelisk was not met, although on 8 August work did begin to cover and remove what were considered the most ideological works. This action affected one tablet celebrating the Fascist resistance to the League of Nations sanctions following the invasion of Abyssinia, and a single mosaic containing the Fascist oath (Corbi, 1960: 6); quite how another celebrating the conquest of Italy's Empire was not considered ideological is unclear. Suspended almost immediately, the cover-up fuelled neo-Fascist intransigence. Mussolini's former press secretary, the Fascist president of CONI, and MSI parliamentary deputy at the time, Lando Ferretti, rushed to what he considered a 'massacre' and declared, in a direct reference to the Fascist era, 'We have stopped today's pigmies from cancelling the work of the giant of a recent, glorious past' (Corbi, 1960: 6).

A protest of over 150 'Missini' (MSI members) on 10 August led to a number of arrests, while night after night the *New York Times* reported that the MSI activists painted slogans praising Mussolini along the Tiber's walls and on public buildings across the city. That there is no mention of this in the Italian press may be indicative of how, as the conflict grew, the issue attracted international attention and comment, not so much for the Fascist symbols, but more for the activity of the Italian Communist Party (*Partito Comunista Italiano*, PCI), which some of the American press interpreted as Soviet trouble-making by proxy (Modrey, 2008: 700–701). With Italy a critical border in the West's battle against communist expansion, what was essentially a domestic argument over the representation of Republican Italy became a Cold War political football, and the Games a pawn in international politics.

Cold War apostles

1960 was a tense year in East–West relations: Gary Powers' U2 spy plane was shot down over Soviet airspace; the Soviet premier Nikita Khrushchev walked out of a four-powers summit meeting in Paris; US President Eisenhower cancelled a planned visit to the Soviet Union; the USSR promised to defend Cuba with missiles if necessary; and, on the eve of the Games, Powers was publicly tried for espionage in Moscow. Could Rome 1960 really be apolitical, as the IOC and the Italian Organizing Committee wanted? Recalling how the Greeks had suspended all hostilities during the ancient event, at the opening of the Olympic Village the Christian Democratic Party deputy and future five-times prime minister Giulio Andreotti expressed hope for the Games' positive international impact: 'Lifting the spirits even for a short period can have an incalculable value [. . .] and who knows if, at some point in the future, some recognition might be given to the XVII Olympic Games for easing a grave moment of international tension' (Anon., 1960a: 5).

There were nonetheless a number of stresses and contradictions within the Olympic movement itself, such as the 'united' German team that was more or less single-handedly forced to compete as one by the American IOC President Avery Brundage. There were also no representatives present from the People's Republic of China, which had withdrawn from the Olympic movement two years earlier in protest at the IOC's recognition of Taiwan. Protesting itself at being considered part of Chinese territory, the Taiwanese delegation entered the opening ceremony carrying small signs declaring 'Under Protest', which *L'Unità* 'unsurprisingly' deemed ridiculous (Anon., 1960b: 6). American athletes were also pressed into action by the CIA, in an attempt to encourage Soviet defectors. The sprinter Dave Sime was given the specific target of Igor Ter-Ovanesyan, while all squad members boarded their flights armed with a Berlitz Italian phrasebook, copies of the US Declaration of Independence and a booklet on the virtues of the American lifestyle. Printed in Russian, they were to be passed on to Soviet team members (Maraniss, 2008: 25–26; 29).

The Games also provided the Vatican with an international recruitment opportunity. Despite the Church's ambivalence and occasional hostility to sport since the mid–late-nineteenth century, the founder of the modern Olympic movement Baron Pierre De Coubertin was granted an audience with Pope Pius X in 1905 during his visit to Rome, to assess its bid to host the 1908 Games. As the 1960 Games opened, Pope John XXIII referred to this in his audience with over 4000 athletes in St Peter's Square: 'Having expected you for a long time, now we can finally welcome you' (De Santis, 1960b: 1). Flanked by fourteen Cardinals, the Pope also shared the stage with the IOC Chairman Avery Brundage, Italian Olympic Committee president Giulio Onesti, the Games Organizing Committee president Giulio Andreotti, as well as the head of the Italian Sporting Centre (*Centro Sportivo Italiano*, CSI), the Church's sports organization, Luigi Gedda. Significant among those blessed, noted the *Corriere della Sera*, was a small contingency of Soviet athletes:

> It wasn't the first time that Soviet citizens entered Saint Peter's Square and visited the Vatican like you do a museum. It was, on the contrary, the first time that ten Soviet citizens mixed among the people crammed before the heir of Peter and stayed for some hours to hear his words and be blessed. Can

one suggest that the Olympic ideal might be so great as to really bring together the most disparate people and to speak in a universal and pious language, capable of erasing all of the rifts of their lives and to suggest a longing for piety?

(De Santis, 1960b: 2)

As *L'Unità* claimed, the Church's exploitation of the Games, supported by the friendly media, was closely connected to the Cold War and financed by the USA. Propaganda leaflets that were translated into twenty different languages for Afro-Asian athletes and socialist athletes were apparently distributed. Clerical and lay activists were to develop an anti-communist and pro-Church campaign among Italian and foreign tourists, while offering their services as guides to monuments and places of national interest (Perria, 1960b: 1). This was refuted by the Christian Democrat mouthpiece *Il Popolo*, which also protested against *L'Unità*'s series of 'offensive' cartoons depicting athletes receiving divine help (Anon., 1960d: 3). In many respects, the spat reflected Italy's long-standing division between the Communist left and religious right as much as the Cold War and the country's strategic border with Yugoslavia, which solidified each group's already entrenched position.

Epic coverage

Despite its political overtones, Rome 1960 saw the transformation of the Olympics into a truly global event. Deemed the first 'non-amateur' or professional Games, athlete numbers almost doubled from Melbourne, four years earlier, while the sale of nearly 1.5 million tickets reflected the booming economy and a rediscovered confidence among Italians. Television coverage was key in the projection of Italy's new or desired identity and the new style of Olympics. Run by the Italian Organizing Committee, rather than by the IOC, it claimed sole rights to establish broadcasting contracts. The first Games to be transmitted live, the competitions reached eighteen European countries immediately, and the USA, Canada and Japan with only a few hours' delay. Indicative of the quality of the Italian transmission was the US cyclist Jack Simes' diary entry. 'I'm surprised that the European TV is clear, too. Hartman [Jack Hartman, his cycling team-mate] once said it's because they have more lines on the screen than we do. I thought everything was supposed to be better in America and we invented TV' (Maraniss, 2008: 375).

The Italian network RAI's coverage wasn't appreciated by all, however, especially *L'Unità*'s Arturo Gismondi. Taking issue with what he considered to have been biased reporting, he drew attention to the whistles and howls of abuse directed at the American boxer Eddie Crook after his victory over the Pole Tadeus Walasek, which RAI's commentator claimed were 'expressions of joy of the many Americans present'. Special ire was reserved for the commentary on the women's 800 metres final that focused on the battle between Australia's Brenda Jones and Germany's Ursula Donath, to the almost total exclusion of the Soviet athlete Lyudmila Lisenko: 'Here's Jones, on the finishing straight [. . .] a few metres left, she approaches the tape [. . .] In fact [. . .] she's come second'

(Gismondi, 1960: 2). Overtaken by her Soviet rival in the last few metres, the commentator continued to laud Jones's great race 'as if the winner didn't exist'. Television, Gismondi complained, 'gave an incredible demonstration of incivility, provincialism, narrow-mindedness. We are a bit ashamed of it for sure, as these things happen in our country' (Gismondi, 1960: 2). Given that RAI-TV was dominated by a Christian Democrat board of control, Gimondi's account doesn't seem too exaggerated, even if *L'Unità*'s celebration of Soviet successes disclosed its own partiality.

The Games was recorded in a feature-length documentary produced by the Italian National Film Institute (*Istituto Luce*) and directed by Romolo Marcellini, a Fascist-trained documentary maker renowned for his epic productions.[9] As the Official Report later noted: 'tens of millions of spectators, even more attentive and critical, gathered in cinema [*sic*] to follow in the brief space of two hours the coloured re-evocation of the Rome Olympic Games' (Organizing Committee of the Games of the XVII Olympiad, 1960: 650). Aware that it was primarily through this medium that the new Italy would be seen, the Olympic Organizing Committee scheduled the events to avoid clashes and help the directors. With a musical score bearing all the hallmarks of the era, it created an atmosphere somewhere between a 1960s heist movie and *Carry On up the Capitol*, conveying a relaxed, sun- and fun-filled nation.[10] The footage also provided a distinctive, beautifully shot, evocative record of Italy, Rome and the 1960 Games, and received an Oscar nomination for the best documentary in 1962.

One of its most notable chapters was the Olympic flame's passage from Greece to the capital, which 'bore reference to the two apexes of classical civilization, Athens and Rome, and [. . .] would pass through the sites of Magna Grecia' (Organizing Committee of the Games of the XVII Olympiad, 1960: 199). Arriving from Athens on an Italian naval training ship in Siracuse, Sicily, it was thereafter carried by local athletes from each of the provinces it passed. After crossing the Straits of Messina onto the Italian mainland, its path hugged Italy's south-western coast to Taranto before returning east. It was here in Lucania, in the depths of southern Italian poverty, that *L'Unità*'s correspondent Arminio Savioli ironically reported a peasant's appeal for him to draw attention to the deprivation and hope-lessness rather than the 'real' news, that of the flame's arrival at Paestum, as wit-nessed by the 'Queen of Holland and her chubby daughter':

> While the bands played and the fireworks exploded, I thought a lot about the words of our comrade Laus. I see the peasant dressed in incredibly miserable clothes, the children's ruined shoes, their filthy legs that haven't had the benefit of soap for weeks (still, today is a bank holiday, the mayors have hung out the tricolour flag [. . .] the military bands have been mobilised and some millions spent on flowers, flags, cans of paint to whiten the house fronts, so the misery won't be seen on television screens and in the documentaries that will be projected in all of Italy's cinemas).

> (Savioli, 1960: 8)

As Luca Pavolini's editorial added: 'the Italian newspapers have rediscovered that the South is poor, backward, it's hungry. And they haven't been able to do anything other than describe it in a tone somewhere between surprise and scandal' (Pavolini, 1960: 1). His attack was directed against those the left considered historically responsible for that hunger: the 'great financial monopolies of the north' who 'reaffirmed President Luigi Einaudi's thesis' that salaries needed to remain higher in the north than the south in order for capital to flow. Thus, by exploiting the flame's passage, he drew attention to how southern poverty and the consequent, constant supply of cheap labour was fuelling Italy's economic miracle. Passing through the ancient sites of Pompei, Herculaneum, Naples, Cuma, Terracina, the papal residency of Castel Gandolfo, before reaching the Appian Way, the Capitol Hill and the Olympic stadium, enthused crowds, peasants, tourists and locals in traditional dress were captured celebrating the torch's passage in southern Italian towns and villages decked in red, white and green. On finally reaching Rome, the documentary took an aerial tour over the city's principal attractions before swooping in and out of the packed stadium and across the Milvian Bridge,[11] where the athletes were marching from the Olympic Village to the opening ceremony to hear the President of the Republic, Giovanni Gronchi, declare the Games of the XVII Olympiad officially open.

The Ethiopian aria

Kings, queens, princes and princesses, and Hollywood stars flocked to the Eternal City, adding lustre to the glitz and glamour of the rejuvenated nation in the throws of the *dolce vita*. Bing Crosby made a specific detour from London, and Sammy Davis Jr added to the 'brat-pack' contingent, as celebrities created work at Ciampino airport, Termini station, hotels and bars for the newspaper chroniclers and *paparazzi*. There were 'celebrated actors (or almost)', including Sandra Dee, Joan Collins, plus the '"diva number one", cinema's prima donna [. . .] Elizabeth Taylor', recorded at the opening ceremony wearing a 'generously low-cut dress' (Josca, 1960: 7). Cary Grant, Rock Hudson, Alain Delon and Gina Lollobrigida were among the screen stars who mingled with the athletes at an organized event on Saturday 4 September.

***

Italian athletes also evidenced the dramatic changes that their society was undergoing. No longer just an escape from hunger, poverty and misery, or a preserve of the wealthy elite, sport had become a middle-class leisure activity and a working-class means of social mobility. The thirty-four women among Italy's 249 competitors provided another indication of change, even if Christian Democracy's sexual paranoia saw all clergy banned from attending women's events (Anon., 1960g: 2). These new, honed female athletes were barracked behind a two-and-a-half-metre high fence, beyond which men were strictly forbidden after the apparent discovery of an extravagant *paparazzo* plan to photograph 'nude Swedes and Americans in the shower'. In what *L'Espresso* termed 'the Olympic Village harem', unstoppable curiosity was stoked by rumours of American and English athletes passing between rooms and corridors in bra and knickers only (Cederna, 1960: 12). In attempting to avoid a potential diplomatic incident, the publicity encouraged binoculared-boys onto the overlooking Corsa Francia Viaduct, which had its uses even if providing a platform for peeping toms wasn't intended to be one of them.

Italy's thirty-six medals and overall third-place finish (behind the USSR and USA) was its best-ever Olympic result. The nation's traditional strengths came to the fore: five cycling medals, plus six in fencing and three in boxing. In the boxing tournament, in which Mohammed Ali (Cassius Clay) also won gold, Giovanni 'Nino' Benvenuti became welterweight champion. The son of a fisherman who practised one of the most hunger-driven sports imaginable, he rejected his humble origins and 'exaggerated in showing his self-taught acculturation: he made it known that he read Hemingway, owned a Picasso, studied Voltaire and prepared for fights by relaxing to Beethoven's violin concertos' (Bassetti, 1999: 174).

In total contrast was middle-class Livio Berruti, who came from a completely different background and further demonstrated how Italy was changing. Equalling the 200 metres world record in qualifying for the final, the twenty-one-year-old was the first sprinter of real world class in sixty years of Italian athletics history. Most unusually, however, while his adversaries warmed up before the final, Berruti concentrated on his university text books in preparation for an imminent exam. Already noted for his apparent coldness and indifference and seen as arrogant by his rivals, Berruti claimed to be retaining composure and conserving energy. Any concerns that he harboured were unfounded, as the outsider repeated his record-equalling time to take gold. Ignoring his bourgeois background, *L'Unità* celebrated the victory, along with that of the German Armin Hary in the 100 metres, as 'a clamorous defeat for the USA in the sprints that were traditionally its preserve' (Colorni, 1960: 1–2). The celebrations, however, soon became controlled admiration for the reserved chemistry student from a well-off Turin family. Unlike previous Italian champions, whose social and geographic origins were evident in a variety of unrefined local dialects, Berruti's command of Italian matched that of his interviewers. A product of his education and leisure time, he contrasted with predecessors who had been toughened by physical labour and motivated by hunger:

> In Berruti, every contradiction, even internal, was resolved. His was not a poem of strength but of smooth agility; his poem was not a fight with nature but rather a harmony with it. In the eyes of the Italians he seemed emblematic of the economic transformation.
>
> (Bassetti, 1999: 172)

An apparent victory for his class as much as the nation, Berruti showed not only how sport connected with Italy's social and economic changes, but also how Italians would increasingly prefer their idols to achieve their goals, or not, with the minimum effort possible.

***

The final event of the Games was the crowning chapter in *Istituto Luce*'s documentary: no leisurely stroll, but an exhausting, spectacular tour of ancient Roman landmarks. Small, lean, barefooted, wearing bright red shorts and a green vest, the Ethiopian Abebe Bikila, a private in Haile Selassie's Imperial Army, did not conform to the image of the modern athlete as he stood waiting for the start of the marathon. None of his competitors took his challenge seriously, with his unofficial personal best for the 42.2 kilometres chauvinistically dismissed as impossible. Bikila had brought running shoes to Rome, but training in the month prior to the Games had ruined them. With new ones causing his feet to blister, he chose to run barefoot, having already toughened them with miles of shoeless training in Ethiopia. Raising eyebrows and interest, it was the significance of his victory that fascinated, as much as the ease with which he consumed the capital's kilometres, coming less than twenty-five years after Mussolini's forces had conquered his own Addis Ababa at the end of a cruel colonial war.

Starting from the Campidoglio, Rome's civic centre set above the Forum, the athletes followed Mussolini's triumphant thoroughfare, the Via dei Foro Imperiali, past the Colosseum, the Palatine hill and the former chariot-racing circuit, the Circus Maximus. Here, at the back of the leading pack, Bikila passed the second–fourth-century Axum obelisk that Fascist forces had plundered from Abyssinia in 1937.[12] Continuing south along the Via Cristoforo Colombo, the marathon passed through EUR before exiting the city and entering the countryside. Turning back at Acilia and bizarrely following a section of the Grande Raccordo Annulare – Rome's outer ring road – the runners turned at the thirty-second kilometre mark onto the Appian Way, which had connected ancient Rome with Brindisi on Italy's south-eastern coast.

Breaking with the tradition of holding Olympic marathons in daylight hours and having them conclude in the stadium, the early evening start maximized the spectacle by conducting the athletes along eight kilometres of the cypress-tree lined Appian Way in darkness. To the rhythm of Bikila's bare feet kissing the uneven stones, the half moonlight, illuminated ancient Roman monuments, and hundreds of torch-bearing soldiers intensified the atmosphere and drama. As Alberto Cavallari wrote in his race report: 'The mixture of the Greek race and Roman sites made it a concentration of charm in its own right. But then the escaping Abyssinian, barefoot, gave it a strong colour [. . .] Arches, marble, columns and the Ethiopian at the final triumph. It wasn't a marathon it was "Aida", with the Romans roadside making up the chorus' (Cavallari, 1960: 14). Re-entering the city at the Porta (Gate) San Sebastiano, with impeccable timing Bikila left his sole pursuer as he re-passed the Axum obelisk. Sealing victory under the Arch of Constantine, in 2 hours, 15 minutes and 16 seconds, he set a new world record.

Seventeen days earlier, Bikila and the small Ethiopian team had marched into the Olympic stadium along Fascism's Via dell'Impero, nearby the controversial mosaics and past the tablets of stone commemorating the regime's 'achievements', one of which was dedicated to the conquest of Abyssinia. Protesting prior to the Games, *L'Unità* had argued that: 'Many of these Italian and foreign athletes and tourists, besides any political reaction, will feel personally offended, in love for their country, perhaps even in remembering painful family tragedies' (Anon., 1960f: 1). Arguably so, but on his nation's behalf Bikila had made a definitive point.

In the days before the rise and dominance of East African athletes, in the context of Italy's two invasions of Ethiopia and its post-1936 colonization, following the decolonization of so many African states in 1960, in the presence of the all-white South African team that the IOC chose not to contest, and against vastly better-funded and equipped Soviet, US and European athletes, Bikila's marathon victory made an enormous impression upon the Games and left a huge mark on the sport that transcended his, admittedly incredible, lack of shoes, for which he is most fondly remembered.[13] His triumph was also that of Rome and the Games, dramatically closing the event under the lights and arch of a long-departed Emperor who, along with his predecessors and successors, continued to inspire the modern city under whatever regime ruled it. For all of the debates in parliament and the Fascist graffiti, there was no better, more apt or significant indication of the break from the past than the comparison of mass, Fascist sport with the celebration of this glorious individual victory by an ex-colonial subject. As the editor of the British Olympic Committee's magazine *World Sports* condescendingly concurred in his report from Rome:

> It is a scene to remember – a moment of theatrical drama; a moment so unusual in modern world athletics when a virtual unknown from an insignificant country crosses the seas and conquers the heroes. It is a fine, unsophisticated, illogical victory [. . .]
>
> This [. . .] was an historic Olympic marathon both in terms of performance and backcloth [. . .] its drama was in its setting, presentation and outcome.
>
> (Pilley, 1960: 27)

Conclusion

In 1934, under the pseudonym of Ettore Bianchi, the author Carlo Levi published a scathing article denouncing the futility of sport, which he argued 'had reduced [the masses] to interesting themselves, like babies, in the gratuitous bounce of a ball' (Bianchi, 1934: 47). Having railed against sport distracting from the class struggle and the battle against Fascism, his words that concluded *Istituto Luce*'s documentary exposed the dramatic change in the new Italy.

> And so, the Olympics were over, and even Rome returned to its daily life like all the cities, villages and countryside untouched by them, where there is never a break from work or need. The Games were a beautiful spectacle from every perspective: colours of peace, flags, strength, youth and the fascinating test of the limits of man's strength. They were a spectacle so beautiful that even the old impenetrable Romans, these body-armoured tortoises, these lizards encrusted by time on their walls, ended up taking an interest.[14]

As Ciro Verratti confirmed, even the Roman antis and sceptics were convinced:

Not only have we provided a confirmation of our organisation that will be memorable to the rest of the world, not only have we got undreamed of victories but we have made a conquest that nobody would have imagined and which was the most difficult, we have conquered the Italians [. . .]

The gold medals of the azzurri's athletes have almost become the gold medals of all Italians. Perhaps our greatest conquest is right here, having shown the Italians the fascination of the Olympics, having won them over to our cause.

(Verratti, 1960: 13)

Levi and Verratti were not wrong. Rome 1960 was a triumph for the city, country and nation, projecting the new Republic as fun-filled, organized, successful, civilized and welcoming. In the midst of the economic boom it confirmed the 'Made in Italy' brand and publicized the seal of quality that was fundamental to its huge export of goods, electro-domestics in particular, which saw the country thrive in the new European Community. Yet beneath the glitz, film stars, and impressive new and restored sporting facilities, there was a darker side. The infrastructure developed for the Games was not only disastrous in terms of the city's congestion and urban future, it revealed the corrosive presence of significant political self-interest at best, or outright corruption at worst. At the same time, while Roman speculators and northern heavy industrialists cashed in, the Games had virtually no impact upon the poor of the capital and the south. This poverty was studiously avoided, for fear of tarnishing the image, by those reporting and recording the event.

Undoubtedly successful, its achievements were still ephemeral, which was demonstrated most clearly by the tournament's greatest and most enduring aspect having been totally unplanned. It was Abebe Bikila, the intriguing underdog who mixed the unexpected with drama to create a scriptwriter's dream and a memory that transcended the tournament's politicization. For all of Rome 1960's successes and failures, it was this small, barefooted former colonial subject who made the greatest impact, remaining longest in the memory, doing most to rehabilitate the nation. He was the greatest symbol of a new, rejuvenated, post-Fascist Italy, which was all, and more, than those who had envisaged the Games, some ten years earlier, could have desired.

Notes

1 For tourist planning, see Ministero del Turismo e spettacolo (ed.), (1960), *Lo stato italiano e le olimpiade di Roma*, Roma: Editalia.
2 All translations by the author.
3 See chapter sections on the reconstruction of CONI, the 1960 Olympic Games and the politics of Italian sport in S. Martin, (2011), *Sport Italia: The Italian Love Affair with Sport*, London: IB Tauris.
4 For an overview of infrastructure developments for the Games, see Rossi (2003): 203–05.
5 For a detailed explanation of the SGI and the Council's role in land speculation see Cancogni, (1960): 3.
6 For *Il Popolo*'s complete review of facilities built for the Games see editions of 2–7 and 9–12 August 1960.

7   The velodrome was demolished in 2008 due to its lack of use, the need for costly structural works and its prime building location.
8   The 'Missini' were members of the MSI.
9   On Marcellini see A. Cori, (2009), *Il cinema di Romolo Marcellini: tra storia e societa dal colonialismo agli anni '70*, Recco: Le Mani.
10 'Carry On. . .' was a series of twenty-nine British comedy films made between 1958 and 1978 that mixed parody, farce, slapstick, innuendo and *double-entendres* to laugh at British institutions and culture.
11 The oldest bridge in Rome, built in 109 BC, the *Pons Milvius* had served as the principal access to the city from the north and the Via Flaminia. It was here, in 312, that Constantine defeated Maxentius, paving the way for the Christianization of the Roman Empire.
12 After decades of negotiation and promises, the obelisk was finally returned to Axum in 2005 and re-erected in 2008.
13 Marking the fiftieth anniversary of Bikila's win, the 2010 Rome marathon was dedicated to his memory. Ethiopia claimed a men's and women's double, with Ethiopian women finishing first, second and third. The men's race winner, Siraj Gena, also picked up the €5000 bonus offered by the race organizer for completing the final 300 metres barefoot.
14 C. Levi, quoted in DVD of the Rome 1960 Games, CONI/LUCE, *La Grande Olimpiade*, 2001.

References

Anon., (1960a), 'Aperto il "villaggio olimpico" che ospiterà oltre seimila atleti', *Corriere della Sera*, 26 July: 5.

——, (1960b), 'Folla e atleti protagonisti della giornata inaugurale', *L'Unità*, 26 August: 6.

——, (1960c), 'La schedina del Totocalcio ha finanziato le Olimpiadi', *L'Unità*, 26 July: 3.

——, (1960d), 'Latino sotto accusa', *Il Popolo*, 14 August: 3.

——, (1960e), 'Lo scandolo delle scritte fasciste', *L'Unità*, 2 August: 1.

——, (1960f), 'Un obelisco da scalpellare', *L'Unità*, 2 August: 1–2.

——, (1960g), 'Vietato al clero di assistere alle gare femminili', *L'Espresso*, 21 August: 2.

Avarello, P., (1999), 'L'Urbanizzazione', in L. De Rosa (ed.), *Storia di Roma dall'antichità a oggi: Roma del Duemila*, Bari: Laterza: 159–201.

Bassetti, R., (1999), *Storia e storie dello sport in Italia. Dall'unitá a oggi*, Venezia: Marsilio.

Benedetti, A., (1960), 'Un record Italiano. Affari e Olimpiadi', *L'Espresso*, 21 August: 1.

Bianchi, E., (1934), 'Sport (Dall'Italia)', *Giustizia e libertà*, 10 February: 46–50.

Camera dei Deputati, (1959), in *Atti Parlamentari dell'Assemblea, Anno 1959, III Legislatura, Discussioni*, Seduta 6 Ottobre: 10612–18.

Cancogni, M., (1960), 'Dietro il sorriso di Rebecchini Quattrocento Miliardi', *L'Espresso*, 11 December: 3.

Cavallari, A., (1960), 'Un abissino dai piedi scalzi ha reincarnate Filippide', *Corriere della Sera*, 11 September: 14.

Cederna, A., (1960a), 'La Città Eternit. Roma Marcia', *Il Mondo*, 30 August: 13.

——, (1960b), 'La Quarta Roma', *Il Mondo*, 23 August: 13.

——, (1965), *Mirabilia Urbis: Cronache romane 1957–1965*, Torino: Einaudi.

Cederna, C., (1960), 'L'Harem Sportivo del Vilagio Olimpico', *L'Espresso*, 28 August: 12–13.

Colorni, G., (1960), 'Livio Berrutti mondiale trionfa nei 200 metri', *L'Unità*, 4 September: 1–2.

Corbi, G., (1960), 'La cancellazione delle scritte Fasciste', *L'Espresso*, 21 August: 6.

Cori, A., (2009), *Il cinema di Romolo Marcellini:tra storia e societa dal colonialismo agli anni '70*, Recco: Le Mani.

De Santis, (1960a), 'Dopo il primo non felice collaudo', *Corriere della Sera*, 9 August: 7.

——, (1960b), 'L'udienza in Piazza San Pietro', *Corriere della Sera*, 25 August: 1–2.

Gismondi, A., (1960), 'Anche nell'Olimpiade la Rai-TV ha voluto portare la Guerra Fredda', *L'Unità*, 12 September: 2.

G. R., (1960), 'Altri sottovia veicolari progettati dal Comune', *Il Popolo*, 1 August: 4.

Insolera, I., (1962), *Roma Moderna: Un secolo di storia urbanistica*, Torino: Einaudi.

Josca, P., (1960), 'Spettatori d'eccezione per il più grande spettacolo', *Corriere della Sera*, 26 August: 7.

Kirk, T., (2005), *The Architecture of Modern Italy Volume II: Visions of Utopia 1900–Present*, New York: Princeton Architectural Press.

Maraniss, D., (2008), *Rome 1960: The Olympics that Changed the World*, New York: Simon & Schuster.

Martin, S., (2011), *Sport Italia: The Italian Love Affair with Sport*, London: IB Tauris.

Ministero del Turismo e spettacolo (ed.), (1960), *Lo stato italiano e le olimpiade di Roma*, Roma: Editalia.

Modrey, E. M., (2008), 'Architecture as a mode of self representation at the Olympic Games in Rome (1960) and Munich (1972)', *European Review of History – Revue européenne d'histoire*, 15 (6): 691–706.

Organizing Committee of the Games of the XVII Olympiad, (1960), *The Games of the XVII Olympiad, Rome 1960: The Official Report of the Organizing Committee, Volume One*, Roma: Stav. Colombo e Rotografica Romana.

Pavolini, L., (1960), 'La fiaccola nel Mezzogiorno', *L'Unità*, 24 August: 1.

Perria, A., (1960a), 'Lo Stato del Vaticano ha vinto le Olimpiadi', *L'Unità*, 2 August: 3.

——, (1960b), 'Suore, preti e giovani di A.C. all'assalto degli olimpionici', *L'Unità*, 31 July: 1, 10.

Pilley, P., (1960), 'The editor speaks from Rome', *World Sports: Official Magazine of the British Olympic Association*, October: 7–27.

Rossi, P. O., (2003), *Roma: Guida all'architettura moderna 1909–2000*, Bari: Laterza.

S. B., (1960), 'La "Via Olimpica" supera il collaudo della curiosità', *Il Popolo*, 8 August: 2.

Savioli, A., (1960), 'La fiaccola passa tra la miseria della Lucania', *L'Unità*, 23 August: 8.

Silvestri, G., (1960a), 'Una pista che scorre sulla città', *Il Popolo*, 5 August: 5.

——, (1960b), 'Un quartiere per la vita', *Il Popolo*, 4 August: 5.

Telesca, G., (2006), 'Tra Berruti e l'Immobiliare: Le Olimpiadi del 1960 e la trasformazione di Roma', *Passato e Presente: Rivista di Storia Contemporanea*, XXIV (67): 43–68.

Verratti, C., (1960), 'Il successo dei Giochi di Roma in una intervista con Onesti', *Corriere della Sera*, 13 September: 13.

6   Sport on Soviet television

Robert Edelman

As elsewhere in the world, Soviet television came to occupy a tiny chunk of cultural space during the late 1930s. Only Muscovites and Leningraders took in the new medium, which could be watched on a few hundred TV sets at factory workers' clubs and other public places (Evans, 2010: 1). The limited menu consisted of films and live, in-studio plays and concerts. Further progress was then abruptly halted by war and reconstruction, but by the late 1940s the latest equipment had been purchased from the West. Soon there were a small number of large sets with tiny screens in the homes and offices of the nation's elite. It also became possible to broadcast from locations outside the studio, and the very first such transmission was a football match played at Dinamo Stadium in the spring of 1949.

This was the 'Golden Age' of Soviet soccer. Fans flocked to the city's arenas in record numbers. The 55,000 seat Dinamo Stadium was often stuffed with chaotic crowds of 80,000 to 90,000. For really big matches, another half million would gather outside to be near the action and possibly gatecrash. These were not the cowed citizens portrayed by Orwell in the novel *1984*. Instead, excited fans pushed and shoved their way past turnstiles to sit in aisles and on each other's laps. Dinamo Moscow's successful 1945 tour of the UK had convinced them they were seeing a world-class spectacle (*Sovetskii sport* (SS), 16 April 1949). Their emotions were stirred by intense and compelling battles on the field, which often produced scenes of disorder in the stands. Many games were broadcast on the radio by the era's great commentator Vadim Siniavskii. Still, this was not enough to induce the capital's many 'lovers of football' to stay home and out of trouble. The idea of providing another way for Moscow's largely male masses to see the game was surely attractive to the city's guardians of order. Yet, at this early stage of television's history, it was far from a mass medium capable of influencing the behaviour of millions.

From Stalin to Chernenko

In television's infancy, its form, content and purpose was the subject of worldwide discussion. In the West, politicians, artists and intellectuals thought television had enormous potential to educate. Soviet politicians, artists and intellectuals were no less excited and uncertain about the paths television might take (Evans, 2010: 5). Viewers could learn important life lessons, but they could also terminate the transmission without consequence. In the minds of some Soviet thinkers, the new medium created the possibility of a second artistic *avant-garde*, last seen in the 1920s with the advent of radically different film styles. At the same time, the pressures of the Cold War led to a focus on television, leading to often inflated expectations of what it could do, as both sides viewed it as a powerful, non-lethal weapon in the struggle for the world's hearts and minds (Caute, 2003: 3–4).

Yet live broadcasts were minefields of unintended consequences. A soccer match which was supposed to inspire workers to exercise could also expose the uninitiated to the disorderly behaviour of fans. Given the small numbers of viewers and their largely elite character, this contradiction did not lead to unwanted political conse-quences. The combination of sport's essential unpredictability and the uncertainties of live telecasts would pose special dangers for a party-state that prized control over the often unruly masses. Regardless of the sport, badly behaving players or incompetent, perhaps dishonest, referees could have a dangerous impact on those in the stands and, with them, those watching at home. It was feared young people would make heroes of 'hooligan' players who, by the 1960s, would disdain authority by wearing their hair long and refusing to tuck in their shirts when not attacking referees and each other (*Zhurnalist*, 4, 1972: 26–27). One television critic even chastised the directors of televised hockey games for rewarding those guilty of on-ice misdeeds by focusing on such miscreants sitting in the penalty box (*Zhurnalist*, 3, 1969: 25).

There were other dangers. After decades of so many falsehoods, the telecast of a live sporting event amounted to an island of authenticity that could not easily be manipulated. If viewers could see what actually happened, commentators could only spin the events that had just been shown on the screen. The factuality of what may have just transpired could not be so easily explained away. As such, televised sport in the USSR, despite the many well documented pathologies of Soviet media, retained a certain core of honesty throughout its entire history, resulting in many less than honest political elites being cautious in embracing the new medium (Roth-Ey, 2007: 290). Additionally, the traditional Russian intelligentsia, always uncomfortable with sport, the human body and popular culture, looked down upon television.

By the mid-1950s, TV sets were being manufactured in greater numbers, and a regular diet of sports was soon provided to Soviet fans. Initially, nearly all the events took place in Moscow and were limited to an audience not far from the capital. By 1980, Soviet television had expanded to cover all eleven time zones, and with the great move of millions into private apartments, nearly every home had purchased a set – one of the few consumer goods made in adequate numbers and at affordable prices. The long-stated goal of the spectator sport industry had been to demonstrate the joys of fitness in order to produce better workers and soldiers. Television now made it possible to carry this message to millions. At the same time, there was the fear that socialist television could produce the same numbers of passive, chubby couch potatoes and frustrated football widows found in capitalist homes (Roth-Ey, 2007: 283).

Soccer and the still infant sport of Canadian-style ice hockey were among the earliest events to be shown. Newsreels, previously seen only in theatres, often had stories about sport. A five-minute segment at the end of the nightly newscast was devoted to both physical culture and high-performance sport. The 1956 soccer season was the first to receive extensive coverage, and the 1957 world hockey championship, held in Moscow, was televised. Over time, major cities and most republics had their own channels, which showed selected games of local teams. More people and more parts of the country became aware of sports than ever before. What had been a big city phenomenon now became national. What had largely been a Russian show now became multi-national. This process had a direct and positive impact on Soviet performances in elite sport, as more young men and women throughout the USSR were inspired to become athletes (SS, 6 September 1956).

Because of the limited technical capacity of early Soviet television, the majority of games came from Moscow. This practice inspired complaints from provincial fans, who felt Moscow-based commentators favoured the capital's clubs. By the late 1960s, however, the centre of power in football had shifted away from Moscow, and television's capacity to show matches outside the centre had improved. By 1967, satellites permitted the transmission of sport throughout the entire USSR (Roth-Ey, 2007: 285; Evans, 2010: 35). With this development, the problem of objectivity took on a new hue, as Moscow fans complained that provincial commentators, largely unregulated by the centre, were biased against teams from the capital (SS, 6 September 1956; 28 February, 25 and 27 April 1957; Edelman, 1993: 166).

The one personality who transcended location was Nikolai Ozerov, a former tennis champion for the Spartak Sport Society, an actor at the Moscow Art Theatre and a member of the Spartak reserve football team. Ozerov, who did not lack self-esteem, did for televised sport what Siniavskii had done for radio (SS, 1 May 1990). Less intense and florid than Siniavskii, Ozerov brought an emotional approach to commentating. He understood that television required less detail than radio, and felt it was possible to embellish his accounts with analysis and reflection. He sought to hide his Spartak allegiance when covering domestic matches, but held little back when working an international event. He particularly did not spare the drama when covering Olympic Games, World Cups or other world championships:

Of course, for a commentator it's always pleasant to report on the victories of Soviet athletes. Your voice takes on a major [as opposed to minor] tone, and you don't have to search for words. But when there is a defeat, believe me, it's not easy to tell about it.

(SS, 30 August 1970)

Although Ozerov was already possessed of an outsized personality, he had been encouraged to adopt such an approach. In 1957, the head of Soviet sports television would write:

The television commentator is the viewer's friend. He can tell jokes and laugh together with them, pose questions, teach the sport, describe exciting moments with great emotion and give his opinions about the game. Every commentator [not just Ozerov] must strive for close contact with the viewer.

(SS, 28 August 1957)

The inculcation of patriotism had been one reason for showing international events, and Ozerov served this purpose well. Yet, over time his monumental ego produced a reaction as other commentators adopted a more rational, understated approach.

While the print media had always been critical in its coverage of sport, television, not surprisingly, took a more positive approach. Yet it cannot be said that commentators made boastful, ideological claims in pursuing their work. Domestic contests were presented without political overtones even when such overtones, like those of the Spartak–Dinamo rivalry, were obvious to most of those watching. When Ozerov was not on duty, commentators such as Evgenii Maiorov, Ian Sparre and Vladimir Maslachenko took a more subdued approach.

In general, most Soviet sport was presented in the Victorian spirit of 'rational recreation' with the goal of educating intelligent viewers who would choose to exercise in order to emulate their high-performance heroes, but football and hockey players could behave violently, undermining their assigned duty as role models (SS, 18 November 1961). These kinds of incident created problems for commentators and directors, who could not easily ignore such bad examples for Soviet youth (*Zhurnalist*, 3, 1969: 24–26). While sport could and did play a positive instrumental role, it was also an arena of pathologies which were harder for commentators to explain.

The televising of sports events produced many of the same problems as in the West. Stadium directors protested that showing games cut down home attendance, while television's defenders argued that the medium increased the size of the total audience. As elsewhere, the pessimists were eventually proven wrong. By the early 1960s, the amount of sports programming on Soviet television's two main and many local channels had reached the level it maintained until 1991. In non-Olympic years, between 500 and 600 sports programmes were shown nationally. Roughly fifty or sixty were football matches. Under Brezhnev, coverage of hockey expanded to similar levels. Basketball, during its vogue in the late 1960s and 1970s, was also shown frequently. The rest of the sports television diet consisted of extensively edited national, European and world championships (Edelman, 1993: 168).

Even before the advent of cable television in the West, the menu of televised sport in the USSR was much smaller than that on contemporary American or even British television. Starting in 1968, however, Soviet viewers were finally able to watch the Olympics. In contrast to the regular slim pickings, the Olympic Games occupied between 150 and 190 hours over sixteen days, much more than contemporary Western coverage. Forced to rely on the international feed, Soviet producers had less control over their images than did their US colleagues. Nevertheless, coverage of international events reflected the regime's goals rather than popular desires. The Games were supposed to be the great showcase for the state sport system, and the desire to produce a parade of medal-winners, even in so-called minor sports, took momentary precedence over football and hockey. The ethos of the Games, an Olympism underpinned by state-centric medal ceremonies, flag-raising and national anthems, allowed the regime to promote its political goals, and popular preferences played a role in the construction of the viewing schedule only in non-Olympic years.

Glásnost' and *perestroika*

By 1985, Soviet citizens, like their capitalist counterparts, had come to watch most of their sports on television. While the print media continued its critical tradition, so-called 'new thinking' was less likely to be found on the airwaves. Yet if sport on television was not particularly critical, it was, at the same time, virtually free of ideological reference and overt political meaning, positive or negative. Even before *perestroika*, one rarely heard specific arguments that a particular victory proved the superiority of Communism. Patriotic pride was acceptable, but rarely did commentators take such emotions further. Instead, political claims were reserved for the nightly newscast's final five minutes, which were devoted to sport. Ozerov's enthusiasm and self-congratulation were eschewed by the new generation of commentators, who were eventually able to discuss some of the negative elements of Soviet sports (Edelman, 1993: 200).

Before and during *perestroika*, Soviet viewers were never able to view as much sport as their counterparts in the West, a distinction that became even starker with the advent of cable television in capitalist countries. In 1986, an average of twelve sports programmes were shown per week. Two years later, this number had declined to nine, as political discussion shows and rock concerts took over a portion of the time previously devoted to sport. At the same time, American audiences could see fifty events per week on cable and over the air (Mickiewicz, 1988: 153–54; Edelman, 1993: 200). In four separate two-week periods in late 1987 and early 1988 (one period for each season of the year), seventy sports events were shown in each period. Of these, twenty-three were devoted to football, fourteen to hockey, and only four to men's basketball.

Again, the Olympic Games were always exceptions to the normal limited diet. Both national channels alternated coverage of the Winter and Summer Games, with some events spilling over to local programming. In 1988, the US National Broadcasting Company showed what was then an unprecedented 179 hours of the Seoul Games, while Soviet television showed its usual 190. Soviet commentators were able to provide on-site interviews with their own athletes for only the second time; the first had been during the 1980 Moscow Games. Yet they continued to rely on the international feed, unlike US companies that could produce their own programming, for which they had paid enormous rights fees. On Soviet TV, events were covered continuously for long periods. The weak as well as the strong were shown, and there was no concentration on the athletes from any particular country. As a result, the internationalism and broad participation of the Games were highlighted in Soviet coverage, as opposed to a focus on winners and specific nations, i.e. their own.

There was little hopping from one venue to the next, as is still common on American broadcasts. The Soviets showed entire football, hockey and basketball games without interruption. Important events that did not involve their athletes also received significant air time. Until 1988, there had been no commercials during Soviet sports events, but coverage of the Seoul Games was interrupted by highly visual commercials for Pepsi-Cola. The segments were Western-produced with Russian voice-overs. They appeared unannounced in previously taped segments, and no notice was paid when the programme returned. If most sports on Soviet television had few, if any, commercials, it also must be said that they contained no hidden commercials for the state and party. While viewers may have drawn a variety of possible political conclusions from what they watched, overt politics and ideology were almost entirely absent after 1985, and rare before that date. There were also few attempts to create false drama in the search for higher ratings. The irrational aspects of sport were downplayed, with commentators taking a detached, straightforward, even scientific tone. Maiorov, the former hockey star, was famous for his unemotional approach that involved an unchanging monotone, even when goals were scored (Edelman, 1993: 183).

Commentary was nearly always done alone, and one rarely got more than a second's glimpse of the commentator's face. There were few interviews and no pre- or post-game shows. Instead, the always well prepared commentators established the context, gave line-ups and provided background during the early moments of a game. The absence of commentary before and after matches meant less setting of the scene than in Western broadcasts. There was no false build-up or hype to convince the audience a particular game was a 'crucial match-up'. Rarely if ever were two sports programmes going on at the same time. There was no competition for higher ratings. Indeed, there were no internal or secret ratings kept by Soviet television. US commentators always told their audiences not to 'go away' before commercial breaks. In the USSR, there was no need for such desperate tactics.

When a competition ended, the transmission ended, leaving it up to the viewer to decide the meaning of what had just transpired. In this way, television, which many outsiders had considered to be one of the regime's most potent methods of control, proved to be less controlling than that of its Western counterparts. The live telecast and the unknown result specific to sport made it a 'bad fit' for mind control and failsafe didacticism. Ironically, attempts to impose political, cultural and even athletic meanings on the games were stronger in the West than in the USSR. Post-game analyses and later highlights shows, especially in the USA, assigned importance to factors that may or may not have been all that important. By contrast, when the games ended in Soviet living rooms, the arguments began.

Additionally, Soviet television was less technically sophisticated than that of its contemporary Western counterparts. Slow-motion replays had been used as early as the 1970s, but camera angles were minimal and on-screen graphics primitive. Directors did not switch quickly from one camera to another. There were no reaction shots of crowds. Fans were shown only during lulls in the action. By 1989, however, these practices began to change. Attractive computer graphics were introduced, and excited fans were now quickly interspersed with the on-field play. The quality of presentation also began to improve under external commercial pressure. In January 1989, Soviet television began showing games of the US National Basketball

Association and the North American National Hockey League, financed by the sale of commercial time to foreign firms hoping to cash in on the increasingly open Soviet market.

While television was always less critical than the periodical press, it eventually got swept up in the impact of *glásnost'*. Commentators spoke about the need to 'restructure' the particular sport they were covering. The dour Maiorov consistently criticized the organizers of the hockey league for contributing to an attendance crisis between 1985 and 1991. At the same time, Maiorov avoided joining the storm of print criticism in 1988 that surrounded Viktor Tikhonov, the national hockey team coach, who sought to prevent his players from seeking work in the West.

Soviet commentators had always felt free to challenge the tactical decisions of coaches or to chastise players for poor performances. More startling and out of keeping with previous practice was a tendency for sport commentators to speak critically on matters with direct political import. In 1988, Vladimir Pereturin covered a regular-season football match between Spartak and Zhalgiris Vilnius. He spoke about the recently completed European Championship, in which the Soviets made the final only to lose to an excellent Dutch team, and the special brilliance of Marco Van Baasten. Everyone throughout the Soviet sports world had been pleased by the result. Pereturin, however, noted the lack of Soviet fan support at the final, played in Munich. Left unsaid but perfectly understood was the fact that, even at this late date, travel to the West was difficult if not impossible for the vast majority of ordinary Soviet citizens. Forty thousand Dutch supporters attended, in stark contrast to a few hundred Soviets. Without saying the result would have been different, Pereturin noted the relationship between fan support and team performance:

> We think this is incorrect. Our life is changing – in football, travel and pro-fessionalism. People should be able to go to various countries. The process of filling out forms should be made faster. It is necessary that our fans should go abroad to support our teams.
>
> (Gosteleradio, channel 2, 14 July 1988)

Given the historical, if conflicted, propaganda function of Soviet television, it would have been reasonable to expect that sports programming would have been equally, if not more, didactic than in the West, but this was not the case. American audiences were repeatedly told the Dallas Cowboys football team from politically conservative Texas team was 'America's team', making them somehow more patriotic and admirable than their opponents. Despite the regime's preference for the teams of the police and army, no particular club was ever described as *the* Soviet team. That role was only assigned to the USSR's actual national team in any particular sport.

My own experience of more than twenty years of watching sports on Soviet television, both before and during *glásnost'*, removed whatever exoticism the games may have held. Westerners, myself included, who expected to see events interpreted through an ideological framework, were disappointed. The most striking feature of sports on Soviet television was their utter ordinariness. Few attempts were made to enhance drama that may have been lacking in the event itself, and this pedestrian quality most distinguished it from its capitalist counterparts. To Western eyes, the telecasts of events seemed less than compelling, and no attempt was made to hide the fact that a particular match was boring. Indeed, since the arranged 0–0 draw was the curse of late Soviet football, commentators could signal to their listeners that the 'boring' match they were watching was most likely rigged (Edelman, 1993: 207).

The limited amount of sport on Soviet television does reflect the limited importance of sport in Soviet society. To be sure, sport was always popular. Millions of people attended stadiums and watched at home, while the national sports paper, *Sovetskii sport*, had a daily print run of 5 million. Yet it would not be correct to say the USSR was sports-crazy. Large chunks of the population were untouched or unmoved by sport. Women were not big consumers of televised sport, and the rural population was not deeply interested either. The traditional Russian intelligentsia was so consumed with the life of the mind that most of its members passed through life oblivious to the needs and pleasures of the human body. Much of the energy devoted to sport, especially Olympic sport, came from the state. Even the more popular spectator sports were presented by agencies of the state. Soviet fans, the majority of them male, came to pick and choose from an ever-changing menu of attractions provided by the state. Certain sports would become fashionable. Others would lose their audiences. Basketball was in vogue in the late 1960s and 1970s, especially after the USSR's triumph at the 1972 Olympics. After the defeat in 1976, the sport was seen less often on Soviet screens. The same was true for figure skating. If the State Sports Committee wanted sport to play its assigned role in producing fitter and more patriotic citizens, then those citizens had to be watching. While it would be vastly overstating the case to claim televised sport in the USSR played an important role in the collapse of Communism, it would be equally wrong to argue television was an efficient weapon in the regime's cultural arsenal. Rather, it was, as it has been elsewhere, what Kuper (2003: 27) has called a 'slippery tool' in the hands of authoritarian regimes. Both sport and television were ripe with unintended consequences. Much the same could be said for Soviet life in general.

Soviet television and me(mory)

Here, I must temporarily abandon my stance as professional historian and replace it with that of participant–observer. Much of what I have related here is based on my own viewing of Soviet television since 1970. Before *glásnost'*, this 'research' was accomplished by watching in various places on various research trips to the USSR. After 1986, it became possible to receive one Soviet channel in the West. Columbia University and the Rand Institute in Santa Monica spent tens of thousands of dollars on immense satellite dishes. Even so, there were problems with this breakthrough. Pre-internet, one had little advance access to schedules. We simply turned on the VCR and recorded the entire day. An assistant then scanned the offerings and alerted researchers to items of interest. I would then take the tapes home, pop open a beer, lie down and work. Today, I get every Russian channel on my computer, schedules are posted for days in advance, and shows can be watched on demand.

During the academic year 1970–71, I lived in the dormitory at Moscow State University. My Russian at the time was fairly rudimentary, as was my knowledge of Soviet sport. There was a lounge on each floor and a rarely used television in each lounge. One evening, however, I passed by a lounge and found it packed with students from all over the world watching Lev Yashin's farewell testimonial match. The great goalie's Dinamo Moscow side was playing a team of world selects. I had no idea who Yashin was, but I did like football and so watched. Ozerov was on full display, wowing the student audience by consecutively interviewing members of the world side in five different languages. Later, I would be taken to several matches at Lenin Stadium, usually involving Spartak, but I did not watch on television, nor did I then understand the comforting pleasures of reading the sports press. The only homes I visited at the time were those of dissidents who disdained sport.

My next long stay came in 1975, and much had changed. My best Soviet friend, an Armenian, had graduated, and was working for the youth music division of Gosteleradio and living in an apartment on Prospekt Mira with his Finnish wife. Needless to say, he owned a television set, and we watched a fair amount of football, usually at my urging. He had a friend who loved hockey, and I would watch at his house as well. I then decided I wanted to watch when I was not at their places, and so I went to a hard currency shop and bought a small television. Such devices were not permitted in the dorms, but somehow I succeeded in sneaking in my new prize. I hid it in a big trunk and took it out every night. My Russian improved dramatically, and I came to learn the names and teams of the sports world. Soon, I had a topic of shared discourse with people, usually men, who were outside the sport-hating academic world of which the social circle of most foreigners was composed.

I got to watch two big events in my friend's apartment. The first was the famed 'Thrilla in Manila', the final and most incredible fight for the heavyweight championship between Joe Frazier and Muhammad Ali. So great was Ali's global authority that the Soviets televised the first professional fight in their history. My friends were stunned by both fighters' abilities and the ferocity of a bout that far exceeded anything they had ever seen. The next event was the second (away) leg of the 1975 football Super Cup, in which Dinamo Kiev defeated the great Bayern Munich side of the era. My friends, one an Arrarat man (as you would expect of an Armenian) and the other a Spartak fan, watched with a combination of curiosity and tension. None of us found the efficient, hyper-rationality of Dinamo's total football (without the Dutch charm) to our liking. We all thought the team sponsored by the Ukrainian secret police to be an enemy side. Nevertheless, we did share a bit of guilty pleasure that a Soviet team had actually won a major, if contrived, trophy.

Over the next sixteen years, I watched in friends' homes in Moscow, Leningrad, Kiev, Tblisi, Vilnius and Yerevan. I cannot say I saw any broadly generalizable behaviour. Some places we watched quietly and politely, drinking at roughly the normal level for a Soviet evening. In most such cases, women were present. Football watching was, nevertheless, a heavily masculinized activity, and my experiences in these homo-social environments usually involved more drinking, leading to a loosening of tongues. Russian is an incredibly rich language, with such bizarre and convoluted curses as *moi khui tebe na zakuske* (literally: 'my cock to you on an *hors d'oeuvre'*). The worst curses were reserved for poorly performing players from the favourite club of my particular host of the day or evening. A few of the cleaner terms were *pederast, alkgolik* and *gomoseksualist*. The onamatopoetic *v zhopu* does not require translation. Less profane but equally colourful words were also used. Spartak was demeaned as 'the shopkeepers' (the team had been sponsored by the retail trades) and, following the consumer connection, they were also called 'meat'. Dinamo were the *kokhli* (the cops) or *mussor* (garbage). The army team (TsSKA) was the *koni* (grooms of horses). Such cries as 'kill the cops' or 'kill the grooms' were usually uttered without consequence by Spartak and other fans in Moscow stadiums. Of course, these chants had less semantic force if uttered in an apartment, where the targets could not hear the words. Referees were, of course, not exempt. Bad decisions provoked the cry of *sudya na mylo*, which according to the twisted syntax of this particular idiom meant 'turn the referee into soap'. This, too, was more likely to be heard on the stands than in a living room. Commentators also came in for colourful criticism, published and unpublished (*Zhurnalist*, 7, 1976: 78–79). For myself, I cannot remember which was more difficult, keeping up with the vodka consumption (cognac if it were Dinamo Tblisi or Arrarat) or making sense of the rich flood of profanity (even now a difficult task).

These impressionistic accounts of sports TV watching are more or less confirmed by recent, more systematic research carried out by the young German scholar Manfred Zeller in the form of archival work (mainly fan mail) and interviews with former Soviet citizens of a certain age. In a recent article that focuses on Kiev in the 1960s, he suggests two important ways in which television changed the experience and meaning of watching soccer. First, by the 1960s the game was broadcast all over the vastness of the USSR:

> The extension of television's broadcasting range created trans-local and trans-national modes of consumption and identification that helped citizens integrate themselves into a Soviet order imagined and negotiated by themselves through semi-public [activities].
>
> (Zeller, 2011: 54)

This 'integration' could simultaneously have a centrifugal impact when it came to questions of nationality. Citizens from many non-Russian republics came to identify with Dinamo Kiev's relatively recent and highly powerful challenge to the Russian centre. In 1961, they became the first provincial side to take the Soviet championship.

Second, as television became the primary source for watching football and sport, viewing was carried out in the porous privacy of the newly constructed Soviet apartment – porous because walls were thin, rooms were small and bugging devices were easily installed. While the stadium was also a place where the public and private could collide and mix, this was even truer of the apartment. It was probably no accident that the Nazis restricted the viewing of television to public places (Roth-Ey, 2007: 302). Watching football, according to Zeller, was 'private and public at the same time'; in other words a liminal space, and what sort of human activity could be a better fit to occupy such a space than sport, one of the most liminal human activities of all (Zeller, 2009). It occupies public spaces (the stadium), semi-public spaces (the street, courtyard and pub) and theoretically private spaces (the apartment). Here, it is worth remembering there is no word in Russian for 'private', and that Soviet apartments were often crowded, multi-generational spaces. Such seemingly individualized spaces undermined the authority of the party-state, which ultimately found itself unable to intervene successfully in many aspects of private life. Yet the distinction between the public and the private was always complicated and shifting in Soviet history. A man's (or woman's) home was not necessarily his (or her) castle.

Zeller describes the 1960s Kievan viewing experiences as relatively orderly, cultured and rational. He attributes this to the varying degrees of a female presence at the time of viewing. To this one might add the low-key, unemotional tone of most Soviet commentators other than Ozerov. Much of these observations (well, not the profanity) track with my own highly personal experience. While the authorities were often perplexed by what they had wrought in making apartments so broadly available, the consequences of the privacy and individualism they afforded appeared to have outweighed the dangers to public order posed by the rampant and potentially dangerous masculinity of the stadium.

In the 1960s, television did not have a negative effect on the size of crowds, but attendance did plummet during the 1970s. This was largely a reaction to the global triumph of negative football, extensive match-fixing and the spread of fan violence. These pathologies reached their nadir in May 1972, when Dinamo Moscow faced Glasgow Rangers in the final of the Cup-Winners' Cup. With Rangers ahead well into the second half, Dinamo Moscow put on a burst of energy that threatened to tie the score. At this point, Scottish fans invaded the pitch in such large numbers that the game was halted, and with it Dinamo's momentum. Rangers went on to win. Watching in the warmth of their Moscow apartments, young Spartak fans were inspired by this 'intervention' in the sporting process. The next year they appeared in the stands of Lenin Stadium in semi-organized groups, seeking to emulate the Scots' behaviour. Soon the fans of other Soviet clubs, many wearing home-made scarves, did the same. Fan violence, touched off by television, became more common. By the late 1970s, gangs of young football supporters in Moscow were roaming the streets of the capital, adorning walls with graffiti and doing battle in public spaces with each other (Bushnell, 1990: 29–68).

At the same time, the footprint of Soviet football greatly expanded. Scores of growing provincial cities, spurred by industrial expansion and improvements in transportation and communication, formed teams and built stadiums. Their patrons, usually local party leaders, used all means, fair or foul, to get their clubs promoted to the highest possible levels. Here television may have played a positive role by keeping latent interest in football alive despite the rampant cynicism and corruption of the late Brezhnev period. As the sheer numbers of arranged matches threatened to strangle the Soviet game during the 1970s, television was there to bear witness to the rot. There was no diminution in the number of games shown, and I have seen no evidence to suggest that viewership dropped off. As a result, there was both public and official pressure on the state sports committee to find remedies. The problems could not, as was so common under Brezhnev, be ignored.

Communism or good, clean fun? The historian returns

It would be stretching the evidence way too thinly to suggest that the televising of sport in the USSR provoked anything that could consistently be called transgressive behaviour leading to regime change. Still, as Evans (2010) has argued, the medium's earliest champions saw it as a space for the display of sincerity and authenticity; a space for truthfulness. Naive as this may seem, television found in sport an activity with an unavoidable core of honesty. If nothing else, commentators had to get the score right. The same was true for the print media. In a land of rumours, lies and much disinformation, the bracing empiricism of an actual score was not something to be taken for granted.

For years, a more than likely apocryphal tale circulated in the offices of the national sports daily, *Sovetskii sport*. In the late 1940s, the odious and brutal head of the People's Commissariat for Internal Affairs (*Narodnyy komissariat vnutrennikh del*, NKVD), Lavrenti Beria, maintained his passionate and meddling support for the Dinamo Moscow soccer team. One night, around two in the morning, the bullying Beria called the night editor at the paper to get the result of that day's Spartak–Dinamo derby. 'What was the score?' he demanded. '1–0 Spartak', came the reply. Violating the truth, Beria, said, 'Print it 1–1'. Unable to violate the honesty and truthfulness of a sports score, the scared but self-respecting editor printed nothing. He knew that 60,000 Muscovites had witnessed the match, and all doubtless told their friends the result. Beria's intervention was pointless. There was no hiding the fact his team had lost. Surely, much the same could be said about live television as well.

Soviet fans produced what Hall (1981: 232) has called 'negotiated responses' to the sporting spectacles placed before them by the only agency that could produce them – the party-state. The goals of the organizers of those spectacles were rarely the same as those of the organized. The state may have been made uncomfortable by so irrational a game as football, but so great was the public's love of the game that not providing such sporting entertainments would have been an act of political suicide. Audiences watched in a variety of places, with a broad range of reactions to what they saw. If the games were dull, the 'lovers of sport' were not motivated to go out to the stadium, or to play the games themselves.

The power of boredom proved to be powerful indeed. Questing for excitement, Soviet fans came to choose their own favourite games and teams, and television helped them do that. No policeman stood by the set and forced 'lovers of sport' to watch. If a game was awful, they could always turn it off. Through their limited, but still free, choices, these citizens of the now defunct USSR came to create meaningful identities and recapture some small piece of themselves. Such identities were political, social and cultural, and highly gendered. Over the entire course of Soviet history, those identities were highly fluid and multiple. Certain shared identities like team support could divide Soviet citizens from each other. At the same time, sporting identities also provided a way for Soviet men and women to act together, undermining those processes of atomization that were so long thought to buttress the authority of Soviet power. Sport on TV was a slippery tool indeed.

References

Bushnell, J., (1990), *Moscow Graffiti: Language and Subculture*, Boston: Unwin Hyman.

Caute, D., (2003), *The Dancer Defects: The Struggle for Cultural Supremacy During the Cold War*, Oxford: Oxford University Press.

Edelman, R., (1993), *Serious Fun: A History of Spectator Sports in the USSR*, Oxford: Oxford University Press.

Evans, C., (2010), 'From Truth to Time', PhD thesis, University of California, Berkeley.

Hall, S., (1981), 'Notes on Deconstructing the Popular', in R. Samuel (ed.), *People's History and Socialist Theory*, London: Routledge & Kegan Paul.

Kuper, S., (2003), *Ajax, the Dutch and the War*, London: Orion.

Mickiewicz, E., (1988), *Split Signals: Television and Politics in the Soviet Union*, Oxford: Oxford University Press.

Roth-Ey, K., (2007), 'Finding a Home for Television in the USSR, 1995–1970', *Slavic Review*, 66 (2): 278–306.

Sovetskii sport, 16 April 1949, 6 September 1956, 28 February 1957, 25 April 1957, 27 April 1957, 28 August 1957, 18 November 1961, 30 August 1970, 1 May 1990.

Zeller, M., (2009), 'Soccer and the Living Room: Sport reception and Private Life in the Late Soviet Union', paper presented at annual convention of the American Association for the Advancement of Slavic Studies, Boston, 12 November 2009.

Zeller, M., (2011), 'Our Internasionale 1966: Dinamo Kiev Fans between Local Identity and Transnational Imagination', *Kritika*, 12 (1): 53–82.

Zhurnalist, (1969), (3): 24–26.

Zhurnalist, (1972), (4): 26–27.

Zhurnalist, (1976), (7): 78–79.

7 *Jeux avec Frontières*

Television markets and European sport

Stefan Szymanski

The development of television in Europe: state regulation in a divided Europe

In 1950 only the UK and France had regular television broadcast schedules; services did not start in the Netherlands until 1951, Germany 1952, Belgium 1953, Italy 1954, and Spain 1956. While the United States already had about 4 million TV homes in 1950 (10% penetration), in the UK there were only 344,000 (2%) and in France only around 15,000. The speed with which television penetrated into the house-hold was astonishing. By 1960 it was in 87% of households in the United States, 55% in the UK, 21% in Germany, 13% in Italy, 12% in France, and 2% in Spain. By 1970 the figures were 95% in the United States, 92% in the UK, 69% in Germany, 54% in Italy, 59% in France, and 28% in Spain. By 1980, the United States and most of Europe were fully saturated (Noam, 1991: 79).

The regulation of television closely followed the pattern set by that of radio, which had been developed in the 1930s. The American model involved asserting public ownership of the airwaves and then licensing scarce bandwidth to broad-casters within defined territories (of which there are several hundred in the United States), the licences being issued by a Federal agency (the Federal Communications Commission, FCC) (Walker and Ferguson, 1998: 18). While competing broad-casters initially tried to produce their own content, the economies of scale in broadcasting the same content across many broadcast territories gave rise to the network system, first in radio and then in television, where CBS, NBC and ABC emerged as the dominant suppliers to a national network of local broadcast affiliates. The cost of delivering programming through a signal that can be picked up free over the air by a television set is recovered by the sale of advertising. Thus, seen as an economic proposition, television is a medium for the sale of audiences by broadcasters and networks to advertisers.

The content of television programmes in the American model is thus driven by what broadcasters believe will attract the largest audiences. However, some regulatory restraints are imposed. While there is no direct censorship, failure to meet standards set by the FCC, Congress and the courts can mean that a licence will not be renewed. The FCC also makes provision to ensure there is a supply of educational content, which is currently the responsibility of the Public Broadcasting Service.

The European model of television broadcasting also followed the radio model, which in Europe involved much closer state regulation than in the United States. Radio broadcasting in most of Europe came under the control of the Post Office, itself a politically controlled organization. A monopoly broadcaster was then created, often in collaboration with producers of radio sets who wanted to see their product penetrate the market. The motives for monopolization were varied, an obvious one being the desire to control the medium for political purposes. While fascists and communists expressed this motive quite openly, this motivation was evident across the political spectrum. For example, John Reith, the BBC's first director general, repeatedly denied Winston Churchill airtime to warn against the threat of fascism, not only because he disliked his views but also because the Prime Minister Neville Chamberlain disapproved of broadcasts that criticized the government's policies (Coase, 1950: 166–6; Noam, 1991: 120).

Broadcast signals prior to the development of encryption technologies have the characteristics of a public good, which in economics means that the good is both non-rivalrous (consumption by one does not limit the consumption by another) and non-excludable (there is no mechanism to exclude some consumers while including others – if the broadcast signal is transmitted, everyone in the region covered by the signal can receive it). Typically it is argued that a public good will be under-supplied, given that non-excludability limits the capacity to recover costs directly. While the funding through advertising model was demonstrated to be viable in the United States, commercial forces tended to be weaker in Europe, and suspicion of commercial motives much stronger. Moreover, since spectrum is scarce, and the delivery of a service over time requires a stable frequency from which to broadcast, some kind of licensing system is necessary to give service providers secure property rights and a basis to invest. However, it was seldom the case in Europe that an extensive debate took place on the merits or otherwise of monopoly licensing. Coase (1950) describes the process by which the BBC was given a monopoly of radio broadcasting, arguments involving the alleged chaos in the United States, low quality of US programming, and the (clearly false) claim that a monopoly was necessary for technical reasons.

Many of these arguments were applied in the creation of television broadcasting monopolies. In the post-war democracies, the regulation of state monopolies generally involved the establishment of Boards, which in theory gave representation to a cross-section of political interests. However, in many countries such as France or Italy (especially in the 1960s and 1970s), control rested effectively with the government of the day. While state-controlled monopoly was the norm, the funding model varied. Although the British chose not to allow advertising on publicly owned broadcast channels, thus relying exclusively on licence fees, others permitted advertising as a supplement.

How television changes sport

The impact of broadcasting was to create gigantic audiences for music, drama and sport. The effect on music and drama was less significant because recording technologies at the end of the nineteenth century, and moving pictures at the beginning of the twentieth, had already created substantial audiences. Sport had not benefited from sound and video recording because one of its most attractive features is uncertainty of outcome: once the sporting outcome is determined (and reported in the newspapers), the interest is substantially diminished. Live radio, and then live television coverage, allow event organizers to reach an audience during the game that is many magnitudes greater than the number of spectators that could be accommodated within a stadium.

But broadcasting does not just change the size of the audience equally across all sporting activities. Some benefit more than others, shifting the balance of power within sport and creating pressures for change. These pressures have been politically contested in both the United States and Europe. It makes spectators more dis- criminating, because they are better able to compare the abilities of players. Broadcasting also tends to undermine the loyalty of fans, or to attract new types of fans who are more interested in the contest, if it is close enough, rather than the contestants. Thus broadcasters who want to attract large audiences in order to generate income from advertising usually focus on the more attractive teams or dominant players, tending to enhance their dominance and reduce interest in smaller teams or lower-level competitions. To make money, the sport also has to be made attractive to a broad television audience, implying a level of moral conduct and behaviour that would not necessarily be required in the absence of broadcasting. Appealing to a wider audience may also require simplifying the structure of the game, and, ideally, the passage of play needs to be broken down to create slots that are attractive to advertisers.

The first sport to be broadcast successfully on radio was boxing, and boxing was also popular in the early period of television (Szymanski, 2009: 428). But in the United States it was baseball that really grew in the radio era by contract- ing with local radio stations to reach local fans in their own homes. Thus, for baseball teams, broadcasting was merely an extension of the local market, a model that continued into the television era, each club negotiating its own contract with local stations and treating these revenues as they would their gate revenues. The great innovator in television sports in the United States was the National Football League (NFL), which introduced a collective approach to marketing the sport on television. While the role of the commissioner in baseball has always been contested, the NFL commissioner from the 1950s created an atmosphere of cooperation among the owners. This perhaps reflected the NFL's relatively low status. Since baseball was the national sport, and college football was far more popular than the professional game, the NFL had an incentive to embrace the new technology and exploit it to the full. It did so by focusing on the delivery of a high-quality broadcast picture and ensuring that each game played would be as competitive as possible. Competitive balance – enshrined in the famous quotation 'On any given Sunday, any team can beat any other team' – became the mantra of the owners, shored up by a number of agreements among the teams sharing gate, merchandizing and television revenues, limiting roster sizes, capping salaries, and rewarding weak teams with early draft picks (most of these measures, incidentally, also having the effect of restricting economic competition and therefore enhancing profitability).

The NFL sold its rights to the networks, who broadcast nationally rather than locally, and this is arguably one reason why football, rather than baseball, has come to be seen as America's national sport. While not initially in a strong bargaining position, the NFL was able to get airtime thanks to intense competition among the networks; once established, it was able to extract growing sums of money from the sale of its rights. Much the same is true of the Olympics. The early Games were covered on television by arrangement with the host nation, with little or no money changing hands, and it was not until 1960 that a substantial television contract was written (CBS paid $440,000 for the Rome Games), and not until 1972 that the International Olympic Committee (IOC) changed its rules to give itself a major share in the television revenues. Since then, competition among the networks has driven up the value of the rights dramatically (Guttmann, 1994: 148).

Once competition drives up the value of rights, the money has to be distributed. While the organizers of competitions (whether organizers of events like Wimbledon tennis, or of teams like the Yankees or Real Madrid) have attempted to control these revenue streams, they have inevitably tended to end up with the players. Competition for the services of the best players, who attract the largest audiences, tends to ensure that this is the case. Where leagues or other competition organizers have attempted to impose restraints, collective action by the players, backed up with the threat of strikes, has tended to force the organizers to distribute a larger share to the players. Sports stars have thus become like recording artists or movie stars.

In the European context, this development was initially stifled by the structure of national television markets. With broadcast monopolies funded by licence fees, advertising restricted and bandwidth limited, the demand for sport by broadcasters was limited. In the early days, public service broadcasters did not consider sport important, and when they deemed events worthy of coverage, they expected to obtain rights for nothing (or merely nominal sums). Even if there were commercial broadcasting opportunities, the existence of national borders meant that the economies of scale, so important to the US networks, were not available in Europe. The organization of sports on a national basis meant that there was little interest on the part of most league and competition organizers in taking advantage of these opportunities. In fact, most sports administrators viewed television with suspicion. Without the ability to generate significant income from the sale of broadcast rights, most football club administrators were primarily concerned that television would encourage fans to watch at home and so threaten the takings at the turnstiles; consequently they opposed live broadcasts. For viewers, however, sport on television was a compelling proposition. Starting with competitions such as the Fédération Internationale de Football Association (FIFA) World Cup and the Union of European Football Associations (UEFA) club competitions that developed from 1956, together with the European Nations Cup from 1960, the coverage of football on television began to attract large audiences. It is claimed that the 1966 World Cup had a television audience of 400 million, predominantly in Europe (Szymanski and Zimbalist, 2005: 155).

European competition in football was not developed with the purpose of generating television audiences in mind, but the accumulation of audiences started to bring changes. The possibility of generating income from the sale of rights was further limited by the European Broadcast Union (EBU), a cartel of national broadcasters that negotiated sports rights on behalf of its members and thus eliminated competition. The EBU was formed in 1950 as an organization for sharing information about technical developments in broadcasting and agreeing common standards, rather like a trade association. However, as with trade associations, the EBU quickly recognized that, by pooling the bargaining power of its members, it could achieve better terms when negotiating with suppliers of content such as the IOC and FIFA. The contrast with the US networks was stark; for example, in 1996 NBC paid $456 million for the Atlanta Games while the whole of western Europe paid only $250 million. Nonetheless, television made top athletes into international stars and made fans more aware of competition outside national borders. Some sports had always used international benchmarks to measure success (e.g. track-and-field, thanks to the Olympics), but other sports, notably football (soccer), became less parochial as television coverage introduced fans to foreign teams. By the 1980s, most football fans would identify the best team as the European champion, not the national champion.

Any comparison between sport in Europe and the United States in the early 1980s would focus on difference rather than similarity: difference in the extent of television coverage, difference in the financial rewards on offer, and difference in the breadth of appeal of the top teams and players. Above all, US sport was clearly organized along commercial lines, while European sport was not. This reflected the different traditions of Europe and the United States, and pre-dated the advent of television. A commercial outlook made US sports suitable for adaptation and promotion by television, while the non-commercial principles of European sport presented an obstacle to the development of sport on television. For example, when the English Football League finally negotiated an agreement for BBC and ITV to carry live coverage of a small number of league matches for a negligible fee, this fee had to be divided among all ninety-two league members, despite the fact that only a small number of teams were actually shown on television. No-one in football had much incentive to develop television broadcasting on this basis, since they stood to gain next to nothing (Inglis, 1988: 239–40).

As several of these examples suggest, one of the most noticeable ways in which television has changed sport has been to increase the amount of money entering sport. There is little doubt that the sums involved today are much larger than in the past, due, to a significant degree, to the influx of TV money. For example, in 1980 the annual income of Manchester United was £2.5 million (Szymanski and Kuypers, 1999: 361), while in 2008 the club generated an income of £257 million (Jones, 2009, appendix 2). The share of television revenues in this income stream has risen; back in 1980 there were no live league matches shown in England and the income from highlights rights was negligible, while today TV income accounts for over one-third of the total. In the NFL, the significance of TV income is even greater. But it is important not to overstate either the contribution of TV to revenues or the scale of the sports business. Most clubs in most sports generate most of their income from ticket sales and the sale of merchandizing (for figures on European football leagues see e.g. Jones, 2009: 13). And most clubs remain relatively small businesses by normal commercial standards. Manchester United is one of the biggest clubs in any sport, not just football, and yet sales of £250–300 million make it only a medium-sized enterprise. In the spring of 2010, a group of investors declared their intention to launch a bid for the club, valuing it at around £1.2 billion – this valuation would not place the club in the FTSE100, the 100 largest companies quoted on the London Stock Exchange. Television may have helped to achieve universal recognition for the big sports clubs and stars, but it remains something of an overstatement to call sport 'big business'.

Deregulation in the 1980s

The state monopoly of television was starting to be questioned in the 1970s. Right-wing think tanks were starting to question the benefits of state ownership in general, and to point out the potential harm associated with monopolistic practices. The economic consensus that monopoly is harmful (leading to prices well above cost) was augmented by the argument that monopoly in state hands would lead to inefficiency and waste, since there was no incentive to control costs. Now that everyone owned a television and viewing hours had expanded, it became obvious that there existed alternatives to monopoly supply. In some countries, such as the UK, where the state broadcaster was held in awe, the proposition that advertising could fund a broadcast channel was eventually accepted, but the state broadcaster (the BBC) was still prevented from carrying adverts. In other countries, such as Italy, the inefficiency of the state broadcaster caused widespread public dissatisfaction and therefore paved the way for the acceptance of privately funded alternatives.

By the 1980s, most European nations introduced legislation permitting private companies to acquire broadcasting licences. This started to create pressure for competition in the sale of broadcast rights, but the major structural change was the advent of satellite broadcasting in Europe. Satellite broadcasting within the European Union posed a major threat to the established system of national regulation. Terrestrial broadcasters had seldom been capable of broadcasting into foreign territories, and therefore national rules were enforceable. However, a satellite broadcaster could be resident in one country but send a broadcast signal into another. European states had to decide who would have jurisdiction, and the 'Television Without Frontiers' Directive (Council of the European Communities, 1989) determined that it would be the nation in which the broadcaster's business was registered. At once, the supervision of broadcasting was no longer under direct national control, and broadcasters had the opportunity to enter the market and seek to exploit economies of scale.

A key difference between these new entrants and the existing terrestrial broadcasters was the ability to charge viewers directly, thanks to the development of encryption technology. Pay television subscriptions are driven largely by premium content, meaning movies (mostly from Hollywood) and sport. Pay TV in the United States had been driven by the development of cable television networks, which had initially been encouraged by the FCC as a means to reach remote communities, but by the 1980s were increasingly aimed at large metropolitan districts where cable could be laid relatively cheaply. Cable was far less well developed in Europe, but soon became attractive because of the sudden emergence of the internet and the deregulation of telephony, creating the possibility of the 'triple play' – selling a combination of pay TV, internet access and telephone services (for further details see Chapter 8 in this volume).

Legal battles: exclusivity, collective selling, ownership and social protection

If the broadcasting landscape in the 1990s was fundamentally different from what had gone before, so were the regulatory challenges. Governments within the enlarging European Union, and increasingly the European Commission itself, had to determine how to manage competition. The issues are complex. On the one hand, economies of scale render competition among a large number of firms unfeasible and hence the issue of dominance becomes key. On the other hand, the continued existence of state-owned and state-funded public broadcasters raised concerns about a level playing field. In either case, potential entrants and competitors raised fears about the possibility of powerful incumbents delaying the introduction of new services that were emerging. European governments struggled with the conflict between the desire to see an innovative television market in Europe, matching the technological advance evident in the United States, and the desire to protect consumers. While technological development requires large revenue streams in order to finance large investments, consumers were often being asked to pay for content that they had previously received for free. In many cases this played badly with the European sense of equality.

Sports bodies became unwittingly tied up in these debates in a number of ways, causing many to believe that principles of sporting autonomy were being eroded. Here we consider four kinds of dispute that have arisen.

Social protection

The acquisition of the rights to Hollywood movies by pay TV channels raised alarm in some countries that American content would dominate European television, and led to calls to impose minimum EU content on all broadcasters. However, in the face of strong opposition by the US government, and limited enthusiasm on the part of several member states, the requirement was effectively dropped. Once it became clear that pay television broadcasters would also willingly buy up all premium sports content at almost any price in order to drive subscriptions, the member states became more unsettled. It was agreed that member states were permitted to draw up lists of protected events, which could be broadcast only on terrestrial, free-to-air television.[1] Most commonly, the rights to the Olympic Games, the FIFA World Cup and the UEFA European Championship were protected, typically also the home matches of the national football team (the away games being outside the national jurisdiction). Specific games of national interest might also be protected, such as cricket in the UK, the Tour de France in France, and so on. These rules are understandably popular with consumers and free-to-air broadcasters, while not so popular with pay TV broadcasters. The rights owners themselves have tended to be ambiguous. While many resent the prohibition on selling to pay TV and generating larger revenues, others prefer free-to-air broadcasting because of the larger audiences. Indeed, Formula One, which is not listed, and therefore can sell its rights to pay TV, has chosen to stay on free-to-air because of the perceived value of having a wider public. However, this may change in future as a larger fraction of households subscribe to pay TV services. Moreover, even if they would prefer to sell their rights to free-to-air broadcasters, they still benefit from not being listed because the broadcaster must still factor a potential offer from pay TV into their bid calculations. The most notable case in this area has been that of English cricket, which was originally listed, then successfully lobbied to be de-listed and sold its rights to pay TV in 2005, but is currently under threat of being listed again under a government review. Critics advocating listing argue that the governing body is undermining the popularity of the sport, while the sport defends itself by arguing it needs the funds to invest in facilities and player development.

Exclusivity

As mentioned above, innovative services involving large fixed costs need a secure revenue stream in order to raise finance. As a result, pay TV operators have tried to write very long-term contracts with the owners of premium rights. However, by its nature, a long-term exclusive contract also reduces the threat of competition, which may enhance the value of revenue streams but limit the prospect for further innovation. This was a major source of concern to the European Commission in the 1990s, and led to the formulation of policy that viewed any contract involving premium sports rights longer than three years in duration as anti-competitive.[2] To the extent that the owners of sports rights could extract larger profits by signing a longer-term deal, their freedom of action is restrained. Moreover, to the extent that consumers could be attracted by minority sports if these sports benefited from long-term investments, so that they might become substitutes for established sports, then competition in the long term may even be diminished. In general, it is argued that the dominant sports in Europe, especially football but also the Olympics and Formula One, are so entrenched, with consumers so unlikely to find substitutes, that restrictions on exclusivity are justified.

Collective selling

Perhaps the greatest area of conflict in sports has concerned the issue of collective selling. The issue first arose in Spain, largely because of its long tradition of broadcasting live league matches on free-to-air television. Spanish soccer underwent a major restructuring at the end of the 1980s that culminated in the 1990 *Ley del Deporte*, which reorganized the finances and legal standing of clubs. The law gave considerable powers to the national league, which then negotiated an eight-year deal for television broadcasting (Ascari and Gagnepain, 2006). This was then challenged in the courts by television companies that had been excluded from the deal and, in a 1993 decision, the Spanish competition court declared collective selling to be illegal, freeing the clubs to sell their rights individually from the 1993–94 season onwards (OECD, 1997). This outcome has clearly benefited Spain's two giant clubs, Real Madrid and Barcelona. During the 1990s, a patchwork of agreements emerged, with some matches moving to pay-per-view and some remaining on regional free-to-air channels (for further details, see Chapter 8 in this volume).

In Germany, the Bundesliga decided in 1989 to take over the marketing of broadcast rights for matches played by its member teams in European competitions such as the then European Cup and the UEFA Cup. The money generated by the sale of these rights was then divided equally among the Bundesliga teams. In 1994, the German Cartel Office decided that, in fact, the team owned the rights, and therefore the Bundesliga was not entitled to control these rights. The Bundesliga, however, appealed over the heads of the competition authority to the government to grant them an anti-trust exemption, citing the US experience, and this was duly granted (Parlasca and Szymanski, 2002). (For further details, see Chapter 11 in this volume.) In 1996, a Dutch court considered the question of who owns the broadcast rights to matches, following the objection of Feyenoord, a leading club, to the collective sale of domestic rights by the league. Since the broadcaster, Sport 7, collapsed before the judgement was announced, its relevance in this case was moot, but the court did express the general view that rights belonged to the home team. In England, the largest ever competition law case to be tried in court was brought by the competition authority against the Premier League and the collective sale of its rights to BSkyB. In 1999, the court decided that collective selling was justified in the public interest. In the same year, the Italian competition authority concluded that the sale of television rights for Serie A and Serie B matches by the league was a violation of competition law and required the league to permit clubs to sell their rights individually (Szymanski, 2002). However, a decade later, the court's decision was overturned and the clubs were permitted to return to collective selling. In 2001, the European Commission expressed reservations about the legality of UEFA's collective sale of Champions League broadcast rights, and agreed to permit collective selling only after extended negotiations that led to significant restructuring of the deal in 2003.[3] Also in 2001, the Commission started investigating the collective selling of Premier League rights, reaching agreement in 2004 on a restructuring that would ensure that, from 2007, no single broadcaster would be able to have exclusive access to Premier League rights.[4]

The reason that collective selling has triggered so much legal activity in Europe is the precarious nature of competition in European broadcast markets. While the potential for soccer leagues to exploit consumers through collective selling raises anti-trust concerns throughout the world, in a market such as the United States there is at least significant competition among broadcasters. In particular, the free-to-air networks in the United States have hitherto offered a significant quantity of live broadcast events. In Europe, however, most collective deals have been struck on the basis of exclusivity, and since there are no other sports rights that can drive subscriptions in the way that soccer does, the danger has been that each national territory in Europe would succumb to a pay TV monopoly. The fear of the competition authorities is that if pay TV broadcasters can monopolize soccer, they can use this as a means to monopolize the entire pay TV market. In other words, collective sale puts together the most valuable rights in a single package, which then fall into the hands of a single broadcaster. The authorities seem to have hoped that, if the rights could be kept divided by prohibiting collective selling, this would in turn foster competition in broadcasting.[5]

Of course, one might also ask why, in the United States, free-to-air broadcasters have been able to win major league broadcast rights at auction, while Europe's terrestrial broadcasters have not. Here the answer may be the smaller national markets of Europe, combined with restrictions on the ability to advertise imposed by television regulators (for example, the US networks show around 20 minutes of advertising per hour, whereas only seven minutes per hour on average is permitted in the UK on commercial channels, while the BBC carries none). European networks simply don't have the financial muscle to compete with pay TV, and governments are unlikely to permit an increase in the number of advertising minutes per hour on the grounds of social policy.

In specific cases, the major concern has been the excessive restriction of output entailed in collective selling. As part of the settlement with UEFA, the European Commission ensured that all matches that were not sold within the collective deal could be marketed by the individual clubs, so that fans will always have an opportunity to watch games if the demand is there. In the case of the Premier League, however, only one-third of all matches played in a season are currently made available for live broadcast, denying many fans access to games that they would be willing to pay to watch. The League and clubs have claimed that this is required to protect gate attendance, as they have always done. However, there is now a good deal of research into the question of how many fans are lost when a game is shown on television, and almost all the evidence shows that the number is tiny, and that the gate revenue that would be lost in most cases is well below the amount that would be gained from selling extra matches for television coverage (Forrest *et al.*, 2004).[6]

In the eyes of many fans, however, the attempt of the anti-trust authorities to challenge collective selling has been wrong-headed. It was striking that during the UK Premier League case in 1999, all the supporter groups that testified defended the practice of collective selling. The reason for this is that many soccer fans see collective selling as the only way to redistribute income from rich clubs to poor clubs. These fans view the growing disparities in soccer income as undermining the ability of the smaller clubs to compete, which they see as the loss of a valuable tradition. Ironically, this issue is one that often arises in disputes over the application of competition law in Europe and the United States. Most competition law experts agree that the purpose of competition law is to promote healthy competition in the market to the benefit of consumers, not to protect companies from competition. But

US observers often criticize European anti-trust agencies for being too eager to use the law to protect specific competitors. For example, the purpose of using anti-trust law to challenge the conduct of Microsoft was not to protect Netscape, but to ensure that no supplier in the internet browser market is illegally prevented from competing. Applying this perspective to sport, the challenge to collective selling could not legitimately be used to preserve small clubs from the competition of their larger rivals, but simply to ensure that both clubs and broadcasters are able to compete to supply services to consumers. To the extent, however, that a success-ful sports league depends on a degree of parity among its teams, it may still be argued that protecting the revenue of small clubs enhances overall competition. A similar argument can be made for teams' financial stability.

Ownership

At the end of the 1980s, television revenues accounted for less than 10% of the income of a football club. By the new millennium, broadcast income for the clubs in the top division in the larger broadcast markets accounted for about one-third of club income, and was growing. Given that the commercial fortunes of broad-casters and sports organizations were becoming intertwined, it was not unnatural for broadcasters to seek to own them. The integration of broadcasters into sports has been a commonplace in the United States, and indeed broadcasters have often been involved in the attempt to launch new leagues. In Europe, examples of ownership by media interests have included Silvio Berlusconi's ownership of AC Milan and Canal+'s ownership of PSG in France. In the UK in the mid-1990s, a number of broadcasters began to take 10% stakes in large football clubs, which they saw as a way of increasing their influence over the negotiation of broadcast rights. In 1998, Sky launched a full-scale bid for Manchester United, which was then referred to the Monopolies and Mergers Commission. The Commission decided to block the deal on the grounds that it could limit competition in broadcast markets by giving Sky too much power when Premier League broadcast rights were auctioned.

More recently, the trend toward ownership of English football clubs by for-eigners, often from outside the EU, has raised questions about the commitment of clubs to remain within the European system. Proposals such as the Premier League's bid to stage a thirty-ninth game outside England suggest that global broadcast markets may be of more interest to these owners than traditional markets. The influx of American owners in particular (the Glazer family at Manchester United; Randy Lerner at Aston Villa; Hicks and Gillett at Liverpool, now owned by New England Sport Ventures led by John W. Henry; Stan Kroenke at Arsenal) suggests the possible Americanization of the English Premier League (EPL). There are a number of ways in which owners schooled in the American franchise system for sports leagues might seek to make English football more profitable, for example by abolishing promotion and relegation in order to limit the incentive to compete on player salaries. The types of changes they might introduce in the broadcasting arena are less obvious on the face of it, but it is possible that they might try to impose greater control by the League over the way matches are shown, even to the point of setting up an EPL broadcasting channel. American leagues have also made significant advances in the development of internet services, and this represents a further direction in which American owners in the UK might seek to develop media rights.

New media and the future

In both the United States and Europe, the evolution of television and of professional sport has gone hand in hand. Much the same can be said about the evolution of television and sport in the rest of the world; the emergence of the Indian Premier League as the world's most important cricket competition is largely thanks to its phenomenal drawing power on Indian television. This relationship is now threatened by the emergence of new media platforms for the delivery of sports events: mobile telephony and the internet.[7]

Mobile phone rights have generated excitement for some years since operators are attracted by the idea of being able to update fans about events within games (e.g. when a goal is scored), and even the possibility of watching a match in full on the phone. This sometimes appears puzzling, given the tiny screen size, and in any case both connection speeds and picture quality have mitigated against wide-scale take-up. However, the latter two barriers are slowly falling, and it is possible that mobile viewing could become significantly more attractive. As yet, the value of rights appears to be small. For example, in April 2010 ESPN bought the mobile rights to the English Premier League for a sum said to be in the 'single-digit millions', which is relatively small beer compared with the value of domestic TV rights for £1.8 billion and overseas rights for £1.4 billion (Neate, 2010). But mobile operators and rights holders have significant incentives to promote this technology since customers are used to paying high prices for premium services.

By contrast, internet users strongly resist paying anything for content, which has made the delivery of sports matches through the medium much less attractive to rights holders. Nonetheless, the internet is becoming an increasingly important medium for the delivery of sports content, and an increasing fraction of rights are available on this platform. The leader in the commercialization of internet rights has been Major League Baseball in the USA, which launched MLB Advanced Media (MLBAM) in 2000 with a view to exploiting new media rights. The business is currently said to generate revenues of around $450 million per year, and in 2005 MLBAM was valued at around $2.5 billion – far more than the value of any individual franchise in MLB (Brown, 2009). However, the internet is not viewed as an unmitigated benefit to sports rights owners. One of the major concerns of rights owners today is piracy via the internet, and it is often feasible to find games normally sold on pay TV pirated and made freely available on the internet. The issue here is not dissimilar to that faced by the music industry regarding illegal downloads. For the music business, the internet has brought about a fundamental change in the business model, shifting from the sale of vinyl, tapes or CDs to the sale of access via *iTunes* and similar online providers. This transition has proved extremely painful for the music business, reflected in significant falls in revenues. Just as the advent of television caused sports event organizers to change their business model, first in the United States and then in Europe, the same may be true of internet broadcasting. Currently sports governing bodies in Europe (and elsewhere) are devoting significant efforts to lobbying governments for protection from internet piracy, but, as with the music business, this may prove to be a vain quest.

The irony of this is that piracy is a phenomenon frequently associated with the globalization of European sport. Far more than the American commercial sports, European football reaches a global audience, with millions of Real Madrid and Manchester United fans to be found across Africa and Asia, and even in the United States itself. For example, 90% of the audience for the 2005 Superbowl, the premier event in American Football, was American, while less than 40% of the audience for the 2005 Champions League Final between Liverpool (England) and AC Milan (Italy) were drawn from the national TV markets of the two competing teams (Gratton and Solberg, 2007: 179). The EPL currently sells its overseas rights for £1.4 billion (Harris, 2010), almost as much as the £1.8 billion generated by rights sales in the UK (Ziegler, 2010). In seeking to serve these global markets, the rights owners are also creating an opportunity for the pirates to prosper.

Television has changed sport across the world, but the development has been uneven. With its greater reliance on market mechanisms, TV sports markets developed far more quickly in the USA, and it was only after the deregulation of broadcasting in Europe during the 1980s that European sport developed the same TV appeal and, crucially, TV revenue-generating capacity as the USA. In a generation, the landscape in Europe has changed dramatically, and while European sport may not be 'big business', it is certainly big enough to require more professional management and commercial nous than was necessary up to the end of the 1970s. Many regret this transformation and many of its consequences, including the very high salaries paid to a small number of players, the rise of football agents, the expansion of merchandizing, and the greater sense of commercialism that surrounds sports today.

However, one further consequence of the growth of TV (and new media) markets has been the expanding international significance of European sport. In some ways, Europe has always been at the centre of global sport, judged by measures such as the frequency of hosting the Olympic Games or the FIFA World Cup, but before TV this dominance was perhaps masked by the greater commercial orientation of sport in the USA. Now that TV can bring the Champions League into every household around the globe, the power of European sports is becoming more visible, above all in the football world. Of course, there will always be important events and competitions in other parts of the world – witness the phenomenal commercial success of the Indian Premier League (cricket); the international appeal of the National Basketball Association (NBA); and the award of the 2010 World Cup to South Africa and the 2016 Olympic Games to Rio. Nonetheless, the size of Europe's market (450 million relatively wealthy consumers) and the international appeal of football means that Europe, thanks to television, has become, and will continue to be, the Hollywood of sport.

Notes

1 This was implemented in a revised version of the Television Without Frontiers Directive in 1997. The UK Broadcasting Act of 1996 specified the events covered by this form of protection.

2 See, for example, the speech of Mario Monti, then competition commissioner, delivered on 17 April 2000 on competition law and sport: http://europa.eu/rapid/pressReleases Action.do?reference=SPEECH/00/152&format=HTML&aged=0&language=EN&guiLa nguage=en

3 http://europa.eu/rapid/pressReleasesAction.do?reference=IP/03/1105&format=HTML &aged=0&language=EN&guiLanguage=en

4 http://ec.europa.eu/competition/antitrust/cases/dec_docs/38173/38173_134_9.pdf

5 If rights are sold in smaller bundles, the argument would go, smaller broadcast companies would be able to obtain a share of rights. If a single broadcaster tried to acquire all the packages, this would then be treated as an anti-trust violation.

6 However, it is true that broadcasting more live games of teams in the Premier League would undermine attendance at games in lower divisions if they were played at the same time.

7 The issues are much discussed in the business world, but there is relatively little academic work published on the subject.

References

Ascari, G. and Gagnepain, G., (2006), 'The Financial Crisis in Spanish Football', *Journal of Sports Economics*, 7 (1): 76–89.

Brown, M., (2009), 'Understanding the real value of MLBAM and MLB Network', *The Biz of Baseball*, 19 January, www.bizofbaseball.com/index.php?option=com_content& view=article&id=2878:understanding-the-real-value-of-mlbam-and-mlb-network& catid=26:editorials&Itemid=39

Coase, R., (1950), *British Broadcasting: A Study in Monopoly*, London: Longmans, Green & Co.

Council of the European Communities, (1989), *Council Directive of 3 October 1989 on the coordination of certain provisions laid down by law, regulation or administrative action in Member States concerning the pursuit of television broadcasting activities*, 89/552/EEC, http://eur-lex.europa.eu/LexUriServ/site/en/consleg/1989/L/01989L0552–19970730-en.pdf

Forrest, D., Simmons, R. and Szymanski, S., (2004), 'Broadcasting, Attendance and the Inefficiency of Cartels', *Review of Industrial Organization*, 24: 243–65.

Gratton, C. and Solberg, H., (2007), *The Economics of Sports Broadcasting*, London: Routledge.

Guttmann, A., (1994), *The Olympics: A History of the Modern Games*, Champaign-Urbana: University of Illinois Press.

Harris, N., (2010), 'Premier League nets £1.4bn TV rights bonanza', *Independent*, 23 March, www.independent.co.uk/sport/football/premier-league/premier-league-nets-16314bn-tv-rights-bonanza-1925462.html

Inglis, S., (1988), *League Football and the Men Who Made It*, London: Willow Books.

Jones, D. (ed.), (2009), *Safety in Numbers: Annual Review of Football Finance*, Manchester: Deloitte.

Neate, R., (2010), 'ESPN wins exclusive rights to show Premier League on mobile phones', *Telegraph*, 6 April, www.telegraph.co.uk/finance/newsbysector/mediatechnology

andtelecoms/media/7560867/ESPN-wins-exclusive-rights-to-show-Premier-League-on-mobile-phones.html

Noam, E., (1991), *Television in Europe*, Oxford: Oxford University Press.

OECD, (1997), *Competition Issues Related to Sport*, OECD Policy Roundtables, Paris: Organisation for Economic Co-operation and Development, OCDE/GD(97), 61–63, www.oecd.org/dataoecd/34/49/1920279.pdf.

Parlasca, S. and Szymanski, S., (2002), 'The Negative Effects of Central Marketing of Football Television Rights on Fans, Media Concentration and Small Clubs', *Zeitschrift fuer Betriebswirtschaft*, 4: 83–104.

Szymanski, S., (2002), 'Collective Selling of Broadcast Rights to Sporting events', *International Sports Law Review*, 2 (1): 3–7.

——, (2009), *Playbooks and Checkbooks: An Introduction to the Economics of Modern Sport*, Princeton, NJ: Princeton University Press.

Szymanski, S. and Kuypers, T. (1999), *Winners and Losers: The Business Strategy of Football*, London: Viking.

Szymanski, S. and Zimbalist, A., (2005), *National Pastime: How Americans Play Baseball and the Rest of the World Plays Soccer*, Washington, DC: Brookings Institution.

Walker, J. and Ferguson, D., (1998), *The Broadcast Television Industry*, Boston: Allyn and Bacon.

Ziegler, M., (2010), 'Premier League fearful after Sky ruling', *sportinglife.com*, www.sportinglife.com/football/news/story_get.cgi?STORY_NAME=soccer/10/03/31/SOCCER_Pay_TV_Nightlead.html

8 Football and media in Europe

A new sport paradigm for the global era

Miquel de Moragas, Chris Kennett and Xavier Ginesta

Introduction: sport and communication change in the twenty-first century

Twenty-first century communication is conditioned by a series of important changes deriving directly, although not exclusively, from digitization combined with transformations in telecommunications that simultaneously affect communication spaces globally and locally. These changes have an impact on sport in general, and football in particular, from its organization and economy to its practice and consumption.

Manuel Castells (2009), in his book *Communication Power*, synthesizes some of the characteristics that define this new communication ecology, which we will apply to the relations between communication and sport. Castells considers the structure of mass media (radio, television, press) under the new conditions of globalization and digitization, as well as the emergence of new communication networks (horizontal and interactive) created by the development of the internet and mobile phone communication. These new forms of communication – defined as 'mass self-communication' – are integrated in the network society in a unique social space that is both multidimensional and interactive, space in which SMS, blogs, instant messaging, podcasts, video blogs, wikis, etc. circulate to create virtual communities.

According to Castells, communication in the network society has two main dimensions: its nucleus of social interaction (participatory and organizational), and meaning-production (contents, messages). While remaining cautious not to adopt a deterministic position, we understand this new communication ecology as the result of the bringing together of diverse technological transformations: the digitization of communication; the interconnection of computers and mobile devices; advances in software capabilities; increased broadband capacity; and the development of wireless networks (Wifi and Wi-MAX) to access the internet.

These accelerated changes in the communication landscape have had important consequences in the use and consumption of media. Castells (2009) states that a redefinition of space and time as a receiver in these new communication processes is required. The internet has made possible 'flow spaces', in which simultaneity is produced without contiguity. This is combined with 'timeless time' that permits asynchronous interaction. Young people no longer understand dominant concepts from the broadcast era, such as fixed television scheduling. These changes are not limited to reception. New communication scenarios are creating a new dialectic between the local and global that affects the fundamental nature of modern sport. The internet is global, but the contents tend to adapt to local cultures and the diversity of fragmented audiences (Castells, 2009). While evidence exists to support these dramatic claims, caution must be exercised when identifying such seismic transformations in society. It is difficult to foresee what the future levels of autonomy of 'self-communication' by the masses will be in relation to the traditional media and the large, powerful media groups that control them.

The media giants that own media sport have started to integrate and commercialize two communication universes: mass communication and the self-communication of the masses. The media powerhouses continue to play determinant roles in the digital era, holding onto the exclusive rights of key media properties, perhaps the most important of which is sport. The mass media maintain a presence online through the power of their brands, and have extended their reach across new platforms, appropriating online networks and their contents. Many of these brands have taken centre stage in the communication process, usurping the message and becoming the main content. Yet the rise of information and communication technology (ICT) giants such as Microsoft, Apple, Google and Yahoo! is changing the dominant communication ecology, creating opportunities for both collaboration with, and competition against, traditional media.

The transformations that have occurred in television in the digital era have been so far-reaching that a television paradigm shift can be identified between the broadcasting era of the twentieth century and a new paradigm, characterized by four main factors:

1   the importance of 'production' (content) over diffusion (channels)
2   the existence of new media actors, including sports clubs, which have been transformed into media organizations with their own television channels and web pages
3   the globalization of the culture industry and, most importantly, the globalization of televised sport, which maintain – but change – identity and meaning in consumption logic and processes
4   the proliferation of content supply, and audience segmentation and fragmentation.

This paradigm can be applied to analyses of sectors of the entertainment industry other than sports, such as film and music. Sport has a singularity, however, due to the fact that its mass appeal and popularity can accelerate transformations in communication. Sport can decisively intervene in the digital transformation of the audiovisual system, accelerating change, creating and increasing audience loyalty, and establishing strategic alliances between actors.

Some of these tendencies existed in the broadcasting era, for example in the Olympic Games and Fédération Internationale de Football Association (FIFA) World Cups, where sport was a key stage for the introduction and development of audiovisual technologies, including colour television, video, and satellite trans-mission. The difference now lies in the globalization of these processes and the convergence of previously independent key factors: the latter include the economy of sports organizations (particularly clubs), television programming and production, the international sporting calendar, and the regulation of sport.

Many scholars have made reference to the global sport media complex to explain the increasingly complex and changing interrelationships between myriad actors in the production, communication and consumption of sport (Maguire, 1999; Law *et al.*, 2002; Rowe, 2003, 2004; Helland, 2007). Transformations in communication systems play a key role in the configuration of this complex, and particularly in the synergies created within it. The income received by top-flight European football clubs for the sale of media rights has grown exponentially since the mid-1990s, when the communication paradigm shift began to accelerate. This acceleration was driven simultaneously by mediated football and a growing local and global demand for it. This convergence is represented in Figure 8.1, which identifies four main groups of actors in the complex: sports institutions/organizations; the media; commercial interest; and community. The changing relations between these actors in the digital era are examined in this chapter through the case of Europe's 'big five' football leagues (England, Germany, France, Italy and Spain).

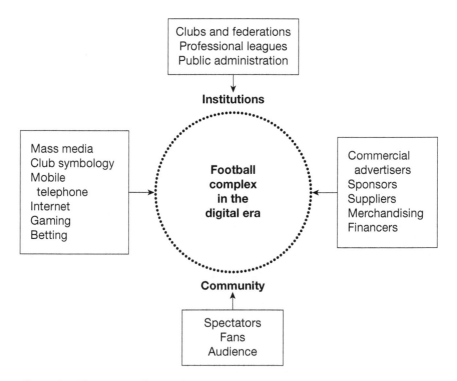

Figure 8.1 The sport media complex

Changes in football consumption in the media

The influence of digitization on communication has occurred in two main ways: the transformation of the supply and forms of television consumption; and the emergence of new media (particularly in the online environment and mobile communication), which, despite their growing influence, have complemented rather than replaced television. Television continues to be the hegemonic medium in the sport media complex, characterized by the growth in supply (number of channels), but also the diversification of platforms (ways to receive television broadcasting) in the aforementioned convergence process. A single audiovisual product (e.g. a football match) can be received in different formats and screens: conventional television; High Definition (HD); 3D mobile devices; personal computer; or even the cinema screen (e.g. FC Barcelona versus Real Madrid, 29 November 2009).

This process coincides with the gradual movement of live football coverage from free-to-view to subscription or pay-per-view (PPV) platforms. Free-to-air broadcasters have gradually lost football media rights to domestic leagues as they cannot compete with media groups in the free market. This tendency has had important cultural consequences despite changes in EU directives on the protection of the broadcasting of events of major public interest (Directive 97/36/CE, European Parliament).[1] The process favours the increased consolidation in the audiovisual sector to the point where – as we shall discuss in relation to what is referred to as the 'Spanish football war' between the broadcasters Sogecable and Mediapro – the acquisition of the media rights for professional football can be a decisive element in the strategic battle for hegemony in this sector. The need for a return on investment has resulted in the leveraging of football media rights by their holders, which has led to almost exhaustive coverage and the continuous broadcasting of games during the weekend at times that fit the broadcasters' schedules rather than the social interests of fans.

Changes in communication also affect the creation of new media by football clubs themselves. Bigger clubs have taken advantage of the multiplication of channels via satellite, cable, digital terrestrial transmission (DTT) and IP (internet) to create their own television channels, such us MUTV (Manchester United), Barça TV (FC Barcelona) or Realmadrid Televisión (Real Madrid). Additionally, digitization has opened up other new and important opportunities for clubs: the creation of their own web pages, and the possibility of using mobile technology as a multimedia and information platform.

The shift to subscription or PPV platforms contributes to 'mass self-communication' (Castells, 2009) in the era of Web 2.0 and the rapid growth of social networks (Facebook, MySpace, Twitter), content-sharing portals (e.g. YouTube), blogs and collaborative 'crowd sourced' platforms (e.g. Wikipedia), which enable communication and interaction between people with shared social and cultural interests, such as football. The rapid emergence of these mass self-communication options produces new complexities and opens a new debate on sport communication processes. The digitization of communication presents an opportunity for clubs to adapt to globalization, creating new 'virtual fan communities' at an international level. As a result, the system of grouping and the association of fans have been transformed, moving beyond the physical grouping of supporters in stadiums on match day (e.g. *tiffosi* in Italy, *peñas* in Spain).

Media rights sales and the privatization of football

The multiplication of television channels in the digital era has seen transference of communication power from broadcast to production. As part of this process, the buying and selling of media rights to certain events has transformed sport, and football in particular, into a product with high economic and strategic value for both sellers (football organizations) and buyers (media organizations). In order to maximize the return on investment in these high-priced rights deals, pay television has become the dominant format for distributing live football coverage in the major European leagues, enabling income generation from subscriptions and/or PPV purchase, as well as through the sale of advertising space.

A further consequence of these major investments in rights purchases is the progressive transformation of the top European leagues into brands (Premier League, Serie A, Bundesliga, La Ligue, La Liga) with the aim of commercializing them internationally. In 2010, Forbes estimated that the most valuable sports brand in the world was the Superbowl ($420 million), while the most valuable club brand value was Manchester United's ($270 million), followed by the New York Yankees ($266 million).[2] Influenced by the experience of the major leagues in the USA, the Premier League was a pioneer in branding and commercialization during the 1990s, driven by News Corp's Sky TV as the media rights holder (Williams, 1994). As an example of the importance of this brand internationally, in 2007 the Premier League had a global reach into 613 million homes covering 202 countries, with an estimated live audience for a single match typically reaching 79.5 million (Harris, 2007).

Broadcast models

Table 8.1 shows the television rights revenues and broadcast models for the five major European football leagues. In 2009 there were five football broadcast models: free-to-air TV; subscription TV channels; PPV TV; IP (internet); and mobile telephone. Spain was the only country of the five in which national law, Act 21/1997, required the free-to-air broadcast of at least one La Liga game per week because the Spanish legislator considered at that moment that football was a general interest content for spectators, so that it had to be protected from exclusivity and, consequently, PPV.[3]

During the 1980s, televised football in Europe was broadcast free-to-air and formed a fundamental part of the public television system, which had almost exclusive access to the rights of major sporting events. This changed with the advent of the first satellite television channels (Sky Channel in 1982, Canal Plus France in 1984, Canal Plus Spain in 1989), which would evolve into multichannel plat-forms. In 1990, Sky and British Satellite Broadcasting merged to form British Sky

Table 8.1 Television rights for the top five European football leagues

Country/ competition	Rights model	Contract	Buyer	Broadcast model	Cost per year (million €)
England (Premier League)	Collective	2007–08/ 2009–10	BSkyB	Pay TV	485
			Setanta (ESPN)	Pay TV	144
Italy (Serie A)	Collective	2010–11/ 2011–12	Sky Italia	Pay TV/IP/ mobile	574
			Mediaset	Free-to-air	217.5
France (Ligue 1)	Collective	2008–09/ 2011–12	Canal+	Pay TV	460
			Orange	Pay TV	300
Germany (Bundesliga)	Collective	2009–10/ 2012–13	Sky Deutschland	Pay TV	225/275
			Deutsche Telekom	IP/mobile	135
Spain (La Liga)	Individual	2009–10/ 2012–13	Mediapro	Free-to-air/ subscription and pay-per-view	350
			Madrid Deporte (Telemadrid)	Free-to-air	50

Sources: Footballeconomy.com, Goal.com, Sportbusiness, Reuters and primary sources from MediaPro.

Broadcasting (BSkyB), branded as Sky. This was followed in 1994 by the creation of the digital platform Canal Satellite Numérique, a subsidiary of Canal Plus (France), and the advent of Canal Satélite Digital in Spain in 1997. Sky, owned by News Corp, and Canal Plus have played a major role in shaping the media rights landscape in the big five European football leagues.

Pay-per-view did not appear until 1991, when Home Box Office (HBO) started to broadcast boxing matches, providing a further example of sport leading innovation processes in the audiovisual sector. This business model for sport media distribution and consumption spread to movies and other sporting contests, including football matches. The creation of the English Premier League corporation by clubs from the Football League was driven by the lure of increased television rights deals offered by the highly competitive BSkyB and the desire to limit revenue sharing to the top-flight clubs. In 1992, soon after the creation of the English Premier League, BSkyB secured its television rights, and this signified a turning point in the communication and commercialization of football in Europe. By 2009, Sky owned part of the main football rights packages in England, Germany and Italy, while Canal Plus owned the main package in France and shared the rights in Spain. Football has established itself as a highly lucrative media product that is used to drive subscriptions in the UK and fight off competition from emerging platforms and substitutes. In order to secure these rights, BSkyB had to pay increasing amounts during the 1990s and into the 2000s, reaching €1.45 billion for the period 2010–13, an unthinkable figure in 1991.

In Germany, two satellite platforms existed in the 1990s: Premiere (analogue), and DF1 (digital). Both were owned by KirchGruppe and were merged in 1999 to form Premiere World, which was renamed 'Premiere' in 2002 and held the rights to the Bundesliga. The decision by KirchMedia (also part of the KirchGruppe) to purchase the rights to the 2002 and 2006 FIFA World Cups plunged it into debt, resulting in its bankruptcy in 2002. An investment group took over Premiere, which was then in turn taken over by Sky Deutschland (part of the News Corporation Group) in 2009 and rebranded as Sky. For the latter deal, Sky Deutschland held the television rights (pay TV) and Deutsche Telekom the mobile and online rights to the Bundesliga (News Corp Group, 2009).

In Italy, two platforms existed at the end of the 1990s: Telepiù (subsidiary of Canal+) and Stream (involving Telecom Italia). BSkyB entered the market in 2000, acquiring control of Stream and merging with Telepiù to create a single satellite platform called Sky Italia. The rights to Serie A played a major role in the merging of the platforms, which was authorized by the European Commission in 2004 under tighter regulatory conditions. For the period 2010–12, the two media rights packages for Serie A were held by Sky Italia and Mediaset in a collective bargaining deal (Ginesta, 2009).

Satellite communication had further repercussions and contributed directly to the globalization of top European football leagues, in particular the English Premier League (Williams, 1994). The international sale of television rights meant that millions of fans around the world could tune in simultaneously to live broadcasts from England, leading to the growth of fan bases for clubs such as Manchester United.

At the end of the 1990s, two new ways of communication emerged: internet (IP TV) and television via mobile telephone. In the telecommunications sector, service providers developed what has become known as the 'triple play', packaging telephone connection and television with broadband. In Spain, Telefónica presented its own brand of IP TV in 2005, Imagenio, which was followed by competition from Jazztel and Orange's triple plays (Vila *et al.*, 2007). In relation to mobile technology, the increased capacity of third-generation data transmission or the creation of specialized networks (DVB-H, DMB or MediaFLO) has created new opportunities for service delivery and, again, sport has played a key role in the development of these services.

Commercialization models

There are two dominant models in the buying and selling of audiovisual rights for football: individual selling and collective selling (or bargaining). Individual selling of rights implies that each club negotiates and sells the rights to cover games played in its home stadium, resulting in multiple sellers and potentially multiple buyers in a theoretically free-market situation. The disadvantage of this model is that less successful and/or popular clubs receive much lower offers and reduced revenues, thus widening the gap between them and the bigger and more successful clubs. This system was in place at the time of writing in Spain, where matters were further complicated by the Spanish Football Federation's regulation that for a game to be televised, both of the participating clubs must be in agreement regarding the sale of rights. This obviously can cause problems when the two clubs have sold their rights to different broadcasters (CNC, 2008).

The collective selling of television rights removes potential conflicts between clubs with different media rights buyers, simplifies the negotiation process and implementation of the deal, and enables clubs to negotiate a potentially higher price by forming a cartel. By bargaining collectively, smaller clubs can negotiate higher sums than would otherwise have been obtained through individual selling. Overall, in Europe, pay TV platforms have come to dominate the broadcasting of top leagues, as Table 8.1 shows. The economic principles of this model are discussed by Stefan Szymanski in Chapter 7. Here, the European football context is overviewed, preceding a closer look at the Spanish exception.

Spain is the only one of the big five European leagues that does not use collective selling, and this has contributed to the dominance of its two giants (FC Barcelona and Real Madrid) and continued economic and sporting inequality in La Liga. For example, the total media revenues from all competitions for the four Spanish clubs that qualified for the UEFA European Champions League (ECL) in the 2006–07 season were: Real Madrid (€114 million), FC Barcelona (€106 million), Valencia FC (€28 million) and CA Osasuna (€10 million). Thus, in terms of media revenues, the top two clubs banked over three times more than any one of their closest rivals, and ten times more than smaller clubs in the same league (Ginesta, 2009: 209).

A further consequence of the escalating value of media rights deals is how football is communicated in journalistic terms. The need to lever the deal and maximize return on investment has meant that many journalists and editors from rights-holding broadcasters fail to maintain neutrality when narrating and representing football, by hyperbolizing and sensationalizing in the interest of maintaining subscribers and promoting the brand they have been instrumental in constructing. In Spain, an interesting example is the changes in the director of communication at Real Madrid during season 2009–10. In January 2009, the president Ramon Calderon appointed Alejandro Elortegui director of communication. Elortegui had worked for eleven years at the sports daily *AS*, whose parent company, Prisa, owned the television rights to Real for that season through another subsidiary, Sogecable. The same month, *Marca*, the other sports daily from Madrid, published a series of articles accusing Calderon of corruption. Eventually Calderon was forced to call presidential elections and Florentino Pérez won, regaining the presidency of the Real Madrid in May 2010. At the end of the season, Pérez replaced Elortegui with Antonio Galeano, from TV station LaSexta, whose parent company, Mediapro, owns the television rights to Real Madrid for the 2010–11 season (Ginesta, 2009).

The football television war (1996–2009): the conflict for audiovisual hegemony in Spain

The symbiotic relations between football and audiovisual organizations are of such significance that they have influenced the regulation of the audiovisual and tele-communications sectors in six main ways, by the regulation of:

* digital television via satellite, cable and DTT
* subscription channels
* PPV
* DTT in terms of new licence allocation and authorization of broadcasters to charge for the system
* competition and public television in the acquisition of sports rights
* free-to-air coverage of certain sports events that are considered to be of general social interest.

In the case of Spain, a law regulating the codification system for satellite television (Act 37/1995)[4] caused the outbreak of what the Spanish journalists dubbed the 'football war' between the two major audiovisual platforms that were fighting not only for audiences but, more importantly, for the hegemony of the Spanish audiovisual system. The first part of the war began as Telefónica (the main Spanish telecommunications operator that was privatized as part of market liberalization policies in 1997 and is now a major international telecommunications player) attempted to snatch the exclusive rights to La Liga from its rival Audiovisual Sport (owned by Sogecable and the Grupo Prisa – owner of *El País* newspaper and the national radio station Ser).

With government support under the Partido Popular (PP), Telefónica launched the digital satellite platform Via Digital in 1997 to compete with the Canal Satellite Digital (CSD) subscription platform that had already been launched by Sogecable. The rights to La Liga were divided between Via Digital (PPV) and CSD (PPV), and the two attempted to outbid each other by inflating prices, even though both platforms were still loss-making ventures. There were not enough subscribers to sustain the two competitors, and by 2001 Via Digital had lost over €600 million. In July 2002, Via Digital and CSD agreed to merge and create a new platform called Digital+, which was owned by Sogecable with participation from Grupo Prisa (56%), Telefónica (maintaining 22% equity but not intervening in the new company's management), and a Mediaset subsidiary (22%). This brought together the rights packages for La Liga on one satellite pay platform, which broadcast each week's La Liga games on PPV except two, one of which was transmitted on its Canal+ subscription channel while the other had to go out free-to-air by Spanish law. This gave Digital+ a near monopoly on La Liga games and drove up subscriptions.

Football television rights therefore had played a fundamental role in this war between two competing platforms, which ultimately resulted in their fusion and the unification of rights packages under one provider. Peace, however, was short lived as Mediapro, a new player, entered the scene in 2006, when Sogecable's contract with La Liga was coming to an end, and waged all-out war on Sogecable's Digital+, snatching the television rights for La Liga club-by-club and redefining the audiovisual landscape in Spain. This marked the second part of the football television war, which raged from 2006 to 2009 and involved continual confrontation between Sogecable and Mediapro, with matters ending up in the high court and requiring parliamentary intervention.

In 2006, Mediapro adopted a direct, aggressive strategy by approaching La Liga clubs one-by-one to make improved offers on their existing deals with Sogecable and acquiring their audiovisual rights. By 2008, Mediapro had secured thirty-eight of the forty-two clubs in the top two Spanish divisions at a cost of over €500 million per season. The key negotiations, of course, were with Real Madrid and FC Barcelona, without whom their plan was doomed to failure. FC Barcelona signed with Mediapro for a record €1 billion over seven years, surpassed by Real Madrid, who signed a €1.1 billion deal for the same period. These deals were historic, and provided both clubs with much needed financial security (Ginesta, 2009: 219). Initially, Mediapro signed a deal with Audiovisual Sport to share the rights, with the latter having control of the pay TV market and the former free-to-air. However, as Mediapro gained the rights to more clubs, conflict arose over what games would be shown free-to-air or on pay TV, forcing the establishment of a new, more specific deal and ongoing negotiations almost on a game-by-game basis. The legal war between the two media organizations involved the boycotting of Mediapro cameras in certain stadiums, and resulted in some games not being televised (Ginesta, 2009). The situation was complicated by the fact that, under the individual rights bargaining system in Spain, in the case that two teams in the same game have sold their rights to different broadcasters, an agreement between the broadcasters must be reached for the game to be televised, according to the Assembly of the clubs of La Liga, 11 July 2002.

During the 2007–08 season, Mediapro took football broadcasting in Spain back to a free-to-air model, broadcasting games on its new national channel La Sexta, which was at that time the only channel through which Mediapro could broadcast as it did not have a pay TV platform. After more than ten years of being restricted to one televised game a week, Spanish football fans suddenly had four or more televised games every weekend to enjoy, including Real Madrid and FC Barcelona's fight for the championship. While the free-to-air broadcasts were achieving large audiences for La Sexta, it was not an economically viable model for the future, and Mediapro started moves to create a pay TV platform.

With the rights to the vast majority of La Liga games secured, Mediapro took a further step in 2009 that would change the legislation regulating the audiovisual sector. Mediapro requested the establishment of a subscription channel on the DTT system, which would be called GolTV and would broadcast La Liga games for a monthly subscription. Government support for Mediapro and its initiatives came from the Spanish Socialist Party (PSOE) and led to the passing of legislation to permit the creation of the channel. This was rushed through parliament in time for the start of the 2009–10 season, as the prospect of football not being televised at all for the nation was apparently too great a risk to bear for all sides. With the media rights to football secured, Mediapro had assumed a very powerful position, not only in the football media cultural complex, but in the Spanish audiovisual sector. Along with Grupo Arbol, Mediapro is a major shareholder in Imagenia, a media holding group that includes companies involved in the different parts of the audiovisual value chain (recording, production, commercialization, distribution, research and development, strategic consultancy) in the areas of film and television programming, including football and other sports such as Formula One.

From one season to the next, Spanish football fans saw live football return to pay television, with the added inconvenience that, in order to receive GolTV, they had to buy a new digital decoder or subscribe to one of the IP TV providers (Telefónica's Imagenio or Organe). Fans wanting to see all the La Liga games had to maintain their Digital+ decoder since Sogecable had the rights to the Sunday night game. Spanish law still stated that one game per week had to be broadcast free-to-air, and this was implemented through Mediapro's La Sexta and regional TV channels. The beginning of the 2009–10 season was chaotic as fans struggled to understand how games would be televised, and how much it would cost them.

It is clear that, during the 1990s and first decade of the twenty-first century, football television rights negotiations in Spain, as in other European countries, played a major role in the establishment of satellite television and the development of the digital television era. This development occurred not only as part of a battle between competing broadcast platforms, but also in the context of a war between media groups that redefined the audiovisual context.

Football clubs and multimedia production

Although an interdependent relationship based on a mutual need for image promotion had been established between football clubs and the media, up to the 1990s they had been autonomous actors. Radical changes have occurred in the twenty-first century, altering this relationship. Media organizations have developed increasingly close relations with sport, including partial ownership (of the clubs directly or the media rights to clubs/competitions), resulting in the loss of a form of journalistic autonomy that characterized earlier times (Harvey *et al.*, 2001; Law *et al.*, 2002; Boyle and Haynes, 2003; Ginesta, 2009). A symbiotic relationship can now be identified between the two groups of actors characterized by its reciprocal dependency. In addition, clubs have transformed themselves into media producers, communicating directly with audiences through their own television channels, web pages and mobile services, which have created new marketing opportunities and reduced their dependence on the traditional mass media. In the near future, mobile devices could become the point of convergence capable of receiving information currently distributed via multiple channels (Boyle and Haynes, 2003; Boyle, 2004).

Mobile technology and football clubs

The use of the mobile telephone as a platform for clubs to communicate with the public is still relatively recent, but the potential for the development of future relationships between clubs and society is evident. Through mobile phones, clubs can offer fans a diverse range of services: news and information updates; images; video; audio; gaming; downloads; ticketing; competitions and so on. These services are delivered via mobile internet connections, SMS and MMS messaging to devices with increasing capabilities for the management and production of new information by the user. This production role for fans closes the communication loop, providing interaction and feedback with the club and its network.

The increased ownership and use of mobile phones and their growing importance as media receptors has seen the establishment of telecommunications operators as key partners for football clubs. Real Madrid, for example, has established important deals with three operators in Spain (Telefónica, Orange and Vodafone) accessing 20,000 users during the 2007–8 season, sending up to six daily SMS alerts. Real Madrid's mobile technology development has not been limited to the domestic market either, with the creation of a mobile web page in 2008 for Japanese users. FC Barcelona has experience with mobile technology dating back to the 2003–04 season. Subscriptions produced revenues of €1.78 million for the 2004–05 season (FC Barcelona, 2005). In 2007, 83,000 club members had subscribed to mobile services, with the club sending around 1 million messages per month. In 2010, two SMS packages were created: a basic pack (information about match schedules and results) that was free for club members; and an enhanced pack (including messages related to news, goal alerts and information on the club's basketball team) at a cost of €0.15 or €0.30 (plus VAT) per text.

Football club web pages

More than a decade has passed since the more innovative football clubs created web pages with a predominantly promotional and informative intent. The communication needs of clubs and the communication potential of the internet (round the clock, around the globe) have enabled the segmentation of audiences, increased interactivity, and the development of virtual communities or networks between fans and partner organizations. The web pages of leading clubs have developed into multifunctional, multimedia communication platforms that can deliver information, products (e-tailing) and services direct to customers and the media.

While the management of club web pages was initially outsourced, clubs have gradually brought content production and design back in-house to control communication with key audiences. In 2010, all the clubs in Europe's top five leagues had web pages, the majority of which were in the process of integrating consolidated multimedia services combining streaming with downloadable files. Despite this, the focus of club web pages was still on providing information (news and statistics), although more interactive services were being introduced (chats, forums, polls, competitions, etc.) – essential aspects of the Web 2.0 era (O'Reilly, 2005). The main form of interaction between clubs and fans, locally and globally, occurred through social- and marketing-based services offered through their websites.

Communication and the football economy

As shown in Figure 8.2, media rights sales have contributed to the dramatic increase in league and club revenues during the past decade. FC Barcelona, for example, earned €42.8 million from media sources in the 2001–02 season (FC Barcelona, 2002). For the 2008–09 season this had increased to €135.5 million (FC Barcelona, 2009). This growth was not limited to the football industry. European broadcasters paid $95 million for the rights to the Barcelona 1992 Olympic Games; and NBC paid $401 million for the US rights. For the Beijing 2008 Olympic Games in the digital pay TV era, prices had increased dramatically, with the European broad-casters paying $443 million and NBC $893 million (IOC, 2010).

During the 1990s, top football clubs' media revenues overtook matchday revenues and became the dominant revenue source in the top five leagues. However, in Figure 8.2 it is interesting to observe that in recent years media revenues have begun to diminish as a percentage of total revenue, with income from commercial sources (merchandising, sponsorship, advertising) becoming increasingly important for clubs. The strategy of commercializing clubs' symbols and identity has

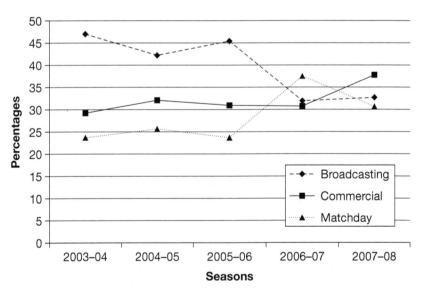

Figure 8.2 Broadcasting, commercial and match-day income percentages in the top five richest football clubs

Note: The clubs that took part in the sample were: Manchester United, Real Madrid, AC Milan, Chelsea and Juventus (2003/04); Real Madrid, Manchester United, AC Milan, Juventus and Chelsea (2004/05); Real Madrid, FC Barcelona, Juventus, Manchester United and AC Milan (2005/06); Real Madrid, Manchester United, FC Barcelona, Chelsea and Arsenal (2006/07); Real Madrid, Manchester United, FC Barcelona, FC Bayern Munich and Chelsea (2007/08).

converted certain teams into global brands (e.g. FC Barcelona, Real Madrid, Manchester United) and their stadiums into an amalgam of entertainment-based theme park and corporate hospitality venue (e.g. the Allianz Arena, Munich). These new revenue sources grow as globalization processes accelerate and international fan bases expand. Clubs can now segment fans as any other commercial organization does, creating geo-demographic and psychographic profiles that enable tailor-made products and services to be developed and promoted in a targeted way. For example, FC Barcelona and Real Madrid have both established publications for specific audiences such as magazines for children, stadium visitors, fans, veterans, sponsors, etc. This process has transformed major football clubs from local, neighbourhood social entities in the pre-broadcast era, to regional, national and international economic entities in the broadcast era, to complex global commercial entities or brands in the digital era.

Figure 8.2 shows the evolution of the revenue breakdowns (by media, commercial and matchday) of the five richest clubs from the 2003–04 to 2007–08 seasons according to Deloitte's Football Money League (Parkes *et al.*, 2007, 2008). For the period from 2003–04 to 2007–08, Manchester United, Real Madrid and Chelsea were placed in the top five every season, and only five other clubs featured (Juventus, FC Barcelona, Arsenal, FC Bayern Munich and AC Milan). The increasing commercialization of clubs is due not only to the sale of shirts or merchandising, but also to the wholesale licensing of clubs' patrimony and symbols. The recent US import of selling naming rights to stadiums, such as the Allianz Arena or the Emirates Stadium, are examples of long-term strategic alliances with sponsors, which have continued the invasion of sporting spaces by commercial messages.

Fans are now witness to the staging of football spectacles in branded spaces: as they walk towards the newly named stadium (or 'venue') they are sold shirts with this season's online betting company on the front; they are distracted by digital advertising hoardings and scoreboards and sponsored promotional half-time contests; while they gaze up to the VIP sky boxes and corporate suites, they might be wondering what is on the menu and why match tickets are so expensive these days. For example, between 2005 and 2009 Manchester United's match ticket prices increased by approximately 50% (James, 2009). The matchday experience has become a marketing exercise focused on maximising revenues and providing an entertainment experience that includes football but does not entirely depend upon it to satisfy customers.

Players as brands and commodities

The complexity of the football economy is also reflected in the players' revenues. Suffice to say that the player with the highest income (on and off the field) for the 2008–09 season was David Beckham, whose sporting career was certainly in decline while his celebrity status continued to rise. The magazine *France Football* produces an annual estimation of the top ten footballers' revenues under three main categories: salary, bonus and commercial (see Table 8.2).

Table 8.2 Salaries of the ten top-earning football stars (million €)

2007–08 season

Player	Team	Salary	Bonus	Comercial	Total
David Beckham	Los Angeles Galaxy	4.2	1.8	25	31
Ronaldinho	FC Barcelona	8.5	0.1	15.5	24.1
Lionel Messi	FC Barcelona	6.8	0.2	16	23
Cristiano Ronaldo	Man Utd	8.5	1	10	19.5
Thierry Henry	FC Barcelona	8	0.3	8.5	16.8
Kaká	AC Milan	9	0.4	5	14.4
John Terry	Chelsea	9.8	0.2	3.9	13.9
Michael Ballack	Chelsea	9.2	0.3	4.2	13.7
Ronaldo	AC Milan	4.2	0.2	9	13.4
Steven Gerrard	Liverpool	7.6	0.3	3.9	11.8
Total		**75.8**	**4.8**	**101**	**181.6**

2008–09 season

Player	Team	Salary	Bonus	Commercial	Total
David Beckham	AC Milan	4.9	1.5	26	32.4
Lionel Messi	FC Barcelona	8.5	0.1	20	28.6
Ronaldinho	AC Milan	6.5	0.1	13	19.6
Cristiano Ronaldo	Man Utd	7.3	1	10	18.3
Thierry Henry	FC Barcelona	8	0.2	8.8	17
Kaká	AC Milan	9	0.1	6	15.1
Zlatan Ibrahimovic	Inter Milan	11	0.5	2.5	14
Wayne Rooney	Man Utd	6	0.7	6.8	13.5
Frank Lampard	Chelsea	8.2	0.3	4.5	13
John Terry	Chelsea	8.4	0.3	3	11.7
Total		**77.8**	**4.8**	**100.6**	**183.2**

Source: Notarianni (2008, 2009).

The top four earners for both seasons took home more from off-the-field commercial activities than from wages and bonuses. David Beckham's commercial ventures earned him five times his salary and bonus, demonstrating the endorsement and advertising value of sports stars as popular celebrities and global commodities.

As part of the interrelations within the sport media cultural complex, media organizations give these individuals the exposure and audience reach desired by corporations to promote their products and brands. Table 8.3 shows the types of products and brands that the highest-earning footballers endorsed and advertised, including clothing, technology and media, food and drinks, financial products and others. Among the most lucrative sponsors of footballers are, unsurprisingly, sports apparel companies, particularly market leaders Nike and Adidas. Recent acquisitions and mergers in the industry have seen Nike's takeover of Converse and Umbro, and Adidas' of Reebok, resulting in the domination of football merchandising deals by two corporations and their sub-brands. The two-pronged strategy of signing deals with clubs on the one hand, and individual footballers on the other, provides these organizations with multiple promotional opportunities and a diverse portfolio of 'products', which will almost guarantee brand exposure.

Nike and Adidas, as leaders in global marketing, have the power to turn footballers into brands that transcend their clubs, national teams and sport in general. The long-term contractual relations established between footballers and these corporations involve extensive promotional obligations and limit player's conduct and mobility. In some cases, they have been cited as influencing the transfer of players between clubs. The influence of the sports apparel giants on the football media cultural complex has undoubtedly increased as clubs and footballers exploit commercial opportunities and maximize revenues.

An analysis of shifts in football club sponsorship and player endorsements demonstrates the increasing importance of ICT companies in the football media complex. While technology companies have a long history in football sponsorship, the entry of telecommunications service providers and computer gaming companies reflects wider changes in the digital era. Sponsors of individual players include:

- telecommunications operators (Telefónica – Messi; Movistar – Ronaldinho; Organe – Lampard)
- computer gaming (Konami – Messi; Electronic Arts – Terry)
- photography/audiovisual recording (Minolta – Ronaldinho)
- electronic accessories (ScanDisk – Messi)
- mobile device manufacturers (Motorola – Beckham; SFR – Henry)
- media groups (Mediaset – Ibrahimovic)

In the 2009–10 UEFA Champions League knockout stages, the title sponsors of seven teams came from the ICT sector, with the rest from online betting, airlines, energy, banks and insurance industries (Table 8.4). These strategic agreements form a key part of the football media complex, enabling clubs to gain revenues by selling part of their commercial rights to interested companies, providing exposure to these companies through the media attention the clubs receive. The majority of top-level clubs have adopted a sponsorship strategy, first developed by the IOC,

Table 8.3 Sponsoring deals of the top ten footballers with the highest annual revenues (data from 2008–09 season)

Player	Clothing	ICT/media	Food and drinks	Financial products	Other brands
David Beckham	Adidas, Armani	Motorola	Pepsi, Findus, GO3 Food		Coty, Sharpie, Gillette, Cabo Sao Roque Ressort, Castrol
Lionel Messi	Adidas, A-Style, Storkman	Konami, Telefónica, SanDisk	Pepsi, Damm, Gatorade, Danone, La Serenissima	Banc Sabadell	M. Mirage, Gillette, Air Europa, Lody for Men, Repsol YPF, Galeno
Ronaldinho	Nike, R10, Omo	Electronic Arts, Ol-Telemar, Konica Minolta, Movistar	Pepsi, Nutrilite (Amway)		
Cristiano Ronaldo	Nike	Konami	Soccerade, Unilever	Banco Espirtiu Santo	Madère Turism Office, Galp
Thierry Henry	Reebok, Tommy Hilfiger	SFR	Pepsi, Pringles, Damm		Gillette
Kaká	Adidas, Armani		Barilla, Guarana Antartica, Ringo		Gillette
Zlatan Ibrahimovic	Nike	Mediaset Premium			
Wayne Rooney	Nike	Electronic Arts	Coca-Cola		
Frank Lampard	Adidas	Orange	Gatorade, Pepsi		
John Terry	Umbro	Electronic Arts			King of Shave

Source: Notarianni (2009).

Table 8.4 Shirt sponsors of clubs qualifying for the knock-out phase of the UEFA
Champions League (2009–10)

Team	Sponsor	Economic sector
Olympique Lyonnais	Betclic	Online betting
AC Milan	Bwin	Online betting
Sevilla FC	12bet	Online betting
Real Madrid CF	Bwin	Online betting
FC Porto	Tmn	Telecommunications
FC Bayern Munich	T Home	Telecommunications
Chelsea FC	Samsung	Consumer electronics
VfB Stuttgart	EnBW	Energy
Olympiacos FC	Citybank	Finance
Manchester United FC	AIG	Finance
PFC CSKA Moskva	Aeroflot	Airline
Arsenal FC	Emirates	Airline
FC Barcelona	Unicef	NGO
FC Internazionale Milano	Pirelli	Automobile
ACF Fiorentina	Toyota	Automobile
FC Girondins de Bordeaux	KIA	Automobile

Source: UEFA (2009).

which involves establishing exclusive product/service/sector categories (such as soft drinks, automobiles, etc.) and different levels of sponsorship (from title sponsors paying the most, down to service providers such as automobiles or foods and beverages).

However, not all sponsorship deals follow the established industry model. The relationship between FC Barcelona and UNICEF, which began in 2006 and was renewed in 2009, raises some interesting issues in the commercialization and communication of football. Until 2006, club policy dictated that the FC Barcelona shirt was one of the few sponsor-free spaces in international professional sport, although it did carry the Nike swoosh. Facing massive debt and the increasing need to maintain domestic and international competitiveness, a motion to allow shirt sponsorship was approved by club members, and speculation began as to which multinational company would spend the estimated €15–20 million a year necessary to secure one of the most sought-after promotional slots in international sport. As interest grew, allegedly, from an online betting company, speculation turned into a social debate about the need to find an appropriate sponsor befitting the club's history and values.

The football industry was surprised when the club finally announced that it would sign a ground-breaking deal with UNICEF. This five-year arrangement saw FC Barcelona making an annual donation of €1.5 million to UNICEF and the establishment of joint educational and health initiatives in developing countries. Barça would wear UNICEF's name on its shirt, and the deal included joint promotional activities such as an advertising spot to promote the relationship, which was broadcast free (due to UNICEF's charitable status) on public television channels around the world. The club also benefited from the sale of these historic shirts.

The agreement received considerable international media attention, the vast majority of which was positive for both parties. While many football clubs were involved in work with NGOs, including UNICEF, this agreement was of particular significance due to its scale and the fact the club had foregone direct investment in the form of a standard title sponsorship deal. In fact, this was an inversion of the typical sponsorship deal, and represented a new kind of strategic alliance based on social responsibility. At the same time, it achieved promotional and brand promotion objectives.

Locating the case in the wider context of the football media complex, certain contextual circumstances need to be considered. First, FC Barcelona won the Champions League in May 2006, in addition to La Liga, making it the highest-profile team in the world, with players such as Ronaldinho and Eto'o established as media stars. Second, and most importantly, the signing of the Mediapro media deal provided the club with an estimated €1 billion over seven years, agreed just two months before the signing of the UNICEF deal in September 2006. And third, the club's renegotiation of its Nike merchandise deal in November 2006 was estimated to be worth €30 million per year. These dramatic improvements to the club's financial performance no doubt facilitated the decision to enter into the agreement with UNICEF.[5]

As previously mentioned, sports betting companies have sealed sponsorship deals with clubs across Europe, as well as securing the purchase of advertising space in stadiums around sports media programming (e.g. 888sport, Bet365, Ladbrokes, StanJames, Betfair, Eurobet, BetClic, Miapuesta, Expekt, bwin, Paddy Power, Gamebookers, Interapuestas, Pinnacle, William Hill, Unibet, Paf). This is an example – albeit an ethically questionable one – of the new digital media paradigm in which football exists. Football provides an ideal vehicle through which to promote online betting on football (and other sports), and companies such as bwin provide an instant, easily accessible global platform (subject to national restrictions). The deal between Real Madrid and bwin brought the club an estimated €30 million per season, although the team was not permitted to wear shirts with bwin's name on in Champions League matches in Switzerland and France, where the promotion of betting is illegal.

Although not direct sponsors of football, the relationship between football entities (e.g. FIFA) and video game producers (e.g. EA Sports) has produced a new set of agreements and the licensing of image rights. Apart from mediated football, a predominantly young profile also consumes hyper-real digital representations and reproductions of football in video games. In the Web 2.0 era, such games can be played online with friends or strangers, giving fans the ultimate interaction of controlling their favourite team and players and even creating their own player.

Conclusions

The paradigm shift from the global broadcast era is by no means complete, but it has certainly accelerated in recent years. The fundamental framework that underpins the sport media complex remains in place, but new actors have entered, and its environment is in flux. As part of wider changes in the communication ecology, digitization created new communications networks and transformed the relationship between sports organizations, commercial interest in sports (sponsors, advertisers, merchandisers), and what were previously understood as broadcast media.

Major media groups are extending their reach across multidimensional and interactive platforms in an attempt to maximize the commercial value and leverage of increasingly expensive football rights packages in the digital era. At the same time, major sponsors, merchandisers and advertisers are trying to maximize return on investment from deals with players, clubs, leagues and federations. While more money is flowing into football entities, the control of meaning-production processes seems to be in the hands of media groups and commercial sponsors. However, the growth of social media and Web 2.0 appears to be transforming communication processes and enabling mass self-communication. In this increasingly complex web of user-driven content, sport, and football in particular, is a theme for discussion, identity construction, communication, and community development on a global scale. Fans have the opportunity to be more active or interactive and to move away from the passive role of audience or consumer in the sport media complex.

Media organizations, even those holding exclusive rights to leagues and events, are no longer the only message broadcasters. Football organizations and footballers, along with the other actors in the sport media complex, have started to establish profiles/channels and participate actively in networks and data-sharing platforms. This could provide new opportunities for intervention, the coordination of initiatives, the convergence of information sources, crowd sourcing, and a shift to the audience as producer. However, the established power brokers in the sport media cultural complex have already begun to exercise their influence in this new environment. Media groups and ICT companies have major interests in social media as channels for corporate communication, continually monitoring and participating in blogs, social networking sites, forums etc., and in some cases acquiring them (e.g. News Corp and *MySpace*). As happened in the broadcast era, these actors are attempting to affect the nature of social interaction and shape messages as part of meaning-production processes.

Challenges for the football industry are emerging as this paradigm shift accelerates and deepens. Media rights sales remain a major source of income for football, and football is still one of the main media products and commercial vehicles for media groups and sponsors. But advances in ICTs and the emergence of more informed audiences mean that, while the rules of the broadcast era may no longer apply, we can see an intensification of the struggle for control of more fragmented and complex communication processes in the digital era.

Notes

1   European Parliament, (1997), 'Directiva 97/36/CE del Parlamento Europeo y del Consejo de 30 de junio de 1997 por la que se modifica la Directiva 89/552/CEE del Consejo sobre la coordinación de determinadas disposiciones legales, reglamentarias y administrativas de los Estados miembros relativas al ejercicio de actividades de radiodifusión televisiva', *Diario Oficial*, L202 of 30/07/1997, 0060–70.

2 See McCullagh (2010). The club brand value refers to 'the portion of their overall value not a result of market demographics and league', that is, team brand jerseys and other such goods (see Schwartz, 2010).
3 See Act 21/1997, Ley 21/1997, de 3 de julio, reguladora de las Emisiones y Retransmisiones de Competiciones y Acontecimientos Deportivos, http://noticias. juridicas.com/base_datos/Derogadas/r0-l21-1997.html.
4 Act 37/1995, Ley 37/1995, de 12 de diciembre, de Telecomunicaciones por Satélite, http://noticias.juridicas.com/base_datos/Derogadas/r1-l37-1995.html
5 In December 2010, though, Barcelona concluded a five-year deal worth more than $200 million in selling shirt advertising to the Qatar Foundation, which would share space on the jerseys with UNICEF. This was announced within days of FIFA's decision to award the 2022 men's World Cup to Qatar. A club statement positioned Barcelona as 'the indisputable brand leader in world football ahead of our international competitors'.

References

Boyle, R., (2004), 'Mobile Communication and the Sports Industry: The Case of 3G', *Trends in Communication*, 12: 73–82.
Boyle, R. and Haynes, R., (2003), 'New Media Sport', in A. Bernstein and N. Blain (eds), *Sport, Media and Culture: Global and Local Dimensions*: London: Frank Cass: 95–115.
Castells, M., (2009), *Communication Power*, Madrid: Alianza Editorial.
CNC, (2008), *Informe sobre la competencia en los mercados de adquisición y explotación de derechos audiovisuales de fútbol en España*, Madrid: Comisión Nacional de la Competencia.
FC Barcelona (2002), *Annual Report*, Barcelona: FC Barcelona.
—— (2005), *Annual Report*, Barcelona: FC Barcelona.
—— (2009), *Annual Report*, Barcelona: FC Barcelona.
Ginesta, X., (2009), 'Les Tecnologies de la Informació i la Comunicació i l'esport: Una anàlisi de la Primera Divisió espanyola de fútbol', PhD thesis, Bellaterra: Universitat Autònoma de Barcelona, Departament de Mitjans, Comunicació i Cultura.
Harris, N. (2007), '160m viewers, 202 countries: Premiership's worldwide pot of gold', *Independent*, 23 January, www.independent.co.uk/sport/football/premier-league/160m-viewers-202-countries-premierships-worldwide-pot-of-gold-433271.html
Harvey, J., Law, A. and Cantelon, M., (2001), 'North American Professional Team Sport Franchises Ownership Patterns and Global Entertainment Conglomerates', *Sociology of Sport Journal*, 18 (4): 435–57.
Helland, K., (2007), 'Changing Sport, Changing Media: Mass Appeal, the Sports/Media Complex and TV Sports Rights', *Nordicom Review*, Jubilee Issue: 105–19.
IOC, (2010), *Olympic Marketing Fact File*, Lausanne: International Olympic Committee.
James, S., (2009), 'Manchester United alone hit loyal fans with season-ticket price increase', *Guardian*, 23 April, www.guardian.co.uk/football/2009/apr/23/manchester-united-premier-league-season-tickets
Law, A., Harvey, J. and Kemp, S., (2002), 'The Global Sport Mass Media Oligopoly', *International Review for the Sociology of Sport*, 37 (3–4): 279–302.
McCullagh, K., (2010), 'Woods, Nike, Man Utd, Superbowl top Forbes list', *Sportbusiness*, 5 February, www.sportbusiness.com/news/171830/woods-nike-man-utd-super-bowl-top-forbes-list?u
Maguire, J., (1999), *Global Sport*, Cambridge: Polity Press.
News Corp Group, (2009), 'News Corporation Increases Stake in Sky Deutschland AG to 39.96 Percent', 5 August, www.newscorp.com/news/news_422.html

Notarianni, R., (2008), 'Les salaries des stars', *France Football*, 8 April, 10–14.

——, (2009), 'Les salaries des stars', *France Football*, 31 March, 4–13.

O'Reilly, T., (2005), 'What Is Web 2.0. Design Patterns and Business Models for the Next Generation of Software', *www.oreillynet.com*, 30 September, www.oreillynet.com/pub/a/oreilly/tim/news/2005/09/30/what-is-web-20.html

Parkes, R., Houlihan, A., Ingles, G. and Hawkins, M., (2007), *Football Money League*, Manchester: Deloitte.

Parkes, R., Houlihan, A., Ingles, G., Hawkins, M. and Ashton-Jones, A., (2008), *Football Money League*, Manchester: Deloitte.

Rowe, D., (2003), 'Sport and the Reproduction of the Global', *International Review of the Sociology of Sport*, 38 (3): 281–94.

——, (2004), *Sport, Culture and the Media*, Maidenhead: Open University Press.

Schwartz, P. J., (2010), 'The world's top sports brands: the Forbes Fab40 values the most powerful names in sports', *Forbes.com*, 3 February, www.forbes.com/2010/02/03/most-powerful-sports-names-tiger-woods-nike-cmo-network-sports-brands.html

UEFA, (2009), 'Fútbol europeo', http://es.uefa.com/footballeurope

Vila, P., Garcia Massagué, M. and Vila, R., (2007), 'Les telecomunicacions', in M. de Moragas, I. Fernández Alonso, J. J. Blasco Gil, J. A. Gimerà i Orts, J. M. Corbella i Cordomí, M. Civil i Serra, O. Gibert i Fortuny (eds), *Informe de la comunicació a Catalunya 2005–2006*, Bellaterra: Edicions UAB: 179–93.

Williams, J., (1994), 'The Local and the Global in English Soccer and the Rise of Satellite Television', *Sociology of Sports Journal*, 11: 376–97.

9 Hosting the Olympic Games

From promoting the nation to nation-branding

Roy Panagiotopoulou

Introduction

Since their inception in Athens in 1896, the modern Olympic Games have attracted international attention (Georgiadis, 2004). Gradually, the media embraced the event, giving it worldwide coverage and enhancing its popularity. The modern Olympics are one of the most mediated events in the world and are a popular cultural expression of our time. Therefore they constitute an important element in the development of global culture (Roche, 2006: 30; Panagiotopoulou, 2010: 233). They have become an emblematic cultural event, symbolizing modernization, in which all countries and institutions want to be present and visible. On the one hand, host cities/countries seek to improve their global image, to increase their international visibility, and to exploit these opportunities for the sake of national interests. On the other hand, the international and local sponsors, the diverse media enterprises, the athletes, the coaches and trainers, the sport federations, and the public have a unique opportunity to achieve worldwide promotion. The culture of consumerism, national antagonisms and superficial multicultural pluralism, in conjunction with the glamour of international promotion, constitute the main traits of the Olympic Games and set the frame in which most citizen-spectators enjoy the event, consume it and, finally, evaluate it (Real, 1998: 20–21; Tomlinson, 2004; Panagiotopoulou, 2010: 254).

These traits define the goals of the Organizing Committees of the Olympic Games. In cooperation with the International Olympic Committee (IOC), the Organizing Committees aim to promote the national profile and defining characteristics of an Olympic Games host city/country and to shape the image of each edition of the Games. At the end of the Games, the international public will have gained new impressions of the organizing city/country and become increasingly interested in the way each organizer tries to use its new infrastructure – the so-called Olympic legacy – and exploit its 'new' international image. The tremendous financial investment in resources has made the staging of the event an issue of public debate and accountability (Horne and Manzenreiter, 2006: 15).

This chapter aims to analyse the interconnection between globalization, nationalism and national promotion in the context of the Olympic Games, Olympic ideology and the IOC's well designed promotional campaign. It presents how national promotion takes place within a cultural and sporting event through the development of the nation as a marketing commodity. Specifically, nation-branding through the Olympic Games as a phenomenon of modernity will be analysed, taking as examples the Olympic Games in Rome in 1960 – where it all began – and those in Athens in 2004, a recent, mature nation-branded city/country.

Globalization, nationalism and promotion of the nation

International sport is one of the main fields in which the process of globalization is evident. The number of people following sports competitions and seeking detailed information through various media platforms has increased. This development has led to the commercialization of sports events and has made sports competitions one of the most popular broadcasting genres. As a consequence, the interest of the sports media, in both traditional and new formats, has risen to the point where journalists far outnumber athletes at the Olympic Games.[1] This interest has also had an effect on the broadcasting rights fees for international competitions and especially the Olympics, which have reached very high levels (IOC Marketing Reports of various editions, www.olympic.org/en/content/Footer-Pages/Documents/Marketing).

The present social context of the Olympics is that of a 'global village' in which people feel that they gain a new cosmopolitan identity as 'citizens of the world' (Maguire, 1999: 144; Roche, 2006: 28; Barnard *et al.*, 2006). The discourse produced by the IOC and the media adopts a clear stance in favour of globalization – an 'active globalizer', as Lee and Maguire (2009: 6) have characterized it – giving people the impression of belonging to a global community (Olympic Games, Youth Olympics fans, etc.).

The interconnection of globalization and nationalism is constantly reinforced through national symbols (flags, anthems, etc.) to identify and evoke nationalistic feelings in an established, internationally defined framework where nations can be seen and recognized, can compete and can be promoted (Bourdieu, 1994: 102–3; Tomlinson, 1996: 587–88; Maguire, 1999). It suits the economic interests of various stakeholders (sponsors, media enterprises, host nations, sports federations, etc.) to promote globalization while branding a specific event in a nationalistic fashion (Tomlinson, 2004; Horne and Manzenreiter, 2006: 13; Lee and Maguire, 2009: 7). As Lee and Maguire noticed:

> [. . .] whole sport reproduces and reinforces the idea of nation and nationhood, it also provides various political and cultural identities which have the potential to transcend national border lines.
>
> (Lee and Maguire, 2009: 9)

This interplay between globalization and nationalism offers the desired prerequisites to using the Olympic Games as a marketing platform to promote a nation.

In the course of reporting on the Olympics, journalists' commentaries have gradually shifted from balanced realism to highly emotional reports, framed by national rivalry and focusing on the dominance of the nation, giving little attention to other sporting events and athletes (Guttmann, 2002; Tomlinson and Young, 2006: 1–6; Billings, 2008). The dominance of a nation becomes, through the media coverage, another competitive issue and thus sport constitutes a part of a nation's fabric and provides proof of its hegemony. These developments strengthened the belief that the Olympics provide one of the best opportunities to intensely promote the image of a nation for a short period of seventeen days, but on a worldwide basis.

The nation as an event

It is widely acknowledged that 'nations are more than geopolitical entities, they are discursively constructed "imagined communities"' (Anderson, 1983). There is a shared sense of the 'character, culture and historical trajectory of a people' (Hogan, 2003: 101–2). Thus media play a decisive role because they create images, symbols and myths, which are embraced by large populations. Globalization has altered the role of the nation-state and created possibilities for new types of communities, new forms of visibility and awareness of the cultural significance of a nation-state. The new elaborated notion of 'homeland' became an important tool for a cultural re-embedding of the nation in a worldwide promotion strategy. This homeland is at the same time old and new, using on the one hand 'invented tradition' (Hobsbawm and Ranger, 1983) and on the other hand new discourses and images of positive notions, contemporary aesthetics, emotions and affective bonding, like any other commodity (Knudsen, 2010: 42). The notion of 'homeland' requires an openness to other cultures and boosts cosmopolitanism and interconnectedness. These new conditions have focused on the everyday, unconscious reproduction or negotiation of the national in ordinary people's lives (Billings, 2008). The national became a constitutional part of specific events and is promoted in an idealized, simplified way. Nowadays, these events provide a public source of information and images from which the majority of people construct perceptions or stereotypical opinions about a foreign nation.[2]

All individuals, collective entities, institutions and nations need a connection to their past. This provides the nation with provenance, authenticity, credibility, cohesion and solidarity, and offers a rich set of experiences and an indispensable link to tradition and heritage.[3] Media events are very well tailored to represent a nation because they combine different functions: they are commemorative, restorative and transformative and they celebrate reconciliation with the new, improved national identity (Dayan and Katz, 1992: 8, 20).

Characteristic examples of media mega-events are Olympic Games' opening ceremonies, which provide the host nation with an opportunity to present its narrative and to demonstrate its past in a selective, idealized way (Hogan, 2003; Panagiotopoulou, 2010). The representation of the nation in dream terms is reflected in the words of IOC President Jacques Rogge who, in his closing ceremony speech at the Athens 2004 Games, thanked the host nation using the expression 'These Games were unforgettable, dream Games' (Rogge, 2004). This narrative serves as an affirmation of national identity and provides an extended advertisement for the host nation. It is an opportunity to promote tourism and international corporate investment and trade, to improve its bargaining position in international negotiations, to impede a political ideology highlighting domestic social inequalities, and to strengthen cultural diplomacy (Hogan, 2003: 102; Panagiotopoulou, 2010: 240).

The nation as a commodity

Place-branding, which initially emerged from the need to promote places for tourism, is not new, but is not always a straightforward process leading to common acceptance and understanding. Branding has been applied systematically to many consumer products since the beginning of the twentieth century, but the idea of promoting nations or destinations emerged only in the 1990s (Morgan *et al.*, 2010: xxiii). Early examples of place-branding can be found in the history of many states as governments sought to build a sense of purpose and reputation for their political, economic and cultural decisions.[4] World Expos and the Olympic Games can be seen as attempts to establish national trademarks (e.g. 'Made in . . .', although they are rarely labelled as such), and as promotional events for the host nation-state (Roche, 2000: 33–64).

The concept of place-branding has two major dimensions: one refers to public or cultural diplomacy; the other to nation-branding as a specific marketing approach. Public diplomacy focuses on the ways in which a nation-state (or multilateral organization) communicates with citizens in other countries and societies to promote a certain image of itself, which is then used as an instrument for advancing international political relations. This can be achieved using activities and interventions from official and private individuals and institutions (Bolin and Stahlberg, 2010: 82). Public diplomacy stresses the view that dialogue is often more effective than bland power pressure to achieve the goals of foreign policy.[5] It embraces the entire promotional campaign, positioning and repositioning a country in the complex field of international relations with the aim of sustaining a positive image and a favourable climate for interrelations. In effect, it constitutes a part of the official foreign policy of a nation-state.

On the other hand, nation-branding may primarily address the global market with the political agencies of secondary concern.[6] A brand is a promise, and branding a place or a nation is all about making the experience of a place/nation as positive, memorable, different and exceptional as it can possibly be.[7] The intention to promote a place contains a certain notion of place competitiveness aiming either to boost tourism or to enhance the international political positioning of a city/country (to attract inland investments, increase negotiation power, boost exports, etc.). Bolin and Stahlberg note that

> [. . .] in the era of neo-liberalism the 'nation' is becoming something quite different from the imagined community of bygone days, and that nation branding has become a historical specific form of producing images of the nation.
>
> (Bolin and Stahlberg, 2010: 79)

This indicates that nation-states are increasingly acting in the same way as commercial enterprises (Anholt, 2007a, 2010: 28; Dinnie, 2008: 17–19; Bolin and Stahlberg, 2010), adopting similar corporate strategies to promote themselves.[8]

Nation-branding in neoliberal times seems to offer a cultural identity created for political consumption (Bolin and Stahlberg, 2010: 94). Promotional campaigns have specific aims, including increasing the 'value of a nation' in the international market; attracting an external audience; promoting specific places as commodities (as tourist destinations); and diversifying the internal market in order to cover as many distinctive consumer demands as possible. While nationalism is preoccupied with history and tradition, nation-branding treats the past superficially and focuses more on the future. Historical facts and monuments serve only to support a new narrative for the city/country promotion. However, both nationalism and nation-branding are highly flexible, even interchangeable, concepts, which can be used individually or in tandem with each other. This adds another element to our understanding of what represents the nation and how it is constructed in the contemporary world.[9]

Nowadays, when the power of the media is unquestioned and the mediated landscape is changing rapidly, influential communication, through all forms of media, is crucial to any kind of promotion. Especially for nations, the need to be promoted globally has become indispensable for establishing and maintaining competitive advantage in all sectors of economic, political and cultural activities. Effective nation-branding requires a strategic action plan with well defined ideological and value-laden priorities. It is crucial that such a plan has a lengthy timeframe and includes cooperation between all stakeholders (foreign policy, international organizations, NGOs, entrepreneurs, etc.). An Olympic Games can become the flagship for a promotional campaign, but only for a limited period. They must be accompanied with a series of other activities that help to develop the post-Olympic effect more systematically.

In order to measure this complex phenomenon of international acceptance and competitive identity,[10] there have been many attempts to construct indices and other statistical tools. One index in widespread use is the Nation Brands Index (NBI), constructed by Simon Anholt, where six areas of national competence are measured. These six areas of competence (tourism, exports, governance, investment and immigration, culture and heritage, and people; also called the nation-brand hexagon) reflect people's perceptions of a country and serve as a global opinion barometer.[11] However, cities are different from countries, in size as well as in their economic and socio-political importance to their country and the international community. They are simpler, smaller and easier to think of as a single entity. When considering cities, people often think of quite practical issues that may affect their living there, including transportation, traffic, air pollution, clean city environment, climate, cost of living, shopping, efficiency of public services, cultural and leisure activities, monuments and sight-seeing attractions, sports facilities, criminality and many other criteria (Anholt, 2007a: 59). Thus a specific City Brand Index (CBI) similarly consists of six components – presence, place, potential, pulse, people and prerequisites.[12]

Nation-branding and the Olympic Games

Modern Olympic Games have an unprecedented capacity to attract people. They are connected with multiple connotations, but primarily they represent hope (of a peaceful, better world, promoting fair competition in sport) and prosperity (in the sense of economic, social and political development). They are events with deep roots in the past, that provide values, ideals, pedagogical premises and ethical codes (Guttmann, 2002: 1–5). As leading sports marketer John Davis points out:

> The Olympic Games have succeeded in capturing the popular imagination around the world, and this broad-based appeal is attractive to companies for obvious commercial reasons.
>
> (Davis, 2008: 6)

Undoubtedly the power of sport affects the consumption patterns of audiences at the national, regional and sometimes global levels.[13] TV viewing figures demonstrate the importance of the Olympics to media and advertising companies. The worldwide Olympic television audience is constantly increasing,[14] and during the Beijing Games reached a peak of 4.7 billion viewers, or 70% of the world's population, who watched highlights of the Olympics (not less than six minutes) (Nielsen, 2008).[15]

So it seems that the Olympics represents the perfect platform for nation and product advertising that stands for friendship, cosmopolitanism, global connectivity, fair play and joy in effort, and at the same time for local differentiation, excellence, excitement, broad-based consumer awareness, innovation and many other values and virtues (Maguire *et al.*, 2008: 2050–52). This development has changed the organization, scope and size of the Olympics, particularly since the 1984 Los Angeles Games, when the commercial potential of the Olympic Games was first identified. These Games were the first to record a profit, and sparked a new relationship between the IOC and international corporate sponsors (Tomlinson, 1996: 585, 590–93; 2004: 160; 2005: 183–86; Lenskyj, 2000: 96–97; Guttmann, 2002: 175; Preuss, 2004: 16).[16] Since then, commercialization, commodification and gigantism have become the striking characteristics dominating the organization of recent Olympic Games.

It is widely acknowledged that the Olympic brand is one of the most globally recognized because it manages to present a fresh face with specific national characteristics in each new edition. It sells itself as the most prominent, recurrent global event of our time (Tomlinson, 2004: 147). The protection of the Olympic Games franchise is therefore rigorous, and use of the symbols, emblem, name, mascots, etc. registered to it is closely guarded and legally defended (Payne, 2005; IOC, 2009).

As Tomlinson outlines, there were entrepreneurs within the IOC who recognized the commercial potential of the Games and, with the help of Horst Dassler (the owner of Adidas), in the early 1980s set up the International Sports Leisure (ISL) marketing company. A partnership between ISL and IOC was established, aiming to create a worldwide marketing strategy for promoting the Olympics (Payne, 2005: 21–22; Tomlinson, 2005: 181). From the early 1980s up to the IOC Congress in Copenhagen in 2009, where the new elaborated marketing priorities for the upcoming digital revolution were presented, the marketing landscape changed considerably. Many new marketing partners have entered the stage (Payne, 2005; Maguire *et al.*, 2008; Sorrell, 2010: 186–90) and planning for the future is oriented solely towards improving marketing opportunities deriving from the use of the new digital technologies. The discourse about Olympic ideals, values, symbols, etc. has become increasingly protective of its brand[17] and demonstrates, in an unmistakable way, that the Olympic product is extremely stable and can be merchandised in various forms and packages.

The 1960 Rome Olympic Games: launch of brand nation

Parallel to the athletic competition, the notion of spectacle in the modern Olympic Games has always played a major role. Rome, the Eternal City, with its ancient history and impressive monuments was, next to Athens, a perfect stage for the Games in the idealized vision of Pierre de Coubertin, who wanted to offer 'an international homage to Roman antiquity'. He expressed his wish in the IOC meeting in London in 1904 that the next Olympic Games of 1908 should be celebrated in Rome, a city with strong symbolic importance for the event:

> I desire Rome only because I wanted Olympism, after its return from the excursion to utilitarian America, to don once again the sumptuous toga, woven of art and philosophy, in which I had always wanted to clothe her.
>
> (Guttmann, 2002: 28)

Those Games never took place in Rome because they were declined due to political disagreements and a natural catastrophe (the eruption of Mount Vesuvius), and the honour passed to London. Rome finally got its chance to host the Olympic Games fifty-four years later, in 1960. In these Games, which took place from 25 August to 11 September, 5338 athletes (611 women) from eighty-three countries participated in seventeen sports and 150 different events (IOC, 2010b).

Italy, at the time of winning the bid to host the Games, experienced a period of rapid development and prosperity. It re-entered the international diplomatic arena and tried to play a major role as an important partner in international affairs (membership of the United Nations, a leading role in developing the constitution of the European Economic Community, etc.), and experienced economic growth, instigated regeneration projects and increased social mobility. Italian politicians and elites wanted to demonstrate these changes, and the progress made within Italian society, to the international community to counter the negative perceptions of Italy following the Second World War (see Chapter 5 in this volume). Staging the Olympics offered a significant opportunity to achieve this goal.

The 1960 Games saw a close relationship between sport and culture in a city with a rich historical past. The Italians made the most of their ancient history, and the eternal city was a mix of the past and present for the athletes. The wrestling events were held in the Maxentius basilica, a full 2000 years after similar competitions took place there. The marathon start line was at the Capitol and ended at the famous Via Apia, near the Constantine triumphal arch, while the gymnastics events were held in the Caracalla thermal baths. Additionally, new venues including the Olympic Stadium and the Sport Palace were constructed.

The promotional strategy for the Games included a Roman makeover of the emblems; the torch and official poster were adorned with Roman motifs and symbols. The decision to use a nationalistically loaded aesthetic and symbolic narrative presenting the Italian nation was the forerunner to the later, more advanced, strategies for nation-branding.

However, connecting the Games to Roman antiquity and history and providing a sense of provenance and authenticity would not guarantee success unless accompanied by worldwide promotion through the media. This requirement was met as the 1960 Games were the first Olympics to be fully covered by television, including live broadcasts.[18] Italian television company RAI broadcast live to eighteen European countries.[19] From then on, the Olympics were gradually transformed into a truly global event.[20] The USA, Canada and Japan could follow the competitions, with a few hours' delay, through taped footage that was flown to New York and Tokyo at the end of each day. The Olympic content was broadcast in the USA on the CBS television network, which paid $394,000 for the first broadcasting rights fees (Horne and Manzenreiter, 2006: 4; Moreland 2006).[21]

In total, 93 hours 40 minutes of Olympic coverage was recorded. This was divided into three daily programmes. The Italian National Film Institute (*Istituto Luce*) produced a documentary film from the recorded material showing highlights from the Games, including epic commentaries of the athletes and beautiful images of the host city. The *cinecitta* film industry complemented the Olympic media promotional project by producing films dealing with issues inspired by Greek and Roman history and mythology. These films had international appeal and were produced between the early 1950s and the end of the 1960s.[22] The stories, characterized as the 'sword-and-sandal' genre, served as a popular culture teaser to stimulate people's interest in antiquity and the historical connections with the ancient Olympic Games. This kind of synergy between the media and entertainment industry was not new, but it was systematically utilized in the case of Rome 1960 to draw attention not only to the event, but also to the city/country that was staging it.

Awe-inspiring promotional campaigns may guide the international media, creating the desired worldwide impression and providing a positive national image to the public. However, sometimes individual achievement can surpass all pre-planned campaigns and the best advertising messages to put their mark on an event. This happened in Rome with the unexpected victory of barefooted Ethiopian athlete, Abebe Bikila, who won the marathon, becoming the first athlete from an African country to win a gold medal (see Chapter 5). The moment of his groundbreaking victory bears the true essence of drama, spectacle and myth (MacAloon, 1984) and, even to this day, provides one of the most striking moments in Olympic Games history. This unexpected incident gave added allure to the Games, helping the organizers to present a successful, modern, fun-filled, spectacular, well designed and carried out event that strengthened the brand 'made in Italy'.

Following the 1960 Games, Italy became one of a handful of 'megabrand countries' (Anholt, 2010: 29) whose public image remains powerful and all pervasive. Italy is currently globally recognized for food, fashion, lifestyle and sexiness (Anholt, 2007a: 98; 2010: 29). These rather superficial attitudes are backed up with strong cultural connotations of past and present (the Roman Empire; the Renaissance, including da Vinci, Michelangelo, Dante and Galileo; opera, including Verdi and, more recently, Pavarotti; cinema, including Sophia Loren and Benini). Italy seems to have successfully applied the rules for promoting a nation at an early stage and, since then, has implemented them consistently.

In the case of the 1960 Rome Olympics, nationalism, links to antiquity, modern heritage and heroic human stories provided the essence for the promotion of a nation-state emerging from a painful past. Italy succeeded in producing a fresh, regenerated image of a nation capable of playing a major role in European and international affairs. The Olympics promoted that image, giving Italy broad visibility and recognition. The Games marked the beginning of the promotion of nations through a strategy of combining popular cultural events with international media campaigns.

The Olympic Games of Athens 2004: an adventurous nation-branding affair

Forty-four years after the 1960 Games in Rome, the size, scope, organization and popularity of the Olympic Games has changed so much that a rough comparison with the respective statistics for the 2004 Athens Games indicates that almost all figures concerning participation have doubled.[23]

The ancient history of Rome served as a suitable ideological and aesthetic frame to promote the continuity and authenticity of the Olympics. The election of Athens as the host city for the 2004 Games aimed to revive a similar link between past and present, with Greece's historical connections to Olympia. As in Rome, Athens decided to stage some competitions in Olympic-related monuments/sites to increase the global impression and nation-branding effects. The shot put took place in the original stadium of Ancient Olympia nearly 3000 years after the first ancient Olympic Games. The archery competition was held, and the women's marathon finished, in the marble stadium where the first modern Olympics in 1896 were celebrated. These events not only demonstrated the historical continuity of the event, but provided a strong sense of affiliation for the organizers and generated deep emotions in spectators and television viewers.

The emphasis on the history of the event and the narrative of the antiquity (Panagiotopoulou, 2003) should help the Olympic movement to recover from scandals relating to the intensive commercialization and gigantism of the Games by emphasizing their ancient values and ideals (Lenskyj, 2000: 21–39; Burbank *et al.*, 2001: 2–4; Guttmann, 2002: 176–77; Payne, 2005: 258). After the over-commercialization of the 1996 Atlanta Games, the IOC was eager to convince the world that the Olympic ideal had not been sold to commercial interests. Athens seemed to be the perfect choice to rejuvenate the tired Olympic narrative, although it proved to be a considerable risk to trust the organization of such a complex and costly project to a small, and not very wealthy, country. Payne observed:

> At the Athens 2004 Olympics, the world experienced one of the greatest and most symbolic Olympic Games ever.
>
> (Payne, 2005: 256)

When Greece won the bid to host the Olympics in 1997, it had put forward some broader socio-political goals. The political and economic leadership of the country presented the Olympic Games as a major opportunity for the country to overcome the confines of its geographical restrictions and become well known worldwide, and to participate in international decisions – at least with regard to the Balkans and the Middle East – as a new and upcoming power. The Games were also seen as an opportunity for Greece to upgrade its role within the framework of an enlarged EU, and to attract international investments in fields as yet undeveloped (Panagiotopoulou, 2009a: 146).

Domestically, the Olympic Games offered an opportunity to improve commercial and tourist infrastructure by upgrading many services and facilities, including transportation, the port of Piraeus, the public roads network and wastewater management. Aesthetic improvement projects were also undertaken, such as the beautification of many public buildings and the renovation of museums (Gold, 2007: 275–78; Panagiotopoulou, 2009a: 149). A unique element in the organization of the Athens Olympics was the impact the Games had on the image of the city/ country and how they achieved, admittedly on a temporary basis, the broad support of the people. Few Olympic cities changed as much as Athens did due to the public works that took place, or were fast-tracked, to meet the upcoming event. Following the Games, the city's infrastructure has improved considerably and this has helped to decisively rebrand Greece as a country (Payne, 2005: 271).[24]

The return of the Olympics to their birthplace, to see the Games in their 'original light', meant a lot not only to the Greek people, but also to the Olympic brand. Provenance, authenticity and historical background had always formed an important tool for marketing in general and especially for the Olympic brand (Davis, 2008: 15). It was necessary that this strong marketing message was believed by IOC officials, international and national sponsors (who were reluctant to support the Games), and the media (who saw every action by the Athens Organizing Committee (ATHOC) for the Olympic Games as a potential failure). The 2004 Athens preparations were among the most scrutinized of any Olympics, with a relentless barrage of international media criticism (Payne, 2005: 263). The criticism was based primarily on two main issues: first, security and the measures planned for its implementation by Greece in order to deal with possible terrorist actions; second, delays in the completion of many building projects related to the organization of the Games. Press reports repeatedly questioned whether Athens would finally be ready to host the Games. However, it should be acknowledged that the organizers kept the public guessing until the final moments as to whether the venues would be ready on time (Payne, 2005: 264, 269; Gold, 2007: 279; Davis, 2008: 87; Panagiotopoulou, 2009a: 158; 2009b: 51–52).

The ongoing negative reports provided an important barometer of the host city's image and the Olympic Games brand. By and large, both ATHOC and the Greek government did not manage to come up with an effective communication strategy that would help to overcome the overall negative atmosphere. The same can be said for the IOC, which on some occasions, instead of backing ATHOC, expressed concerns about the progress of the Games' preparation (Payne, 2005: 264). The communication strategy, especially the part dealing with the international media, was not very successful for the nation's image improvement. In contrast, the marketing campaign concerning sponsorship and protection of the brand from ambush marketing proved to be very successful (Payne, 2005: 265).

The torch relay was a pivotal moment in nation-branding that helped, at the most critical point, to switch a negative international stance towards Greece to a positive one. Greek officials had originally organized the shortest torch relay ever (from Olympia to Athens) but decided to expand it to the longest ever.[25] This idea gave important impetus to the promotion of the nation-brand. It provided the media with a perfect platform to start a delayed countdown to the upcoming Olympics, which was loaded with emotions, expectations, tradition, beautiful images of cities, and people participating all over the world.

At the time of the bid, Greece did not have a particularly positive international image (Panagiotopoulou, 2009a: 149; 2009b: 50–52).[26] International awareness and the reputation of Greece is associated with the systematic promotion of various tourism destinations and historically/culturally significant sites. Nation-branding attempts before the Olympics were aimed at attracting tourism and reinforcing Greece's position as a major tourism destination. This narrowly focused campaign did not address the need to present a modern, ambitious society willing to play a more decisive international role in south-east Europe and eager to convince the international public that, alongside the beautiful landscapes and historical sites, a modern, dynamic society was emerging.[27] Comments by the chief marketing official of the IOC, Michael Payne, confirm the change of focus in ATHOC's nation-branding strategy as the Games took place:

> The images and media reports from the Games transmitted around the world helped to re-brand Greece as a country. The world ended up discovering a new Greece – mythological and traditional images combined with modern, dynamic design.
>
> (Payne, 2005: 271)

The staging of the Olympics benefited the small country as a whole, not just the city of Athens. According to the Anholt NBI of 2007, Greece was ranked in seventeenth place (Anholt, 2007b: 6). While this ranking cannot be seen as a direct result of hosting the Olympic Games,[28] some characteristics of brand Greece can be identified. The major advantages of the country lay in its tourism and its leading position among European nations in culture and heritage (classical and con-temporary). However, Greece received a low ranking in exports (the lowest of the Eurozone member states), investments and immigration, and governance. Summing up, Greece still has a lot to do to improve its international reputation; the Olympics were a key moment in attracting the world's attention, but this did not last for long. Anholt's commentary on the impact of staging the Olympics for Athens indicates:

> [. . .] as Athens discovered rather too late after hosting the Olympics – probably the biggest PR opportunity that Greece had enjoyed since the sacking of Troy – the event itself doesn't automatically do anything for the country's brand. It's a media opportunity, not a branding activity in its own right, and the most important thing for countries as they prepare for such events is to know precisely what they are going to say and prove about themselves while the show is in the town and the global media spotlight is switched on.
>
> (Anholt, 2007a: 110)

The main weakness of the Greek promotional campaign was the lack of a strategic nation-branding promotional plan that would remain in place following the Olympics. This deficit was due to lack of experience in managing such a large project as the Olympic Games, restricted financial resources, and, primarily, to the internal fighting and bickering among Greek political parties, politicians, bureaucrats and ATHOC. The result was that ATHOC followed its own plan to brand the Olympics and the Athens Games, and the Ministry of Tourism organized a separate campaign to boost tourism (Singh and Hu, 2008). These conditions severely restricted the opportunity the Olympics provided to exploit the benefits of being at the centre of the world's attention and thus to adequately promote the nation.

Ultimately, Greece kept its promises to the Olympic movement, delivering a very successful Games[29] and adding its own magic to the event by linking the Olympics to its original creators. Athens looked better than perhaps at any time in its recent history, offering a truly festive atmosphere. For the international com-munity, the choice of Athens presented an unquestionably symbolic dimension and a forceful cultural message. For the local community, the Games delivered un-forgettable moments of national pride and celebration while serving to build the confidence of a new generation of Greeks.

Conclusion

The Olympic Games constitute one of the biggest mediated phenomena and are an expression of the popular culture of our time. Therefore they are an important element in the development of global culture. Their popularity makes them an emblematic cultural event for modernization in which all countries want to be present and visible. Host cities/countries compete to gain the right to host the event, aiming to improve their global image and to increase their international visibility.

The same applies to sponsors, the diverse media enterprises, athletes, sports federations, etc. All of them seek to increase visibility and reputation, which, in turn, increases their income and power. In this interplay, the media play an essential role in presenting and representing the nation and the Games actors.

In the global era, nation and nationalism coexist and by no means exclude each other. This relationship proves particularly useful for the mediation and promotion of any kind of ideas and products, even nations. The global–national nexus becomes a constitutional part of many global events, and in this framework specific national characteristics or historical periods are showcased in an idealized, banalized way. However, this relationship is constantly challenged in times of alleged globalization. Place-branding emerged from the needs of countries to become visible and to compete at the international level. This form of promotion primarily addresses the global market and indicates that nation-states increasingly act like commercial enterprises. The Olympic Games provide an ideal platform for nation promotion because the brand of a city/country can be directly connected to the strong brand of the Olympics.

The strategies and practices for promoting a nation through the Olympics were demonstrated by examining two Olympic Games which took place nearly fifty years apart. Despite the time difference, the 1960 Rome and the 2004 Athens Olympics have many common characteristics. Both cities based their promotion campaign on their specific relationship to the ancient history of the Games, to tradition, heritage and targeted ideals, using historical sites to stage some of the competitions. Both countries at bid time were in a period of socio-political upgrading, and national elites wanted to use the popularity and publicity of the Olympics to increase their international position and launch a new, positive national image. They understood the importance of the media and tried to exploit them as effectively as possible, with distinctive results.

However, there were also substantial differences. First of all, the size and complexity of the organization of the Olympics has risen considerably, and international interest in following the preparation, staging and post-Olympic use of the infrastructure has increased. These factors ensure that hosting the Games is a volatile and unpredictable undertaking.

Rome, in the early stages of nation promotion, made systematic efforts to promote the promising sides of the city/country. It finally succeeded in establishing a strong brand, 'Made in Italy', synonymous with style, fashion, gastronomy, etc. The Olympics provided the starting point for an ongoing, systematically planned, national promotion campaign. The pivotal role of the media was recognized very early on, and the Organizing Committee of Rome oversaw the creation of a live transmission network for television for the first time in history, gaining the approval of all media. In other words, they succeeded in delivering a well organized promotion of the nation long before the globalization era and ensured that all kinds of interrelationships began.

Athens, in contrast, began the organization of the Games in a phase of mature globalized relationships and at an early stage of nation-branding as a recognized marketing approach. Greece had long experience in destination branding, implemented mainly in the tourism sector. However, the country had no experience in organizing complex projects like the Olympics, had restricted financial resources, and could not manage to overcome internal political dissent. These deficits were quite obvious from the beginning of the preparation period and led to continuous critical reporting throughout the media. Athens received more negative media coverage than any other host city.

ATHOC and the Greek government followed different paths for promoting the nation, with an unsurprisingly reduced outcome. Neither party developed a well thought out, long-term, strategic plan with clear goals. Under these conditions, the staging of the Olympics provided only limited opportunities for successful nation-branding. The entire world recognized the great effort of a small country to stage the Games, but after two or three years the post-Olympic effect has vanished. Additionally, later negative developments (the December 2008 riots and the 2009–10 economic crisis) have turned the faintly positive image of the country into a rather negative one.

It is true that the Olympic Games have the power to shape the international image of a nation for a short period. However, the decisive elements in creating and maintaining such an image are based more on the socio-political conditions, the vision of the local elite and the state of the economy, and less on the Olympic 'impressions', which are merely temporary. The question of whether nation-branding in the era of globalization offers an effective marketing tool to enhance a country's international reputation remains open. However, one question can be answered for sure: the Olympic ideals, values and educational/pedagogical notion, as declared by de Coubertin and once accepted as the 'universal vision', have gone for good, leaving the stadiums empty of meaning but full of consumerism and commodification. The new era of digital technology is only enhancing such developments.

Notes

1 In the Athens 2004 Olympics, 10,500 athletes participated and 21,500 journalists (twice as many as the athletes) worked, broadcasting the event in the press, radio and 300 television stations worldwide. In total 35,000 hours of programming were transmitted (Exarchos, 2006). These figures were exceeded at the Beijing 2008 Olympics, where 10,942 athletes took part and the media coverage was undertaken by 24,562 journalists (IOC, Beijing 2008, www.olympic.org/en/content/Olympic-Games/All-Past-Olympic-Games/Summer/Beijing-2008). 61,700 hours of dedicated broadcasting programme was transmitted (IOC Marketing Report, Beijing 2008, 24: http://view.digipage.net/?userpath=00000001/00000004/00040592).
2 In the globalized discourse about a nation, we encounter a set of stories, images, landscapes, historical events, national symbols and rituals that stand for the shared experiences that give meaning to a nation (Hall, 1992: 293). This discourse is used mainly by the media, but also by other agencies such as museums, exhibitions, tourism pamphlets, travel advertisements, etc.
3 The classical example of a culture constructing an identity that is based on the past using myths veiled in history is nationalism. Oblivion, or even forgery, of history constitutes a decisive factor in the constitution of a nation (Hobsbawm, 1998: 324–25). The recognized historiographers of a nation usually carefully select, shape, reshape or even

falsify decisive 'events' in order to construct the 'narrative of the nation' (Hall, 1992: 293).

4   The turbulent French history of the eighteenth and nineteenth centuries is often demonstrated as an example of place branding. From the French Revolution of 1789 to Napoleon's Empire; from the restored Bourbons, the Second Republic and the Second Napoleonic Empire to the adventures of the Third Republic and its efforts to establish democratic government and basic human rights, there have been continuous efforts to develop a self-conscious, homogeneous society and to gain public acceptance and international respect (Olins, 2010: 19–21). It has long been stated that 'as nations emerge they create self-sustaining myths to build coherent identities. When political upheavals take place [. . .] the nation reinvents itself' (Olins, 2010: 22; see also Anholt, 2003a: 213).

5   Public diplomacy (or soft power) includes government-sponsored cultural, educational and information programmes, citizen exchanges, and broadcasts used to promote the national interests of a country through understanding, informing and influencing foreign audiences. Many scholars distinguish public diplomacy from propaganda based on the premise that propaganda is by definition deceptive and manipulative. Advocates of public diplomacy insist that creating a bond of trust between governments and foreign nations is critical, and is best achieved through honest and open communication about a country's foreign policy goals.

6   'It could very well be an asset to public diplomacy' (Bolin and Stahlberg, 2010: 82).

7   Dinnie defined nation branding as 'the unique, multi-dimensional blend of elements that provide the nation with culturally grounded differentiation and relevance for all of its target audience' (Dinnie, 2008: 15).

8   While many marketers believe that branding a nation is not exactly the same as branding a company or a product, they agree that many of the branding techniques are similar, because people working in a company, consuming products, or living in a country can be motivated, inspired and manipulated in the same way (Olins, 2010: 24). Anholt (2010: 28) points out that the idea that countries behave like brands has become more and more familiar to many marketers, economists and politicians. It helps to answer the question as to how countries can position themselves in the global marketplace to gain competitiveness, reputation and, ultimately, wealth.

9   Concerning the volatile relationship between nationalism and nation branding, Bolin and Stahlberg (2010: 96) point out that '[nation-states. . .] what they are marketing is the access to a consumption force to be exploited by foreign capital. Nation branding, then, relates to nationalism similarly to how branding does to advertising.'

10   The term 'competitive identity' stands as a key concept in defining national reputation. According to Anholt (2007a: 26), 'The basic theory behind competitive identity is that when governments have a good, clear, believable and positive idea of what their country really is, what it stands for and where it's going, and manage to coordinate the actions, investments, policies and communications of all six points of the hexagon [of the Nation Brands Index] so that they prove and reinforce this idea, then they stand a good chance of building and maintaining a competitive national identity both internally and externally – to the lasting benefit of exporters, importers, government, the cultural sector, tourism, immigration and pretty much every aspect of international relations.' This definition is rather instrumental and does not try to capture the phenomenon in its initial causal relationships; additionally, it stresses the benefits for the market, not the community.

11   These areas are: tourism (first-hand experience of visitors), exports (provenance of various types of merchandise, quality judgment), governance (policy decisions), investment and immigration (favorable business environment, recruitment of foreign talents and companies), culture and heritage (desire to consume foreign cultural products) and people (friendliness, behavior to foreign people, celebrities, etc.) (Anholt, 2003b: 333–35, 2007a: 25–26, 2007b, 2–3). The NBI is a ranking of the world's nation brands based on a worldwide panel of 25,000 people and including thirty-five countries, which

pay to be included in the measurement. Some nations hosting international events are occasionally included in the NBI as guests.

12 The city-brand hexagon includes the following components: the presence (city's international status and standing); the place (physical aspects, climate, environment); the potential (economic and educational opportunities, job offers); the pulse (vibrant urban lifestyle, excitement); the people (inhabitants' behavior towards foreigners); and the prerequisites (perception of the city's qualities, possibility to live there) (Anholt, 2007a: 59–60).

13 At the recent XII Olympic Congress of the IOC in Copenhagen in October 2009, the keynote speaker for the section Digital Revolution was not an athlete or an academic, but a well known chief executive manager of the WPP Group Plc and marketing consultant to the IOC, Sir Martin Sorrell, who said 'Brands that have sponsored sporting events have benefited from their popularity. [. . .] This is because consumers who are sport fans have a much stronger attachment to the brand when compared with consumers who are not sports fans. The power of sport to generate value for brands remains a significant opportunity' (Sorrell, 2010: 186).

14 TV viewing figures for recent Olympic Games: Atlanta 1996, 3.2 billion viewers; Sydney 2000, 3.6 billion; Athens 2004, 3.9 billion; Beijing 2008, 4.7 billion. The huge increase in viewership of the most recent Olympics was due to the increased interest of the Chinese population and to the US viewers (211 million) (Seidman, 2008).

15 The Beijing 2008 Games were the first Games with a fully digital coverage. Internet and mobile telephony use increased rapidly, and it is estimated that this trend is only in its infancy. Recent data concerning the development of broadband technologies and their connection to the Olympic Games demonstrate that at the end of 2008, the worldwide broadband penetration average was at 24% (in the USA the respective percentage was 73%), with 1.6 billion people online and about 4 billion mobile phone users (Sorrell, 2010: 187). New digital devices (3G mobile phones, wireless internet, etc.) allow sports fans to follow and interact with their favorite sport, friends, family, etc. Consumers have many ways to consume sports and Olympic content, and the way people interact with this content is changing rapidly. Consequently, the media content produced for these purposes is constantly increasing and becomes more and more diversified and specialized. In research conducted by NBC, the average amount of time internet and television viewers spent watching the Olympics was roughly double the amount of time television-only viewers spent on this event (about 6 hours 57 minutes for internet and TV viewers, compared with 3 hours 26 minutes for TV-only viewers) (Carrion, 2010: 191; Sorrell, 2010: 188). Given the rapid development of new media technologies and their relationship with sports and the Olympics, we can conclude that 'the more options we are offered, the more we will consume' (Carrion, 2010: 191).

16 Tomlinson (2004: 148) remarks sharply that 'The LA Olympics not only symbolized the survival of a shaky antiquated-sounding ideal, but also shook and stirred that ideal into a new shape, and international sporting events of this profile were never to be quite the same again. It could be seen as the pivotal moment when the Olympics were steered down a path towards their Disneyfication.'

17 The following excerpt of the *Final Report of the IOC Coordination Commission, Games of the XXIX Olympiad, Beijing 2008* (IOC, 2010a: 32), under the subtitle *Protecting and Promoting the Olympic Brand*, is characteristic of the prevailing discussion: 'With Beijing 2008, our brand was given an even stronger universal and inspiring dimension – touching the lives of millions of people across the globe. [. . .] However, many groups tried to use the Games' unparalleled platform to promote their own causes. Let's be realistic: this will always be the case! As a result, our brand can sometimes be tainted by wrongly targeted campaigns or demonstrations. Nonetheless, surveys show that, thanks to our brand's strength and resilience, it was able, ultimately, to emerge from these Games stronger than ever. [. . .] The Olympic brand is obviously heavily reliant on image and values. As a result, its flagship product – the Olympic Games – despite

its strength can nevertheless become vulnerable. We must be aware of that reality and the risks that result from permanent exposure. Our challenge flows from the fact that we license the use of our brand to a vast number of stakeholders, including our organising committee partners. The IOC therefore needs to more carefully manage, coordinate and control all uses of the Olympic brand, image and values.'

18 The very first international television transmission occurred in the 1956 Winter Games in Cortina d'Ampezzo in Italy. The broadcasting signal reached eight European countries (Billings, 2008: 1). RAI took the first step in linking the various broadcasters on an international level, and at Rome 1960 they developed the experience in a technologically more complex environment and organized for the first time what, after some years, became the Olympic broadcasting system. For a detailed description of the organization of radio and television live transmission and the technical and organizational difficulties encountered see: www.la84foundation.org/6oic/OfficialReports/1960/OR1960v1.pdf

19 Twenty-one countries in total were linked to television coverage of the Games: fourteen countries in Eurovision (Austria, Belgium, Denmark, Finland, France, West Germany, Great Britain, the Netherlands, Italy, Luxembourg, Norway, Sweden, Switzerland and Yugoslavia); four Intervision (Czechoslovakia, East Germany, Hungary and Poland); the United States and Canada through the medium of the CBS organization; and Japan through NHK. For a detailed description of the organization of radio and television live transmission see: IOC, Official Report of the Organizing Committee for the Games of the XVII Olympiad Rome 1960 (Volume 1), www.la84foundation.org/6oic/Official Reports/1960/OR1960v1.pdf

20 Since the very beginning of broadcasting, sports had been an integral part of television programming. Amateur and professional sport competitions were frequently shown on television, attracting an increasing – mostly male – audience. The Rome 1960 Games is one of the key milestones in the globalization and commercialization of the modern Olympic Games. See also Encyclopedia Britannica, Rome, Italy, 1960 www.britannica.com/EBchecked/topic/428005/Olympic-Games/59615/Rome-Italy-1960? anchor=ref364543

21 This huge operation is presented in detail in the Official Report on the XVII Olympiad of Rome 1960 (IOC, www.la84foundation.org/6oic/Official Reports/1960/OR1960 v1.pdf). The entire revenue for the IOC that derived from broadcasting fees for these Games was $1,200,000 (Olympic Broadcasting Services, Beijing Olympic Broadcasting (2008), www.obs.es/beijingolympicbroadcasting2008.html).

22 Some selected examples of this genre production having direct connection with Greek and Roman antiquity are: *The Sins of Rome* a.k.a. *Spartacus* (1952), *Ulysses* (1954), *Attila* (1954), *Hercules* (1958), *The Argonauts* (1958), *The Colossus of Rhodes* (1960), *Queen of the Amazons* (1960), *Siege of Syracuse* (1960), *The Minotaur* (1961), *Slave of Rome* (1961), *Perseus the Invincible* (1962), and many others.

23 At the 2004 Athens Olympics, 10,625 athletes (4329 of whom were women) took part; women's participation rose from 11.4% in Rome to 40.7% in Athens; the countries from 83 to 201; the sports from 17 to 28; the events from 150 to 301. Additionally, 21,500 journalists were accredited for the Athens Games. See for Rome, IOC http://www.olympic.org/en/content/Olympic-Games/All-Past-Olympic-Games/Summer/Rome-1960 and for Athens, IOC http://www.olympic.org/en/content/Olympic-Games/All-Past-Olympic-Games/Summer/Athens-2004.

24 This is despite the fact their final cost is seen as very high, and for the economic capabilities of the country almost prohibitive. For more details see Apostolopoulou and Papadimitriou (2004: 182); Panagiotopoulou (2009a: 150–53).

25 The flame's international journey should cross five continents, last thirty-three days, and pass through twenty-six countries and thirty-three Olympic cities, and the torch should be carried by 3600 torchbearers. A total of 260 million people had the opportunity to see the torch relay (Jaquin, 2004: 7). Obviously, this was the primary incentive for the two sponsor companies Coca Cola and Samsung to undertake organization of the relay.

26 To a large extent, this remained the case throughout the entire preparation period up to one or two months prior to the beginning of the Games. The main negative aspects highlighted were: air pollution, chaotic traffic, garbage in the streets, the absence of a particular architectural and cultural urban character in the city, etc. Quite often, such stereotypical criticism was combined with strong prejudice which failed to recognize some gradual improvements in the city and was mostly related to tourist activity and the problems that tourists encountered in Greece.

27 These were the main findings of an international survey ordered by ATHOC and conducted by TNS ICAP in December 2003 in six countries (Japan, USA, United Kingdom, France, Germany and Spain) with thirty interviews of opinion leaders in each country (Fola, 2007: 197).

28 Greece was included in the NBI measurement of 2007 as a guest nation. Its placement in the NBI cannot be seen as influenced by the Olympics because there were no previous measurements.

29 For example, *The Times* titled its article just after the opening ceremony as 'From tragedy to triumph', (Barnes, 2004), and after the ending of the Olympics 'Shame on us for having little faith – Greeks pulled it off with style' (Slot, 2004). Another publication was an open letter from the president of the television network NBC, D. Ebersol (2004), to the Greeks, the Organizing Committee and the Government, 'NBC: sorry and congratulations'. The praise and the 'apologies to Greece' came too late to make up for the small numbers of foreign visitors to the Athens Games.

References

Anderson, B., (1983), *Imagined Communities*, London: Verso.

Anholt, S., (2003a), 'Branding places and nations', in R. Clifton and J. Simmons (eds), *Brands and Branding*, London: The Economist/Profile Books, 213–26.

——, (2003b), 'Editorial', *Place Branding*, 1 (4): 333–46.

——, (2007a), *Competitive Identity: The New Brand Management for Nations, Cities and Regions*, London: Palgrave Macmillan.

——, (2007b), *The Anholt Nation Branding Index – Special Report*, Q2 2007 Special Report, 1–7, www.simonanholt.com/Publications/publications-other-articles.aspx

——, (2010), 'Nation brands and the value of provenance', in N. Morgan, A. Pritchard and R. Pride (eds), *Destination Branding, Creating the Unique Destination Proposition*, 2nd revised edn, London: Butterworth-Heinemann, 26–39.

Apostolopoulou, A. and Papadimitriou, D., (2004), 'Welcome home: motivations and objectives of the 2004 Grand National Olympic sponsors', *Sport Marketing Quarterly*, 13 (4): 180–92.

Barnard, S., Butler, K., Golding, P. and Maguire, J., (2006), 'Making the news: the 2004 Athens Olympics and competing ideologies?', *Olympika*, 15 (1): 35–56.

Barnes, S., (2004), 'From tragedy to triumph', *The Times*, 14 August, www.timesonline.co.uk/tol/news/world/article469521.ece

Billings, A., (2008), *Olympic Media: Inside the Biggest Show on Television*, London: Routledge.

Bolin, G. and Stahlberg, P., (2010), 'Between community and commodity: nationalism and nation branding', in A. Roosvall and I. Salovaara-Moring (eds), *Communicating the Nation: National Topographies of Global Media landscapes*, Göteborg: Nordicom, 41–58.

Bourdieu, P., (1994), 'Les Jeux olympiques: programme pour une analyse', *Actes de la recherche en science socials*, 103: 102–3.

Burbank, M. J., Andranovich, G. D. and Heying, C. H., (2001), *Olympic Dreams. The Impact of Mega-Events on Local Politics*, London: Lynne Rienner.

Carrion, R., (2010), 'The impact of the digital revolution on the Olympic movement', in *IOC XII Olympic Congress Copenhagen 2009 Proceedings*, Lausanne: International Olympic Committee, 190–92.

Davis, J., (2008), *The Olympic Games Effect: How Sports Marketing Builds Strong Brands*, Singapore: John Wiley and Sons.

Dayan, D. and Katz, E., (1992), *Media Events: The Live Broadcasting of History*, Cambridge, MA: Harvard University Press.

Dinnie, K., (2008), *Nation Branding: Concepts, Issues, Practice*, London: Butterworth-Heinemann.

Ebersol, D., (2004), 'NBC: sorry and congratulations', *Naftemporiki*, October 9.

Exarchos, G., (2006), 'Olympic Games and television: the global image and the Greek heritage', in R. Pangiotopoulou (ed.), *Athens 2004 Post-Olympic Considerations*, Athens: Athens National Publishing House, 106–16.

Fola, M., (2007), 'The image of Greece in the international community: an analysis on the occasion of the Olympic Games in Athens', in Chr. Vernardakis (ed.), *Public Opinion in Greece 2005–2006*, Athens: Savalas Publishing, 197–223.

Georgiadis, K., (2004), 'The press and the promotion of the Olympic Games in the 19th century in Greece', *Zitimata Epikoinonias*, 1: 121–28.

Gold, M. M., (2007), 'Athens 2004', in J. R. Gold and M. M. Gold (eds), *Olympic Cities: City Agendas, Planning and the World's Games 1896–2012*, London: Routledge, 265–85.

Guttmann, A., (2002), *The Olympics: A History of Modern Games*, 2nd edn, Urbana: University of Illinois Press.

Hall, S., (1992), 'The question of cultural identity', in S. Hall, D. Held and T. McGrow (eds), *Modernity and its Future*, Cambridge: Polity, 273–326.

Hobsbawm, E., (1998), *On History*, Athens: Themelio.

Hobsbawm, E. and Ranger, T. (eds), (1983), *The Invention of Tradition*, Cambridge: Cambridge University Press.

Hogan, J., (2003), 'Staging the nation', *Journal of Sport and Social Issues*, 27 (2): 100–122.

Horne, J. and Manzenreiter, W., (2006). 'An introduction to the sociology of sports mega-events', in J. Horne and W. Manzenreiter (eds), *Sports Mega-events: Social Scientific Analyses of a Global Phenomenon*, Oxford: Blackwell, 1–24.

IOC, (2009), *Marketing Media Guide*, Beijing 2008, Lausanne: International Olympic Committee.

——, (2010a), *Final Report of the IOC Coordination Commission, Games of the XXIX Olympiad, Beijing 2008*, Lausanne: International Olympic Committee.

——, (2010b) 'Rome: 1960', www.olympic.org/rome-1960-summer-olympics

Jaquin, P., (2004), 'The Games', *DIFFUSION online*, 32, European Broadcasting Union, www.ebu.ch/en/union/diffusion_on_line/sport/tcm_6–13856.php

Knudsen, B. T., (2010), 'The nation as media event', in A. Roosvall and I. Salovaara-Moring (eds), *Communicating the Nation: National Topographies of Global Media Landscapes*, Göteborg: Nordicom, 41–58.

Lee, J. W. and Maguire, J., (2009), 'Global festivals through a national prism', *International Review for the Sociology of Sport*, 44 (5): 1–24.

Lenskyj, H. J., (2000), *Inside the Olympic Industry: Power, Politics and Activism*, Albany: SUNY Press.

MacAloon, J., (1984), 'Olympic Games and the theory of spectacle', in J. MacAloon (ed.), *Rite, Drama, Festival, Spectacle: Rehearsals Towards a Theory of Cultural Performance*, Philadelphia: Institute for the Study of Human Issues, 241–79.

Maguire, J., (1999), *Global Sport, Identities, Societies, Civilizations*, London: Polity.

Maguire, J., Barnard, S., Butler, K. and Golding, P., (2008), 'Olympic legacies in the IOC's "Celebrate Humanity" campaign: ancient or modern?', *International Journal of the History of Sport*, 25 (14): 2041–59.

Moreland, J., (2006), 'Olympics and Television', *The Museum of Broadcast Communications*, www.museum.tv/eotvsection.php?entrycode=olympicsand

Morgan, N., Pritchard, A. and Pride, R., (2010), 'Introduction', in N. Morgan, A. Pritchard and R. Pride (eds), *Destination Branding: Creating the Unique Destination Proposition*, 2nd revised edn, London: Butterworth-Heinemann, 3–16.

Nielsen, (2008), 'The final tally – 4.7 billion tune in to Beijing 2008 – more than two in three people worldwide', 5 September, www.nielsen.com/us/en/insights/press-room/2008/the_final_tally_-.html

Olins, W., (2010), 'Branding the nation: the historical context', in N. Morgan, A. Pritchard and R. Pride (eds), *Destination Branding: Creating the Unique Destination Proposition*, 2nd revised edn, London: Butterworth-Heinemann, 17–25.

Panagiotopoulou, R., (2003), 'Join us in welcoming them home: the impact of the ancient olympic games' legacy in the promotion campaign of the Athens 2004 Olympic Games', in M. de Moragas, Chr. Kennett and N. Puig (eds) *The Legacy of the Olympic Games*, International Symposium Lausanne 2002, Documents of the Museum, Lausanne: International Olympic Committee, 346–52.

——, (2009a), 'The 28th Olympic Games in Athens 2004', in G. Poynter and I. MacRury (eds), *Olympic Cities and the Remaking of London*, London: Ashgate, 145–62.

——, (2009b), 'The image of Athens and Greece in the international and Greek press during the preparation and staging of the Olympic Games Athens 2004', in *International Olympic Academy 11th International Seminar for Sports Journalists, Proceedings*, Athens: International Olympic Committee, 48–64.

——, (2010), 'Sports events: the Olympics in Greece', in N. Couldry, A. Hepp and F. Krotz (eds), *Media Events in a Global Age*, London: Routledge, 233–49.

Payne, M., (2005), *Olympic Turnaround: How the Olympic Games Stepped Back from the Brink of Extinction to Become the World's Best Known Brand*, www.michaelrpayne.com/downloadables/chapter1.pdf

Preuss, H., (2004), *The Economics of Staging the Olympics: A Comparison of the Games 1972–2008*, Cheltenham: Edward Elgar.

Real, M., (1998), 'MediaSport: Technology and the commodification of postmodern sport', in L.A. Wenner (ed.), *MediaSport*, London: Routledge, 14–26.

Roche, M., (2000), *Mega-Events and Modernity: Olympics and Expos in the Growth of Global Culture*, London: Routledge.

——, (2006), 'Mega-events and modernity revisited: globalization and the case of the Olympics', *Sociological Review*, 54 (2): 25–40.

Rogge, J., (2004), IOC President's speech at the closing ceremony of the Games of the XXVIII Olympiad, 30 August 2004 – press release, www.olympic.org/media?q=rogge+2004&chkcat=111&searchpageipp=10&searchpage=10&articlenewsgroup=-1&articleid=52375

Seidman, R., (2008), 'Beijing closing ceremonies have best U.S. ratings since 1976 Games in Montreal', 25 August, http://tvbythenumbers.com:80/2008/08/25/beijing-closing-ceremonies-have-best-us-ratings-since-1976-games-in-montreal/4771

Singh, N. and Hu, C., (2008), 'Understanding strategic alignment for destination marketing and the 2004 Athens Olympic Games: implications from extracted tacit knowledge', *Tourism Management*, 29 (5): 929–39.

Slot, O. (2004), 'Shame on us for having little faith – Greeks pulled it off with style', *The Times*, 31 August.

Sorrell, M., (2010), 'The impact of the digital revolution on the Olympic movement', in *IOC XII Olympic Congress Copenhagen 2009 Proceedings*, Lausanne: International Olympic Committee, 186–90.

Tomlinson, A., (1996), 'Olympic spectacle: opening ceremonies and some paradoxes of globalization', *Media, Culture and Society*, 18: 583–602.

——, (2004), 'The Disneyfication of the Olympics? Theme parks and freak-shows of the body', in J. Bale and M. K. Christensen (eds), *Post-Olympism? Questioning Sport in the Twenty-first Century*, Oxford: Berg, 147–63.

——, (2005), 'The commercialization of the Olympics: cities, corporations and the Olympic commodity', in K. Young and K. Wamsley (eds), *Global Olympics: Historical and Sociological Studies of the Modern Games*, Amsterdam: Elsevier, 179–200.

Tomlinson, A. and Young, C. (eds), (2006), *National Identity and Global Sports Events*, Albany, NY: SUNY Press.

Websites

Encyclopedia Britannica, Rome, Italy, 1960, www.britannica.com/EBchecked/topic/428005/Olympic-Games/59615/Rome-Italy-1960?anchor=ref364543

IOC, Athens 2004, www.olympic.org/en/content/Olympic-Games/All-Past-Olympic-Games/Summer/Athens-2004

IOC, Beijing 2008, www.olympic.org/en/content/Olympic-Games/All-Past-Olympic-Games/Summer/Beijing-2008

IOC, Final Report of the IOC Coordination Commission, Beijing 2008, www.olympic.org/Documents/Reports/EN/Br-Beijing-ENG-web.pdf

IOC, Marketing Report, Beijing 2008: http://view.digipage.net/?userpath=00000001/00000004/00040592

IOC, Official Report of the Organizing Committee for the Games of the XVII Olympiad Rome 1960 (Volume 1), www.la84foundation.org/6oic/OfficialReports/1960/OR1960v1.pdf

IOC, Rome 1960, www.olympic.org/en/content/Olympic-Games/All-Past-Olympic-Games/Summer/Rome-1960

Olympic Broadcasting Services, Beijing Olympic Broadcasting 2008, www.obs.es/beijingolympicbroadccasting2008.html

10 Regulatory regimes in European sport

Anthony King

Introduction: the end of disorganized capitalism

In their widely read histories of Europe, Mazower (2000) and Judt (2005) provide a broadly similar account of the basic contours of the post-war landscape. Decisively, the decades following the Second World War from 1945 to 1970 were unified by the advance of Keynesian welfarism in Europe. For Mazower and Judt, the post-war economic miracle was facilitated and, indeed, characterized by a strong system of state regulation; 'This "unexpectedly dazzling" revival of capitalism took place, of course, in a world where the extension of state power was accepted not only in the economic sphere itself, but also in the sphere of social welfare' (Mazower, 2000: 298). Indeed, while this 'Golden Age' (Mazower, 2000: 327) was most evident in western Europe, the fascist and communist regimes that dominated southern, central and eastern Europe might be seen as alternatively authoritarian versions of Keynesian regulation committed to state-management of the economy, full employment and the provision of at least a basic standard of living. Mazower himself notes the extent of industrial development in the Soviet Union in the 1950s (Mazower, 2000: 277). Both Mazower and Judt describe how this state-centric political order fragmented in the crisis of the 1970s to be replaced by neoliberal, increasingly globalized regimes from the early 1980s. Thatcher and Berlusconi were the most obvious proponents of the market, but Mitterand, Chirac, Kohl and Schroder all introduced important deregulatory legislation. The financial crisis of 2008–09 has been widely interpreted as the end of this free market period of globalized capitalism, with which Mazower and Judt conclude their studies. In 2010, it seems that Europeans now stand on another historic watershed when the neoliberal regime, dominant since the 1980s, is itself about to collapse.

The apparent end of neoliberalism has encouraged a renewed interest in the mid-twentieth-century system of economic regulation and Keynesianism, in particular. Suddenly, after almost three decades of disfavour, Keynesianism has once again become attractive to governments, commentators and bankers. As Joseph Stiglitz, Nobel Prize-winner and former chief economist for the World Bank, noted:

> We are all Keynesians now. Even the right in the United States has joined the Keynesian camp with unbridled enthusiasm and on a scale that at one time

would have been truly unimaginable. For those of us who claimed some connection to the Keynesian tradition, this is a moment of triumph, after having
been left in the wilderness, almost shunned, for more than three decades. At
one level, what is happening now is a triumph of reason and evidence over
ideology and interests.

(Stiglitz, 2008)

Governments have been compelled to intervene in the economy, and the quasi-
nationalization of prominent financial institutions has followed. Close state control
of national economies seems to be becoming the norm once again.

It is widely recognized by scholars that, historically, sport is typically closely
connected to the historical conditions in which it occurs. In particular, professional
sport is organized within, and influenced by, the regulatory regime of which it is
both a part and a manifestation. If the neoliberal regime which has been dominant
since the 1980s is collapsing, then it seems highly likely that sport is about to go
through a period of regulatory reformation, especially since it has become so
intertwined with global capital flows in the past twenty years as a result of its
increasing dependence on television and sponsorship. In February 2009, Michel
Platini drew a pessimistic parallel between football and the financial crisis,
predicting that if current economic practices were allowed to continue unchecked,
the game could collapse: 'European clubs are telling [UEFA] that our system is
in danger of financially imploding in the medium term' (Harris, 2009: 54). The
question that confronts scholars today is how will the credit crunch and the
apparent collapse of disorganized capitalism affect sport in Europe? In the preface
to the *Philosophy of Right*, Hegel famously maintained that the Owl of Minerva
flew only at dusk (Hegel, 1967: 13). It was impossible and inappropriate for
philosophy – or by extension the social sciences – to predict the future. Self-
conscious understanding necessarily followed the moment of particularistic
objectification; it could not precede it. However, although care needs to be taken,
it may be possible to sketch some of the critical contours that may define the
coming decades of sport in Europe.

This chapter does not attempt to provide a comprehensive guide to the future of
sport in Europe. It examines two sports (football and cricket) and a sporting 'mega-
event' (the Olympic Games) in order to map the historical trajectory of European
sport and to outline its likely future. Only football can genuinely be described as
European, since it is the prime sport in all major European countries. However,
although the Olympics have become an indisputably global movement, Europe has
historically dominated the Olympics in terms of administration and political
influence: of the seventeen Summer Games between the end of the Second World
War and 2012, eight will have taken place in Europe (if Moscow is included). The
Olympics, then, provides some useful insight into the development of European
sport. Cricket can by no means be described as a European sport. It is an English
game played, as a result of English influence, intermittently on the Atlantic rim of
Europe, in the Netherlands, Spain, Ireland and Portugal. Yet, as a rapidly globalizing
game in which England, as a populous part of a major European member state,

still plays a key role, cricket might illustrate the future of sport (albeit in this case a minority one) in Europe.

The regulation of sport in the twentieth century

Football

In his figurational analysis of global sport, Maguire drew on Robertson's (1992) work on globalization to claim that the development of sport can be usefully periodized. Specifically, Maguire proposes that the twentieth century can be divided into two main 'global sportization phases', the first running from the 1920s to the 1960s, and the second from the 1960s to the 1980s.[1] The first phase more or less coincided with the Fordist and Keynesian regime, which Mazower and Judt describe, and is characterized by heavy state involvement in the administration of sport. For Maguire, this dominance begins to fragment from the 1960s with the waning of Western control over global sports and an outright crisis of state hegemony in the 1970s (Maguire, 1999: 85–86). Maguire does not explicitly define a third phase of global sport in the twentieth century, but one is certainly implicit in his discussions of the 'global media–sports complex'. There he explores the new deregulated economic dynamics of the 1990s. Again referencing Robertson, he emphasizes the 'reassertion of local identities', the decline of the nation-state and the emergence of transnationalization (Maguire, 1999: 21–22).

Maguire's periodization of the twentieth century was intended to apply to sport in general, but the periods can be clearly seen in the development of European football. One of the principal aims of *The European Ritual* (King, 2003) was to elucidate the connections between the transformation of football and the wider trajectory of European integration. Accordingly, *The European Ritual* argued that the development of football in post-war Europe might be usefully understood in terms of three periods: 1955–70, 1970–86, and 1986 (and especially after 1990) to the early 2000s. In the first successful 'international' period, competition between European football clubs, organized by sovereign federations and coordinated by the Union of European Football Associations (UEFA), coincided with the success of the initial phase of European integration after the Treaty of Rome in 1957. In the 1970s, the early optimism of the international era collapsed in the face of a perceived decline in playing standards, corruption, foul play and hooliganism. Football suffered its own Eurosclerosis, a crisis which reached its nadir in 1985 with the deaths of thirty-nine Juventus fans at the European Cup Final in the Heysel Stadium in Brussels. In the 1990s, football underwent a revolution. The revenue from deregulated television, increased sponsorship, reformed competitions (above all, the Champions League) and, in 1995, the liberalization of the European player market with the Bosman ruling, introduced a new transnational geography in which economic and sporting power was concentrated in a small number of major city clubs in increasingly close cross-border communication – and competition – with each other. The emergence of a new hierarchy in football was most obviously demonstrated by the creation of the G14 in 1998 to challenge UEFA. In this new order, national leagues and national federations remained important, but their sovereignty had been compromised and subverted by the rise of a transnational network of concentrated super-clubs.

The European Ritual provided one description of this process, but scholars in the sociology of the sport noted the phenomenon much more widely. Manzenreiter and Horne's (2006) work on mega-sport events, itself referencing Maurice Roche's (2000) research, also provides a similar chronology highlighting the importance of deregulation to the globalization of sport in the 1990s. In his monograph on global football, Giulianotti (1999) understood the development of football in terms of 'traditional', 'modern' and 'postmodern' periods but, in his more recent work with Roland Robertson, Giulianotti has described the defining features of late twentieth- and early twenty-first-century football in a manner that accords closely with Maguire's and my own chronologies. Giulianotti and Robertson (2004) maintain that from the 1980s the deregulation of television and player contracts has transformed the institutional structure of football into a series of empowered localized nodes in a global network. Simultaneously, they note the transformation of fan identities as a result of these processes, whereby localized collective identities have begun to supersede national allegiances.

Most recently, Goldblatt has proposed a model manifestly similar to those already extant in the literature and especially *The European Ritual*. Goldblatt divides European football after the Second World War into three periods. Running from 1955 to 1974, he calls the first period 'the glamour and glory: high industrial football in Europe', referring to the fact that the sport was a manifestation of the post-war economic boom, regulated on a national basis and reflecting the new affluence and optimism of the time. This era was followed by 'the European crisis of 1974 to 1990', culminating in a final period of deregulated, media-dominated football, 'through the looking-glass', from 1990 to 2006. At that point, 'the unparalleled commercialization of European football in the closing decades of the twentieth century signalled the ideological and institutional victory of capitalism' (Goldblatt, 2007: 684). Goldblatt notes the revolutionary impact of new television revenue and the deregulation of the player market for European football: 'In the 1990s European football's long economic decline was spectacularly reversed; the ailing rustbelt of Fordist football was transformed into a booming post-industrial sector awash with money and hubris' (Goldblatt, 2007: 688). Significantly, Goldblatt identifies a dynamic of concentration to be central to European football since the 1990s, as money and playing power congregated in a small number of super-clubs: 'The degree of economic concentration in European football was extra-ordinary' (Goldblatt, 2007: 690).

There is general consensus, then. After the breakdown of stably regulated post-war football in the 1970s, the sport has been transformed into a post-Fordist, globalized ritual. This process has been characterized by the concentration of economic and playing power in a network of 'super-clubs' within Europe, which now compromise the authority and autonomy of national leagues, federations and UEFA. The credit crunch might signify the decline of this liberal transnational regime in which clubs have been increasingly dominant forces.

It seems likely that in the immediate future, another historic reform of European football is about to take place, which may be no less significant than the emergence of the deregulated regime out of the crisis of the 1970s. A new system of regulation may be appearing out of the kernel of the old order.

The Olympics

The Olympic Games follow a similar historical trajectory to that of European football. In his analysis of the summer games, Tomlinson (2005) proposes that Olympic history can be broadly classified into three periods: 1896–1928, 1932–84 and 1984–2000. In the first period, the Olympic Games were 'relatively low profile, politically and commercially' and were, before the First World War, typically appended to national exhibitions. For Tomlinson, in the 1930s and especially at the notorious Berlin Olympics (Guttmann, 2006), the Games started to be used for international power politics, which continued up to 1984. For instance, after the Second World War the Games were consistently compromised by Cold War politics as the Soviet Union and USA sought to gain political advantages. The selection of Mexico in 1968, for example, resulted substantially from the fact that Soviet members of the International Olympic Committee (IOC) would not vote for candidate cities from NATO countries (Brewster and Brewster, 2006: 105–5): 'In this explicitly nationalist second phase in the history of the Olympic Games, they prospered primarily on the basis of their usefulness as a vehicle for the articulation of political meanings and national rivalries' (Tomlinson, 2005: 56). Nevertheless, while Tomlinson's claim that all the Olympics from 1932 to 1984 represent a historical unity is plausible, he himself notes the growing crisis in the Olympic movement from 1968: 'the Olympic project veered from crisis to crisis in the crisis-ridden "M" years from 1968 to 1980, rocked by political protest (Mexico, 1968), terrorist incursions (Munich, 1972), unprecedented losses (Montreal, 1976) and major boycotts (Montreal, 1976, and Moscow, 1980)' (Tomlinson, 2005: 56).

Consequently, without significant conceptual violence, it might be possible to revise Tomlinson's periodization to align it with the history of football. While it is certainly true that the Olympic movement was small, exclusive and even arcane before the First World War and, perhaps, even into the 1920s, it was, even at that point, conceived and organized as an international event. For Baron de Coubertin, the Games idealized the muscular manliness he felt essential for national progress and survival in the competitive international system of the late nineteenth and early twentieth centuries (Mosse, 1985). The Games themselves were intended to provide a peaceful forum for international intercourse and competition. However, de Coubertin's concept of an international competition resonated with nationalist sentiments at the time and the Games became an appropriate forum for the expression of international rivalries, especially after the First World War. Therefore it may be possible to reconceive Olympic chronology. Instead of dividing the Olympics into two phases, initial and international, running from 1896 to 1928 and from 1932 to 1984, it might be more useful to understand the Olympics as having gone through an international phase from 1896 to 1972. This long period might be subdivided into separate early and mature international phases, pre- and post-1932. Throughout this long period, the Games were a venue for inter-state interaction, competition and consensus, and were administered on an international basis between states, their representatives, the National Olympic Committees and the IOC.

The crisis of the 'long decade' of the 1970s, running from 1968 to 1980 (Tomlinson's 'M' Olympics), might be viewed as a distinct era of dramatic transition, representing the collapse of the existing system of Olympic regulation. From the late 1960s, the international administrative structure, in which states played an almost exclusive role, began to be challenged by new political and economic currents. Misappropriation of the Games for political purposes was typical, as Guttmann has emphasized (2002: 1), but the actions of black athletes at Mexico and, especially, Black September's attack at Munich, were novel in that they were the first time sub-state actors had so demonstrably hijacked the event for political purposes. The states' international monopoly over the Games was being compromised. That monopoly was further eroded at Montreal, which accrued $1 billion of debt to bankrupt the city. States had always paid for the Olympic Games in the past, but the relatively small scale of the costs, the political benefits of staging the Games, and, in the 1950s and 1960s, sustained economic growth reduced the significance of that expenditure. Finally, in 1980, the tensions between the USA and the Soviet Union were so heightened as a result of the latter's invasion of Afghanistan that the USA withdrew from the Moscow Olympics altogether. The political and economic tensions of the 1970s undermined the viability and validity of the Olympics themselves as an international event. Indeed, at the closing ceremony of the Moscow Olympics, the IOC President Lord Killanin publicly admitted that the difficulties evident over the past three festivals jeopardized the future of the Olympic movement itself: 'I implore the sportsmen of the world to unite in peace before the holocaust descends' (Young, 2006: 112). Scholars have concurred: 'the terrorist massacre of the Israeli team at Munich in 1972 and the spiralling costs of staging the Montreal Games in 1976 had left the Olympics looking like a terminally tarnished product' (Tomlinson, 2006: 164). Although of a very different form from that of football, the Olympic Games went through its own crisis in the 'long' 1970s.

While the Soviet Union boycotted Los Angeles, these Olympics constituted an important transition point in the history of the Games. The influence of commercial forces had accelerated from the Winter Games in 1968 (Guttmann, 2002: 128) but 1984 marked the first genuinely commercial Games, which occupied 'a pivotal place in the history of modern sports events' (Tomlinson, 2006: 163). Frightened by the debts accrued by Montreal, the Los Angeles Olympic Organizing Committee established itself on a purely commercial footing and sought to exploit television and sponsoring rights, staging the Games without public financing. Decisively, Rule 4 of the Olympic Charter allowed for a non-state organization to administer the Games for the first time. ABC paid $225 million for the television rights, while thirty corporate sponsors invested a further $130 million. As a result, Los Angeles 1984 made a profit of over $200 million (Guttmann, 2002:163). These Games denoted a profound shift in the organization of the Olympics from a state-centric international regime to commercialized globalism. The entrepreneurialism of the Los Angeles Olympics was reflected in changes at the level of the IOC itself. The patriarchal presidency of Lord Killanin, which 'the Olympics was reputedly lucky to survive' (Guttmann, 2002: 171), was succeeded by that of Juan Antonio Samaranch, who commercialized the institution aggressively. Decisively, he formed an alliance with Adolf Dassler's International Sports, Cultural and Leisure Marketing (ISL) in 1985. As a result of his sports equipment company, Adidas, Dassler had been a key figure in the marketing of sport since the 1970s and, working closely with Samaranch, he developed a new strategy by which the IOC could exploit the television and sponsorship rights of the Games. The Olympic Games were transformed into a commercial venture. Of course, states still played an important role. For instance, London could not have won the 2012 Olympics without the intervention of Tony Blair, and the Beijing Olympics was intended as a demonstration of Chinese national power. However, the Games were no longer simply a state-dominated international event. The IOC was increasingly partnering television companies and corporate sponsors whose influence over the venue and format of the Games was growing.

The new globalized politics of the Games gave rise to a distinct form of scandal from the 1980s onwards, which Andrew Jennings has doggedly exposed. The IOC was no longer a forum of international tension and dispute, but an institution exploiting the multiple opportunities of a deregulated global system to maximize its profits and interests (Simson *et al.*, 1992; Jennings, 1996). From Los Angeles 1984 to Beijing 2008, the Olympics Games, lurching as always from controversy to controversy, was administered by a globalized and commercial regime. States remained important actors, but the Games became a transnational event in which non-state actors, above all multinational media, sponsoring corporations and cities, had increasing influence. The financial crisis of 2008–09 may once again denote a new era of Olympic history. With the credit crunch, the Beijing Olympics might be seen as the last Games of the neoliberal era. London 2012 is likely to have the dubious distinction of being the first Games of a more austere regulatory regime.

Cricket

In football and the Olympics, a similar threefold trajectory of historical development is observable. Both were regulated by an international regime during the twentieth century (especially since the Second World War), in which nation-states and their national federations, coordinated by an international body, were dominant. In the 1970s, this order underwent a fundamental crisis and, as a result of globalization, a new deregulated, transnational order emerged in the 1980s in which sub-state actors, transnational corporations, cities and clubs became critical agents in each. It may be possible to understand the development of international cricket in the twentieth century by reference to a similar threefold periodization: 1900–70, the 1970s, and the 1980s to 2008. Cricket was one of the longest-standing sports in England, pre-dating the invention of 'modern sports' at elite public schools by over

100 years. It assumed a recognizable form in English rural society in the early decades of the eighteenth century, where it involved proto-forms of professionalism and was a focus of extensive gambling. It was disseminated internationally through the empire, becoming embedded in British India, South Africa and Australia (Kaufman and Patterson, 2005). However, while international matches were played in the late nineteenth century, the concept of international cricket as a regular, organized event was institutionalized in 1909 with the formation of the Imperial Cricket Conference (ICC), consisting of England, Australia and South Africa. Dominated by England, the Conference was based in the Marylebone Cricket Club (MCC) at Lords. Despite the long history of English cricket, the formation of the ICC institutionalized international cricket in a manner closely consonant with football and the Olympics. In the late 1920s and early 1930s, New Zealand, India and the West Indies joined the Conference; Pakistan, following Partition, did likewise in 1952. As with the Olympics, there were very substantial international disputes during this period, including the infamous bodyline tour of 1932–33. However, neither the authority of the ICC (and England in particular) nor the structure and hierarchy of international cricket were fundamentally questioned.

In the late 1960s, accelerating into the 1970s, political and economic tensions became increasingly acute. In 1968, the England team was scheduled to tour South Africa and was likely to re-select a successful South African all-rounder, Basil D'Oliveira, who had been one of England's best players in 1967. The partly Asian D'Oliveira had emigrated to England because he had been banned from representative cricket in apartheid South Africa. It was unlikely that the South African authorities would have allowed him to return in 1968 (Williams, 2001: 56). In the event, with accusations of cravenness, the MCC did not select D'Oliveira. Nevertheless, the race issue was only postponed, and in 1971 the ICC banned South Africa from international cricket as a result of political pressures from both within and outside the game, to be re-admitted only in 1992 after the end of apartheid. The changing political dynamics within international cricket were also beginning to be demonstrated on the pitch, as the dominance of England (and Australia) was challenged by the originally subordinate cricketing countries, India, Pakistan and the West Indies. This shift of power was illustrated perhaps most clearly in 1984, when the West Indies, refining a new pace-attack system, demolished England 5–0 in a test series in England. At the same time, economic forces began to infiltrate the game. New one-day competitions, television and sponsorship first appeared in the 1970s but, decisively, in 1977 Kerry Packer introduced his World Series Cricket (Sen, 2005: 100). The Series continued for only two seasons, but Packer demonstrated the commercial potential of the game by hiring the best professional cricketers in the world to play in one-day matches which maximized the potential of television and sponsorship. The World Series indicated the possibilities for cricket if it could restructure itself to emergent global realities. The 1970s and early 1980s were a transition for cricket in which the old England-led international system of governance was being replaced by globalizing imperatives.

Paralleling changes in football and the Olympics, major institutional reforms began to take place from the 1980s. In 1964, the ICC had replaced the outmoded title Imperial with International and, in 1989, it renamed itself as the International Cricket Council. In a deeply important change in 2005, the ICC then relocated itself from Lords to Dubai. Rumford (2007) has highlighted this move as evidence of the 'post-westernization' of the game. The Asian sub-continent, and especially India, which accounted for 60% of cricket's global income, had now superseded England and its white satellites as the centre of gravity for world cricket. Dubai was also a more suitable venue for orchestrating the financial interactions that had become increasingly important to international cricket. The ICC was deliberately positioning itself on a nodal point in the new geography of global capitalism. Successive ICC presidents Jaymohan Dalmiya and Elsan Mani have sought to institute the commercial approach adopted by Samaranch's IOC and Havelange's *Fédération Internationale de Football Association* (FIFA). As Marqusee has noted: 'the paternalistic, Anglocentric system was replaced by an elected president and the beginnings of full-time administration' (Marqusee, 2005: 257). Specifically, the ICC oversaw the development of new competitions such as the Indian Premier League, which maximized the patronage of television and sponsorship companies through the staging of a transnational sporting event in which the global stars of cricket played for artificially created teams. Global cricket has been increasingly organized by a commercialized, 'post-western' ICC in collaboration with sponsoring and television corporations. Indeed, Tim Lamb, chairman of the England and Wales Cricket Board (ECB), fully recognized the new situation: 'Sport is a business. We are a company and we have signed contracts for a multi-million pound event. This is not a game of beach cricket' (Marqusee, 2005: 253). Cricket, then, has followed a historical trajectory compatible with both football and the Olympics. A period of relative regulatory stability during the middle decades of the twentieth century, when the game was organized on an international basis from London, was ended by a crisis in the 1970s and early 1980s, followed by a dramatic period of globalization in the 1990s. The question is, how will cricket respond to the new financial situation that confronts it?

The regulation of sport in the twenty-first century

There is evidence that a process of re-regulation of football, explicitly connected to the financial crisis, has already begun. In 2009, UEFA President Michel Platini stressed the need to regulate football in the light of new economic circumstances: 'In football, as in the economy in general, the market is incapable of correcting its own excesses, and it was not the UEFA president who said so, it was Barack Obama' (Harris, 2009: 54). Platini's concerns were a response to the growing economic problems in European football. In England, for instance, most of the major clubs were heavily leveraged with apparently unfeasible debts, while Southampton and Portsmouth were in the process of financial collapse. In order to stabilize the sport, Platini proposed that club spending, player salaries and other costs should be limited: 'We are looking at the idea of limiting a club's expenditure on staff – salary and transfer fees combined – to an as yet undecided percentage of its direct and indirect sporting revenue.' Platini wanted to introduce a system of regulation where club finances and debts are monitored centrally with wages and spending limited in proportion to club income. Platini's calls for a restricted economy in football recall the managed, 'Keynesian' system of football administration that was predominant in Europe in the 1950s and 1960s. At that time, the legal status of the clubs, the transfer and retention system, and the authority of the federations restricted the clubs' economic activities. In March 2009, Platini renewed his calls for regulation with a further proposal. Concerned with spending levels, UEFA proposed that the major clubs be taxed and their excess revenue redistributed to poorer clubs. For UEFA, this proposal had a number of advantages. It would potentially equalize disparities in play: in 2008, Olympique Lyonnais had won France's Ligue 1 for the previous seven years, while Porto had claimed Portugal's Liga for six of the previous seven seasons (Blitz, 2009: 1). Moreover, it would introduce financial discipline into the sport by limiting the spending of major clubs. UEFA officers visited Major League Baseball in the United States to investigate how redistributive models operate in those competitions.

Platini also wanted to re-inscribe stabilizing national boundaries onto football:

> If you bring people from Qatar and there is no-one from Liverpool or Manchester at the club, where is Liverpool or Manchester? I think it is not good. I think the Qataris should invest in Qatar. Do you want in Liverpool an Arab sheikh as president with one Brazilian coach and nine or eleven African players? Where is Liverpool in that? We have to make some rules. What is football? Football is a game and this game has become popular because of the identity. You have to have identity, that is where football's popularity lies.
>
> (Mole, 2008)

It is clear, therefore, that he wants to restrict the ownership market in order to protect the connection between clubs, national leagues and the nation. The reaffirmation of national borders in European football is a means of reversing the process of radical transnationalization that followed the Bosman decision. For UEFA, re-nationalization and re-regulation is a means of stabilizing football financially. In 2010, Platini had some success in implementing his regulatory reforms. The European Club Association, UEFA's forum for clubs, accepted his 'financial fair play' rules, which will enter UEFA statutes in the 2013–14 season. These rules limit the proportion of turnover that a club can spend on players, with a view to equalizing playing differentials in Europe.

The renewed authority of UEFA suggests a re-subordination of the clubs and return to the post-war system of international administration. There seems to be some evidence that the decline in the clubs' authority, which Platini would desire, has indeed occurred. Most significant here is the demise of the G14, the lobby group of Europe's biggest clubs. In late 2007, the G14 engaged in a long-standing debate with UEFA and the national federations over compensation for the release of players for national duties. In January 2008, the dispute was finally resolved. Federations would compensate the clubs for players. In return, the G14 agreed to disband as an autonomous body outside of UEFA. A new European Clubs Association (ECA), consisting of 103 clubs representing all the leagues in UEFA, was instituted. Sepp Blatter, FIFA President, regarded the disbanding of the G14 as a triumph: 'Something very special has happened today. The clubs, which are the basic cells of our game and fundamental to its thriving, are at last to become a part of the pyramidal football organization' (Ziegler, 2008: 31). The quietus of the G14 was taken as clear evidence by Blatter that UEFA and FIFA had re-asserted the primacy which they had enjoyed over clubs in the mid-twentieth century.

The reality of this nascent regime, however, may in fact be very different from Blatter's conception of it. It is notable that G14 clubs are over-represented on the ECA. The ECA consists of a group of seventeen clubs, defined as founding members, alongside a further eighty-six. The seventeen founding members include eight of the original G14 (Manchester United, Bayern Munich, Juventus, AC Milan, Ajax, Porto, Real Madrid and Barcelona) and a further two clubs from the expanded group of eighteen clubs (Olympique Lyonnais and Valencia). All the other G14 clubs (Inter, Borussia Dortmund, Arsenal, Liverpool, PSV Eindhoven and Bayer Leverkusen), except for the always less influential Marseille and Paris St German, are normal members of the ECA. In addition, the ECA consists of a senior transitional board, of which five out of seven represent major G14 clubs. It seems almost certain, given the over-representation of the G14 in the ECA, that the super-clubs will have a disproportionate impact over policy decisions and the regulation of the game. Indeed, Blatter himself unwittingly affirmed the power of the major clubs in the coming era. When he discussed the 'special' moment of the clubs' incorporation into UEFA, he seemed to take this as evidence of their subordination. The fact that he could view their representation in UEFA as a normality signified the new status which they now enjoyed. In the post-war period, the notion that the clubs would have had direct influence over, and interaction with, UEFA was unthinkable. Yet by 2008, Blatter accepted that the clubs have an inalienable place in the administration of the European game.

One of the defining features of the deregulated era of the 1990s was the concentration of economic and playing power at the biggest clubs. The credit crunch does not seem to have arrested this process of concentration. The major clubs still continue to attract the largest investors since they enjoy the greatest patronage from television networks and sponsors, for whom they attract a global audience. In 2005, Manchester United signed a record four-year shirt sponsorship deal with AIG worth £56.6 million but, following the collapse of the company, AIG confirmed that it would not be renewing its contract after 2010. The club has been in discussion with an Indian corporation, Sahara, which offered £19 million. The new deal is smaller than the record AIG contract but it is still very large – especially in relation to other European clubs. The transnational geography, which began to crystallize from 1990, is likely to be affirmed and consolidated with the largest clubs, now officially part of UEFA, in a better financial and political position. These clubs are likely to continue to dominate European and domestic competitions and, therefore, sustain and indeed increase their popular appeal and public profile. In addition, with the creation of the ECA, these major clubs are likely to play a decisive role in the regulation of the game.

Overall, football is likely to be regulated by a multi-polar arrangement of differing and convergent interest groups – clubs (uniting in shifting groupings and alliances), federations and UEFA. Regulation is likely to be more intrusive than it has been, especially since the Bosman ruling in 1995, but a return to a Keynesian international order is unlikely. It might be more accurate to argue that European football is entering an era of regulated transnationalism. In short, the future would not seem to be a return to the organizational regime of the 1950s in which sovereign federations controlled their own leagues and the clubs within them. Rather, the new regime is likely to involve a complex organizational structure in which UEFA coordinates the regulation of football through negotiations with complicit clubs and federations. In this institutional complex, the clubs are no longer subordinate, but are at least as important as the federations and UEFA themselves. Major European clubs, as part of a transnational network, are likely to constitute a critical nexus in this new geography, but interactions and competition between them may be mediated by collective agreements between multiple actors: the clubs themselves, UEFA, the federations, the European Commission, national governments, all heavily influenced by the media and sponsors. The fundamental features of the transnational geography that emerged in the 1990s, however, are unlikely to be reversed. Borders will remain porous in football, and the transnational links between concentrations of playing and economic power (the super-clubs) are likely to remain a defining feature of the new era. It is apparent that football's neoliberal transnational regime has merely undergone a moderate revision.

A similar dual process of immediate crisis and moderate reform seems to be evident in the Olympics and in international cricket, in both of which an era of regulated transnationalism, or regulated globalization, may be discernible. The 2008 Beijing Games successfully merged nation-state politics with globalized commercialism. The London Olympics of 2012 may become the debt Games, a reflection of the economic crisis in which they have been organized and will be staged. The projected costs were raised by government from £3.3 billion in 2006 to £9.3 billion in 2009, but by November 2008 a figure of £20 billion (ten times the original estimate) was widely accepted as a more plausible total (Lea, 2008). If the cost of the games is even close to £20 billion, they will induce significant economic and fiscal stress on London and the UK, especially in the light of major reductions in public sector spending announced in 2009. Conceived in an era of growth and overconfident entrepreneurialism and founded on seriously underdeveloped plans, the Games, a year before they are due to take place, seem to be overleveraged with a level of debt which the event itself has no prospect of recovering. It is dangerous to speculate out to 2016 but, if London becomes the Montreal of the twenty-first century, it is possible that the IOC and the Olympic Organizing Committee in Rio might institute a less ambitious Games in which the state and private sector coordinate more modest investments. Although, given the current growth of the Brazilian economy, such austerity measures may be unnecessary even by 2016. Despite the potential financial problems for London, it seems unlikely, therefore, that the regulatory structure and commercial priorities of the Games, instituted by Samaranch and Dassler in the 1980s, will be fundamentally revised in the next decade. The IOC is currently exploiting the commercial potential of the London Games through alliances with global capital, especially television and sponsoring corporations, candidate cities and states. Early indications suggest that Rio in 2016 will be no different. It seems improbable that the IOC's commercialized, global strategy will fundamentally change in the next decade. Like football, some marginal revision of the administration of the Olympic Games is possible to produce a regime broadly equivalent to football's regulated trans-nationalism, but a return to the purely international, state-oriented regulation of the twentieth century is almost inconceivable.

A similar future seems to be detectable in cricket. International cricket has experienced an immediate financial – and political – crisis, which has induced moderate regulatory reforms without fundamentally altering the structure of post-westernization. In 2008, the ECB signed a three-year contract with Sir Allen Stanford, an Antiguan-based British businessman, to play a series against an invitation side of international stars for a prize of $20 million. The Stanford tournament was a direct and extreme manifestation of the globalization of cricket where market considerations determined the organization of the tournament:

> Of all the short-form matches currently being organized, the conclusion is easily reached that Stanford Superstars v. England is the most offensive. It has no context as a proper sporting competition, it is neither country versus country, club versus club or invitation XI versus invitation XI. It is a rococo hybrid. It has money but nothing else going for it.
>
> (Brenkley, 2008)

The Stanford Super Series represented commercialization at its most extreme. In 2009, however, the ECB withdrew from it when Allen Stanford was accused of fraud and financial irregularities exposed by the credit crunch. The collapse of the tournament was similarly a product of the crisis of the neoliberal system that gave rise to it in the first place. The collapse of Stanford's Super Series was indicative of the vulnerability of an increasingly commercialized and deregulated world cricket, and it seems likely that cricket authorities will be more cautious about the organization of tournaments in the future.

In addition, there are now substantial political threats to the Indian Premier League. Echoing the Munich crisis of 1972 and a manifestation of global terrorism, the threat of an assault on the Indian Premier League, especially following the Mumbai attacks in November 2008 in which 173 were killed, may precipitate the withdrawal of western players from the tournament, effectively undermining the competition. This would be a serious threat to globalized cricket. However, even if the Indian Premier League is abandoned, it is unlikely that the basic contours of post-westernized cricket will be fundamentally undone by either these economic or political problems. The ICC in Dubai has not significantly altered its strategy for the promotion of international cricket. The nexus of television, sponsorship and new forms of international and transnational competition, in which India and the Asian sub-continent play an increasingly important role, will almost certainly be sustained. The market opportunities are too attractive to ignore. Indeed, recent global developments have increased the financial pressures on western national cricket federations accelerating the search for new formats. The ECB is currently exploring the possibility of introducing a new, city-based 20/20 tournament to be played at the major test grounds in England, specifically to rival the Indian Premier League (Hoult and Bolton, 2010). At the national level, then, the financial crisis has not fundamentally undermined the interconnections between cricket, television and sponsors. On the contrary, it might be argued that financial pressures have accentuated the importance of these commercial, transnational strategies.

Conclusion

Sport has always reflected and been influenced by wider historical conditions. The credit crunch signals the end of one kind of 'disorganized' capitalism. The recession, and the new regulatory regime that seems to be emerging from it, is likely to have a significant impact on European sport in the early twenty-first century. However, despite the frequent appeals to Keynes, a genuine return to heavy nationalist economic management is unlikely. States are likely to control the financial sector in coordination with other governments, but they are unlikely to try and take control of the commanding heights of the economy as they did in the post-war period. Similarly, in European sport the emergent regulatory regime seems to represent a moderate institutional reform, not a revolution. In European football, UEFA, in close cooperation with the major clubs, is likely to introduce some relatively modest reforms around salaries and expenditure. Such regulation will be important, but it will not fundamentally alter the trajectory of concentration and transnationalization that has been evident in European football since the 1990s. The network of major European clubs is likely to develop and strengthen throughout the recession and into any future recovery. Similarly, it seems unlikely that the new institutional structures which appeared in the Olympic Games and international cricket from the 1980s are about to be fundamentally revised. Processes of globalization may have been slowed by the financial crisis, and international sports federations may be more cautious in the future about investment, but the basic pattern of regulation seems unchallenged. European sport has gone too far down the path of globalization to return to the now comforting simplicities of the international era. In the twentieth century, political disputes predominantly contoured around the simple axis of international power. In the coming decade, disputes are likely to germinate with renewed intensity between fans, players and administrators along a multiplicity of fracture lines, which characterize the global order.

Note

1   Maguire describes five phases, the first three referring to the nineteenth and early twentieth centuries. I focus here on Maguire's fourth, fifth and (implied) sixth phases, which divide the twentieth century into three periods.

References

Blitz, R., (2009), 'Richest football clubs could be forced to pay tax on star players', *Financial Times*, 26 March: 1.

Brenkley, S., (2008), 'Winner takes all, even the game's soul', *Independent*, 26 October, www.independent.co.uk/sport/cricket/stephen-brenkley-winner-takes-all-even-the-games-soul-973759.html

Brewster, C. and Brewster, K., (2006), 'Mexico City 1968: sombreros and skyscrapers', in A. Tomlinson and C. Young (eds), *National Identity and Global Sports Events: Culture, Politics and Spectacle in the Olympics and the Football World Cup*, Albany: State University of New York Press: 99–116.

Giulianotti, R., (1999), *Football: A Sociology of the Global Game*, Cambridge: Polity.

Giulianotti, R. and Robertson, R., (2004), 'The globalization of football: a study in the glocalization of the "serious life"', *British Journal of Sociology*, 55 (4): 545–68.

Goldblatt, D., (2007), *The Ball is Round: A Global History of Football*, Harmondsworth: Penguin Viking.

Guttmann, A., (2002), *The Olympics: A History of the Modern Games*, Urbana: University of Illinois Press.

——, (2006), 'Berlin 1936: the most controversial Olympics', in A. Tomlinson and C. Young (eds), *National Identity and Global Sports Events: Culture, Politics and Spectacle in the Olympics and the Football World Cup*, Albany: State University of New York Press: 65–81.

Harris, N., (2009), 'Platini warns of "impending implosion"', *Independent*, 19 February: 54.

Hegel, G., (1967), *Philosophy of Right*, Oxford: Oxford University Press.

Hoult, N. and Bolton, P., (2010), 'English cricket looks again at city franchises for Twenty20', *Telegraph*, 13 April, www.telegraph.co.uk/sport/cricket/counties/7583184/English-cricket-looks-again-at-city-franchises-for-Twenty20.html

Jennings, A., (1996), *The New Lords of the Rings: Olympic Corruption and How to Buy Gold Medals*, London: Pocket Books.

Judt, T., (2005), *Postwar: A History Of Europe Since 1945*, London: Heinemann.

Kaufman, J. and Patterson, O., (2005), 'Cross-national cultural diffusion: the global spread of cricket', *American Sociological Review*, 70 (February): 82–110.

King, A., (2003), *The European Ritual: Football in the New Europe*, Aldershot: Ashgate.

Lea, M., (2008), 'London 2012 could cost £20 billion. . . TEN times original budget, ex-Olympic chief predicts', *Mail Online*, 9 April, www.dailymail.co.uk/news/article-558211/London-2012-cost-20billion-TEN-times-original-budget-ex-Olympics-chief-predicts.html

Maguire, J., (1999), *Global Sport: Identities, Societies, Civilizations*, Cambridge: Polity.

Manzenreiter, W. and Horne, J., (eds) (2006), *Sports Mega-Events: Social Scientific Analyses of a Global Phenomenon*, Oxford: Blackwell.

Marqusee, M., (2005), 'The ambush clause: globalization, corporate power and the governance of world cricket', in S. Wagg (ed.), *Following On: Cricket and National Identity in the Postcolonial Age*, London: Routledge: 251–65.

Mazower, M., (2000), *Dark Continent: Europe's Twentieth Century*, New York: Vintage.

Mole, G., (2008), 'Michel Platini: Qataris should invest in Qatar, not English Premier League', *Telegraph*, 9 October, www.telegraph.co.uk/sport/football/leagues/premierleague/3163583/Michel-Platini-Qataris-should-invest-in-Qatar-not-English-Premier-League-Football.html

Mosse, G., (1985), *Nationalism and Sexuality: Respectability and Abnormal Sexuality in Modern Europe*, New York: Howard Fertig.

Robertson, R., (1992), *Globalization: Social Theory and Global Culture*, London: Sage.

Roche, M., (2000), *Mega-Events & Modernity: Olympics and Expos in the Growth of Global Culture*, London and New York: Routledge.

Rumford, C., (2007), 'More than a game: globalization and the post-westernization of cricket', *Global Networks*, 7 (2): 202–14.

Sen, S., (2005), 'History without a past: memory and forgetting in Indian cricket', in S. Wagg (ed.), *Following On: Cricket and National Identity in the Postcolonial Age*, London: Routledge: 94–109.

Simson, V., Jennings, A. and Nally, P., (1992), *The Lords of the Rings: Power, Money and Drugs in the Modern Olympics*, London: Simon & Schuster.

Stiglitz, J., (2008), 'Getting bang for your buck', *guardian.co.uk*, 5 December, www.guardian. co.uk/commentisfree/cifamerica/2008/dec/05/us-economy-keynesian-economic-theory

Tomlinson, A., (2005), 'Olympic survivals', in L. Allison (ed.), *The Global Politics of Sport: The Role of Global Institutions in Sport*, London: Routledge: 42–56.

——, (2006), 'Los Angeles 1984 and 1932: commercializing the American Dream', in A. Tomlinson and C. Young (eds), *National Identity and Global Sports Events: Culture, Politics and Spectacle in the Olympics and the Football World Cup*, Albany: State University of New York Press: 163–77.

Tomlinson, A. and Young, C. (eds), (2006), *National Identity and Global Sports Events: Culture, Politics and Spectacle in the Olympics and the Football World Cup*, Albany: State University of New York Press.

Williams, J., (2001), *Cricket and Race*, Oxford: Berg.

Young, C., (2006), 'Munich 1972: re-presenting the nation', in A. Tomlinson and C. Young (eds), *National Identity and Global Sports Events: Culture, Politics and Spectacle in the Olympics and the Football World Cup*, Albany: State University of New York Press: 117–30.

Ziegler, M., (2008), 'G14 axed after deal with FIFA and UEFA', *Birmingham Post*, 16 January: 31.

11 The Europeanization of football

Germany and Austria compared

Arne Niemann, Alexander Brand
and Georg Spitaler

Introduction

Sport, in so far as it constitutes an economic activity, is subject to European Community (EC) law. Since the Bosman ruling of 1995, EU-level policy-making in the domain of sport has been considerably more prominent and significant than in previous decades of European integration. However, not all developments on the EU level are as well known as the Bosman case.

Going beyond EU/European level developments, the actual impact of EU law and EU policy-making on the domestic (sports) arena is particularly under-researched.[1] Decision-making at EU level affects a range of areas with an impact on the broad structures and institutional set-up of domestic sport in European states as well as on actors such as associations and clubs. By focusing on the impact of European integration at the domestic level, our research interest reflects the evolution of research agendas in the study of EU integration: after four decades of attention to developments of integration at the European level, in the early to mid-1990s scholars have increasingly begun to examine the effect that European integration may have on domestic settings, a process that has been termed 'Europeanization'.

Our study concentrates on football, the sport that has been subject to most (well known) European-level cases and decisions. Football is the most popular game and the sport with the greatest economic significance in Europe. Its influence cuts across political, economic, social and cultural spheres, and should illuminate other sectors of European sport. Our empirical analysis focuses on German and Austrian football, and particularly on three sub-cases: (1) the nationality issue related to the Bosman ruling of the European Court of Justice; (2) transfer rules resulting from the Bosman ruling, and (3) the issue of Bundesliga broadcasting rights.

Germany and Austria have been chosen as cases studies for several reasons. The two countries/leagues contrast in important dimensions, and thus allow us to probe the relevance of Europeanization mechanisms in varying contexts. First, the German Bundesliga, along with the English, French, Italian and Spanish leagues, constitutes one of the major football leagues in Europe, whilst the Austrian Bundesliga is one of the smallest. Second, Germany is one of the founding members of the EC and a country in which the European integration process has traditionally been held in high esteem by both the political elites and the public. The German case therefore allows us to explore the impact of European integration on domestic sport under favourable conditions. Austria, by contrast, only joined the EU in 1995 and its political elites and public have, especially in recent years, been more Eurosceptic in outlook. Moreover, an analysis of these two countries/leagues is of particular interest because of the special and precarious relationship in football between Germany and Austria as neighbours sharing a language and – to some degree – historical–cultural heritage.

Europeanization

Research on Europeanization has gradually increased since the mid-1990s and developed into an academic growth industry over the past decade in particular. In the field of political science alone, the term 'Europeanization' is used in a number of different ways to describe a variety of phenomena and processes of change (Olsen, 2002). Most frequently, Europeanization refers to domestic change in areas such as policy substance and instruments, processes of interest representation and policy style as well as (political) structures and institutions (Radaelli, 2000). The Europeanization research agenda arguably focuses on a set of very important research questions, related to *where, how, why*, and *the extent to which* domestic change occurs as a consequence of EU integration and governance at the European level.

As a starting point, Europeanization is understood here as the process of change in the domestic arena resulting from European-level governance. However, it must be stressed that Europeanization is viewed not as a unidirectional, but rather as a two-way-process which develops, furthermore, in both top-down and bottom-up directions. Top-down perspectives largely emphasize vertical developments from the European to the domestic level (Ladrech, 1994; Schmidt, 2002). Bottom-up accounts stress the national influence on European-level developments (which in turn feed back into the domestic realm). This latter perspective highlights that EU member states are more than passive receivers of European-level pressures. They may shape policies and institutions on the European level to which they have to adjust at a later stage (Börzel, 2002).

Beyond top-down (downloading) and bottom-up (uploading) accounts, we would like to highlight a further aspect that has been neglected in scholarship and which is relevant for some of our empirical analysis below: the societal/transnational dimension of Europeanization. This dimension encapsulates two elements: (1) the *level and sphere* of change; (2) the type of *agency* generating or resisting change. Hence the societal dimension addresses the fact that regulation and jurisdiction from Brussels is likely to induce adaptational pressure in societal contexts beyond the political level, such as the realm of sport and, for our purpose, football. The transnational dimension captures how societal actors (e.g. football clubs, football associations or the media) either react to the EU's attempts to regulate them, or create transnational spaces which in turn have an impact on the governance of football.[2]

An important caveat, before we begin our analysis, is the fact that Europeanization should not be limited to simple 'EU-ization' (Brand and Niemann, 2007: 184–85).

In sport, for instance, the early transnational networks that defined Austrian football in the first half of the twentieth century cannot be ignored. Due to the multinational heritage of the Austro-Hungarian monarchy, Austrian football was internationally oriented from the outset and already substantially internationalized or Europeanized. Early football in Austria focused on the urban regions, especially Vienna, where the first continental professional league was established in 1924 (Horak, 1992; Horak and Maderthaner, 1996). Some players in the inter-war period came as migrants or refugees from Hungarian, Bohemian and Moravian regions, and many were children of migrants. At the same time, hundreds of Austrian football players and coaches went abroad to work in other European leagues, especially in France (Lanfranchi, 1994; Barreaud, 1998: 56). In the inter-war years, Viennese teams had already fairly international squads, even by today's standards. Before the Second World War, the most important focus for Viennese clubs was the so-called 'Central European Triangle', a tri-party competition between Vienna, Prague and Budapest. Some authors even talk about a Central Europe football space – a trans-boundary space of action that developed out of frequent contacts, matches and peer-group orientation (Marschik, 1998; Marschik and Sottopietra, 2000). In 1927, this led to the so-called Mitropa Cup, a club tournament contested chiefly within this triangle (but also including Yugoslavia and Italy), and the International Cup for national teams. Both tournaments have been described as forerunners of now well established competitions at European level (Mittag and Legrand, 2010). This Central European football space (1) served as a means for normalizing relations between states that belonged to the former Austro-Hungarian empire; and (2) serviced financial interests and the will to generate extra revenue (Marschik, 2001). After the Nazi occupation in the late 1930s, the Central European football sphere largely ended, and never really recovered after 1945.

This brief historical detour demonstrates that there is an obviously important pre-Bosman dimension to the Europeanization of Austrian football. In Germany, by contrast, such Europeanization processes are not evidenced in the first half of the twentieth century. Further, the more recent history of European football, not least the establishment of the Champions League in the 1990s, also points to an important layer of the Europeanization dynamic which is not reducible primarily to EU-related pressures.[3]

Comparative analysis of German and Austrian football

Case 1 – Bosman I: the nationality issue

Important trends in German and Austrian football over the past decade can be interpreted as symptoms of an ongoing Europeanization. This is because a whole complex of such trends – the increased influx of foreign-born players, attempts to restrict their numbers along with efforts to promote young local talent, and the search for a new 'transfer regime' – has its roots in the seminal Bosman ruling of the European Court of Justice (ECJ) in 1995. In essence, the ruling consisted of two general findings: first, the traditional system of paying transfer fees for out-of-contract players infringed upon the right of every European (worker) to move freely under Article 48 of the Treaty establishing the European Community (TEC) and thus had to be abolished; and second, that 'nationality restrictions' imposed as a means to limit the number of foreign players in a football club were illegal in so far as they discriminated against players from countries within the European Union (Foster, 2000: 42).

In Germany, football was affected by both aspects, although one could claim that the latter had a more 'visible' effect for the football community as a whole. The abolishment of general nationality restrictions[4] and opening up of the market for players from all other EU countries already implied an increase in the number of foreign-born players. But the German Football Association (*Deutscher Fußball-Bund*, DFB) liberalized even further and extended the right to play professional football in Germany without being considered a foreigner, not only to EU residents (so-called *EU-Ausländer*) but also to players from all fifty-two member associations of the European Football Association (*Union des Associations Européennes de Football*, UEFA). Thus, in the two German professional leagues at least, after Bosman the status of *EU-Ausländer* really meant *UEFA-Ausländer*, and EU resident equated to UEFA resident.

This arrangement was exceptional in Europe and requires some explanation. One possible cause is the special socio-political situation in Germany after reunification. The DFB and its leading actors were still influenced and impressed by the dramatic political changes in Europe and the 'unification' of the continent that had taken place only a few years previously, and simply 'did not want to erect new walls or barriers', especially towards national associations in Central and Eastern Europe, with which they had strong institutional links.[5] In a similar vein, some were convinced that the ongoing process of European integration would at any rate soon render any differentiation between certain types of European meaningless.[6] A second major factor is that the extension created a larger market from which German football clubs could sign players, not least from Central and Eastern Europe. With the loss of out-of-contract transfer fees, Bosman, after all, had eliminated a central source of financing for clubs. German clubs, in particular, are subject to relatively strict licensing procedures, which force them to pursue relatively sound economic policies. Opening up the market certainly had a compensatory effect, as it was generally less expensive to sign players from Poland or the Balkans. Both explanations – the socio-political and the financial – were certainly in play at the same time.

It is hardly surprising that the DFB's decision led to an influx of players from all over Europe. Developments in the first division of the Bundesliga are instructive in this regard. Pre-Bosman, at the beginning of the 1990s, the ratios of player groups categorized according to origin were fairly stable: approximately 80% of players were German-born, 12–14% UEFA residents (excluding Germans), 5–7% non-UEFA residents. After Bosman and the DFB's expansive decision, the proportion of German-born players steadily decreased (to 50% in 2005). Both the proportion of UEFA residents and that of players from other continents substantially increased, although the latter remained relatively small (between 12 and 14% in 2003 and 2004) compared with the former (up to 38% in 2005).

The decision to open the market for all Europeans might seem liberal, but the DFB did not fully liberalize until 2006–07, when it decided to abolish the limit on all foreign players in professional clubs, albeit with the provision that a certain number of players have to be signed who are eligible for a German national team and/or stem from the youth system of a German club (UEFA's 'home-grown players'). In turn, the shortage of talented young German footballers, which became an obvious problem at the end of the 1990s, was at least in some part attributed to Bosman and the way it had been specifically implemented in Germany. At this point, the DFB became concerned about the promotion and protection of the talent pool for its national teams. In collaboration with the German Football League (*Deutsche Fußball Liga*, DFL), it tried to play a steering role by establishing certain rules for professional and amateur clubs, which aim at developing young German players as far as possible within the limits of domestic and European law. Licensing rules oblige every club in the Bundesliga to maintain a training centre for young players (*Nachwuchsleistungszentrum*). Amateur clubs attached to professional teams are now allowed to field only three players over twenty-three. The number of non-EU players in German amateur teams has been cut back from a maximum of six (2002) to three (2004). This kind of 'steering policy' was supported by the German Ministry of the Interior, which in 2002 issued a directive that in effect made it impossible for non-EU players to get a work permit unless they were signed by a team in the first or second Bundesliga. In 2003, the follow-up to this directive specified that non-EU players must be signed to play in the first team and cannot be farmed out to the amateur ranks of professional clubs (Franzke, 2003).

In sum, the parts of Bosman that related to issues of nationality generated strong pressure for change on the German FA, which reacted in the mixed fashion of the DFB. While there were counter-reactions, no strong, fully-fledged counter-pressure to European institutions ensued. Transposition varied from the progressive (the decision to extend the definition of 'EU resident') to the more conservative (measures to promote German talent). Overall, however, the nationality issues embedded in Bosman changed the structures and landscape of German football. Above all, the constitution of the Bundesliga has become above all less German, more international, and, in a wider sense, more European. The degree of change is most aptly captured by the notion of 'system transformation', which denotes a paradigmatic or core policy change.

Prior to Bosman in Austria – except for a total ban on new signings between 1974 and 1977 – regulations allowed either two or three foreign players per team in the first division, a total later extended by two additional 'assimilated' players under UEFA's '3+2 rule'. Central European ties had been weakened since the 1940s and 1950s, but Austrian football still profited from the inflow of players and managers from neighbouring states, most notably Czechoslovakia, Hungary and Yugoslavia, which produced a continuous migratory movement of players, especially from the early 1960s (Liegl and Spitaler, 2008: 36–73). Pre-1989, some players and managers from Hungary and Czechoslovakia received permission from their sports authorities to move to their neutral neighbour state. The fall of the Iron Curtain in the late 1980s turned Austria into a country of football transit and immigration (mostly in the lower leagues), as transfer restrictions were abolished in Central and Eastern Europe and players made use of their freedom to travel (Duke, 1994: 159). But Austria gradually lost its special appeal as a destination for Central and Eastern European players.

With Austria's accession to the EU in 1995, the Bosman ruling became effective there too. As in Germany, Austria not only liberalized its football market for EU foreigners, but in 1996 the relevant ministry decreed that up to five third-country nationals would be permitted per club. Later this number was increased to seven.[7] Austria liberalized beyond what was strictly required by the Bosman ruling for several reasons. Given that the two professional leagues still mainly attracted foreign players from Central and Eastern Europe (including the former Yugoslavia) (Liegl and Spitaler, 2008: 36–73), Austrian clubs did not want to lose the opportunity to acquire moderately priced players. Also, the pressure to Europeanize was accompanied and paralleled by the more general trends of globalization (of economy and capital as well as migration), liberalization and deregulation (of domestic markets) (Lanfranchi and Taylor, 2001: 222; Giulianotti and Robertson, 2007). As a result, the proportion of foreign players increased sharply in the post-Bosman era, doubling from 19% in 1995 to around 38% by 2000. The proportion of players from Eastern Europe and neighbouring countries fell, while that of the rest of (essentially) EU-Europe more than doubled for a time (Liegl and Spitaler, 2009: 247).

By the turn of the century, both the football community and the mainstream media believed that Bosman and the seemingly liberal transposition it caused had adversely affected Austrian football, with the hampered development of young Austrian talent prominent in debate. This perception led both the Football League and political actors to take counter-measures. First came the so-called 9+9 rule, a gentlemen's agreement to which the clubs obliged themselves voluntarily, whereby at least nine players who could be selected for Austrian national teams had to be listed on the match sheet. This was greatly driven by politicians of the right-wing populist Freedom Party of Austria, which had entered government in 2000. Clearly, the 9+9 rule did not conform with the basic tenets of the Bosman ruling. However, regulations were only challenged in the second professional league, where the rules were even more restrictive, when the Austrian Federal Court of Justice ruled in favour of five claimants in 2001 to the effect that the promotion and cultivation of young talent did not justify discrimination against EU citizens (Karollus, 2006: 67). The 9+9 rule was also short-lived due to almost instant non-compliance by one of the bigger clubs, Sturm Graz, which led the club chairmen of the Bundesliga to devise an extended premium system that rewarded the use of Austrian players. Via this so-called *Österreicher-Topf* (the Austrians' pot), money earned from broadcasting rights is paid to clubs if they achieve a quota of eleven Austrian players among eighteen players on the match sheet (fielded players and substitutes), and according to the minutes for which players, who can be selected for Austrian national teams, were actually fielded. Legally, this arrangement is somewhat dubious since it introduces incentives to discriminate against EU-foreigners (Skocek and Weisgram, 2004: 323). But it has not yet been challenged, largely because it is voluntary. Finally, since 2004 the general admission of third-country nationals to Austrian professional football has been governed by legislation covering foreign employees who possess special qualifications (*Schlüsselarbeitskräfte*). There is no longer a legal restriction per club, and running alongside the aforementioned incentive system this amounts to almost *de facto* full liberalization.

Both the German and Austrian cases show interesting parallels: on the one hand, a liberalization beyond what was strictly implied in the Bosman ruling, motivated in large part by the desire to purchase moderately priced players from Central and Eastern Europe; on the other hand, counter-measures intended to curb the impact of an influx of foreign players on the training of young and talented players eligible for the national teams. While the Germans were more subtle and operated apparently more in accordance with EU law, the Austrian measures were more questionable in terms of compliance. Another interesting difference arises from the key actors involved in the respective countries. While in Germany the football association has been of central importance, supported at times by the ministry of the interior, in Austria it was the media (promoting a discourse against 'mediocre foreign players'), parts of the FA, the league, and influential politicians who took the lead. In sum, however, Bosman and its implementation has certainly changed the composition of football squads in both countries: foreigners account for around 50% of players in the German Bundesliga and approximately 40% in the Austrian Bundesliga (Liegl and Spitaler, 2009: 247).

Case 2 – Bosman II: the new 'transfer regime'

The second major consequence of the Bosman ruling was the complete revision of the traditional transfer system, after the payment of transfer fees for out-of-contract players was found to infringe upon the right of free movement within the EU. Since the transfer system was subject to international agreement and regulated via the world body *Fédération Internationale de Football Association* (FIFA), it became clear during the second half of the 1990s that this part of Bosman was not just (EU- or UEFA-related) European business, but implied a revision of the global transfer system. The European Commission pushed this view and suggested that football constituted a normal business activity which should be regulated in accordance with competition law. By contrast, the national and regional associations as well as FIFA promoted the opposing view that football and sport fulfilled special social functions and therefore should be treated differently. These and other actors – such as clubs, leagues, media and lawyers – formed 'advocacy coalitions' to promote their opinions in the negotiation process (Parrish, 2003). The overhaul of the international transfer system has been a long process, in which the national associations and FIFA/UEFA, to some extent, managed to assert themselves. Although the Commission finally forced them to the table by threatening another ruling through the ECJ in 2000 (Croci, 2001: 7), the new transfer regime agreed upon in 2001 suggested that the Commission had loosened some of its initial demands. This is especially the case with contract stability, which (as opposed to 'normal' periods of notice) still has to be guaranteed except for narrowly defined situations, as well as the introduction of a new system of training compensations

(Weatherill, 2003: 68). The Commission's change in attitude merits attention and needs to be explained. How was it possible, as Croci and Forster put it, that after reaching the compromise agreement with the European Commission in 2001, FIFA President Sepp Blatter 'publicly thanked Competition Commissioner Mario Monti with words that gave the impression that the Commission had simply acted as a consultant to FIFA to improve its transfer rules' (Croci and Forster, 2004: 16)?

Possibly the Commission was persuaded by arguments put forward by FIFA (and the DFB) about the peculiarities of organizing football and the presumed consequences of a fully liberalized transfer regime. Indeed, some leading German football officials interpret the negotiation process with the Commission as a successful act of lobbying that created more awareness within the Commission, for instance, about the inoperability of leagues in the context of highly volatile player markets.[8] Indeed, the fact the Commission gradually reformulated its position throughout the 1990s, as evidenced in the so-called Helsinki Report on Sport from 1999 (Brown, 2000: 139) – a report from the Commission to the European Council dealing precisely with the functions of sport within the Community against the background of ongoing internationalization as well as commercialization – might support this interpretation. Moreover, several national football associations, not least the German DFB, lobbied and convinced their governments to exert some political pressure on the institutions of the Community.[9] Access to policy-makers and the ability to explain the possible adverse implications of a fully liberalized transfer regime for the most popular sport in Europe therefore proved a crucial resource for the DFB and other big national football associations.

The case of Austria, however, seems to suggest that smaller countries with less impressive football leagues mostly remained on the sidelines. Our research has not produced any substantial results regarding the involvement of the Austrian Football Association (*Österreichischer Fußball-Bund*, ÖFB) in these debates at the European level. The reasons for this apparent lack of activism are obvious. As a relatively small member and a newcomer to the EU in the second half of the 1990s, Austria has had other (more) important interests to pursue. Similarly, the ÖFB is a relatively small association,[10] whose expertise, resources and personal contacts at the European level, especially in relation to the relevant political institutions, have been limited. Apart from the successful bid for the 2008 European Championships (together with Switzerland), the Austrian FA has not acted visibly on the European level.

Undoubtedly, the common stance of some national governments, spurred not least by the lobbying efforts of influential sports associations, exerted indirect political pressure on the Commission, which can act with some degree of autonomy in competition policy but does not take decisions in a political vacuum. Thus, one can clearly see both engagement (attempts to modify the pressure of the ECJ's ruling and the Commission's claims) and more confrontational modes of action (attempts to resist and oppose pressures through organizing political counter pressure) in the reactions, for instance, of the DFB and FIFA. Two of the most important aspects of the new transfer system agreed upon by FIFA and the Commission, besides the rules concerning contract stability, are the fixing of training compensations for players under the age of twenty-three, and the principle that clubs involved in the training and education of young players should be duly rewarded. Such compensation is in some ways a continuation of the old transfer fee payments for out-of-contract players, albeit at a lower level, with regard to young and amateur players. Hence the 'new transfer regime' agreed upon by FIFA and the Commission does not so much represent a complete overhaul of the old system as, rather, a case of 'heavy adjustment' (where existing policy cores are left – largely – unchallenged but substantial changes are made/absorbed). As the White Paper on Sport stated in 2007, the Commission thus considers the new transfer regime 'an example of good practice that ensures a competitive equilibrium between sports clubs while taking into account the requirements of EU law' (European Commission, 2007: 16). Nevertheless, the introduction of compensation payments by the DFB was ruled illegal in Germany in 2004 by the Regional Superior Court of Oldenburg, which argued they infringed the freedom to choose a profession (Article 12, German Basic Law).[11] In essence, this judgement constituted a 'national Bosman ruling' with special relevance to amateur football. Given that the Court acknowledged the DFB may have complied with FIFA rules, but argued that the rules of private organizations such as FIFA have nonetheless to abide by national *as well as* European law, it is evident that the 'new transfer regime' hardly constitutes the end of the debate.

In sum, while the 'Bosman nationality regulation' led to a 'system transformation' in German, Austrian and other domestic football, the 'Bosman transfer regulation' has had less far-reaching implications. In the latter instance, Europeanization led only to some 'heavy adjustment' due to somewhat less forceful top-down Europeanization pressure (with the Commission relaxing its stance) and more considerable counter-pressure (associations and, to a lesser degree, clubs conducting substantial lobbying).

Case 3 – broadcasting rights: the Bundesliga marketing system

Over the past decade, the transformation of the broadcasting sector has had a significant impact on professional football in most European countries, including Germany and Austria. Overall, broadcasting is a key element in the increased scale of commercialization in sports (and above all football) in Europe, which led EU institutions and Community law to intervene in the sector. The Commission's preoccupation with football has been driven by its need to monitor the broadcasting sector, where it seeks to preclude practices that facilitate incumbents' ability to impede new entrants to the market (Weatherill, 2003: 74).

One of the most contentious issues concerns the marketing system of broadcasting rights. The central marketing and joint sale of broadcasting rights on behalf of individual participants is an established commercial practice in European football and the European sports sector more generally, the system offering prospective buyers the opportunity to compete for only one package which comprises a league's entire output. Purchasers are unable to complete deals with individual clubs. Such collective selling is an equalizing arrangement which ensures that revenues are distributed more evenly than in a decentralized model. For instance, broadcasting rights for the Bundesliga, the English Premier League and the UEFA Champions League are (essentially) marketed centrally by the DFB/DFL, the Premier League and UEFA, respectively. In the decentralized system, the allegedly more attractive clubs would take significantly more of the pie than smaller clubs. The main argument in favour of the collective system is that it helps sustain vibrant (inter-club) competition, a crucial element of any sporting activity.

From the perspective of EU law, two issues were important here: first, whether preventing clubs from entering into individual agreements with broadcasters amounts to a restriction of competition and thus falls within the scope of Article 81 (1) TEC; second, whether the collective selling of broadcasting rights is necessary to ensure the survival of the financially weaker participants in the League. If the solidarity argument is accepted, an exemption under Article 81 (3) from the application of Article 81 (1) TEC may be granted (Parrish, 2002: 9). Although the Commission generally has very significant competencies in competition policy, it had already insisted that it did not aspire to become a general sports competition policy regulator. The Commission also increasingly deviated from an orthodox articulation of Articles 81–82 in its communications and became ever more eager to respect the social and cultural benefits of sports in recent years (Weatherill, 2003). Hence, the overall level of top-down pressure (exerted in this instance by the Commission) was less significant than in the previous two sub-cases.

In 1999, largely contrary to the Commission's (original) policy line, the DFB requested an exemption from the application of Article 81 with regard to the central marketing of television and radio broadcasting rights for professional football matches in Germany. In doing so, it was not only concerned about the balance of inter-club competition. If the Commission was to rule in favour of a decentralized model, the DFB and DFL would lose substantial property rights over broadcasting. Aided by UEFA and German policy-makers, and backed by a large majority of clubs, the DFB sought to reduce initial EU-level pressures to decentralize their broadcasting rights scheme.

Under the German collective selling system, the DFB leases the broadcasting rights to the DFL, which markets the rights and redistributes the revenues gained to the clubs. The DFB application for derogation from Article 81 was supported by claims about the solidarity function, which the central marketing system supposedly fulfils. Most officials from the DFB and DFL, as well as the vast majority of clubs, supported this stance, with only Bayern Munich, Borussia Dortmund and Bayer Leverkusen (of the thirty-six professional clubs) favouring a decentralized model due to their capacity to raise considerably greater revenues on their own. Although these clubs sporadically threatened to pursue exit options, such as a European breakaway league, all clubs eventually accepted the collective selling system.[12]

In the pursuit of an exemption from EU anti-trust rules, the DFB and the DFL went to considerable efforts to influence matters, mainly via UEFA. As a member of the UEFA Executive Committee and the Executive Committee Working Group on matters related to the European Union, former DFB President Mayer-Vorfelder was well connected, and within the UEFA framework DFB officials participated directly in talks with representatives from the European Commission, members of the European Parliament and national ministers responsible for sport. In addition, top DFB officials cultivated direct relations with Commissioners Reading (Education and Culture) and Monti (Competition). The DFB's use of UEFA as a channel was convenient since the latter – simultaneously with the DFB case – was itself involved in talks with the Commission, having applied for an exemption from Article 81 concerning the collective marketing of commercial rights to the UEFA Champions League. This lobbying (via UEFA) has retrospectively been judged a success.[13] Rather than applying direct (political) pressure, it was important in the discussions with the Commission and other EU circles to specify the implications of a vigorous application of Community antitrust rules to professional football in Germany. In addition, a certain amount of political pressure spilling over from the Bosman case and the subsequent talks concerning transfer rules provided an additional rationale for the Commission's decision to exempt the new system for marketing Bundesliga broadcasting rights.

In January 2005, the Commission closed the case as a result of certain commitments made by the DFL. Most significantly, media rights are now offered in several packages in a transparent and non-discriminatory procedure, but the new marketing system contains core DFB/DFL demands. The new model has been described as 'essentially a centralized system of marketing broadcasting rights with some decentralized elements on the fringes'.[14] Most importantly, collective marketing of TV rights will broadly continue in one key aspect: clubs have only limited scope for selling their games.[15] Overall, these changes, spurred by EU-level pressures, can be described as 'partial adjustments', since only moderate/modest alterations were made and important policy cores remained untouched.

In the case of Austria, the national football authorities have not been visible in the struggle over the collective selling. Beyond the explanations advanced above, it is safe to assume that the smaller national associations took part in this process merely as interested spectators, monitoring (if at all) what the larger associations and the representatives of bigger clubs were trying to negotiate *vis-à-vis* the European Commission.[16]

Two further specific explanations for this lack of Austrian agency seem promising. On the one hand, the relationship between the (big) clubs in Austria and the national association is relatively harmonious[17] and free of the dualism symptomatic of other cases (such as Germany). Hence the need to go to Brussels to engage EU institutions over specific matters (such as decentralized marketing of TV rights) has arguably been lower. On the other hand, broadcasting rights do not constitute a major issue for the (larger) Austrian clubs, since the rights sold collectively by the League are at a relatively low rate and thus generate only a small sum of money for distribution. From 2007–10, the Football League received a total of €14.33 million per year, from both Austrian public television (ORF) and pay TV (*Neue Kronen Zeitung*, 4 July 2007: 56), a sum dwarfed by the €1.4 billion of the English market or the €440 million in Germany at that time. Broadcasting revenues therefore make up a relatively minor share of the average club's total annual earnings, the average Bundesliga team spending around €10 million per year.[18] This does not mean that the general question of the legal permissibility of collective selling schemes is not applicable to Austria as well; rather, it indicates that the (big) clubs – main drivers of Europeanization in the German case – have shown little activism in pursuing any interest concerning a decentralization of broadcasting rights via (or *vis-à-vis*) Brussels.

In contrast to the German case, where broadcasting issues have enormous implications for the clubs' finances, the revenue structure of most big clubs in Austria has been characterized by a special feature: financial backing by a large sponsor and hence structures of patronage. According to Deloitte, 60% of the football league members' revenues derive from sponsoring (season 2007–08), which represents the highest number among ten researched Western European leagues (Sinnreich, 2009: 49). This alternative source of income explains why most Austrian clubs have not placed the issue of broadcasting rights (plans to generate much more from them via a decentralized system) high on their priority list. However, in January 2010, Rudolf Edlinger, chairman of Austria's most popular football club Rapid Vienna, opposed the new television contract negotiated between the Austrian Football League and pay TV channel Sky, insisting among other things that a further reduction of games in free terrestrial TV would adversely affect the media presence of the club's many corporate sponsors. He threatened to sell television rights for Rapid's home-games individually (Hackl, 2010), which caused the League conference of club chairmen to reject the initial tender and call for new bids.

Explaining similarities and differences

The two country cases presented in this chapter display a number of similarities. First, with regard to the nationality aspect of Bosman, both countries liberalized beyond what was strictly necessary, partly because of similar desires to sign additional moderately priced players from Central and Eastern Europe. Second, this triggered very significant changes amounting to a system transformation in both countries. Third, both countries took counter-measures several years later.

Overall, however, the differences outweigh the similarities, with German football post-Bosman more obviously responding to, engaging with, and being driven by Europeanization processes and pressures than its Austrian football counterpart. (1) While the German clubs and association were actively engaging with (or mostly against) the Commission's liberalizing efforts with regard to broadcasting and the transfer regime, the Austrian football association and clubs remained merely interested spectators. (2) Although counter-measures were taken in both countries against the nationality aspect of Bosman, these proved rather different: the Germans were more subtle and EU-law-compliant, whilst the Austrians' actions were, at best, questionably compliant. (3) Although Austrian football had undergone an important (Central) Europeanization period long before Bosman, a process that was not paralleled in Germany, some more recent developments at the European (but not EU) level such as the Champions League (which could not be analysed here), have been of much more importance for German football.[19]

How can we account for these differences? The two dichotomies outlined in the introduction offer some explanation: the 'big–small' dichotomy; and the contrast between long-standing EU members paired with pro-integration political elites and public and those states that have recently become members along with a less EU-phile political elite and public. These seem relevant in (at least partially) explaining the differences, except perhaps for the latter one (3). Additional factors also played a role, such as the lesser dependence of Austrian clubs on broadcasting money (due to the reliance on sponsors), varying levels of harmony in the relationship between the national football association and the (bigger) clubs, and Austria's regional heritage as a Central European football power with regard to different levels of multi-nationality in its pre-Bosman demographic make-up.

More generally, we conclude that domestic factors can substantially condition Europeanization processes. Domestic-level actors such as clubs, associations and leagues, and transnational actors such as UEFA, may constitute important conditioning elements and buffers to EU-level pressure. Although the EU can exert substantial adaptational pressure, there have been ways of escaping some of the consequences of adaptation or of weakening the pressure itself. The impact of European integration is most effectively mitigated if domestic and transnational agents involve themselves during the formation of policy and negotiation process, as the German sub-cases 2 and 3 have indicated. Yet, in the implementation stage too, a 'conservative' transposition of law may, to some extent, compensate this impact, as the measures taken to promote young German and Austrian players have shown in case 1.

Conclusion

In recent years, debates about the ever-increasing professionalization and excessive forms of commercialization of European football have proliferated. While linked up with these processes, but not reducible to them, we have focused on dynamics of Europeanization within two national football cultures: German and Austrian football, and their respective mixtures of commercial appeal and cultural values. In this, we were guided by an interest in processes of transformation and trans-figuration within the societal sphere, which can, in turn, be attributed to the impact of direct EU policies, indirect pressures emanating from EU-level policies, as well as a host of bottom-up processes of engagement and resistance towards such policies.[20]

More general patterns of development emerge if one is to broaden the view across a multitude of nationally defined football cultures in Europe. First, national structures in European football have undoubtedly internationalized substantially, in some cases, such as the German and the Austrian, going beyond what was necessary after the Bosman ruling of 1995. Thus, following this ruling and the European Commission's investigation on FIFA's international transfer system, the players market is the only sector of European professional sport that has been truly internationalized and liberalized. Other structures and markets in the sport sector remain far more organized along national lines. Such liberalization, on the other hand, does not mean homogenization, as policy and sports actors had (and still have) considerable leeway in deciding upon how to transpose such regulations. At the same time, the pressure that could be marshalled on behalf of national football associations and big clubs in the respective national markets differed markedly. Bigger associations – in terms of membership, market size and visibility at the European level – as well as countries with a host of clubs that regularly compete at the top European level – were far more inclined and successful at 'steering' liberalization dynamics than their smaller counterparts. Smaller countries and their respective football associations have, as the Austrian case indicates, certainly sought to find a way to cope especially with the ensuing crowding out of young talent eligible for national teams. However (and this makes the Austrian case a special one), a historically determined, fairly high level of liberalization pre-dating any EU pressures or other configurations of the national football sector, together with the adaptational pressures on behalf of the EU since the 1990s, might have led to more volatile situations, where media, less EU-phile publics and politicians gained at least temporarily more influence on sports policy than elsewhere.

Second, as the politicization of the transfer issue system (more than the various transpositions of the Bosman ruling concerning 'nationality quota') has shown, such rather defensive gestures countering EU-induced transformational pressure have been articulated not only during the policy implementation phase, but frequently also during policy formulation. Here, the results are fairly unambiguous: bottom-up responses in the sense of policy input on behalf of national sports actors have been the business of bigger countries/leagues, while the reactions of most smaller countries/leagues has been characterized more by 'acquiescence'. This is aptly demonstrated by the contrast of German sports actors and politicians heavily involved in the respective negotiations *vis-à-vis* the spectator role of their Austrian counterparts.

Although this is somewhat paralleled by the dynamics of the European (de-)regulation within the football broadcasting market – intervention of actors from 'bigger' countries in order to modify pressures stemming from the Commission's initial policy agenda, most visible in the German case, and far less engagement on behalf of smaller countries/associations/leagues, e.g. Austria – additional factors must be taken into account. Hence, and third, the strength of bottom-up engagement with European sports – and football, for that matter – policy might vary according to the very structures of the respective markets. The more general pattern that has emerged in European football, whereby collective selling (central marketing) is accepted by the competition watchdogs at the European level as long as TV rights are divided into small packages of several games that then can be sold to different operators, can be explained safely by the successful bidding attempts of the representatives of the larger leagues, as described above. Inaction or 'acquiescence' regarding the issue of football broadcasting rights, as could be regarded in the case of smaller countries with a lower level of professionalization and commercialization (e.g. Austria), however, might also be due to the specific revenue structures in their markets. A fairly high level of patronage and private sponsorship for football clubs might thus have an inhibiting effect on policy activism at the European level.

Not least, the 'Europeanization' of football across Europe cannot be reduced to the interplay of top-down (EU-level) and bottom-up (national-level) pressures alone. Any further analysis of the ongoing transformation of the European football scene should also incorporate the transnational level more thoroughly. This is because European football clubs, transnational elite club groupings, as well as the European football association UEFA and its widely successful model of club competition (Champions League, and to a lesser degree the newly created Europa League) have helped developing sport actors' networks across Europe far beyond any EU-induced change. It is these dynamics, recently paralleled at the level of pan-European supporters' organizations as well, that might contribute substantially to the processes analyzed here.

Notes

1 For the developments at European level, see Brown (2000), Foster (2000), Parrish (2002, 2003), Weatherill (2003) and Parrish and Miettinen (2008). The impact on the domestic sphere has not completely escaped academic attention. For work that links domestic-level football developments more systematically to European integration, see: Brand and Niemann (2007); Manzenreiter and Spitaler (2011 forthcoming); Niemann *et al.* (2011 forthcoming).

2 For a more detailed elaboration of the societal/transnational dimension of Europeanization and its application to football, see Brand and Niemann (2007).

3 For further analysis of such transnational, non-EU-induced dynamics in both cases, see Brand *et al.* (2010).

4 Before the transposition of Bosman, the so-called '3+2 rule' applied. It allowed European teams to field three foreign players and two 'assimilated players', i.e. those who had played in the respective country for at least five consecutive years.

5 Interview with Dr Theo Zwanziger, then Managing President of the DFB, by telephone, January 2005.

6 Interview with Gerhard Mayer-Vorfelder, then President of the DFB, by telephone, January 2005.

7 Since 1976, the employment of non-national football professionals (as of all other migrant workers) was subject to the Federal Act on the Employment of Foreigners (*Ausländerbeschäftigungsgesetz*, BGBl. 218/1975). For reasons of public interest, work permits for football players were normally granted more easily by the public authorities than in some other sectors of employment.

8 Interview with Gerhard Mayer-Vorfelder, then-President of the DFB, 2005.

9 See the joint statement by Gerhard Schröder and Tony Blair in the run-up to the Nice Summit (Meier, 2004: 14).

10 It has approximately 590,000 members, as compared with the 6.5 million members of the German DFB. It is small not in relation to its membership/inhabitant quota, but as a structure of representation within the European system of governance.

11 Ruling of the Regional Superior Court Oldenburg, Az.: 13 O 1195/04, 29 October 2004. See also the confirmatory ruling of the Regional Appeal Court Oldenburg, Az.: 9 U 94/04.

12 Later it was revealed that Bayern Munich came on board mainly because of a 'secret' marketing agreement with the Kirch-Group, which had secured the rights for the period 2000–04. As a result, the club *de jure* agreed to the central marketing model, while *de facto* securing the financial rewards of a decentralized system. See Kruse and Quitzau (2003: 13–14).

13 Interview with Gerhard Mayer-Vorfelder, then President of the DFB, 2005.

14 Interview with Dr Christian Hockenjos, Managing Director at Borussia Dortmund, by telephone, January 2005.
15 Clubs can sell their games for various media only after the match. Time frames for selling these rights differ across the different media. For full details see European Commission (2005). However, the central marketing model has not been unchallenged. In 2008, the domestic federal anti-trust agency opened an investigation, provoked mainly by Bayern Munich's questioning of the deal reached between the DFL and the Kirch subsidiary KF 15 (Franzke, 2008).
16 This is confirmed by the fact that Austria follows the German model in having established a system of collective selling of rights with some modifications.
17 Interview with Peter Klinglmüller, Chief Press Officer at the Austrian Football Association (ÖFB), by telephone, May 2009.
18 Reliable data are hard to compile. The Bundesliga is not allowed to compile data on the clubs' budgets (let alone make them public), while the clubs are reluctant to make them transparent. Austria Vienna has a budget of about €15 million annually, after the club's sponsor, Frank Stronach, drastically reduced its sponsorship and eventually left the club (Adrian and Schächtele, 2008: 43). With the exception of Red Bull Salzburg, this sum seems to be the upper limit at other Austrian clubs. In the case of Austria Vienna, television revenues represent 12% of the overall budget of €15 million (season 2008–09), compared with 70% from sponsor revenues and 15% from ticket sales (*Kurier*, 2009).
19 See Brand *et al.* (2010) as well as Brand and Niemann (2007) on the Champions League and other genuinely transnational activities such as club fora and fan networks.
20 The following conclusions are drawn on the basis of a more comprehensive account of the transformation of European football; see García *et al.* (2011 forthcoming). Both cases analysed here are hence contextualized against the background of more general trends and dynamics of the Europeanization of football.

References

Adrian, S. and Schächtele, K., (2008), *Immer wieder, nimmer wieder: Vom Schicksal des österreichischen Fußballs*, Cologne: Kiepenheuer und Witsch.

Barreaud, M., (1998), *Dictionnaire des Footballeurs Etrangers: Du Championnat Professionnel Français 1932–1997*, Paris: L'Harmattan.

Börzel, T., (2002), 'Member state responses to Europeanization', *Journal of Common Market Studies* 40 (2): 193–214.

Brand, A. and Niemann, A., (2007), 'Europeanisation in the societal/trans-national realm: what European integration studies can get out of analysing football', *Journal of Contemporary European Research* 3 (3): 182–201.

Brand, A., Niemann, A., and Spitaler, G., (2010), 'The Europeanization of Austrian football: history, adaptation and transnational dynamics', *Soccer & Society*, 11 (6): 761–74.

Brown, A., (2000), 'European football and the European Union: governance, participation and social cohesion – towards a policy research agenda', *Soccer and Society* 1 (2): 129–50.

Croci, O., (2001), *Taking the Field: The EC and the Governance of European Football*, paper presented at the 7th ECSA-USA International Conference, Madison, Wisconsin.

Croci, O. and Forster, J., (2004), 'Webs of authority: hierarchies, networks, legitimacy, and economic power in global sport organizations', in G. T. Papanikos (ed.), *The Economics and Management of Mega Athletic Events: Olympic Games, Professional Sports, and Other Essays*, Athens: ATINER: 3–10.

Duke, V., (1994), 'The flood from the East? Perestroika and the migration of sports talent from Eastern Europe', in J. Bale and J. Maguire (eds), *The Global Sports Arena: Athletic Talent Migration in an Interdependent World*, London: Routledge: 153–67.

European Commission, (2005), *Details of Broadcasting Rights Commitments by the German Football League*, press release MEMO/05/16, Brussels.

——, (2007), *Background Paper: Sport Governance in Europe* – White Paper Consultation by Commissioner Jan Figel with the European Sport Federations, JK D(2006) 9809, Brussels.

Foster, K., (2000), 'European law and football: who's in charge?', in J. Garland, D. Malcolm and M. Rowe (eds), *The Future of Football – Challenges for the Twenty-First Century*, London: Frank Cass: 34–51.

Franzke, R., (2003), 'Nicht EU-Spieler nicht in den Amateur-Teams. Schily zieht Rote Karte!', in *Kicker Online*, 27 January.

——, (2008), 'Die Liga zittert: Platzt der TV-Vertrag?', in *Kicker*, 10 March: 8–10.

García, B., Niemann, A. and Grant, W., (2011 forthcoming), 'Conclusion: A Europeanised game?', in A. Niemann, B. García and W. Grant (eds), *The Transformation of European Football: A Process of Europeanisation?* Manchester: Manchester University Press.

Giulianotti, R. and Robertson, R., (2007), 'Recovering the social: globalization, football and transnationalism', *Global Networks*, 7 (2): 144–86.

Hackl, C., (2010), 'Ein Bruderzwist im Hause Fußball', *Der Standard*, 13 January.

Horak, R., (1992), 'Austrification as modernization: changes in Viennese football culture', in R. Giulianotti and J. Williams (eds), *Game Without Frontiers. Football, Identity and Modernity*, Aldershot: Ashgate: 47–71.

Horak, R. and Maderthaner, W., (1996), 'A culture of urban cosmopolitanism: Uridil and Sindelar as Viennese coffee-house heroes', *International Journal of the History of Sport*, 13 (1): 139–55.

Karollus, M. M., (2006), 'Gemeinschaftsrechtliche Schranken für Ausländerklauseln im Sport, insbesondere auch gegenüber Drittstaatsangehörigen', in A. Grundei and M. Karollus (eds), *Aktuelle Rechtsfragen des Fußballsports IV*, Vienna: Linde: 67–91.

Kruse, J. and Quitzau, J., (2003), *Fußball-Fernsehrechte: Aspekte der Zentralvermarktung*, Diskussionspapier 18, Hamburg: Universität der Bundeswehr, Fächergruppe Volkswirtschaftslehre.

Kurier, (2009), 'Lizenz zum Zittern: Fit-mach-mit vor dem Millionenspiel', 10 March: 29.

Ladrech, R., (1994). 'Europeanisation of domestic politics and institutions: the case of France', *Journal of Common Market Studies*, 32: 69–88.

Lanfranchi, P., (1994), 'The migration of footballers: the case of France, 1932–82', in J. Bale and J. Maguire (eds), *The Global Sports Arena: Athletic Talent Migration in an Interdependent World*, London: Routledge: 63–77.

Lanfranchi, P. and Taylor, M., (2001), *Moving with the Ball. The Migration of Professional Footballers*, Oxford: Berg.

Liegl, B. and Spitaler, G., (2008), *Legionäre am Ball. Migration im österreichischen Fußball nach 1945*, Vienna: Braumüller.

——, (2009), 'Zwischen Transnationalität und Identitätspolitik – Österreichische Migrationsregimes und der Profifußball (1945–2008)', *SWS-Rundschau* 49 (1): 234–55.

Manzenreiter, W. and Spitaler, G., (eds) (2011, forthcoming), *The European Spectacle: Governance, Citizenship and the New European Football Championships*, London: Taylor & Francis.

Marschik, M., (1998), 'MITROPA: representations of Central Europe in Football', *International Review for the Sociology of Sport*, 36 (1): 7–23.

——, (2001), '"Even the parliament interrupted its session . . .": creating local and national identity in Viennese football', *Journal of Sport and Social Issues*, 22 (2): 199–211.

Marschik, M., and Sottopietra, D., (2000), *Erbfeinde und Hasslieben. Konzept und Realität Mitteleuropas im Sport*, Münster: LIT.

Meier, H. E., (2004), 'From Bosman to collective bargaining agreements? The regulation of the market for professional soccer players', *International Sports Law Journal*, 3 (3–4): 4–13.

Mittag, J. and Legrand, B., (2010), 'Towards a Europeanisation of football? The history of the UEFA European Football Championship', *Soccer & Society*, 11 (6): 709–22.

Niemann, A., García, B. and Grant, W. (2011 forthcoming), *The Transformation of European Football: Towards the Europeanisation of the National Game*, Manchester: Manchester University Press.

Olsen, J. P., (2002), 'The many faces of Europeanization', *Journal of Common Market Studies* 40: 921–52.

Parrish, R., (2002), 'Football's place in the Single European Market', *Soccer and Society* 3 (1): 1–21.

——, (2003), *Sports Law and Policy in the European Union*, Manchester: Manchester University Press.

Parrish, R. and Miettinen, S., (2008), *The Sporting Exception in the European Union Law*, The Hague: Asser.

Radaelli, C., (2000), *Whither Europeanization? Concept Stretching and Substantive Change*, European Integration Online Papers No. 4 (8), http://eiop.or.at/eiop/texte/2000–2008a.htm.

Schmidt, V., (2002). 'Europeanization and the mechanics of economic policy adjustments', *Journal of European Public Policy*, 9: 894–912.

Sinnreich, D., (2009), 'Fairplay und Folklore', *ballesterer*, 46: 49.

Skocek, J. and Weisgram, W., (2004), *Das Spiel ist das Ernste: Ein Jahrhundert Fußball in Österreich*, Vienna: Echomedia.

Weatherill, S., (2003), '"Fair play please!" recent developments in the application of EC law to sport', *Common Market Law Review* 40 (1): 51–93.

12 Why are the European and American sports worlds so different?

Path dependence in European and American sports history

Maarten van Bottenburg

Introduction

In the nineteenth and twentieth centuries, European and American sports formations and cultures developed along quite different lines. First, different sports became popular in the United States than in Europe. Baseball, basketball, ice hockey and 'American football' were the most prominent in the United States, set against 'global' football ('association' or 'soccer'), tennis, cycling and gymnastics as the most popular sports in Europe. Second, these sports were developed, organized and practised in different contexts: that of schools, colleges and universities in the United States, and that of voluntary clubs and associations in Europe. Third, American sports commercialized and professionalized earlier and much more thoroughly than European sports. Fourth, as a business, professional sports in the United States were organized in closed leagues of competing franchises, while both amateur and professional sports in Europe formed part of open competitions based on the principle of promotion and relegation. Fifth, America's closed professional leagues remained national in scope and meaning for a long time, and were established under profit-oriented managerial control without any international regulatory body. This often led to the formation of competing leagues in the same branch of sport. In contrast, Europe's open sport competitions had an international or even global appeal and were governed by international non-profit federations. And sixth, compared with Europe, the American government hardly influenced the development of the sporting formations and cultures. Sports in the United States were market-driven and developed independently of the state, while governments in Europe increasingly intervened in the world of sports, especially after the Second World War.

Because the American sporting formation and culture seems to be the anomaly in this respect, American authors have come to speak of 'America's sports exceptionalism' (Markovits and Hellerman, 2001: 39–51; Sparvero *et al.*, 2008: 269). This fits with the American self-image and pride in being fundamentally unique, different from the rest of the world. It also elaborates on the scholarly literature of American exceptionalism, going back to classical studies like de

Tocqueville's *De la démocratie en Amérique* (1992; 1835–40) and Sombart's *Warum gibt is in den Vereinigten Staaten keinen Sozialismus?* (1906). The American exceptionalism thesis, however, has also become the subject of considerable debate with respect to not only the causes of America's alleged uniqueness, but also – and more fundamentally – the questions of whether this concept is a reality or a myth, and what empirical evidence can be found for both positions (e.g. Shafer, 1991; Tyrrell, 1991; Lipset, 1997; Lockhart, 2003; Hodgson, 2009). Recently, this wider discussion has been extended to the world of sports. Pope, for example, has tried to overcome a strictly national focus on American sport history and to endorse a critical, transnational mode of analysis. He interprets the American story not as an exception to dominant patterns of national power in a world of nations, but 'as a particular, and constantly changing expression of complex forces' (Tyrrell, quoted in Pope, 2007: 95). In line with this, Nafziger argued that the variations in sporting practices in the United States, as well as the much neglected similarities between features of the European sports model and the actual organization of sports in the United States, call into question both the reality of a North American sports model and the extent to which its features differ materially from those of its European sibling. Moreover, Nafziger noted that trends of globalization and commercialization continue on both sides of the Atlantic, accelerating a convergence of the European and North American sports model in many respects and on all levels of competition (Nafziger, 2008).

The problem, however, is that systematic comparisons of the European and American sporting configurations are hard to find in spite of an increasing interest in this topic by politicians, journalists and scholars. There are too many monographs and articles on European and American sport to mention. However, only a few authors (e.g. Naul, 1991; van Bottenburg, 2001; Markovits and Hellerman, 2001; Halgreen, 2004; Hofmann, 2004; Nafziger, 2008; Szymanski, 2008; Stokvis, 2009) have tried to describe and explain their differences and similarities on the basis of a systematic comparison from a historical, sociological, economic or legal perspective. As a result, many questions concerning the social origins and implications of the differences between American and European sporting formations and cultures remain unanswered.

One of the most intriguing questions in this respect is why voluntary clubs have become the organizational principle for practising sport across broad areas of Europe, whereas schools and colleges have become fundamental to the organization of sport in the United States. Was it not the emphasis on voluntary associations in America that so impressed de Tocqueville, Weber, Gramsci and other foreign observers as one of the distinctive characteristics of the 'new' versus the 'old' world (Lipset, 1991: 20)? Following this puzzling question, other issues arise. Why did American high school and intercollegiate athletics, most of which is publicly funded, develop in the direction of a nationally oriented market model, in which a few, elite athletes perform for the benefit of paying customers, and become connected with personally owned, business-like leagues? In contrast, why did private clubs and associations in Europe in many sports resist commercialization for so long, initiating and dominating a global network of amateur sport organizations and competitions as well as becoming closely connected to national sports policies in their countries? To what extent have these differences been challenged by broader processes that have been felt in all western societies since the Second World War, such as the growth of affluence, the extension of secondary and higher education, the replacement of manual labour by office-based jobs, and, more recently, accelerated processes of globalization, commercialization and mediatization? Have these trends led to convergence and reconfiguration, or are they counterbalanced by the 'path-dependent' national dynamics of sport on both sides of the Atlantic?

Building on monographs and articles on European and American sports formation and culture, and on a selection of systematic comparisons, this chapter aims to answer these questions and thus to explain the main differences between the two sports configurations. Inspired by insights from historical sociology and historical institutionalism, the explanation will be based on three basic principles. The first is that the current differences between European and American sporting configurations will be analysed from a historical perspective. European sport and American sport are far from static systems. On the contrary, they have moved from and towards each other, although we do not yet understand exactly why, to what extent, and with what result. Second, as each sporting configuration has developed within a specific society, the differences between the two systems will be analysed by connecting the (changing) sports configuration with the (changing) societal system. And third, the differences between Europe and the United States will be explained by making use of a 'path-dependent' analysis (Mahoney, 2000; Pierson, 2004).

According to Mahoney, 'path dependence occurs when a contingent historical event triggers a subsequent sequence that follows a relatively deterministic pattern' (Mahoney, 2000: 535). He further suggests that a path-dependent analysis has three defining features. First, path-dependent analysis involves the study of causal processes that are highly sensitive to events that take place in the early stages of an overall historical sequence. Second, in a path-dependent sequence, early historical events are contingent occurrences – or 'critical junctures' – that cannot be explained on the basis of prior events or 'initial conditions'. Third, once contingent historical events take place, path-dependent sequences are marked by self-reinforcing mechanisms that reproduce a particular institutional pattern over time. Initial steps in a particular direction induce further movement in the same direction (Mahoney, 2000). The critical junctures are characterized by the adoption of a particular institutional arrangement from among two or more alternatives. 'These junctures are "critical" because once a particular option is selected it becomes progressively more difficult to return to the initial point when multiple alternatives were still available" (Mahoney, 2000: 513). The choices made during these critical junctures close off alternative options and lead to the establishment of institutions that generate enduring and self-reinforcing processes (Capoccia and Kelemen, 2007).

It is important to be explicit and clear about the use and meaning of the terms 'path dependence' and 'critical junctures'. According to Mahoney, the term 'path dependence' is often used too loosely and without clear definition, meaning only that what has happened earlier will affect later sequences of events (Mahoney, 2000: 510). Similarly, Capoccia and Kelemen argue that 'critical junctures' and their synonyms are too often treated as 'bookends' or as a '*deus ex machina*' in otherwise carefully constructed stories of institutional development. They emphasize that researchers should not stop at simply identifying a critical juncture, but must instead deepen the investigation of the historical material to identify the key decisions (and the key events influencing those decisions) steering the system in one or another direction, favouring one institutional equilibrium over another (Capoccia and Kelemen, 2007: 343).

A four-part analysis follows of the critical junctures and path-dependent sequences in the history of the organization of sport in Europe and the United States. This needs to start by acknowledging that European sport itself is highly differ-entiated. In the first section, I provisionally distinguish a few archetypical models in the organization of sports in Europe and compare these with the model that is archetypical for the United States. In the subsequent sections, I concentrate on an explanation of the two most fundamental differences between the European and American archetypes. The second section focuses on the critical juncture that led to diverging structuring principles of sport participation on both sides of the Atlantic: voluntary clubs in Europe (club structure) versus educational institutions in the United States (school structure). The third section places the critical juncture at the heart of the analysis that initiated differences in professional sport competitions: associations as part of globally operating federations in Europe (association structure) versus franchises affiliated to personally owned business-like leagues in the United States (commercial structure). Hence the second section focuses mainly on what is called 'grassroots sports' or 'sport for all', and the third section on 'professional (high-performance) sports'. This is followed by an analysis of the causal, self-reinforcing, path-dependent processes initiated by these critical junctures in the fourth section, and a discussion of the impact of converging dynamics on these processes, resulting from broader social, economic and political changes in the second half of the twentieth century.

Archetypical models of sport

Much of the grassroots sport in the United States is provided by schools, colleges, universities, public parks and recreation departments, as well as club-like businesses such as fitness and health centres. In addition to these sport providers, there are large multi-sport organizations that function as private not-for-profit enterprises, such as the YMCA, Boys & Girls Clubs of America, and Jewish Community Centres. These organizations provide sport as part of their educational and social service mission. Moreover, there are also private, independent clubs in several branches of sport, spread throughout the country, especially in those sports – like handball – that have not been established in the school system, or sports such as tennis and golf that are (also) played by older adults, often in quite expensive country clubs (Slack and Parent, 2008; Sparvero *et al.*, 2008). In general terms, the list of the main sport providers in Europe does not deviate from this. Here, too, sport is provided by educational institutions, sport and recreation departments of local governments and commercial clubs for fitness-related activities and sports such as squash, bowling, martial arts and adventure sports (van Bottenburg *et al.*, 2005).

The difference between the United States and Europe, however, lies in the relative importance of these providers. In the United States, an educational–commercial configuration has become predominant. This configuration is characterized by a system in which schools and colleges and commercially managed sports centres form the main organizing principle of sport participation. Voluntary clubs and public authorities have had negligible impact on this configuration compared with their European counterparts. In Europe, on the other hand, a voluntary–governmental configuration has become the principal system. Voluntary sports clubs and associations assumed a strong position. In many European countries, these voluntary organizations have been confronted with, and supported by, an increasingly active public sector, while the influence of the business community and educational system remained relatively weak until the last decades of the twentieth century.

Of course, the overall picture of the European sport model is heterogeneous. Each country and region has had its own specific national history and sport development. The tradition of voluntary sports clubs is strongest in northern and western parts, and weakest in eastern parts of Europe. In recent decades, commercially managed sports centres have become important for sports participation, especially in north-western European countries such as Sweden, Denmark, UK, Ireland, the Netherlands, Belgium and Germany, and in southern European countries such as Spain and Italy. In countries such as Luxembourg, France, Austria and Finland, the strong position of voluntary sports clubs goes hand-in-hand with the weaker position of commercially managed sports centres but also a more active role for public authorities. Finland scores the highest in sports participation and physical activities in Europe, and seems to be characterized, quite atypically, by a strong missionary state, a high level of informal sport participation, and a lower level of sport participation in sports and health clubs. Even more atypical are the eastern European countries. Here, a relatively weak (though strengthening) position of both sport clubs and commercially managed sports centres goes hand-in-hand with a relatively strong (though diminishing) presence and role of public authorities. With all kinds of differences between these countries, this governmental–educational configuration predominates in Poland, Estonia, Hungary, the Czech Republic, Slovakia, Lithuania, Slovenia and Cyprus. In these countries, the sports participation structures still show the marks of their long-term dependence on the state-regulated and -financed educational system (schools and universities), although new commercial and voluntary structures are rising (Figure 12.1).[1]

Club versus school structures

The contrasts between the dominant configurations in Europe and the United States are all the more intriguing if one realizes that, in its early stages, modern sport was

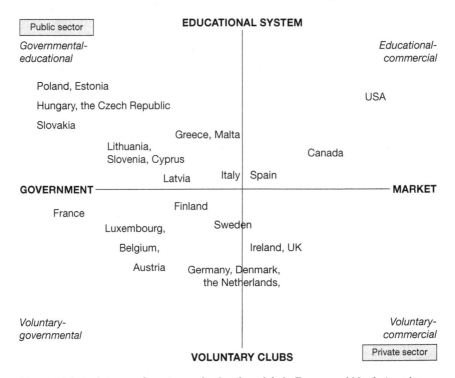

Figure 12.1 Archetypes of sport organizational models in Europe and North America

organized in clubs in both Europe and the United States. In line with the quickly spreading voluntary associations in the English-speaking world in other fields of social activity (politics, religion, art, music and trade), the club became the basic organizational unit of modern sport on both sides of the Atlantic. The creation of clubs was an expression of the right of individuals to associate freely without the interference or oversight of the state (Szymanski, 2008). Moreover, it was quite a simple process. Groups of boys, young men or adults just followed democratic procedures that governed voluntary associations. They chose a name, wrote and ratified a constitution and bylaws, listed the financial and personal obligations of each member, and searched for playing space (for example, see for Europe: Holt, 1981, 1989; and for the US: Kirsch, 1989).

The associative model was more or less adopted from the British, who dictated the development of modern sport in its earliest decades both on the European continent and in the United States. However, between the mid-nineteenth and mid-twentieth centuries, sport in America developed along an entirely different path than it took in Europe (Rader, 1983; Mandell, 1984; Guttmann, 1988; Markovits and Hellerman, 2001). This was made possible because the United States underwent a relatively autonomous modernization process, surpassing the European countries in several respects by the end of the nineteenth century. Most of the inhabitants were European immigrants or their descendants but, especially after the Civil War, they increasingly emphasized their independence and cultivated their national traits. As the United States became a key player on the world stage, its citizens' early admiration of English culture was replaced by self-confidence in their country's own achievements. In line with this, they took the liberty of reinterpreting English sports culture. The products of this were new sports such as baseball, football and basketball, which they were proud to call American (Kirsch, 1989; van Bottenburg, 2001).

The development of a principle, which deviated from Europe, in the organization and regulation of these sports was yet another expression of this. The initial process of club formation in the field of sport by young men was stimulated unintentionally in Europe and the United States by the rise of secondary and higher education in the second half of the nineteenth century. Being brought together in schools or colleges, they started all kinds of activities in self-organized debating societies, fraternities and sororities, and also athletic organizations. Initially, in both the United States and most European countries, this process of club formation by young students took place independently of school programmes. In the second half of the nineteenth century, however, the club-based sport competitions increasingly met with opposition from school authorities. They criticized the new craze for sport, which, it was claimed, was detrimental to study and caused problems with injuries and unruly behaviour. Nonetheless, the school authorities in Europe did not try to gain control of the club-based sport participation of their students, nor did they – or only slowly and partly – allow the students to organize sports in the context of their schools (Stokvis, 2009). Conversely, in the United States, educators across the country tried to increase their authority over their students' sport activities. This led to the development of the comprehensive high schools, which supplanted the academic-oriented high school between 1890 and 1920. In these comprehensive high schools, special attention was given to the participation of pupils in common extracurricular activities such as sports, social activities and the government of the school (Rader, 1983).

These contingent events in Europe and the United States took place in a relatively short period, but would trigger path-dependent processes that constrained future choices and thus produced distinct legacies. In the United States, the organization of sport became included in the extracurricular programmes of the educational institutions, whereas clubs and schools remained separated in most European countries. Before discussing the self-reinforcing path-dependent processes that resulted from this critical juncture, I will go more deeply into the key factors that steered the system in one or the other direction. In a recent publication, the Dutch sociologist Stokvis has attempted to provide an explanation for the watershed in the history of the organization of sport on both sides of the Atlantic (Stokvis, 2009). In this article, Stokvis refers to four interrelated factors. The first is that American high schools in the first decades of the twentieth century were increasingly comprised of more heterogeneous groups of students than secondary schools in many European countries. The United States developed a concept of education that emphasized the inclusion of large numbers on all levels. Secondary schools in

European countries were, on the other hand, often split up and organized according to intellectual performance, social background and – in some countries – religion. Here, higher education remained the preserve of a privileged few until the education explosion of the late 1960s and early 1970s (Markovits and Hellerman, 2001). The increasingly heterogeneous composition of the student population at American high schools stimulated a reform of the classical curriculum, with special attention being paid to extracurricular activities. This change was strongly supported by middle-income parents, who saw high schools not as academic institutions designed to prepare students for entrance into colleges, but rather as places to equip their sons with the social skills required for white-collar occupations (Stokvis, 2009).

This parental support for school reform with extracurricular sport activities under adult control is related to a second factor that distinguished the American from the European situation. As Stokvis observed in an earlier publication (Stokvis, 1989: 91), parents of students in the United States have always had a greater say in school policy than in Europe, where the school curriculum has been brought under the control of central governments. This parental participation in school governance created stronger ties between educational institutions and local communities in the United States than in Europe. This enhanced the development of community activities such as sport competitions within high schools and colleges. In contrast, students in Europe turned – and still turn – their back on the schools after school hours to practise sport or play music in autonomous clubs. Wilson strengthens this argument by adding that American high schools, much more than their European counterparts, are governed locally on a township, county or school district basis. The supreme authority at the grassroots level is the school board. These boards are typically filled by elections won by 'practical men' with a business background and not by those interested in the intellect. Most of them are males who favour both material symbols of education and sport competitions. Schools and universities in Europe, on the other hand, devote themselves mainly to education, including physical education, while private clubs provide opportunities to practise and watch sports at all levels (Wilson, 1994).

Moreover, the sport programmes had – and still have – an important additional function. This is a third factor: educational leaders recognized that interscholastic athletics could be used in solving the problem of giving a common identity to this heterogeneous mass of students, with all its potential class and ethnic conflicts. Markovits and Hellerman emphasize that:

> As in the case of major European soccer clubs with their clear identities, milieus, and networks, the football and basketball teams of American universities became essential representatives of the identity and culture of their respective regions, states, cities and towns. On the European continent, sports never entered the realm of the universities, since these were seen as research institutions, training grounds for state bureaucrats, or domains of the church. In all three cases, they remained strictly in the realm of the mind and had little, if any, tolerance for pursuits of the body.
>
> (Markovits and Hellerman, 2001: 43)

Apart from interscholastic athletics, the public high schools had no common goals that could inspire the allegiance of the student population as a whole. Varsity sport, including the various accompanying ceremonies, however, could create a positive attitude towards the school and enhance the identification of the community with the school (Wilson, 1994; Stokvis, 2009). As Rader observed, the results of this could – and can – be seen in salaries and facilities. School boards typically pay the coach more than any other teacher, and invariably place a higher priority on the construction of a gymnasium or a football field than a laboratory or a library (Rader, 1983: 163). Everywhere in the United States, high schools and colleges appointed professional coaches who developed coaching and managerial rather than pedagogical skills. This professionalization of coaching reinforced the control of the college administration over the sports participation of the students (Wilson, 1994).

In addition to the more homogeneous student population, the educational ethos and the stronger government control of the school curriculum in many European countries, Stokvis points to another decisive difference between both sides of the Atlantic that hindered the introduction of extramural sport programmes in European schools, namely the opposition of physical education teachers to modern English sports in the second half of the nineteenth century. In the mid-nineteenth century, these physical education teachers had successfully propagated gymnastics. In many European countries, gymnastics was included in the school curriculum as a means to improve discipline and strengthen the nation. When modern sports were introduced a few decades later, they often met with strong opposition from physical educationalists. The practice of sports outside schools or in extracurricular pro-grammes could undermine the status of gymnastics. Moreover, the propagandists of gymnastics argued that sports without proper supervision would produce fanaticism to the detriment of homework and students' futures. In their pleas for gymnastics and opposition to modern sports, the physical education teachers addressed – and were backed by – the central government, notably in countries that were confronted with escalating political tensions or military confrontations. As noted above, European states controlled the school curriculum more than the federal or state government in the United States. As a result, the playing of sport remained separate from gymnastics, and thus exceptional at schools in many European countries. Instead, sport was confined to private clubs until well into the twentieth century (Naul, 1991; Riordan and Krüger, 2003; Pfister, 2006; Szymanski, 2008). Physical educators in the United States, on the other hand, intended not to eliminate interscholastic sports, but to position physical education as their foundation. However, they did not succeed in this, as athletic competitions moved irresistibly to dominate programmes of physical education (Wilson, 1994).

Association versus commercial structures

As Holt rightly argues in his seminal *Sport and the British*, it was not the provision of sport for profit that was remarkable in the nineteenth and twentieth centuries, but the degree to which commercial forces were excluded from sport (Holt, 1989:

281). Modern sports evolved out of traditional pastimes that had a long tradition of prizes in cash or in kind. However, this tradition was interrupted by an era of amateurism, which lasted from the second half of the nineteenth century to the end of the twentieth century (Stokvis, 2003).

The amateur rule originated in England as a means of class distinction and class exclusivity. It was rooted in a combination of increased social tension in mid-Victorian England and the growing popularity of sport among the working classes in this period (Holt, 1989: 108). With the spread of English sports to the European continent, this amateur rule was more or less enforced in many sports and countries. Because athletes from outside England were allowed to compete with the English only if they could demonstrate that they did not play for pay, their national governing bodies had to guarantee their amateur status. The English could demand this from athletes abroad because England enjoyed such a lead over other countries in most sports that these foreign athletes were honoured and keen to compete with the English. In some spectator sports, for example (association) football, cricket, boxing, horseracing, cycling, tennis and golf, professionalism was accepted, but only as part of an international sport system which was governed by middle-class amateurs in national and international amateur associations. As such, in many European nations – and indeed elsewhere in the world – professional leagues and competitions developed into a kind of non-profit-making cartels, which remained under the auspices of their national amateur governing bodies (Holt, 1989: 285). This, however, was not the case in the United States. Although amateur sports emerged here too after the Civil War, the American sports world came to diverge from the European with the creation of competing personally owned commercial leagues. These leagues came to operate quite independently of the rest of the global sporting system.

At least four factors led to this critical juncture. First, it is generally agreed by scholars that the distinction between professional and amateur proved to be less tenable in the United States than in Europe because of differences in the class structure (Rader, 1983; Mandell, 1984; Guttmann, 1988). According to Mandell, sports business, sports spectatorship and sports heroes were smoothly integrated in the new society, which was 'equalitarian, literate, accomplishment oriented, optimistic, materialistic, relatively traditionless and geographically dispersed' (Mandell, 1984: 192). In nineteenth-century England, with its more rigid class structure, boundaries between classes were crossed with the greatest difficulty. Sports were one of the many status markers in this class conflict. In the United States, class sensitivities were not as keen, thus creating more freedom to transcend class boundaries in sport (Wilson, 1994: 70).

Second, Americans were hardly involved at all in the foundation of international governing bodies in sports such as (association) football, athletics, tennis, (field) hockey, swimming and gymnastics. Contrary to European sport history, they produced new sports of American origin, such as baseball, (American) football and basketball, which came to dominate the national sports scene. In these sports, several local and regional leagues developed which were hardly influenced by English or international sporting governing bodies (van Bottenburg, 2001). On the European continent, many English sports were adopted at the end of the nineteenth and the beginning of the twentieth century. During this period, there was greater inter-dependency between these nations than ever before. In the light of their diverging languages and cultures, there was a clear need for international regulation and standardization in many fields. In the sports field, this led to the foundation of authoritative international organizations with a variety of regulatory functions, preventing or discouraging initiatives by other organizations to start competing, commercial leagues (Stokvis, 1989). The American sports world, however, developed in relative geographical and cultural isolation from this process of organization, regulation and standardization in the 'Old World', giving Americans more room for all kinds of commercial initiatives to establish closed professional leagues under profit-oriented managerial control, especially in the American sports (Mandell, 1984; Markovits and Hellerman, 2001). Commercial and professional sports competitions in Europe thus became far more international in scope than those in the United States (Wilson, 1994).

A third factor is that, as I argued in the previous section, the educational institu-tions became the main organizers of play in the United States whereas the voluntary associations came to dominate in Europe. Soon after the introduction of inter-collegiate sports, groups of colleges formed committees to regulate competition. This gave rise to several conferences, all over the country, rearranging the structure of college sports away from a hierarchical, single-sport arrangement, which was dominant in the international sporting system, to a horizontal, multi-sport system. The constitution of the international sport federations provided that in each country, a single organization in each sport should exercise control over the national competition. In the United States, however, the National Collegiate Athletic Association (NCAA), formed in 1910, refused to work within these international rules and isolated itself from the international – and Olympic – sports movement (Wilson, 1994).

Fourth, in this college setting, the Americans imposed their own particular interpretation of amateurism, which was quite unlike that found in the club tradition in the United States or amateur sports in England.

> As early as the 1870s, college teams were competing against each other for both cash and non-cash [. . .] prizes, competing against professionals, charging money at the gate, [. . .] spending heavily on recruitment and support of athletes, and hiring professional coaches. [. . .] Yet because they tied sports to college attendance, they could use the expansion of higher education as a basis for the argument that their version of amateurism was more democratic and open than were the private, voluntary efforts of club sports.
>
> (Wilson, 1994: 71)

As such, high school and intercollegiate athletics, most of which were publicly funded, developed in the direction of a market model. Interestingly, the team and league owners were careful not to compete with the college teams for playing talent. They agreed not to raid colleges for talented players until their eligibility as defined by the NCAA had expired. At the same time, this agreement allowed and enabled professional leagues to connect themselves to the intercollegiate leagues as their 'farm system' where talents are nurtured (Wilson, 1994). In Europe, the nurturing of talent is one of the functions of local sports clubs. These clubs are connected to national and international governing bodies that organize local, regional, national and international (open) competitions for different age groups and have developed selection procedures and systems of promotion and relegation. The American system of personally owned commercial (closed) leagues lacked this system. As alternatives, they have allied themselves to intercollegiate competitions and started minor leagues.

Self-reinforcing sequences on both sides of the Atlantic

The critical junctures examined here had diverging consequences for the further development of American and European sporting formation and cultures. In the United States, each school, college and university developed an athletic department, created sports facilities and venues, and became culturally interpreted as the setting for sports activities. In large parts of Europe, on the other hand, it was principally in the voluntary club where sports provision could be found, where the expertise to organize sports competitions was developed, and which parents thought of when they wanted their children to play the sports they liked.

Hence, when the rising level of education and prosperity in the western world led to an explosive growth in sport participation, this was absorbed in the school system in the United States and in the club system in Europe. It was this institutional arrangement that offered the most and best sport facilities, coaches and competitions. It was the schools and colleges in the United States and the sport clubs in Europe that came to be seen as the normal, logical and 'natural' settings for organizing and practising sport. As more and more investments were made, and more and more expertise was concentrated in one or other of these systems, it became progressively more difficult to return to the initial point where both alternative forms of institutional arrangement still could be put forward as an equivalent option, and to transform the dominant pattern. Once adopted, the school system in the United States and the club system in Europe delivered increasing benefits as they developed, and this led to dramatically different paths in the history of sport. As these processes progressed, they evolved mechanisms that reproduced their distinctive institutional pattern over time (Mahoney, 2000).

A further self-reinforcing sequence was that the American system became more elite sport-oriented and the European system more directed towards sport for all. Sports practised at the American high schools, colleges and universities became highly competitive and achievement-oriented. Interscholastic sports grew into an institution governed not by the participants themselves, but by faculties, administrations and alumni, who focused primarily on the effect sport can have on the prestige of their schools and colleges, and the identification with the school by students and the local communities (Guttmann, 1988; Stokvis, 2009). The coaches and athletic directors modelled their programmes on professional or high-level elite sport with the emphasis on winning and on the higher-profile sports. Their goal became to be ranked, rather than to respond to the needs of all students in their schools (Slack and Parent, 2008). As Wilson points out: 'coaches were rarely trained in physical education, athletic facilities were not designed for mass participation, and interscholastic contests were confined to a few sports with no recognized carryover value into adult years' (Wilson, 1994: 289). Varsity athletes – the most talented and competitive students – came to enjoy institutional support through provision of facilities, coaching, trainers, and the costs of attending competitions, while less talented students had the opportunity to participate in college-based 'club' sports. These, however, were not – or less well – supported and regulated by the athletics departments of the educational institutions (Sparvero *et al.*, 2008).

In western European countries, on the other hand, the dominant trend in the second half of the twentieth century was to facilitate 'sport for all' and to open sporting clubs to everyone. This was partly the result of increased government interference in the field of sport. In response to the growing number of sports participants, governments increasingly subsidized clubs in western European countries for the construction of sporting facilities and the training and coaching of youngsters. For the clubs, however, this government support also resulted in increased pressure by government authorities to open their doors for everyone, put less emphasis on competition and achievement sport, and create more possibilities for recreational sports participation. This was clearly linked to the welfare policy principles of the 1960s and 1970s in western European 'welfare states' (Houlihan and White, 2002; Bergsgard *et al.*, 2007).

In eastern Europe, the communist authorities also encouraged sport after the Second World War, but this policy change was driven primarily by their wish to gain international repute and bind people more firmly to compatriots, their unions, and the party. State support in eastern European countries targeted first-class athletes whose achievements would boost the country's international prestige, emphasizing the amateur sports that had been integrated in the Olympic programme. As with sporting culture in the United States, so sport in eastern Europe became highly achievement-oriented, focusing on a specific group of sports and creating particular sports academies to prepare young talented athletes for international sporting competition (e.g. Hoberman, 1993; Girginov and Sandanski, 2004). This was, however, the product of state support and promotion, whereas sports development in the United States has been an example of a *laissez faire* system. In Eastern Europe, the responsibility for providing sport opportunities was often taken over by publicly funded and managed educational institutions, and to a lesser extent by local governments and quasi-public voluntary agencies (Wilson, 1994).

Related to the process just mentioned, sports in the United States became dominated – both at school and university level – by a spectator- or audience-centred perspective, whereas – at least at the club level – a player- or participant-centred approach prevailed in Europe (Stokvis, 2003). As a result of the audience-centred perspective in the United States, only a limited number of sports are included in the high school and college athletic programmes. The particular mix of sport varies from school to school, but in general those sports that attract the most public attention are widely included: the most commercialized and professionalized sports (football, basketball, baseball, tennis); the most appealing Olympic sports (track-and-field, swimming, gymnastics); and sports such as ice hockey, rowing, soccer, volleyball, and wrestling are well covered in most but not all regions. Most other sports, however, are rarely, if ever found in the high school and college sport systems (canoeing, shooting, handball, skiing). As a result of this, athletes are typically channelled into sports for which there are opportunities to compete in school (Sparvero *et al.*, 2008).

Both critical junctures in the organization of sport therefore not only reserved many sports opportunities to those attending schools and colleges, it also had a powerful effect on the kind of sport experience they had (Wilson, 1994). It is true that Title IX of the Education Amendments of 1972 has secured or improved the position of some women's sports (Suggs, 2005). This, however, has been accompanied by the elimination of some 'minor' Olympic sports for men in order to obtain percentages of participation that appear equal for both sexes. Moreover, the American sport system also implies that sport participation has traditionally peaked during childhood and adolescence. The 40-year-old, unfit and unhealthy alumnus, watching sport on television, with beer and snack food at hand, is a well known American stereotype. Public money for sport facilities is mainly channelled through schools and universities. Adults who are beyond their school and college years are therefore not served as well as the young. The school sport programmes concentrate on the biggest team sports that students in their later life seldom play, and offer athletic facilities that are only open to their students. Private enterprise is expected to fill the gaps in sport provision (Sparvero *et al.*, 2008: 243–50).

The western European club system is based less on spectators and viewers than on participants. In general, the club facilities are created by or with the financial support of the government. This is generally based on the needs of the participants, with the number of club members as the main indicator. Children and adolescents are overrepresented in the European club system – just as white males and higher-income groups are – but in countries such as Sweden, Norway, Denmark, Ireland, England, the Netherlands, Belgium, Luxembourg, France, Switzerland, Austria, Spain and Italy, sports clubs represent 10–30% of the entire population, including many people in their thirties, forties, fifties and even hardy types in their sixties and seventies (van Bottenburg *et al.*, 2005). While Americans usually abandon serious participation in sports after graduation from high school or college, many sport participants in Europe continue their membership of a sporting club when they are over twenty.

There is a further diverging institutional outcome that derives from these critical junctures and the subsequent processes of self-reproduction and path dependency. This is the contrast between the nationally oriented closed leagues of American professional sports versus the internationally oriented open competitions in European professional sports. Sports clubs in Europe founded regional, national and international federations, and organized a pyramid structure on the basis of a system of promotion and relegation, which created a top professional level in most sports. In contrast to this, baseball, basketball, football, and other sports that were commercialized in the United States were organized and professionalized independently of the rest of the global sporting system. Being developed in relative autonomy from the 'processes of sportization' that took place in the internationally interconnected European sports world (Elias and Dunning, 1986; van Bottenburg, 2001), the Americans did not feel any pressure to formulate the rules of their sports and sport competitions in an international federation of national sport associations. Nor were they compelled to bring their rules into line with what was regarded as the 'international standard'. First in baseball, and later in other American sports as well, an alternative model of competition evolved (Szymanski, 2008). Professional leagues became joint ventures of constituent teams. Operating as franchises, these teams collaborate outside the sporting field in order to promote their mutual economic interests. As such they have formed a closed system – for example, the National Football League – in which eligibility of teams is not managed by a system of promotion, relegation and qualification – as is the case in the Champions League – but by co-optation (Nafziger, 2008). As the reputation and interests of the professional leagues on both sides of the Atlantic increased, it became more and more prestigious and profitable for the teams and clubs to function within their system and remain loyal to it. Although commercialization processes put pressure on the open European system and globalization processes challenge the closed American system, resignation from the European (international) leagues or opening up the American (national) leagues is (still) seen as too risky an enterprise. Both systems have become trapped in their own structures of competition and governance from which only a new 'critical juncture' in history may be able to release them.

Further processes of commercialization and globalization may lead to such a transformation. They create converging dynamics that intermingle with diverging trends (Nafziger, 2008). A principal example of this in the sport participation sphere is the popularization of fitness, running, and so-called 'alternative' sports such as skating, climbing, surfing and snowboarding. These sports have caught on in both Europe and the United States, and have been organized neither in the school system nor in the club system. On both sides of the Atlantic, they have been practised in different organizational frameworks, or in no organizational context at all. This represents a challenge to the existing school sport and club sport structures. These 'alternative' sports were developed in the context of new commercial relationships and on the street. They became popular mainly among young people, for whom these sports expressed a freer, more individual, egalitarian and pleasurable image, and gave the impression of being either not controlled or less controlled by adults than conventional sports. Fitness, aerobics and running have become popular among people who are a generation older than the average sport participant at an American school or in a European club. These sports are mainly practised to keep healthy and manage the body – motives that are radically different from the social and sporting reasons for competing in varsity or club sports (Stokvis and van Hilvoorde, 2008). The popularization of these 'new' sports thus led to the extension of the existing school- and club-based sport cultures in the United States and Europe, respectively. This convergence in sporting formation and culture, therefore, does not occur because either of the established institutional patterns has displaced the other, but because of the emergence of new sporting forms and arrangements on both sides of the Atlantic

Conclusions

Although we should overlook neither significant variations within the European and American sporting configurations nor their similarities, we can conclude that there are indeed fundamental differences between both models. The two most striking differences are their organizational arrangements with respect to sport participation (club versus school model) and to professional sport competition (open versus closed leagues). Rather than interpreting these differences from the perspective of American exceptionalism, they are analysed in this chapter as 'changing expressions of complex forces'.

These forces are explained here by looking back in history for contingent occurrences – critical junctures – that have produced differing institutional arrangements and have induced self-reinforcing, path-dependent mechanisms. As comes to the fore from this analysis, the critical junctures that led to the split in the organization of sport participation and professional sport competitions can be understood by analysing broader societal differences and specific differences in the school system – student population composition, educational ethos, government control – and the international orientation of the early governing bodies.

The processes that were responsible for the genesis and split of the European and American model were different from the processes responsible for their reproduction (Mahoney, 2000: 512). Once the school model had become dominant in the United States and the club model in Europe, they triggered other self-reinforcing, path-dependent processes that enforced the cultural preferences and financial benefits of the existing model, and marginalized the advantages of adopting an alternative institutional arrangement. However, the analysis also indicates that the existence of these self-reinforcing mechanisms does not imply an ever-widening divergence of both sporting configurations. General processes of commercialization and globalization produce converging dynamics that intermingle with the diverging trends. This creates dynamic tensions between local, national, and continental sporting configurations in the twenty-first century and opens the possibility of new critical junctures that may change the course of sport history.

Note

1 Figure 12.1 is an adaptation of a typology of national sports systems in the European Union developed by Camy *et al.* (Vocasport, 2004) in a study supported by the European Commission (DG Education and Culture, Contract no. 2003–4463/001–001). Their typology was based on four parameters: the role of public authorities in the regulation of the system (particularly the state); the degree and form of coordination of the various actors involved in the national sport system; the distribution between the three types of providers (public, voluntary, commercial); and the suitability of supply to changes in demand. On the basis of these parameters, four types of configuration in Europe were identified: a bureaucratic configuration, characterized by the very active role that public

authorities take in regulating the sport system (Belgium, Cyprus, Czech Republic, Estonia, Finland, France, Greece, Hungary, Latvia, Lithuania, Malta, Poland, Portugal, Slovakia, Slovenia, Spain); a missionary configuration, characterized by the dominant presence of a voluntary sports movement with great autonomy to make decisions (Austria, Denmark, Germany, Luxembourg, Sweden); an entrepreneurial configuration, characterized by the regulation of the system arising from the social or economic demand for sport (Ireland, UK); and a social configuration, characterized by the presence of the social partners within a multi-faced system (the Netherlands). As the stress on the presence of social partners in the social configuration indicates, this model was developed in the context of a study on the labour market (vocational education and training) in the field of sport.

The figure elaborates on this typology, but refers to the types of providers of sports participation (voluntary sports clubs, commercially managed sports centres, PE in primary and secondary schools) and the presence and influence of public authorities in this respect. The figure is based on an analysis of comparable empirical data on five parameters: sport participation in general (*Eurobarometer 62.0*, European Commission, 2004); sport participation in clubs (*European Social Survey*, Centre for Comparative Social Surveys, 2002 and *Eurobarometer 62.0*); sport participation in the health club industry (IHRSA, 2006); PE in primary and secondary education (Hardman, 2008); and the role of the state in the sport systems of the EU member states (Vocasport, 2004). The main results of this analysis are summarized in Table 12.1. Unfortunately, comparable data for other European as well as North American countries are lacking. The typology of the United States and Canada in Figure 12.1 is based on secondary literature (Wilson, 1994; van Bottenburg, 2001; Markovits and Hellerman, 2001; Nafziger, 2008; Stokvis, 2009).

Further research is needed to refine and extend this international comparison and validate this typology. Ideally, this should also include a parameter for the role of the state, market, educational institutions and voluntary organizations with respect to the organization of elite sports. Here, the typology used in Figure 12.1 serves mainly as an illustration of (1) the differences between the educational–commercial configuration in northern American countries and the voluntary–governmental configuration in northern and western European countries; and (2) the differences within Europe, contrasting a voluntary–governmental configuration in most northern and western European countries and an educational–governmental configuration in several eastern and southern European countries.

References

Bergsgard, N. A., Houlihan, B., Mangset, P., Nodland, S. I. and Rommetvedt, H., (2007), *Sport Policy: A Comparative Analysis of Stability and Change*, Amsterdam: Elsevier.

van Bottenburg, M., (2001), *Global Games*, Urbana and Chicago: University of Illinois Press.

van Bottenburg, M., Rijnen, B. and van Sterkenburg, J., (2005), *Sport Participation in the European Union: Trends and Differences*, Nieuwegein: Arko Sports Media.

Capoccia, G. and Kelemen, D., (2007), 'The study of critical junctures', *World Politics*, 59 (4): 341–69.

Centre for Comparative Social Surveys, (2002), *European Social Survey*, London: City University.

Elias, N. and Dunning, E., (1986), *Quest for Excitement: Sport and Leisure in the Civilizing Process*, Oxford: Basil Blackwell.

European Commission, (2004), *The Citizens of the European Union and Sport: Special Eurobarometer 62.0 213*, Brussels: TNS Opinion and Social c/o EOS Gallup Europe.

Table 12.1 Level of sports participation, club membership, fitness penetration and governmental interference in twenty-five member states of the European Union

Country	Active or very active in sport and exercise	Members of sports clubs (%)	Sports clubs as preferred provider for exercising (%)	Fitness penetration rate	Minimum time allocation for PE in primary and secondary schools	Governmental interference
Finland	++++	+++	++	++	++	+++
Sweden	++++	++++	+	++++	++	+
Denmark	++++	++++	++++	+++	++	+
Ireland	+++	+++	+++	+++	+	+
UK	+++	++++	++	++++	+	+
Netherlands	+++	++++	++++	++++	++	++
Germany	++	++++	+++	+++	+++	+
Belgium	+++	++++	+++	+	++	++
Luxembourg	++	+++	+++	n.a.	++++	++
France	+++	n.a.	+++	++	++++	+++
Austria	++	+++	+++	++	+++	+
Portugal	+	++	++	+	++++	+++
Spain	++	+++	+++	++++	++++	++
Italy	+	++	++	+++	+++	++
Greece	+	+	+	++	+++	++
Malta	++	n.a.	+	n.a.	+++	++++
Cyprus	++	n.a.	+	n.a.	+	++++
Slovenia	++	+++	+	+	+++	++++
Czech Republic	+	n.a.	++	+	+++	++++
Slovakia	+	n.a.	++	+	++	+++

Estonia	+	n.a.	++	+	++++	++++
Latvia	+	n.a.	+++	+	++	++++
Lithuania	+	n.a.	+	+	+	++++
Hungary	+	++	+	+	+++	++++
Poland	+	+	+	+	+++	++++
Criteria						
++++	≥60%	≥20%	≥24%	≥10%	224–271 min/week	Dominant public agencies
+++	≥50–<60%	≥10–<20%	≥16–<24%	≥7.5–<10%	176–223 min/week	Very significant role of public agencies
++	≥40–<50%	≥5–<10%	≥8–<16%	≥5–<7.5%	128–175 min/week	Fairly significant role of public agencies
+	<40%	<5%	<8%	<5%	80–127 min/week	Relatively low contribution of public agencies
Sources	European Commission (2004); Scheerder and van Tuyckom (2007: 134)	Centre for Comparative Social Surveys (2002)	European Commission (2004); Groll et al. (2008: 78)	IHRSA (2006)	Hardman (2008)	Vocasport (2004)

Girginov, V. and Sandanski, I., (2004), 'From participants to competitors: the transformation of British gymnastics and the role of the eastern European model of sport', *International Journal of the History of Sport*, 21 (5): 815–32.

Groll, M., Koopmann, O. and Hänsch, K., (2008), *Organisational Aspects of Sport in the European Union*, Cologne: German Sports University Cologne.

Guttmann, A., (1988), *A Whole New Ball Game: An Interpretation of American Sports*, Chapell Hill and London: University of North Carolina Press.

Halgreen, L., (2004), *European Sports Law: A Comparative Analysis of the European and American Models of Sport*, Copenhagen: Thomson Reuters.

Hardman, K., (2008), 'Physical education in schools: a global perspective', *Kinesiology*, 40 (1): 5–28.

Hoberman, J., (1993), 'Sport and ideology in the post-Communist age', in L. Allison (ed.), *The Changing Politics of Sport*, Manchester: Manchester University Press, 15–36.

Hodgson, G., (2009), *The Myth of American Exceptionalism*, New Haven and London: Yale University Press.

Hofmann, A. R. (ed.), (2004), *Turnen and Sport: Transatlantic Transfers*, Münster: Waxmann.

Holt, R., (1981), *Sport and Society in Modern France*, London: Macmillan.

——, (1989), *Sport and the British. A Modern History*, Oxford: Oxford University Press.

Houlihan, B. and White, A., (2002), *The Politics of Sports Development: Development of Sport or Development through Sport?* London/New York: Routledge.

IHRSA, (2006), *European Market Report: The Size and Scope of the Health Club Industry*, Boston: International Health, Racquet & Sportsclub Association.

Kirsch, G. B., (1989), *The Creation of American Team Sports*, Urbana and Chicago: University of Illinois Press.

Lipset, S. M., (1991), 'American exceptionalism reaffirmed', in B. E. Shafer (ed.), *Is America Different? A New Look at American Exceptionalism*, Oxford: Oxford University Press, 1–45.

——, (1997), *American Exceptionalism: A Double-edged Sword*, New York and London: W. W. Norton & Co.

Lockhart, C., (2003), *The Roots of American Exceptionalism: Institutions, Culture and Policies*, New York: Palgrave Macmillan.

Mahoney, J., (2000), 'Path dependence in historical sociology', *Theory and Society*, 29 (4): 507–48.

Mandell, R., (1984), *Sport: A Cultural History*, New York: Columbia University Press.

Markovits, A. S. and Hellerman, S. L., (2001), *Offside: Soccer and American Exceptionalism*, Princeton: Princeton University Press.

Nafziger, J. A. R., (2008), 'A comparison of the European and North American models of sports organisation', *International Sports Law Journal*, 7 (3–4): 100–108.

Naul, R. (ed.), (1991), *Turnen and Sport: The Cross-cultural Exchange*, Münster: Waxmann.

Pfister, G., (2006), 'Cultural confrontations: German *Turnen*, Swedish gymnastics and English sport – European diversity in physical activities from a historical perspective', *Culture, Sport, Society*, 6 (1): 61–91.

Pierson, P., (2004), *Politics in Time*, Princeton: Princeton University Press.

Pope, S. W., (2007), 'Rethinking sport, empire, and American exceptionalism', *Sport History Review*, 38 (2): 92–120.

Rader, B., (1983), *American Sports: From the Age of Folk Games to the Age of the Spectator*, Englewood Cliffs: Prentice Hall.

Riordan, J. and Krüger, A. (eds), (2003), *European Cultures in Sport: Examining the Nations and Regions*, Bristol: Intellect.

Scheerder, J. and van Tuyckom, C. (2007), 'Sportparticipatie in de Europese Unie: Vlaanderen vergeleken met het Europa van de 25', in J. Scheerder, C. van Tuyckom and A. Vermeersch (eds), *Europa in beweging: Sport vanuit Europees perspectief*, Gent: Academia Press, 123–58.

Shafer, B. E. (ed.), (1991), *Is America Different? A New Look at American Exceptionalism*, Oxford: Oxford University Press.

Slack, T. and Parent, M. M., (2008), 'Sport in North America', in B. Houlihan (ed.), *Sport and Society: A Student Introduction*, London: Sage, 471–91.

Sombart, W., (1906), *Warum gibt is in den Vereinigten Staaten keinen Sozialismus?* Tübingen: Mohr.

Sparvero, E., Chalip, L. and Green, B. C., (2008), 'United States', in B. Houlihan and M. Green (eds), *Comparative Elite Sport Development*, Amsterdam: Elsevier, 242–71.

Stokvis, R., (1989), *De sportwereld: Een sociologische inleiding*, Alphen and Brussels: Samsom.

——, (2003), *Sport, Publiek en de Media*, Amsterdam: Aksant.

——, (2009), 'Sport en middelbaar onderwijs in de VS en Nederland', *Sociologie*, 5 (4): 484–501.

Stokvis, R. and van Hilvoorde, I., (2008), *Fitter, harder & mooier: De onweerstaanbare opkomst van de fitnesscultuur*, Amsterdam and Antwerpen: De arbeiderspers and Het sporthuis.

Suggs, W., (2005), *A place on the Team: The Triumph and Tragedy of Title IX*. Princeton: Princeton University Press.

Szymanski, S., (2008), 'A theory of the evolution of modern sport', *Journal of Sport History*, 35 (1): 1–32.

de Tocqueville, A., (1992, originally published in 1835 and 1840), *De la démocratie en Amérique (part 1 and 2)*, Paris: Les Éditions Gallimard.

Tyrrell, I., (1991), 'American exceptionalism in an age of international history', *American Historical Review*, 96 (4): 1031–55.

Vocasport, (2004), *Vocational Education and Training in the Field of Sport in the European Union: Situation, Trends and Outlook*, Lyon: EOSE.

Wilson, J., (1994), *Playing by the Rules: Sport, Society, and the State*, Detroit: Wayne State University Press.

Afterword

Toby Miller

This afterword is not an exegesis on the excellent chapters that precede it. Much of what I have to say may even seem tendentious to my fellow authors, but the analysis is indebted to them. I elected to use this opportunity to ponder questions that arise from my reading of their work and the present conjuncture as it shapes this volume's key terms – sport, Europe and cities – and to propose a future research agenda.

The political–economic argument underpinning what follows is that nine processes characterize twenty-first-century sport: globalization, governmentalization, Europeanization, Indianization, Sinization, televisualization, urbanization, environmentalization and commodification:

1 a return to levels of global investment seen routinely in the age of empire, before the First and Second World Wars and sizeable tariff barriers;
2 the redisposal of what Barthes (1973) referred to as 'governmentality' – regions, states and cities claiming responsibility for, and legitimacy from, economic and sporting success. Foucault (1991) modified this term to describe the investment of capacities in the population to undertake the work of growth and governance, a concept animated in policy terms by Sen (2009) and applied to sport as both an ethical exemplar and a generator of well trained workers, in addition to a site of transnational civil society as per the *Union des Associations Européennes de Football* (UEFA), the *Fédération Internationale de Football Association* (FIFA) and the World Anti-Doping Agency (WADA);
3 how European wealth reasserted itself in the management of world football to undermine the voting hegemony of the Global South in FIFA, thereby returning the sport to control by a white plutocracy;
4 the emergence of India as the financial hegemon of cricket, albeit one whose residual subaltern status still clouds its decision-making influence over others;
5 the emergence of China as the first dominant manufacturer and lending power with a taste for state-funded Olympism and a peasant class in the hundreds of millions becoming an internationally competitive *lumpenproletariat*;
6 the formative role of television sports coverage and the spread of television itself across the world and into the inner workings of sports teams;
7 the role of cities in transforming everyday life and as indices of globalization;

8   the environmental consequences of global sport; and
9   the way that sporting personalities, goods, and even nations have become
     commodified to earn money for both private gain and the public weal, drawing
     on labor aristocrats as symbols of a supposedly meritocratic domain.

NICL

These developments occur in the context of a new international division of cultural
labor (NICL). The noted economist Jacques Attali (2008) explains that a new
'mercantile order forms wherever a creative class masters a key innovation from
navigation to accounting or, in our own time, where services are most efficiently
mass produced, thus generating enormous wealth'. New eras in knowledge and
communication index homologies and exchanges between militarism, colonialism
and class control. During the 1970s, the Global North recognized that its economic
future lay in finance capital and ideology rather than agriculture and manufacturing
– seeking revenue from innovation and intellectual property, not minerals or masses.
Hence the consulting firm of former US Secretary of State and master of the dark
art of international relations Henry Kissinger advising that the USA must 'win the
battle of the world's information flows, dominating the airwaves as Great Britain
once ruled the seas' (Rothkopf, 1997). This is the backdrop to globalization as
applied to sport, which has become a cultural industry as well as a means of training
citizens and workers.

The NICL has challenged the very idea of 'Europe'. In the past quarter-century,
the European Union has seen arrivals from beyond its borders grow by 75% (Annan,
2003; Castles and Miller, 2003: 4; UNDP, 2004: 30). This mobility, whether
voluntary or imposed, temporary or permanent, is accelerating. Along with new
forms of communication, it enables unprecedented levels of cultural displacement,
renewal and creation between and across origins and destinations (Schweder *et
al.*, 2002). Most of these exchanges are structured in dominance: the majority of
international investment and trade takes place within the Global South, while the
majority of immigration is from there to the Global North, under the sign of the
anti-colonialist slogan 'We are here because you were there'.

Even the 'British–Irish archipelago', once famed 'as the veritable forge of the
nation state, a template of modernity' (Nairn, 2003: 8), has been subdivided by
cultural difference, as a consequence of both peaceful and violent action and a
revisionist historiography that asks us to note the millennial migration of Celts from
the steppes; Roman colonization; invading Angles, Saxons, Jutes, Frisians and
Normans; attacking Scandinavians; trading Indians, Chinese, Irish, Lombards and
Hansa; refugee Europeans and Africans; and the 25,000 black folks in London in
the eighteenth century (Nairn, 2003; Alibhai-Brown, 2005).

Despite this history, a nostalgic presentism is everywhere. Data from the Pew
Research Center for the People & the Press indicate that majorities around the world
oppose immigration, largely because of fear (2004). This has led to outbursts of
regressive nationalism, whether via the belligerence of the United States, the anti-
immigrant stance of western Europe, or the crackdown on minorities in eastern

Europe, Asia and the Arab world (Halliday, 2004). The populist outcome is often violent – race rebellions in British cities in the 1980s; pogroms against Roma and migrant workers in Spain in 2000 and Germany in the 1990s; the *intifadas*; migrant-worker struggles in France in 1990 – on it goes. Virtually any arrivals are subject to racialization, though particular feeling is often reserved for expatriates from former colonies (Downing and Husband, 2005: xi, 7). If one takes the two most important sites of migration from the Global South to the North – Turkey and Mexico – one sees anti-immigrant state and vigilante violence alongside corporate embrace of migrants in host countries (Bauböck, 2005: 9). Thus far, studies of chauvinism and hyper-masculinity have tended to focus on crowd conduct at fixtures, largely neglecting the wider ideological tone of competitiveness and differentiation into which collective identification against an other so easily slides.

Urbanism

The NICL has both facilitated and been stimulated by urbanization. Almost 50% of the world's population lived in cities in 2000, up from 30% in 1960. More people are urban dwellers today than were *alive* in 1960; and for the first time in world history, more people now live in cities than in rural areas. Most of the remainder are desperately poor peasants (Amin, 2003; Observatoire de la Finance and UNITAR, 2003: 19; Davis, 2004: 5).

In 1950, only London and New York were regarded by geographers as mega-lopolises. By 1970, there were eleven such places, with thirty-three projected for 2015. The fifteen biggest cities in 1950 accounted for 82.5 million people; in 1970 the aggregate was 140.2 million; and in 1990, 189.6 million. Four hundred cities today have more than a million occupants, and thirty-seven have between 8 and 26 million (Scott, 1998: 49; García Canclini, 1999: 74; Dogan, 2004: 347). Across the globe, cities have undergone 'macrocephalic' growth (Scott, 1998: 49) to the point where they burst at the seams – not so much with opportunity and difference, but with desperation and sameness. UN-HABITAT (2003) estimates that a billion people reside in slum conditions, a figure expected to double in the next three decades. And in the post-1989 epoch, the crises of *cognitive* mapping – where am I and how do I get to where I want to be? – have been added to by crises of *ideological* mapping – who are we and what do we stand for? (Martín-Barbero, 2000: 336).

Analysts have long suggested that city-states will displace nations this century, with urban radials as new trading routes. Cities such as Milan, Madrid and Mexico City are financial centers of transnational media and sport production and distribution. Each has evolved its own logics and interests, which do not necessarily correspond to those of any sovereign state. The study of these sporting media capitals is not simply about acknowledging the dominance of a place. It must unravel, for instance, how Mexico City negotiates its status as a cultural and economic nexus for Latin American social enclaves around the world. The sporting media capital is a relational concept with varying kinds of flow (economic, cultural and technological) that are radically contextualized at multiple levels (local, national and global).

City-based football is a major site of international labor mobility. Players move in accordance with several factor endowments, beyond issues such as talent and money. There is a clear link between imperial history and job destination in the case of Latin Americans going to Spain, Portugal and Italy, and Africans playing in France, while cultural links draw Scandinavians to Britain. A small labor aristocracy experiences genuine class mobility in financial terms, underpinned by a huge reserve army of labor and ancillary workers, each subject to various, and often quite severe, forms of exploitation. This tendency is so marked that it has given rise to a Professional Football Players' Observatory, which tracks the success and value of players, complete with an interactive online instrument to illustrate migration (www.eurofootplayers.org).

In 1992, Silvio Berlusconi announced that 'the concept of the national team will, gradually, become less important. It is the clubs with which the fans associate' (Miller *et al.*, 2001). The city–club nexus in football now sees teams owning all or some of their visual rights, rather than selling them on to conventional broad-casters – just as they had transcended nations, so they are seeking to do the same with national commerce and become global media and entertainment entities. This is how, for example, Real Madrid and Manchester United split their income in 2003–04: 42% (Madrid) and 27% (Manchester) from merchandising; 24% and 27% from television; 26% and 36% from domestic ticket sales; and the remainder from international tours (BBC News, 2005). It may come to pass that such clubs withdraw from local competitions and TV systems, in favor of a world of administration and revenue that they control – something presaged by the league-like format and the primacy placed nowadays on the European Champions League. Manchester United, Benfica, Barcelona, Middlesbrough, Olympique de Marseille, Real Madrid, AC and Inter Milan, and Chelsea boast their own television channels, for instance.

Environmentalism

We are also seeing the infiltration of environmental consciousness into the governmentality of global sports. So the 2010 FIFA World Cup and the Vancouver Winter Olympics were closely monitored for their environmental impact. FIFA set up an Environmental Forum in response to critics of the 2006 tournament. Its task is to 'green' stadiums, training grounds, accommodation, amenities and so on in accordance with the UN Environmental Program. South Africa used biogas from landfills, wind farms and efficient lighting during the 2010 World Cup (IOL News, 2008). But of course such initiatives do nothing to get at the real issue of such mega-events. Mostly fuelled, if I can use that term, by European travel, the World Cup had the largest carbon footprint of any commercial event in world history: 850,000 tonnes of carbon expended, 65% of it due to flights (Climate Neutral Network, undated).

Then there is golf. Over sixty million people worldwide play this most destructive of the culture industries. Although half of these environmental miscreants live in the USA, the sport is in massive decline there, a problem it is addressing via traditional Yanqui Leninist methods – overseas expansion to deal with domestic overproduction. There are now more than 12,000 courses beyond the USA, mostly in Europe and Japan, and they cover territory the size of Belgium. Japan had seventy-two golf courses fifty years ago. Now it has 2000. The sport's deforestation of a country that had been mostly forest has been so comprehensive that lumber is now an import. The next true believers lined up to participate are in China and India; the Mission Hill resort near Hong Kong is the world's biggest golf course. Again, TV is a crucial player. Whereas the *mythos* of golf declares itself a conservationist's delight, based on the notion that rabbits grazing, birds shitting, and other wild things burrowing in naturally produced St Andrew's grass, the model TV course for the four majors (conducted in just two countries, and reliant on keeping people off course for months and months in advance of media exposure) has become the standard worldwide. This environmental sublime is named after that paragon of racial and gender inclusiveness, the US Masters: 'Augusta National Syndrome' stimulates a chemical fog of cosmic proportions, and the most reckless water use imaginable, both in terms of the courses' need for it and the way that they fail to store water as effectively as virtually the ecosystems they have displaced. This is in addition to the cancers experienced by greenkeepers that are probably caused by pesticides, herbicides and germicides (Winter and Dillon, 2004; Environment South Africa, 2005).

Sport, the crisis and an agenda

It would be misleading to paint the NICL as always and everywhere a source of growth, given the global financial crisis. What can that conjuncture tell us about neoliberalism and the future of sport?

Neoliberalism was one of the most successful attempts to reshape individuals in human history. Its achievements rank alongside those similarly productive and destructive sectarian practices that we call religion, colonialism, nationalism and state socialism. Neoliberalism's lust for market conduct was so powerful that its prelates opined on every topic imaginable, from birth rates to divorce, from suicide to abortion, from performance-enhancing drugs to altruism. It stood rhetorically against elitism (for populism); against subvention (for markets); and against public service (for philanthropy) (Gorbachev, 2009; Hall and Massey, 2010). But neo-liberalism had a grand contradiction at its heart: a passion for intervention in the name of non-intervention. It pleaded for investments in human capital, yet derided social engineering. It called for the generation of markets by the state, but rejected democratic controls on profits. It hailed freedom as a natural basis for life, but policed property relations.

The global economic crisis we are experiencing occurred because of an unusual alliance of policy-makers, neoliberal economists, rentiers, and workers in the Global North. On the one hand, fictive capital sought returns based on financialization rather than the material economy. On the other, workers sought to counter the lack of reward for increased productivity and the threat of offshore production by leveraging home mortgages for credit. This asset inflation was supported by policy-makers and economists anxious to suppress workers' wages and hence increase profit levels while ensuring political quietude (Kotz, 2009; Lucarelli, 2009; Bresser-Pereira, 2010).

It is hard to imagine a better example of collectivity, individuation, substructure and superstructure in tension than European football over the past three decades. Small city businesses that were run rather like not-for-profits, drawing upon and representing local cultures, became first *entities participating* in the NICL, as they sought to purchase talent from elsewhere, then *objects of* that division, as they were themselves commodified and made into creatures of exchange. In the course of this radical transformation, they fell prey to fictive capital, becoming sources of asset inflation used by rentiers to service their debt elsewhere through the cash flow of television money and gate receipts.

So how should we approach the future study of Europe, the city and sport? I suggest that sport studies has seen three tendencies, each of which is on display in various ways in this volume. They cross disciplines and historicities, so while each may be dominant in one field of knowledge or era, there are generally elements of the others at play as well. The trichotomy I propose implies a chronology, but I do not wish to suggest that any segment has succeeded in vanquishing any other.

Sport Studies 1.0 is a mixture of nostalgia and functionalism, emerging in the 1950s across two disciplines. So within history, we find a fan's passion for unearthing details of how sports, clubs and national teams are founded and succeed. Within sociology, we encounter a Parsonian/Panglossian embrace of sport as a release for tensions in the biological/psychological/social body, where a miraculous homology between the 100-meter dash and class politics sees meritocracy at work.

Sport Studies 2.0, which appeared in the late 1960s, is a *mélange* of technical, scientific forms of measurement and coaching alongside neoclassical economics. It veers between kinesiology and management studies, from optimal measures of javelin-throwing to obedience to market ideology. Drawing on positive visions of the sporting and social orders evident in 1.0, it experiments and models in the service of elite athletic and business performance.

Sport Studies 3.0 emerged in the 1970s in reaction against these celebratory and managerial discourses. It takes the form of critique on a class, gender, sexuality and race basis, drawing on cultural policy, Marxism, feminism, queer theory and post-colonialism, and is found across critical sociology and cultural studies.

Each of these discourses has its merits. 1.0 is friendly – it appeals to those who like sport; 2.0 is useful – it appeals to those who decide what sport looks like; 3.0 is critical – it appeals to those who sense that something is wrong with this picture.

If we are to understand and help democratize the future of Europe, cities and sport, we'll need aspects of all three tendencies within our toolkits. For me, 3.0 keeps it real. But as we know, it offers minimal if any *entrée* to populism or power. 1.0 and 2.0 make sense to the broader public and hegemons, respectively, so they can make a mark on policy. The trick for the future is to establish whether the three formations can function within research teams, social movements and policy formations.

The topics we should engage with these toolkits are massively complex and pressing:

- immigration and the recoding of Europe
- media monopoly capitalism
- residual asset inflation parlayed through team ownership
- labor aristocrats versus reservists
- the third sector of sports managerialism and civil society; and
- the environmental impact of sport.

The debates may be heated, but the agenda should be clear.

References

Alibhai-Brown, Y., (2005), 'The dishonesty of the immigration card', *Independent*, 11 April: 33.

Amin, S., (2003), 'World poverty, pauperization & capital accumulation', *Monthly Review*, 55 (5): 1–9.

Annan, K., (2003), 'Emma Lazarus Lecture on International Flows of Humanity', United Nations Press Release SG/SM/9027, 21 November, www.un.org/News/Press/docs/2003/sgsm9027.doc.htm

Attali, J., (2008), 'This is not America's final crisis', *New Perspectives Quarterly*, 25 (2): 31–33.

Barthes, R., (1973), *Mythologies*, London: Paladin.

Bauböck, R., (2005), *Citizenship Policies: International, State, Migrant and Democratic Perspectives*, Global Migration Perspectives 19, Geneva: Global Commission on International Migration.

BBC News, (2005), 'Real Madrid income beats Man Utd', 4 October, http://news.bbc.co.uk/2/hi/business/4307808.stm

Bresser-Periera, L. C., (2010), 'The 2008 financial crisis and neoclassical economics', *Brazilian Journal of Political Economy*, 30 (1): 3–26.

Castles, S. and Miller, M. J., (2003), *The Age of Migration*, 3rd edn, New York: Guilford Press.

Climate Neutral Network, (undated), *Greening 2010 FIFA World Cup*, United Nations Environment Programme, http://unep.org/climateneutral/Default.aspx?tabid=496

Davis, M., (2004), 'Planet of slums: urban innovation and the informal proletariat', *New Left Review*, 26: 5–34.

Dogan, M., (2004), 'Introduction: four hundred giant cities atop the world', *International Social Science Journal*, 181: 347–60.

Downing, J. and Husband, C., (2005), *Representing 'Race': Racisms, Ethnicities and Media*, London: Sage.

Environment South Africa, (2005), 'Japan golf courses and deforestation', www.environment.co.za/golf-courses-polo-fields-effects/japan-golf-courses-and-deforestation.html

Foucault, M., (1991), 'Governmentality', in G. Burchell, C. Gordon and P. Miller (eds), *The Foucault Effect: Studies in Governmentality*, London: Harvester Wheatsheaf, 87–104.

García Canclini, N., (1999), *Imaginarios Urbanos*, 2nd edn, Buenos Aires: Eudeba.

Gorbachev, M., (2009), 'Bring back the state', *New Perspectives Quarterly*, 26 (2): 53–55.

Hall, S. and Massey, D., (2010), 'Interpreting the crisis', in R. S. Grayson and J. Rutherford (eds), *After the Crash: Reinventing the Left in Britain*, London: Soundings/Social Liberal Forum/Compass, 37–46.

Halliday, F., (2004), 'The crisis of universalism: America and radical Islam after 9/11', *openDemocracy*, www.opendemocracy.net/democracy/article_2092.jsp#

IOL News, (2008), 'SA unveils plans for green World Cup', 16 September, www.iol.co.za/index.php?set_id=1&click_id=143&art_id=vn20080916053803370C287052

Kotz, D. M., (2009), 'The financial and economic crisis of 2008: a systemic crisis of neoliberal capitalism', *Review of Radical Political Economics*, 41 (3): 305–17.

Lucarelli, B., (2009), 'The demise of neoliberalism?', *Real-World Economics Review*, 51: 48–54.

Martín-Barbero, J., (2000), 'Nuevos mapas culturales de la integración y el desarrollo', in B. Kliksberg and L. Tomassini (eds), *Capital Social y Cultura: Claves Estratégicas para el Desarollo*, Buenos Aires: Banco Interamericano de Desarrollo, Fondo de Cultura Económica, 335–58.

Miller, T., Lawrence, G., McKay, J. and Rowe, D., (2001), *Globalization and Sport: Playing the World*, London: Sage.

Nairn, T., (2003), 'America vs Globalisation, parts 1–5', 9, 16, 23 January; 4, 20 February, *openDemocracy.net*.

Observatoire de la Finance and UNITAR, (2003), *Economic and Financial Globalization: What the Numbers Say*, New York: United Nations Institute for Training and Research.

Pew Research Center for the People & the Press, (2004), *A Global Generation Gap: Adapting to a New World*, 24 February, http://people-press.org/commentary/?analysisid=86

Rothkopf, D., (1997), 'In praise of cultural imperialism', *Foreign Policy*, 107: 38–53.

Schweder, R. A., Minow, M. and Markus, H. R., (2002), 'Introduction: engaging cultural differences', in R. A. Schweder, M. Minow and H. R. Markus (eds), *Engaging Cultural Differences: The Multicultural Challenge in Liberal Democracies*, New York: Russell Sage Foundation, 1–13.

Scott, A. J., (1998), *Regions and the World Economy: The Coming Shape of Global Production, Competition, and Political Order*, Oxford: Oxford University Press.

Sen, A., (2009), *The Idea of Justice*, Cambridge: Belknap Press.

UN-HABITAT, (2003), 'The challenge of slums', 1 October, www.unhabitat.org/content.asp?cid=3008&catid=5&typeid=6&subMenuId=0

UNDP, (2004), *Human Development Report 2004: Cultural Liberty in Today's Diverse World*, New York: United Nations Development Programme.

Winter, J. G. and Dillon, P. J., (2004), 'Effects of golf course construction and operation on water chemistry of headwater streams on the Precambrian Shield', *Environmental Pollution*, 133 (2): 243–53.

Index

ABC 10, 113, 176

AC Milan: Berlusconi's ownership 123; ECA 181; income 140, 141; player salaries 142; sponsors 145; television audiences 125; television channel 229

Adidas 143, 144, 177

advertising 113, 114, 115, 122, 146

Aicher, Otl 63

Ajax 181

Ali, Mohammed 94, 108

'alternative' sports 219

amateurism: Europe/United States comparison 206–7, 214, 215; France 73; ice hockey 39, 40, 41

American football 38, 205, 211, 214; audience-centred perspective 218; closed competitive system 218–19; television coverage 115–16, 125

Anderson, Dave 46

Andreff, Wladimir 3

Andreotti, Giulio 90

Andrews, David L. 2

Anholt, Simon 154, 160, 161, 164n8, 164n10

Anqueteil, Jacques 73

anti-trust law 122–3, 126n5

Arafat, Yasser 63

archetypical models of sport 208–9

Arsenal FC 140, 141, 145, 181

art, socialist realist 25

association structure 208, 210–11; *see also* voluntary associations

Aston Villa FC 123

athletics 5, 13; East Berlin World Youth Festival 59; France 71, 77; international governing bodies 214; Soviet Union 23; United States 215, 217

Attali, Jacques 227

audience-centred perspective 217–18

Audiovisual Sport 136, 137

Australia 178

Austria: football 12, 13, 187–200; ice hockey 36; missionary configuration 221n1; sports clubs 209, 218; sports participation indicators 222

Avice, Edwige 76

Balbier, Uta 8

Ballack, Michael 142

Barthes, Roland 226

baseball 37–8, 205, 211, 214; audience-centred perspective 218; closed competitive system 218–19; internet rights 124; television coverage 115

basketball 2, 13, 37, 205, 211, 214; audience-centred perspective 218; closed competitive system 218–19; France 71, 74, 80n7; international appeal 125; Soviet Union 23, 103, 104, 105–6, 107

Bassetti, R. 94

Bayer Leverkusen 181, 196

Bayern Munich: broadcasting rights 196, 201n12, 202n15; defeat by Dinamo Kiev 108; ECA 181; income 140, 141; sponsors 145

BBC (British Broadcasting Corporation) 114, 117

Beckenbauer, Franz 38

Beckham, David 141, 142, 143, 144

Beddoes, Dick 36, 42

behaviourism 24

Belgium: bureaucratic configuration 221n1; commercial sports centres 209; ice hockey 36; sports clubs 218; sports participation indicators 222; television 113

Benedetti, Arrigo 84